PORTFOLIO / PENGUIN

GOOD GUYS AND BAD GUYS

Joe Nocera is an op-ed columnist for *The New York Times* and coauthor of *All the Devils Are Here*. He spent ten years at *Fortune* as a contributing writer, editor at large, executive editor, and editorial director. He has won three Gerald Loeb awards for excellence in business journalism and was a finalist for a Pulitzer Prize in 2006. He lives in New York.

Good Guys and Bad Guys

Behind the Scenes with the

Saints and Scoundrels of American Business

(and Everything in Between)

Joe Nocera

PORTFOLIO / PENGUIN

PORTFOLIO / PENGUIN

Published by the Penguin Group

Penguin Group (USA) Inc., 375 Hudson Street, New York, New York 10014, U.S.A. · Penguin Group (Canada), 90 Eglinton Avenue East, Suite 700, Toronto, Ontario, Canada M4P 2Y3 (a division of Pearson Penguin Canada Inc.) · Penguin Books Ltd, 80 Strand, London WC2R 0RL, England · Penguin Ireland, 25 St Stephen's Green, Dublin 2, Ireland (a division of Penguin Books Ltd) · Penguin Books Australia Ltd, 250 Camberwell Road, Camberwell, Victoria 3124, Australia (a division of Pearson Australia Group Pty Ltd) · Penguin Books India Pvt Ltd, 11 Community Center, Panchsheel Park, New Delhi—110 017, India · Penguin Group (NZ), 67 Apollo Drive, Rosedale, Auckland 0632, New Zealand (a division of Pearson New Zealand Ltd) · Penguin Books (South Africa) (Pty) Ltd, 24 Sturdee Avenue, Rosebank, Johannesburg 2196, South Africa

Penguin Books Ltd, Registered Offices: 80 Strand, London WC2R 0RL, England

First published in the United States of America by Portfolio, a member of Penguin Group (USA) Inc. 2008
This paperback edition published 2011

10 9 8 7 6 5 4 3 2 1

THE LIBRARY OF CONGRESS HAS CATALOGED THE HARDCOVER EDITION AS FOLLOWS:
Nocera, Joseph.
Good guys and bad guys : behind the scenes with the saints and scoundrels of American business (and everything in between) / Joe Nocera.
    p. cm.
Includes index.
ISBN 978-1-59184-162-3 (hc.)
ISBN 978-159184-439-6 (pbk.)
1. Businessmen—United States. 2. Capitalists and financiers—United States. 3. Executives—United States. 4. Finance—United States. 5. Journalism, Commercial—United States. I. Title. II. Title: Saints and scoundrels of American business.
    HC102.5.A2N63 2008
    338.092'273—dc22   2008007319

Printed in the United States of America
Set in Minion · Designed by Amy Hill

For Katherine, Amato, and Nicholas

Contents

Introduction   1

1. It's Time to Make a Deal   7
   Texas Monthly, October 1982

2. Jobs Agonistes (Steve, That Is)   47

   The Second Coming of Steve Jobs   49
   Esquire, December 1986

   Good Luck with That Broken iPod   65
   The New York Times, February 4, 2006

   Weighing Jobs' Role in a Scandal   68
   The New York Times, April 28, 2007

3. The Ga-Ga Years   73
   Esquire, February 1988

4. Michael Milken, Mitigated (Well, a Bit)   98
   GQ, December 1992

5. Charlie Merrill and His Stock   107
   GQ, October 1994

6. Lawyers from Hell   125

Fatal Litigation   127
Fortune, October 16 and 30, 1995

The Lawyer Companies Love to Hate   157
The New York Times, July 2, 2006

7. How the Bancrofts Blew It   161

Disgruntled Heiress Leads Revolt at Dow Jones   163
Fortune, February 3, 1997

A Family's Benign Neglect at Dow Jones   175
The New York Times, August 4, 2007

8. Saint Warren of Omaha   179
Money, July 1998

9. The Rise and Fall of Henry Blodget   187

The Cheerleader   188
Money, June 1999

Led into Temptation? Who Wasn't?   191
The New York Times, September 3, 2005

10. The Smartest Guys in the Room   195

A Revenge Fantasy, Except It's Reality   196
The New York Times, January 28, 2006

Mr. Skilling, for the Defense   200
The New York Times, April 15, 2006

Fastow's Long Walk to Less Time   203
The New York Times, September 30, 2006

11. The Quantitative, Data-Based, Risk-Massaging
Road to Riches   207
The New York Times Magazine, June 5, 2005

12. If It's Good for Philip Morris,
Can It Also Be Good for Public Health?   224
The New York Times Magazine, June 18, 2006

13. The Cufflinks That Went to China   243

The Board Wore Chicken Suits   244
The New York Times, May 27, 2006

Overstock's Campaign of Menace   248
The New York Times, February 15, 2006

After Five Years, His Voice Can Still Crack   252
The New York Times, September 9, 2006

Give Me a Double Shot of Starbucks Nostalgia   255
The New York Times, March 3, 2007

Our Love-Hate Relationship with Wal-Mart   259
The New York Times, November 5, 2005

The Cufflinks That Went to China   262
The New York Times, January 21, 2006

14. Return of the Raider   267
Fortune, May 27, 2002

Acknowledgments   283
Index   287

Introduction

In the spring and summer of 1982, just as I was turning 30 years old, I became a business writer, though I didn't realize it at the time. Today, plenty of college kids come out of journalism school steeped in business, eager to compete for jobs at MarketWatch.com or TheStreet.com, *The Wall Street Journal*, or CNBC. They've taken accounting courses, so they know how to dissect a balance sheet. They're conversant with the stock market. They know who Larry and Sergey and Steve and Warren are (as in Google founders Larry Page and Sergey Brin, Apple's Steve Jobs, and Warren Buffett). They know why the Fed raises and lowers interest rates, and the difference between growth and value investing. Then again, who doesn't these days?

But it wasn't like that in the early 1980s. Later, I would come to think of myself as having stumbled upon this wonderful, unexplored subject—business!—but I know that's not really the case. Many fine writers had gotten there long before I arrived on the scene, though most worked for magazines like *Forbes* and *Fortune*, which, despite serious circulations and seriousness of purpose, had the feel of niche publications, aimed at the narrow investing class or midlevel managers. The investing revolution, which would lure the middle class into the market, was in its infancy. The birth of CNBC was still seven years off. *The Wall Street Journal* published a fair amount of first-rate writing, but most of it was expended on nonbusiness features; the *Journal's* business coverage wouldn't become truly energized until Norman Pearlstine became its editor in 1983. At mainstream publications like *The New York Times* or the *Chicago Tribune*, the business section was largely an afterthought, most certainly not a part of the paper you aspired to if you were trying to climb the greasy pole. When I think of the leading lights of business journalism from that era, excluding those who worked for the

1

dedicated business magazines, I stop after four people: Lou Dobbs, who anchored a dedicated half-hour business show on CNN, the then-tiny cable network; Sylvia Porter, the syndicated personal finance columnist; Louis Rukeyser, whose half-hour stock market show ran every Friday night on PBS; and John Brooks, the elegant writer who wrote business stories for *The New Yorker.* Of course, I didn't know about them until much later either.

In Providence, Rhode Island, the dying East Coast city where I grew up, the business climate was characterized less by hostility than by a numbing indifference. (Like many dying East Coast cities, Providence underwent a remarkable renaissance in the 1980s, long after I'd left for greener pastures.) Its most interesting business figure was a man named Royal Little, the founder of Textron, and the inventor of the modern conglomerate. But the first time I ever heard his name was in 1989, when he died at the age of 92— by which time, of course, I was deeply interested in all things business. My most powerful "business memory" growing up—if you can call it that—was seeing huge, boarded-up redbrick factories all over town, with signs that read: "200,000 Sq. Ft. to Let. Will Remodel to Suit." What did these factories once make? Why had they closed? Who had once owned them, and worked in them? I was too young to be curious about the answer, but even as I grew older, it wasn't something people talked about. Those boarded-up factories were the backdrop of the state, part of what Rhode Islanders took for granted.

Although my grandfather had been a classic small entrepreneur, the founder of a thriving corner grocery store and liquor store, I can't ever remember hearing the word "entrepreneur" uttered when I was growing up. It just wasn't in anyone's frame of reference. My mother, a liberal Democrat, viewed business with a liberal's deep suspicion. My father never said anything about business one way or the other. As I note elsewhere in this book, he was a high school teacher, and although he continued to work in the grocery store on Saturdays for most of his life, there was a sense among his brothers and sisters that he was the lucky one; he had escaped the family business, and landed a position that did not require manual labor to put food on the table. But although he had a white-collar job, he was hardly a businessman. Indeed, growing up in the 1950s and 1960s, I'm sure I must have had friends whose fathers were businessmen. For the life of me, though, I can't think of any.

By the time I was a sophomore in college, I knew I wanted to be a journalist. It was the era of Woodward and Bernstein, but their kind of investigative journalism wasn't what fired my imagination. Instead, I was drawn to the work of the so-called New Journalists, writers like Tom Wolfe, who were publishing their immensely ambitious narratives in magazines like *Esquire* and *Rolling Stone*. That's what I wanted to do. I eventually landed in Washington, D.C., where, like most reporters in the nation's capital, I wrote about politics. In my late 20s, I lived in Paris for several years, where I free-lanced sporadically, again mostly about politics. And then one day early in 1982, I found myself in Texas, a brand-new staff writer for *Texas Monthly*, a 10-year-old magazine that prided itself on publishing the kind of immensely ambitious narratives that I longed to write. More precisely, I found myself in the dining room of my first subject, T. Boone Pickens Jr., eating, of all things, fried catfish. (Some details you never forget.) And that's pretty much the moment when I found my calling.

How can I convey how different this experience was from anything I'd known before? It wasn't just the experience of eating fried catfish with Boone that was new and different—though that was strange enough. It was all of it, all of Texas. The cultural divide between Rhode Island and Texas, it seems to me now, was larger than the gulf that I found when I moved from Washington to Paris. The Providence of my childhood was a static place, with an aura of defeatism about it—people sought out nice, safe government jobs, and if they had larger aspirations they moved someplace else. Texas, on the other hand, was anything but static. It was a place crackling with energy, and over-flowing with ambition. I had arrived just in time to experience the state's last great oil boom, and for the first time in my life, I watched people openly, joyously, eagerly trying to get rich. In Texas, I heard people use the word "entrepreneur" all the time. In Texas, business and businessmen were what mattered. It was a revelation.

Boone, of course, was an entrepreneur, and that first night, dining in his home in Amarillo, way up there in the Panhandle of Texas, he must have used the word a half dozen times. He told me his story: his father had worked for Phillips Petroleum, and after graduating from Oklahoma State with a geology degree, he went to work for Phillips as well. But he hated everything about it—hated the bureaucracy, hated the unwillingness of the company to ever take a risk on anything, hated the idea of being a salaried employee working for superiors he didn't respect, expected to wait his turn for a pro-motion or a raise. So one day, at the age of 27, he quit and started his own exploration company. By the time I met him, he had turned that little com-pany, Mesa Petroleum, into one of the largest independent exploration and production companies in the country, and had surrounded himself with a group of young executives who were every bit as hungry as he was. In Ama-rillo, he was the Big Man on Campus, with a house so large it contained an indoor basketball court, if I recall correctly. I'm guessing he was worth somewhere north of $100 million. Even then, it was a lot of money.

Boone had another purpose in dwelling on his entrepreneurial roots that night. He wanted to impress upon me how different he was from the CEOs of America's big companies. I wasn't taking notes that night—the dinner was off-the-record; our mutual purpose was to see if he would cooperate for the profile I hoped to write, which is contained in the first chapter of this book. But I can still recall him railing about the men who ran *Fortune* 500 companies: how they cared more about empire building than building shareholder wealth; how they didn't understand who they were supposed to be working for; how they weren't aligned with the people who owned the company. They were decidedly *not* entrepreneurs, the men who ran America's large corporations; they were—and I can still recall the scorn in his voice—corporate bureaucrats. At that point in his career, Boone hadn't yet conducted his first "corporate raid," and was barely known in business circles outside of Texas. His ideas about the primacy of the shareholder, which were also being developed by a handful of others, including a financier named Carl Icahn, were only just beginning to enter the business culture.

Even so, it felt to me as though I were hearing a foreign language for the first time. Shareholders owned companies? Really? As I listened, I felt some dismay about how little I knew about this world I was about to enter for the first time, but I also felt a growing sense of excitement. I had spent my career up to then interviewing politicians and their staffs. Elected officials were invariably cautious and scripted; you had to go through a press aide to get 15 minutes of their precious time. Alas, most business executives are now just as scripted and difficult to get to—but it wasn't like that then, and it certainly wasn't like that in Texas. This was an entirely new experience—more open, more rough-and-tumble, and ultimately, to me, more interesting. I spent five months working on the story that ensued, which, as you'll see, morphed into an article about Boone's first takeover attempt. Reporting that story was so memorable to me that, 25 years later, I can remember more details of what it was like in the Waldorf-Astoria as Boone was making his first corporate raid than of any story I've done before or since.

I dwell on Boone for several reasons. The first is that meeting him that night, and working on that story, really did set me on a path from which I never turned back. In Texas, I quickly learned, business was the story in much the same way that politics is the story in Washington. It was a story I wanted to tell. My third or fourth article for *Texas Monthly* was about Houston's mayoral politics. It was the kind of subject that had once completely engaged me—but working on it felt like drudgery. I could hardly wait to get back to writing about business. Far more compelling to learn about—and write about—Trammell Crow, the great Dallas real estate developer (the man often credited with inventing the atrium, by the way), or the death of an early Texas Instruments computer, or the end of the oil boom. Because I had never taken any business courses, I was learning on the fly. I struggled to understand income statements and balance sheets (it's still a struggle, if truth be told). But I also quickly realized that the essence of business was not the balance sheet. Business was often as Shakespearean as, well, Shakespeare. Executives did things for reasons of pride and ego and revenge just as often as they did things for purely business reasons. There were rise-and-fall stories and redemption stories—several of which I retell in this collection. Personality mattered—and so did character.

Boone also represents, to my mind, the reason this book is titled *Good Guys and Bad Guys*. As is often the case, the title of this book is the conceit of the book's editor, Adrian Zackheim; it was his way of summing up the quarter century's worth of profiles, narratives, and columns that make up this collection. To be honest, I had never seen my career in those terms before. I had always thought of myself as someone whose role was to explain the innards of business to readers, to draw out the people and stories that fascinated me, and to show why things happened the way they did. I still think that is a lot of what I try to do. Take, for instance, the story "Fatal Litigation," which is in chapter 6. I knew nothing about mass torts when I began the story, but I was fascinated that the plaintiffs' bar could drive a company into bankruptcy, and I wanted to understand how that had happened. Though the story focuses on Dow Corning and silicone breast implants, my larger purpose in writing it was to explain where mass torts came from, how they evolved, and how they work.

Once I started to look at these stories through Adrian's prism, though, I had to admit that he had a point. Journalism is a profession that, by its nature, searches for heroes and goats—good guys and bad guys—and my journalism is no exception. I build my stories around people, and try to understand their motivations, their actions, and their thought processes. I tend to leave the large historical forces to the historians.

But I don't necessarily wind up with the obvious good guys and obvious bad guys—indeed my assessment of who the good guys and bad guys are can be the opposite of what you might expect at first glance. Take "Fatal Litigation" again. My liberal, East Coast upbringing would suggest that I would come to the story with the point of view that the plaintiffs' lawyers were the good guys, bringing justice to the victims of big, bad Dow Corning. But the reality I found was different: the plaintiffs' bar, with no scientific evidence to back up its lawsuits, had nonetheless forced a company into bankruptcy. That didn't seem right to me. It still doesn't.

Although Boone and I eventually had a falling-out that lasted many years (see the last chapter for more details), I've always though of him as one of the good guys. Many people disagree with that assessment, and I understand that. His right-wing politics are the opposite of mine, and he does things that make me cringe, like giving hundreds of millions of dollars to the Oklahoma State athletic department, or funding the Swift Boat Veterans who were out to besmirch the war record of John Kerry. But I long ago came to the view that he was right about the primacy of the shareholder—which is also a view that is now held not just in corporate America but in society in general. And his famous raids, which made him such a figure of controversy in the mid-1980s, struck me then—and strike me now—as one of the most important moments in modern business history. Boone, it turns out, was right about executives being glorified bureaucrats, and companies being bloated and uncompetitive. One of the reasons the corporate raiders were so reviled in their time is that as they forced companies to get "leaner and meaner," employees lost their jobs, and work that had long been done in the United States got outsourced. But the truth is, that needed to happen in order for American companies to become competitive again. Capitalism isn't always pretty. Whether you like him or not, Boone's effect on American business was profound.

Over the past 25 years, I've come to believe deeply in the importance of business—a far cry from where I was when I started down this path. It is as important as politics, as medicine, as religion, as the law—as any of the other large forces driving American society. It can do great harm, and it can do great good. The fact that its fundamental motive is ever-increasing profits does not lead me to view business as inherently suspect, as so many people do. The search for profits can cause businesspeople to do terrible things sometimes—see my Enron chapter—but it can also cause them to do terrific, transforming things. Back when he was managing editor of *Fortune* in the 1990s, my old boss John Huey liked to say that when it came to writing about executives, our job "was to pat them on the back when they deserve to be patted on the back, and kick them in the rear when they deserved to be kicked in the rear."

Good guys and bad guys indeed.

November 2007

CHAPTER 1

It's Time to Make a Deal

Not long after this article was published, in the fall of 1982, Boone Pickens happened to be talking to Robert Cole, the longtime mergers and acquisitions reporter for *The New York Times*. Cole had covered the Mesa–Cities Service battle for the *Times*— indeed, he makes a cameo appearance in this piece—and he and I had met a few times during the course of the deal. He knew, in other words, just how young and green I was. And I could tell that it bugged him. So when he got Boone on the phone, he growled, "Next time you do something like that, give the story to *The New York Times*!" I can't say I blame him for feeling that way.

My very first business story turned out to be quite the coup: nobody had ever before reported on a takeover attempt from the inside. As it turns out, nobody's done it since either. One reason is that it is just too fraught with legal danger. Had Cities Service discovered that I was sitting next to Boone while he plotted strategy with his investment bankers and lawyers—and had the battle ended up in court—the Mesa side could very well have been stripped of its attorney-client privilege. In addition, the merger pros like Joe Flom of Skadden, Arps and Hamilton James of Donaldson, Lufkin & Jenrette really hated the idea that a reporter was writing down what they said and did.

One of my enduring memories of the month I spent at the Waldorf-Astoria reporting this story was sneaking up to the Mesa suite early in the morning, when Boone was still in his bathrobe and only a few of his aides were around—and then trying to stay invisible for as long as possible. Eventually, though, a Flom or a James would start to talk about something sensitive, and somebody would notice that I was still in a corner somewhere taking notes. And so I would get summarily tossed out of the suite—only to sneak back up the next morning and do it all over again. Only on the last—and, thankfully for me, the most dramatic—day of the deal did they all forget I was there. They had too much else to worry about.

So why did Boone let me come back into the suite, day after day? A large part of it was luck. Nicholas Lemann, then the executive editor of *Texas Monthly* (now the dean of Columbia's Graduate School of Journalism and a staff writer at *The New Yorker*), had assigned me to profile Boone even before I'd landed in Texas to join the magazine's writing staff in the spring of 1982. What interested Nick was that Boone was a Texas oilman who didn't have a chip on his shoulder about Wall Street or the business culture of the East Coast; on the contrary, he had a publicly traded stock, and assiduously courted analysts and institutional investors. Nick wanted a story that explored the relationship between a Texas oilman and Wall Street.

It wasn't long, though, before I realized something big was afoot, though Boone wouldn't tell me what it was. I knew so little about business—and securities law—that I even asked him once if he were planning a takeover, not realizing I had just requested inside information. Then, on a Friday afternoon, about two months into my reporting, as I was interviewing Boone's son Mike in Houston, the news broke that Cities Service had struck first, making a tender offer for Mesa before Boone could make a tender offer for Cities Service. I spent the next few days trying to get Boone on the phone, all the while rehearsing what I would say to convince him to let me come to New York to watch him do the deal. I never got to make the speech. When he got on the phone, his first words were "Joe, what are you doing in Texas? The play's in New York."

Hence the luck: Boone let me in the suite because I had gotten to know him over the course of the previous two months—and he had gotten to know me. Despite my lack of business credentials, he had become comfortable with the idea of my writing about the Cities Service deal. He also had his own reasons for wanting the story, no matter how much his advisers objected. He was not without ego; he realized a higher profile could only help him do other, bigger deals; and he understood, at least implicitly, that being on the cover of *Texas Monthly* would catapult him into a different realm of business celebrity than a profile in a business publication. A few years later, when he made his most famous takeover attempt—of Gulf Oil—he wound up on the cover of *Time* magazine. Along with Carl Icahn and a few others, he was the epitome of the corporate raider, a man who made a crusade out of going after underperforming companies. Whatever you think about the raiders' methods and goals, I've always believed that one of the things they did was make business seem interesting, fascinating even. To me, that was the great revelation that came out of reporting this story—I'd had no idea business could be so full of drama. I was hooked.

When I look at this story now, more than 25 years later, there are several things that strike me. One is my own tone—I'm clearly enthralled by what I'm seeing, but I feel a little guilty about it because, as a newcomer to business, I'm not sure mergers make any sense. Today, as a grizzled veteran, I'm still not sure most mergers make sense, but I've taken a "resistance-is-futile" position—as has most everyone in business. The kind of anger that Cities CEO Chuck Waidelich displays toward Boone in this story—anger at the thought that his company is under attack from this *pipsqueak*—just doesn't exist anymore.

I'm also struck at how small this deal now seems, even though, at the time, it would have been one of the largest in history. The takeover tactics both sides employed are primitive. There is a sense throughout that all the players were making it up as they went along—as, indeed, they were. As for the players themselves, it's amazing how many of the biggest names in M&A were involved in the Mesa-Cities deal. Bruce Wasserstein was the king of M&A advisers, and now runs Lazard. Hamilton James is the number two— and heir apparent—at Blackstone, the well-known private equity firm. Joe Flom is retired, but his counterpart, Marty Lipton, is still advising companies and boards. One person on the periphery of the deal was Ivan Boesky, who would later be at the center of the 1980s insider trading scandal. I didn't have the wit to put Boesky in the story, but I have distinct memories of Boone's deflecting his relentless efforts to get some little nugget of information that would give him an inside edge. Clearly, Boone sensed things about Boesky that the rest of us would only discover years later.

There is one other person, I realize in retrospect, who is missing from this narrative: Michael Milken. This story essentially revolves around Boone's increasingly desperate attempts to raise the $1 billion he needed to gain control of Cities. Milken at the time was running Drexel Burnham Lambert's famous West Coast office—he had even invented junk bonds by then—but he had not yet figured out that they could make it possible for people like Boone Pickens to attack large corporations otherwise out of their reach. That he would figure out two years later, when Boone Pickens decided to go after Gulf Oil—and the era of the corporate raider began in earnest.

It's Time to Make a Deal

Texas Monthly, October 1982

Tuesday, May 11, en route to Boston

On the bright, crisp morning of May 11, promptly at ten o'clock, T. Boone Pickens Jr., the founder, president, and chairman of the board of Mesa Petroleum Company, stepped aboard a private plane at Houston's Hobby Airport. Under his arm was a thick folder stuffed with papers and documents, and behind him trailed an aide carrying several more folders bulging with papers. The plane, a sleek Falcon nine-seat jet, cream-colored with blue trim, was one of two corporate jets owned by Mesa Petroleum, and on this day it was carrying Boone Pickens to Boston, where he was scheduled to deliver an address to a convention of financial analysts.

The middle of May was not the best time for Pickens to have a speech on his agenda; he was excruciatingly busy. Two days before the trip, he had cut short a weekend at his ranch near Pampa to attend a late Sunday afternoon meeting at the offices of Baker & Botts, the giant Houston law firm that does most of Mesa's legal work. The next day, he canceled the top management meeting that is usually held every Monday at Mesa's Amarillo headquarters, so that he could continue the Baker & Botts sessions. After the Boston speech and a dinner given in his honor by Morgan Stanley, a New York investment banking house, he planned to fly immediately to New York for still more meetings that would last into the night and through most of Wednesday. If Pickens could have divined a way to avoid the Boston trip, he probably would have done so.

But if there were good reasons for ducking the convention, there was a better one for attending: it was the best way to keep America's oil analysts from knowing what he was up to. Had Pickens canceled his appearance at their convention, the rumors that had swirled around him for over a year would have gathered and swelled like a tornado. Every oil analyst in America would have had the same thought at the same moment: if Boone Pickens is so busy that he has to cancel his speech here, he must be planning something... he must be getting close to making a deal... he must be preparing to make a run at Cities Service Company! Which, of course, was exactly what Pickens was doing. Life in the oil business is a succession of deals, and if Pickens could pull this one off it would be the biggest and most daring deal of all. The rewards were potentially huge and so were the risks, and everybody would be watching to see if he stumbled.

When the Mesa jet had reached its cruising altitude, Pickens picked up a telephone that lay next to his armrest and called his office in Amarillo. "How's the market today?" he asked.

Although Pickens has practically been canonized on Wall Street for his shrewd financial dealings, he gives an impression of ordinariness. He does not exude charisma. He favors unostentatious business suits and shuns accoutrements like flashy rings and cowboy boots. At 54, he is obviously in good physical condition, but no one would ever mistake him for a 35-year-old: the hair around his ears is graying, and his face is lined with the creases of age. His jowls sag. From certain angles, he bears a striking resemblance to our most uncharismatic president, Jimmy Carter. Being a Republican of the hard-rock variety, Pickens finds the comparison odious.

After talking to his office, Pickens made a second call, this one to Alan Habacht, a partner in the New York investment firm of Weiss, Peck & Greer. As an analyst for a firm that has controlled as much as 900,000 shares of Mesa stock, he was an important shareholder. Earlier that morning, Habacht had called Amarillo looking for Pickens, and now Pickens was returning the call.

"Hey, Alan, what's going on?"

Habacht had one thing on his mind: Cities Service. What was Pickens doing? Was he going to make a move anytime soon?

It was no secret on Wall Street that Boone Pickens had long lusted after Cities Service, although at first glance it seemed an improbable dream. Cities was the 39th-largest company in America and the 19th-largest oil company; Mesa hadn't yet cracked the *Fortune* 500. Cities had $6 billion in assets to Mesa's $2 billion. By the measure of annual sales, Cities was twenty times larger than Mesa. But when Pickens looked at Cities, he saw not its size but its 307 million barrels of proven oil reserves, and the 10.6 million unexplored domestic acres on which it held the drilling rights, and, above all, its stock price, which was one third the estimated value of the company's assets. What he saw, in other words, was an opportunity to find oil on Wall Street more cheaply than he could find it by drilling for it.

All this the analysts knew, but what they didn't know was when or how—or even if—he could put together the kind of huge, complicated deal it would take to make a run at Cities. That's just the way Pickens wanted it. For by the middle of May, after months of trying, he thought he finally had it figured out. Boone Pickens was going to try to buy Cities out from under its management by making what is called an unfriendly tender offer for the company's stock—an open invitation to Cities' shareholders to sell their shares to Mesa and, in so doing, put him in control of the company and kick out the old management. The deal he was putting together was indeed huge and complicated—and extremely unusual in the annals of Wall Street. It's almost always the bigger company that goes after the smaller one; for the minnow to try to swallow the whale, as Pickens wanted to do, was unheard of. By the time he went to Boston, a tentative launch date had been set for the Mesa tender offer: it was June 1, just three weeks away.

As anyone who reads the business pages knows by now, Mesa Petroleum and Cities Service did indeed go to war this past June. The fighting lasted three weeks, the battleground was Wall Street, and the weapons were those of American finance. Boone Pickens did not win the war, inasmuch as he failed to gain control of Cities Service, but he didn't really lose it either. The war ended on June 17, when the Gulf Oil Corporation stepped in and agreed to pay $5 billion to acquire Cities in a deal that would have been the third largest in history had it held up. When Gulf pulled out of the deal seven weeks later, Cities was locked into either finding a new multibillion-dollar buyer or liquidating itself. The moment it agreed to the Gulf deal, Cities lost any chance of remaining independent. That would not have been the case had Boone Pickens not tried so hard to buy Cities.

As to why Pickens went after Cities, that is harder to say for sure. The rewards could be tremendous: if he pulled it off, Pickens would be buying oil in the ground at the bargain basement price of $5.50 a barrel, and Mesa would instantly join the ranks of the second-tier oil companies. But the risks were equally large: if he lost this deal, he might lose Mesa, his life's work. Even if he won, he would have to go more than $1 billion into debt. A number of analysts who watch Mesa for a living wondered out loud sometimes whether Cities was worth the risk.

But there was something else at work, something besides the cold logic of numbers and the assessment of risk. The fact is, Pickens loves making deals; they fuel him and excite him and challenge him in a way that the everyday business of his company does not. Perhaps even more than the successful search for oil and gas, Pickens' ability to make good deals has been the key to Mesa's rapid raise. I had tagged along with Pickens on this trip, as I would on all his travels for the next six weeks, and I asked him why he was pursuing Cities so doggedly. He proffered a wry smile, shrugged his shoulders, and said simply, "It's time to make a deal."

Wednesday, May 19, Houston

Boone Pickens harbored a special contempt for Cities Service. In Pickens' opinion, Cities, for the nine years that he had been casting covetous glances at it, had done everything wrong. It made diversification decisions that always seemed to sour. It had all that acreage but wasn't very good at finding oil and gas. Its stock was always undervalued. The Cities management knew full well what Pickens thought of the company, and consequently their dislike of him went beyond pure business judgment. In the summer of 1981, at a time when Wall Street was full of rumors about a possible takeover of Cities Service, Charles J. Waidelich, the company's chairman and chief executive officer, had told reporters that Cities was not interested in being bought; potential suitors, he had said, "should buzz off." He didn't mention any names, but everyone on Wall Street knew he was referring to Boone Pickens and Mesa Petroleum.

In fact, Pickens *had* made his first serious run at Cities that summer. First he bought up 4.1 million shares of Cities stock—5 percent of the company—for $180 million. But he couldn't hope to make a tender offer to go for 51 percent; Mesa was simply too small to be able to borrow the billions of dollars that it would take. Instead, he came up with an unusual idea: he would make his tender offer with the help of partners—other oil companies that saw in Cities the cheap oil reserves that he saw. By early summer he had lined up two companies to go in with him: Freeport-McMoran and Louisiana Land & Exploration.

In mid-August, however, Cities found out about the partnership and began to play very rough. One of its investment bankers called Freeport and Louisiana Land and told them that if they didn't back out, Cities would take *them* over. That was the end of Pickens' partnership. Round one to Cities.

Round two began about a month later, when Pickens started looking for a new set of partners. It was an arduous process, but by late this spring it was falling into place, and by the time Pickens got back to Texas from his trip to see the analysts in Boston, he had decided that it was time to call a meeting. On the Wednesday after his return from the East, his lawyers and his financial people trooped downtown to Mesa's Houston offices in the Dresser Tower to hear him try to talk a group of bankers out of a little money. About $1 billion, to be precise.

To open the meeting, Pickens made a short statement, telling the bankers that he hoped to make a tender offer for Cities stock on June 1 and that he hoped they would keep the information they were about to hear confidential. Then the lawyers and financial people filled the bankers in on the details, such as they were: Mesa would raise $1 billion by selling to a group of partners either stock that Mesa would issue or, later, Cities oil reserves. (The bankers didn't know it yet, but the partners were the Southland Corporation of Dallas, which owns the 7-Eleven chain; the Damson Oil Corporation of

New York; the Madison Fund, a New York investment firm; and the Sunshine Mining Company, a Dallas concern that runs a number of American silver mines.) The partners' $1 billion would serve as collateral for $1.3 billion that the bankers would then lend Mesa to complete the financing. With that much money, Mesa could offer $45 a share for 51 percent of Cities stock—about $10 higher than the stock was bringing on the market.

As his associates talked, Pickens walked out of the conference room with one of his aides. He was pleased to see the deal coming together, but he was worried that it wouldn't remain secret for much longer, because dignified forms of spying are a staple of takeover fights. He turned to the aide. "Look back there and tell me what you see," he said.

"I see a roomful of people," the aide replied.

"That's right," said Pickens. "And they all have one friend they can trust."

Friday, May 28, Tulsa

Pickens was right. Within days of his meeting with the bankers, word of it had leaked back to Cities Service's headquarters in Tulsa. Now Cities realized it was in a battle for its life, and it began plotting its counterstrategy.

That strategy was unveiled two weeks later, and it was consummate hardball. On Friday, May 28, Cities issued a press release that read in its entirety:

> Cities Service Company said it intends to commence a cash tender offer to purchase up to 51 percent of the voting power of Mesa Petroleum Company at $17 a share. First Boston Corporation and Lehman Brothers Kuhn Loeb will act as dealer-managers [meaning Cities' investment bankers] for the offer.

Cities had launched a preemptive strike, and a very clever one at that; for a targeted company to defend itself by going after its attacker was a brand-new strategy in the takeover game. Although there was some question in Pickens' mind as to whether Cities really wanted Mesa or was just trying to scare him off, there was no question at all that it could swallow Mesa if it so desired. So the Cities offer was a real threat. In making the tender, Cities had shown unexpected life—it wasn't the sort of thing plodding companies usually did. And Pickens, so wrapped up in pulling his partners together that he hadn't spent much time thinking about what Cities was doing, had been caught completely by surprise.

Monday, May 31, Houston

To understand the dynamics of a corporate takeover fight, you need mainly to keep in mind one length of time: twenty business days. Under federal law, when a company makes a public tender offer for a block of another company's stock, twenty business days must pass before the tendering company can actually purchase the stock. During that time, stockholders (meaning primarily the major portfolio managers on Wall Street, who control the fate of almost every major American corporation) who want to sell their shares "tender" them to the acquiring company. When the twenty days are over, the amount of stock the offer has attracted is announced and the acquiring company knows whether it has succeeded—that is, drawn 51 percent of the target company's stock—or failed. The waiting period is a frenetic, tense time: Wall Street comes alive with rumors, reporters scramble all over the story, and to the targeted company the twenty days seem like the grimmest of deadlines.

This, then, was the predicament Boone Pickens faced the day after Memorial Day: the Cities offer was about to begin, and the twenty-day clock would start counting down. Pickens did not yet have his partnership lined up, but even if he accomplished that within the next few days and made his own tender offer for Cities stock, Cities would still be in a position to buy Mesa before Mesa could buy Cities. That was an awful thought.

Pickens woke up early on Memorial Day in his Houston condominium. He began his day in typical Pickens fashion: he jogged several miles and then had a breakfast of cereal and fruit. All weekend long he and his advisers had grappled—unsuccessfully—with what to do about the Cities offer, and it was still very much on his mind. After breakfast he stepped into the shower, and that's when it hit him. It was an utterly simple idea. "Why don't we pull an ol' bear-hug deal?" he thought. Within an hour, he was at Baker & Botts.

A bear hug is a "friendly" offer that everyone knows isn't friendly at all—a bit like Russia's embrace of Poland. Unlike a tender offer, a bear hug is an offer made directly to the company's board of directors (rather than to the stockholders) and is contingent upon the board's approval. If the offer is high enough, sometimes a board will feel compelled to accept it, even when it doesn't want to, because of its legal responsibility to act in the best interests of the company's stockholders. That happens, but not often; most of the time a bear hug is simply a way of putting pressure on the board. It generates press coverage, it alerts the company's stockholders that there is an offer out there, and usually it is a signal that there is another, less friendly move in the offing—like a tender offer at a lower price.

Pickens had a little bit of all these purposes in mind when he conceived his bear hug. At the Baker & Botts offices, he laid out his idea to the assembled lawyers. What he wanted to do was call up Cities' chairman and chief executive officer, Charles Waidelich, and offer to buy out his company for

$50 a share. With Cities stock at about $35 a share, that was a 43 percent pre-mium. (In contrast, the Cities tender offer was only 25 cents higher than Mesa's closing price of $16.75 on Friday, May 28.) Such a transaction would cost Mesa about $4 billion, half of which Pickens planned to pay in cash and half by issuing $2 billion worth of Mesa stock to Cities stockholders.

"Is there any reason we can't do this?" Pickens asked.

Then Pickens dialed Waidelich's number in Tulsa. "Chuck," he said, "I want to tell you about an idea we have."

"I'm not interested," said Waidelich.

Pickens persisted. "Wait a second, Chuck, I want you to at least hear me out. The offer is for $50 a share..."

"I'm still not interested," replied Waidelich. "And it's not a formal offer anyway. It's not written down anywhere."

"Hell, we'll have an offer to you in Tulsa in three hours."

"I don't want it," said Waidelich.

"We've got to bring it to you now," said Pickens coyly. "We have a disclo-sure problem. Our stockholders need to know that we've made an offer."

"But it's *not* an offer," insisted Waidelich.

"Aw, Chuck," Pickens said, "you and I have been in business a long time and known each other a long time, and if we in this industry can't call each other up and explain things like this to each other, then we've gone a long way in the wrong direction." Then he added, "We'll get you an offer in the morning, and we'll have to put out an announcement, and I guess you'll need to call your directors on this."

"I have no intention of calling them," replied Waidelich. "We're not interested."

But from Pickens' point of view, it didn't much matter whether Waidelich was interested in the offer or not. The important thing was that the offer was on the table. At last Mesa was in the play.

Tuesday, June 1, New York

On the 39th floor of the Waldorf Towers, the toniest section of one of New York's toniest hotels, the Waldorf-Astoria, there is a large two-bedroom suite that is leased by the investment house of Lazard Frères. It's a businessman's suite, a place where a busy chief executive officer, in town on business, can rest his head by night and do his deal by day. The suite's color scheme is simple and to the point: everything is done in shades of white. Its main room conveys not so much comfort as function. Half the room is a dining area, the other half a living area (sofa, coffee table, oversized chairs), and between the two, acting as a divider, stands a single wooden desk. Although the Waldorf is in the heart of Manhattan, the blandness of the walls and the blandness of the view combine to give the suite a little of the feel of a military bunker, a hideaway 39 stories high. Except for its seven telephones, the suite is cut off from the rest of the world.

This was Boone Pickens' temporary headquarters in New York, the place where, as they say in the Mafia, he had gone to the mattresses. He had the suite thanks to the good graces of a Lazard partner, a fellow Texan named Jim Glanville (Pickens seems to have a good ol' boy network that includes every Texan on Wall Street). Glanville told him to keep the suite "as long as necessary," even though Lazard itself wasn't in the deal.

It had been late Monday night when Pickens arrived in New York. He had come for two reasons. First, and most immediately, he wanted to keep the negotiations with his partners on track and to get them signed up and Mesa's unfriendly tender offer readied within a few days. All he had so far was his friendly bear hug, which the Cities board was likely to turn down. He needed now to back that up with the tender offer—a much more serious threat to Cities because the management couldn't control its outcome. To that end, Pickens had scheduled a Tuesday morning meeting in the New York office of George Gould, the president of the Madison Fund, which was tentatively in the deal for $200 million.

The other reason Pickens was in New York was that, quite simply, that's where the action was. Texas might be where you could find oil and run a company, but only in New York could you do a deal like this. New York was where all the key players were; it was where you could hear all the rumors, and keep track of how "the Street" was reacting to your strategies, and be in constant touch with all the people on Wall Street who would be making decisions upon which your fate depended.

Pickens had brought an entourage with him. There was his special assistant, a former UT basketball player named John Bush, who had been brought in to man the phones in the suite. There was Robert Stillwell of Baker & Botts, who in 1964, as a cocky 27-year-old associate, had worked on the deal that created Mesa in the first place and had been doing legal work for Mesa ever since, becoming with time one of Pickens' most trusted advisers. There was Jesse R. Lovejoy, called Bob, a young partner in the old-line New York law firm of Davis, Polk & Wardwell, who maintained a perfect pinstripes-and-suspenders Wall Street appearance while eagerly helping Davis, Polk to jump into the ungentlemanly merger field. There were two investment bankers from the firm of Donaldson, Lufkin & Jenrette: Joe L. Roby, a senior vice president, and Hamilton James, a tall, gangling 31-year-old Harvard Business School graduate who did merger work for the firm but had never been close to a deal this big before.

For Pickens, there had been good news and bad news in the last few days. The good news was that his bear hug was having some effect on Cities Service. Waidelich might not have considered it a formal offer, but the reporters covering the deal had all treated it as such. Partly as a result of that coverage, there were, as Pickens had hoped, some large Cities Service stockholders—mostly Wall Street portfolio managers—who were calling the company's management and directors to find out what they were going to do about the offer. Through the Wall Street grapevine, Pickens heard that the Cities board of directors was now planning a meeting early the following week to consider Mesa's $50 bear hug. The Cities directors were starting to feel the heat.

The bad news, however, was of much more moment: the collapse of his carefully built partnership. Pickens got the first inkling of disaster during his meeting with Gould on Tuesday morning. A phone call came in to Gould from an acquaintance of his, Henry Breck of Lehman Brothers. Along with First Boston, Lehman Brothers was advising Cities Service in the deal, and it didn't take Gould long to discover that Breck was calling in that capacity. When Breck got on the phone he pointedly told Gould that if he stayed in the partnership with Pickens, "there would be a dirty fight and that Cities has adopted a scorched-earth policy" (as Mesa later contended in a court hearing).

So there they were again: the Cities scare tactics that had worked so well the previous summer. In the face of this threat, Gould did not back down. But the Southland Corporation, it turned out, had also received menacing phone calls from Lehman Brothers threatening a takeover attempt by Cities. And later on Tuesday morning Southland folded its hand.

Suddenly Pickens had lost a partner that had been expected to contribute $500 million to the deal. No lead partner meant no bankers and thus no money to make a tender offer. Last summer, after Cities had chased away Freeport-McMoran and Louisiana Land & Exploration, Pickens had been able to get the deal cranked up again at his own pace. Now he didn't have that luxury. That morning the Cities offer had begun; the twenty-day clock was running. Although the Cities offer, at $17 a share, was very low (Mesa's stock had risen higher than that on the stock exchange that day), there was no doubt that a lot of Wall Street professionals holding Mesa stock would tender it to Cities, on the assumption that Cities would eventually raise the offer. Under the timetable of the offer, Cities would be able to buy the Mesa stock tendered to it at 12:01 A.M. on June 28. On that date, if enough stock had been tendered, Cities would own Mesa Petroleum—unless Boone Pickens could pull a rabbit out of his hat.

. . .

For the past three years, the Mesa Petroleum Company has held its annual meeting in late April in the gymnasium of the T. Boone Pickens Jr. Fitness Center. The center is one of Pickens' favorite things; he is a health buff, and he built it because he wanted everyone at Mesa to be as healthy as he is. Located on the third floor of the parking garage adjacent to Mesa's modern headquarters in downtown Amarillo, the center has, besides the gym, a weight room, a jogging track, four racquetball courts (racquetball is Pickens' favorite sport), carpeted locker rooms, and a small staff in charge of ministering to the health needs of Mesa employees and their families.

At promptly 9:45 A.M. on the day of this year's annual meeting, the creator of the T. Boone Pickens Jr. Fitness Center ambled down the hall with his hands stuffed in his pants pockets. But his eyes were alert and focused straight ahead, and his head was cocked in the direction of an aide who was whispering something to him. Pickens usually has an aide or two hovering nearby; that comes with the territory. The schedule of everyone else at Mesa revolves around Pickens, and indeed his stamp is everywhere evident. Pickens dislikes large corporate bureaucracies, so Mesa gets by with only nine hundred employees. Pickens disapproves of interoffice romances, even when the two people are unmarried, so they almost never take place. Pickens hates smoking—he once fired the band at the company's Christmas party because the bandleader refused to stop smoking—so it is rare to see a lighted cigarette in the Mesa building. As a chief executive officer, Pickens makes a lot of money ($892,129 in 1981), has homes in Palm Springs, Houston, and Amarillo and a ranch near Pampa, and lives a life relatively free of the little daily annoyances that the rest of us face. Perhaps in return, his life is an endless series of phone calls and meetings. This morning was no exception.

As Pickens made his way toward the gym, he stopped periodically to greet some of his local stockholders, many of whom were waiting in the corridor for a chance to say hello. This was a task Pickens handled with the skill and grace of a diplomat at an embassy reception. As pleased as the stockholders were to see him, Pickens seemed equally pleased that so many of them had taken the time to come to his annual meeting. Mesa's Amarillo stockholders are no longer very important to the survival and growth of the company, but Pickens still treats them as though they were.

When Pickens finally reached the entrance to the gymnasium, he took a quick glance at his watch. It was 9:55. By ten o'clock Pickens, visibly anxious to begin, was standing at a podium that had been set up at the back of the gym. "Let's get started here on time," he said. Everybody sat down.

. . .

When Boone Pickens first started out, he couldn't have foreseen that someday he would be chairing the annual meeting of a major exploration and production company. All he knew was that he wanted to break into the oil business and make some money at it. The year was 1955, and Pickens was 27 years old, just four years out of Oklahoma State University's geology program.

By the time he graduated from college, Pickens had a wife and child to support, so when Phillips Petroleum offered him a job as a geologist he took it. For four years he worked for Phillips, and although he was learning his trade, he was never content there. One day, during one of his increasingly frequent harangues directed at the incompetence of his supervisor, a Phillips district geologist, his wife, Lynn, said, "If you don't like working for Phillips, why don't you quit?"

She hadn't meant it to be a serious remark, but the light bulb immediately switched on in Pickens' head—and two days later he was either self-employed or unemployed, depending on which way you looked at it. He had $1,300 in a Phillips thrift plan and, by then, two children.

With most of his savings Pickens bought a sturdy station wagon, which was probably the smartest investment a young man trying to get into the oil business could make; to get work, he had to spend most of his time on the road. Pickens would hear of a hot oil play in, say, Oklahoma, and off he would go to get whatever piece of the action he could find. He would do geological work. Or he would try to do small deals. Or he would do some well completion work. Sometimes he did all of those things at once. "I remember being up in Canadian, Texas, sitting on a well, and spending my time in a telephone booth trying to do some other deal," he says. "It's a hundred and ten degrees outside, and I'm about to get blown away in a windstorm, and all I can think about is that well ten miles away that I should be catching samples from." You could make a living like this, but it was a scramble.

Within a year Pickens had gained a reputation as being both honest and talented. One of the men who was impressed with him was his wife's uncle, a wealthy Amarillo businessman named John G. O'Brien. Together with another well-to-do Amarilloan, Eugene McCartt, the owner of a small grocery chain, O'Brien proposed to Pickens that they form a small oil company. This was exactly the break Pickens had been hoping for, and by September 1956 his first company, Petroleum Exploration, Inc. (PEI), had been formed.

Now he needed people who would invest in PEI, so he began knocking on the doors of businessmen in and around Amarillo who were known to do small-time drilling deals. He and a small staff put together one investor group after another, each with its own multiwell drilling program. As each group succeeded in avoiding too many dry holes, more people lined up to get into one of his investor groups. In 1959 Pickens took $35,000 and headed for Canada for the first time; good, cheap acreage was to be had there, and he formed a second company, called Altair, to get in on the play.

By 1964 both PEI and Altair had outgrown their original purpose. From six employees in 1956, the companies now had 26, and the drilling groups had multiplied to the point where three hundred outside investors owned four thousand separate properties in which the companies had an interest. Keeping track of their dealings had become impossibly complicated. To Pickens the obvious solution was to end the drilling groups and take the companies public. Looking back, it is obvious that going public was the right call; one man who put $80,000 into several PEI drilling groups says that today his investment is worth about $1.5 million. But it wasn't so obvious then, particularly because investors who traded their interest for stock would lose the tax breaks that came with doing individual drilling deals. To persuade his investors to swap their drilling interests for stock, Pickens once again had to knock on doors. By May 1964 he had 239 investors signed up. That month PEI went out of business, replaced by a newly formed public company, Mesa Petroleum, and Altair became a wholly owned subsidiary of Mesa. Mesa issued 420,052 shares of stock to its new stockholders.

The subsequent history of Mesa is a success story of almost fairy-tale proportions. In the oil field Mesa seemed to make all the right moves. It got involved in North Sea exploration, discovered a major field, and then sold out at the optimal moment. In the early seventies, Mesa was one of the smallest companies to bid on federal offshore leases in the Gulf of Mexico; today Mesa has a $1.5 billion investment in the Gulf, and its Gulf Coast division is its largest revenue producer. On Wall Street, Pickens pulled off a coup in 1969, when Mesa took over the Hugoton Production Company, a company with fifteen times Mesa's reserves. That deal instantly made Mesa a much larger company and made possible much of Mesa's subsequent success. Three years later, Mesa bought a second company, Pubco, in Albuquerque, which became the foundation for its Rocky Mountain and Permian Basin divisions. In 1969 Mesa's stock was listed on the New York Stock Exchange, where it rose and then rose some more. Not everything Pickens touched turned to gold, to be sure: Mesa's cattle division took a $20 million bath in 1974 when the bottom fell out of the cattle market. But even that had a silver lining; it taught Pickens that the oil business was what he was good at and what he should stick with. Never again did he try to diversify.

And as Mesa prospered, so did Pickens himself. At the time of the Hugoton deal, he was drawing a salary of $44,167 a year; a decade later it was over half a million dollars. He owns outright about a million shares of Mesa's stock, worth on a good day about $20 million, and has as-yet-unexercised options worth about $120 million. In 1980, after exercising one of his stock options, Pickens was named in several business magazines as the highest-paid executive in the country that year, taking down $7,866,000.

If there was a flaw in the Boone Pickens success story, it was at home. Pickens-watchers in Amarillo like to say that while he was building up Mesa, the one thing he had let suffer was his family. Pickens hates to hear that, because he doesn't think it's true—or at least he doesn't think that any problems at home stemmed from his work schedule. "I never missed a graduation, or a recital, or any of the other things fathers are supposed to do," he says in his own defense. When he wasn't on the road, he had dinner every night with his wife and four children, even if he had to return to the office later. "As long as any of the children had something to say, we would talk," he recalls now. "But as soon as they started some of that silly stuff, well, that wasn't in the program." Today, while he's quite close to his two sons, one a young stockbroker in Houston and the other a student at SMU, he is distant from his two daughters, a fact that pains him.

In 1971 Boone and Lynn Pickens were divorced after 21 years of marriage, and the following year he remarried. His second wife, Beatrice Carr, was from Oklahoma; she and Boone knew each other as children, and for Pickens this was a much more compatible match. Bea Pickens loved being part of his world, and she was caught up in the excitement of watching Mesa grow. He could talk to her about Mesa. She liked to run the ranch. She had expensive tastes, but he was making a lot of money and could indulge her. At the time of the marriage, her youngest daughter was 11 years old. That daughter grew up adoring Boone Pickens, and she still does.

Back in the gymnasium on the morning of Mesa's eighteenth annual meeting, Pickens was launching into a few closing remarks. "We plan," he said, "to take advantage of acquisition opportunities. There are only two ways a company like ours can grow: exploration or acquisition. Those are the only ways to expand the reserve base." And then he opened the meeting to questions.

If Mesa had any disgruntled shareholders, they were not in evidence that morning. Only two stockholders took the floor, the second of whom rose to say, "Mr. Pickens, I'm a stockholder and I just want to applaud you and the company on the job you've done." Everyone clapped at that, and Pickens replied, "Mr. Casey, we appreciate you coming here every year from Houston." On that note, the meeting was brought to an end. Pickens stepped away from the podium and once again glanced at his watch before wading into the crowd. It was 10:45. Exactly.

Wednesday, June 2, New York

It is extremely important to Boone Pickens to be in control of events around him, but now events were in control of him. He had come to New York to take over Cities Service, but Cities seemed much closer to taking over Mesa. He had no partners, and thus no way of putting together a serious tender offer for Cities. The bear-hug offer was on the table, but how often did bear hugs work? Time was running out, too: on June 28 Cities' waiting period would be over and it could buy Mesa.

At that desperate moment, Joseph Flom entered the picture. Flom, a lawyer, is one of the dominant figures in the small industry that has grown up on Wall Street around corporate mergers. He started doing takeover work a decade ago when most New York firms considered it unseemly. Today he is the most important partner in one of the fastest-growing law firms in the country: Skadden, Arps, Slate, Meagher & Flom. The merger in which Joe Flom is not working for one side or the other is rare indeed, and no matter how things turn out for the companies involved, they always turn out well for Flom. He has built his reputation up to the point where he does well even when there aren't any mergers around, because companies keep him on retainer simply to prevent him from ever being on the other side of a deal they might do.

On Wednesday, the day after the partnership fell apart, Pickens and his entourage trooped over to Flom's office and explained their predicament to him. Flom is a leprechaun—a short, white-haired, slightly stooped man whose pipe is never very far from his lips and whose expression is one of continual bemusement. He puffed on his pipe as he listened, asking questions but otherwise not saying very much. When they had finished, he looked up at Pickens and said, in a quiet voice, that yes, he did have an idea.

"Why don't you do a Dome-Conoco deal?" he asked.

Of course! There were some embarrassed glances around the room—why hadn't anybody thought of that before? What Flom had in mind was this: the Conoco-DuPont merger, which had dominated Wall Street the previous summer (and in which Flom had enlisted on Conoco's side), had begun in earnest after a small Canadian company, Dome Petroleum, made a tender offer for 20 percent of Conoco's stock. Dome had no intention of taking over Conoco; all it wanted was enough shares so that it could swap that stock back to Conoco in return for a controlling interest of the American company's Canadian subsidiary. However, instead of getting 20 percent of the stock, Dome was deluged with stock—more than 50 percent of Conoco's shares ended up being tendered to Dome. That was a clear signal to Wall Street that dissatisfaction among Conoco stockholders was high and that the company was ripe for a takeover. Then several huge, acquisition-minded companies—most notably, Mobil and Seagram's—jumped in with tender offers of their own, and the battle was on.

Flom thought that Mesa could do a variation on the Dome strategy. It could tender for whatever amount of Cities stock it could afford to buy without partners, say, 15 percent. Then—and here was the variation—if a majority of the stock was tendered, Mesa would not back away as Dome had done. Rather, it would use the stock as a lure to attract enough new partners to be able to buy not 15 percent but 51 percent, and hence control, of Cities. Nobody had ever tried this before; from now on, the Pickens team would be flying without instruments.

The details were worked out: Mesa would make a tender offer for 15 percent of Cities stock at a price of $45 a share. That was still about $10 a share higher than the stock was trading on the stock exchange. At $45 a share, 15 percent of Cities would cost Mesa just under $600 million, and Pickens knew from previous discussions with his banks that this was probably the most he could borrow for a tender offer. Before the meeting broke up, a launch date had been set. It was Monday, June 7, five days away.

Friday, June 4, New York

"This is supposed to be the best table in the house, you know." Boone Pickens smiled when he said that, and so did the others who were with him, but it was true. They were seated front and center in New York's fabled "21" club. If the Waldorf Towers is where chief executive officers roost when in New York, then "21" is where they dine. It is not a great restaurant anymore (if it ever was), but its reputation remains oddly undiminished; it is still one of those places in New York frequented by well-to-do businessmen simply because other well-to-do businessmen go there. The food and service hardly seem to matter.

Pickens likes to go to "21" whenever he is in New York, but this was the first chance he'd had this time around. Most of his evenings since his arrival on Monday had been spent in strategy sessions, either in the Waldorf suite or in a legal conference room, and most of his meals had been eaten in haste. Tonight he was planning to relax a little and forget about the Cities Service deal for a few hours.

Just as his dinner was served, however, the deal intruded, in the form of a man from another table who walked over and introduced himself to Pickens. Pickens stood up to greet him while the others at the table, most of them lawyers working on the deal, continued eating. The man turned out to be an employee of Cities Service, and he was just drunk enough to say exactly what was on his mind. "I hope you beat the pants off them," he told Pickens. "They're a bunch of f—ing assholes. They don't know what they're doing. The best thing that could ever happen to Cities would be for you to get them."

Pickens grimaced his way through this little diatribe, but when the man left, he happily recounted the conversation for the benefit of the others at the table who had missed it. "Boy," he said, "it's just amazing how much Cities is disliked."

The Mesa tender offer—for 15 percent of Cities Service's stock at $45 a share—was launched on Monday morning, right on schedule. The bank consortium was lined up; the documents were readied and flown to Washington, where they were filed with the Securities and Exchange Commission; and the reporters covering the deal had all received phone calls on Sunday night from Pickens in which he had briefed them on his latest move. By the time the New York Stock Exchange opened at nine o'clock, everyone on Wall Street knew that Boone Pickens was doing a Dome deal and Cities' stockholders had twenty days to tender their shares to Mesa. The clock was ticking.

With the market open, the first question for the people in suite 39-F of the Waldorf Towers was how was Wall Street reacting to the Mesa tender offer? At ten-thirty the first answer came in. Cities stock was at 36⁷/₈, down 1¹/₈ from where it had closed on Friday. A bad sign. If Wall Street had thought Mesa was going to succeed in swallowing Cities, the professionals would have begun buying Cities stock, intending to sell it to Mesa, and the price would have jumped instead of fallen. To find out why that wasn't happening, Bob Lovejoy went into one of the bedrooms and called several Wall Street arbitrageurs.

All the large investment houses have arbitrage departments, which make their money by betting on the outcome of a merger. Arbitrageurs—or arbs, as they are called on Wall Street—buy stock at the market price in the company they expect to lose the battle and tender it to the expected winner at the takeover price, which is always above market. In a small merger fight, the arb community sometimes controls so much stock that it can decide the outcome. The Mesa-Cities deal was far too big for that, but the arbs were still worth talking to, partly because they were the chief conduit of Wall Street rumors and partly because everyone else on Wall Street would be influenced by what the arbs were doing.

Lovejoy emerged a few moments later with his report. "Barry Allardice at Morgan Stanley says this was the perfect play for us, the best move we could have made right now. All the arbs think we'll get over 50 percent of their stock." The problem, Lovejoy continued, was that although the arbs might admire Mesa's move, they still saw Cities as being out in front. The reason was the time difference: the expiration date on the Cities tender offer for

Mesa was Monday, June 28; for the Mesa tender offer for Cities, it was Friday, July 2. Thus even if each side were to get 51 percent of the other's stock, Cities would be in front because it could take over Mesa four days before Mesa could take it over. Although Mesa had finally launched its tender offer, it still had one more mountain to climb. It now had to find a way to eliminate Cities' time advantage. For the people in the suite, that was the new priority.

The suite was filling up now, as it typically did late in the morning. The earliest arrivals were Lovejoy and Bush, who had breakfast with Pickens. Lovejoy had been up all night Sunday overseeing the preparation of the offering documents. But he still looked fresh and alert, and when he came in for breakfast he brought a bag of Granny Smith apples, which Pickens loves. Bush was now sitting at the desk, handling the blitz of phone calls coming in on the two phones there. Stillwell, who had just awakened, was sipping coffee at the table. Bea Pickens made her first appearance of the day before heading off for lunch with a friend; she had flown in from Texas over the weekend. Sitting on the sofa was a rumpled man named Richard Cheney. He was another charter member of Wall Street's merger industry, vice chairman of the public relations firm of Hill and Knowlton who specialized in "takeover and proxy fight PR."

Although objectively nothing of significance was happening, you could sense that the people in the suite were getting wound up. The doorbell rang frequently; most of the time it was the bellhop delivering envelopes for Pickens. Some of them contained telegrams of support from friends; others, wire service clips compiled by Hill and Knowlton; and still others, résumés from job seekers. The people in the suite paced around the room, changed seats, talked in small snippets of conversation, and, most of all, talked on the telephone. In the three weeks Pickens spent in New York, the ringing of the telephone was the sound he heard most often, and in some ways it was the most reassuring. The constant phone calls—from reporters, from Wall Street investment bankers passing along rumors, from stockholders, from his own office—gave Pickens, and everyone else in the room, the sense that suite 39-F was at the very center of the universe. During the time Pickens was there, Menachem Begin arrived in New York to address the United Nations and stayed in the Waldorf Towers. Also, 500,000 people from all over the country demonstrated in New York's Central Park against nuclear power. Pickens, completely absorbed by his own deal, scarcely noticed either event.

Around three o'clock, Pickens got a call from one of Mesa's investment bankers. Somebody turned on the speaker so everyone could listen.

"I talked to Bob Abboud. [A. Robert Abboud is the president of Occidental Petroleum.] He said, 'All of us would like to be involved, but the Doctor' "—meaning Dr. Armand Hammer, Occidental's octogenarian chairman—" 'is worried about an unfriendly deal.' The way to do this is to get Flom to talk to the Doctor. You have to have the Doctor understand how this is different from an unfriendly deal if 51 percent of their stock is tendered to us. [What this meant was that if a majority of the stockholders favored the transaction, the deal would not necessarily be considered unfriendly.] Flom has a long-standing relationship with the Doctor, so he's the one to do it. Anyway, Boone, I think there's a live interest here."

"Great," said Pickens. "I think this deal will be easy to sell if you've got 51 percent in your pocket."

"Right. But we still need to get Flom to sprinkle his holy water on it. And also, Boone, Abboud said if you're in a defensive mode and you need a white knight, they respect you and would be interested in being your white knight."

To this last remark, Pickens made no reply.

Pickens had planned a late-afternoon strategy session, and by five o'clock all the key strategists except Flom—who had a dinner engagement elsewhere—had assembled in the suite. Cities stock had closed at 36¼, down 1¾ from the opening price. The trading volume in Cities had been extraordinarily light for a company that had just been hit with a tender offer 25 percent above its market price.

Pickens slumped into one of the oversized chairs. He looked tired and discouraged. "Except for the papers this morning," he muttered, "this has been a zero day."

Everyone sat down around the coffee table. "I don't know what to say," Pickens said. "I thought we would be getting our presentation ready for the Cities board at this point."

Before he could go on, he was interrupted by a phone call. It was from a large Cities Service stockholder. Because of his holding, he could get through to some Cities directors, but he was unhappy with Cities' management, and for that reason, every time he had a conversation with someone at Cities, he immediately leaked what he had been told to Pickens. He was one of Pickens' main sources of intelligence in the deal; no doubt Cities had sources doing the same for it.

"He says he talked to Waidelich," said Pickens after hanging up the phone. "He said, 'I've got an awful lot of stock and I'm worried. What are you going to do at the meeting tomorrow?' Waidelich told him to hold on to his stock, because there would be no surprises at the board meeting. He complimented

Chuck, said he was absolutely cool and rational. There wasn't any panic in his voice at all."

"You know," said Lovejoy, "they could delay this thing for a month. They could say it's too complicated, it needs further study. That would be the smartest thing they could do."

The phone rang again, and Pickens walked over to the desk to take the call. Two of his own employees were calling in from Tulsa. On Pickens' instructions, they had gone there to see what they could glean from hanging around Cities' hometown. Pickens turned on the speaker.

"How did you do?" he asked.

"Well, we got into the Cities building today," one of them replied. "We applied for jobs. They wouldn't take our applications, Mr. Pickens."

Everyone chuckled at that.

"We had lunch in the Cities cafeteria. Boy, people sure are taking your name in vain around here."

"So if we get a house in Tulsa, you would advise that we get one with a big fence?" said Pickens.

"That's about right, Mr. Pickens."

While Pickens was taking a third call, Hamilton James of Donaldson, Lufkin & Jenrette proposed to the others a new idea that he thought might finally turn the tide in Mesa's favor.

"We need to get the date of their tender offer extended past ours," he said. On this point, everyone was agreed: as long as Cities had that four-day time difference, it was still in the driver's seat.

The way to accomplish this, James thought, was to find someone friendly to Mesa to make a competing tender offer for Mesa stock. The law says that any time there is a competing tender offer, ten days must be added to the timetable of the first tender offer. The loophole that James saw in the law was that there was nothing in the rules that said how much stock the tender offer had to be for. Thus James' scenario would work like this: someone would make a competing tender offer, but for only 10 percent of Mesa's stock. That would force Cities to wait an additional ten business days before it could begin to buy any Mesa stock. In the meantime, Mesa would put together its deal to buy a controlling interest in Cities. When July 2 rolled around, it would buy the Cities stock...and Cities would then become a subsidiary of Mesa Petroleum. Naturally, the new parent company would put a quick end to Cities' tender offer for it.

"It has to be a real tender offer," said Lovejoy. "They would have to come in because they thought it would be a good investment. Boone couldn't promise anything because then it would be a self-tender and the other side would go to court and say it didn't count."

But that was a minor quibble; the Mesa strategists, including Pickens (who had returned to the sofa), all thought that James was on to something.

"Ten percent of Mesa wouldn't be much," said Pickens. "About $140 million."

"I think you should figure a bit higher than that," answered Lovejoy. "More like $150 million to $170 million."

Clearly they would move ahead with James' plan. But it seemed somehow not to interest Pickens fully. "You know," he said, "I still don't think that board is going to turn us down tomorrow."

Tuesday, June 8, New York

Pickens was wrong. Late Tuesday afternoon, Cities Service announced that its board of directors had unanimously rejected Mesa's $50 bear hug and recommended that Cities stockholders do likewise to Mesa's $45 unfriendly tender offer. To underscore the announcement, Cities' chief executive officer, Charles Waidelich, met, for the only time in this deal, with a selected assemblage of merger reporters in the conference room of Cities' Park Avenue offices. He stood at a podium at the back of the room and read from a prepared statement. A civil engineer who had spent thirty years rising through the ranks at Cities, he looked tense and uncomfortable; his jaw was clenched, and beads of sweat were forming on his forehead. His voice was a little jumpy, but there was no mistaking the message: "The Cities Service board of directors is unanimous in its view that the board and not Boone Pickens will make the decision as to whether, when, and upon what terms Cities Service is for sale."

Having taken his little dig at Pickens, Waidelich then threw a new twist into the plot. The Cities board, he announced, had a new proposal—its own bear hug for Mesa. As Waidelich explained it to the reporters, Cities was offering to pay $21 a share for Mesa stock, contingent on the approval of the board of directors of Mesa Petroleum.

No one from Mesa was allowed into Cities' offices to attend the press conference, but somehow Richard Cheney, the PR man, managed to get a tape recording of the conference. Fifteen minutes after it was over, Cheney, Pickens, Bea Pickens, and the half-dozen others in the Mesa command post were listening to Waidelich on tape—and truth to tell, they were enjoying every minute of it. The reporters browbeat Waidelich, and he simply lacked the skill to deflect their questions gracefully. No, Waidelich said in response to one question, Cities had never, ever threatened to tender for any potential Mesa partner. "I just told them that I had looked at their company and they appeared to be very attractive," he said.

"That's the same thing, Mr. Waidelich!" bellowed Robert Cole of *The New York Times*.

Cheney found that exchange so amusing that he replayed it anytime someone new came into the suite.

At another point on the tape, Waidelich said he hoped Pickens would stay on if Cities bought Mesa—"I think Mr. Pickens could make a contribution" were the exact words he used—but his voice was so lacking in conviction that you could hear several reporters snicker.

Pickens barely had time to listen to Waidelich's statement before the phones began ringing; reporters wanted his reaction to the latest Cities move. With the tape recorder still playing on the coffee table, Pickens moved to the desk to be closer to the phones. The first call he took was from Robert Cole, a gravel-voiced man who had been Waidelich's chief antagonist at the press conference.

"How do you analyze the offer, Mr. Pickens?" asked Cole.

"Well," said Pickens, collecting his thoughts as he spoke, "the $21 is not much of an offer, that would be my feeling."

"How would you feel about staying with Mesa if Cities took it over?"

Pickens paused for a second and then grinned. "I would suppose that if Cities took Mesa over, then Chuck would offer me a job as Southwest Kansas district geologist, based out of Ulysses."

Cole chuckled and wrote down the line. "Southwest...Kansas... district..."

"Southwest Kansas district geologist, based out of Ulysses," repeated Pickens. "Did you get that, Bob? You can quote me on that."

Before rejoining the others, who were still playing and replaying the tape of Waidelich's press conference, Pickens took a call from another reporter, Tim Metz of *The Wall Street Journal*.

"Tim," said Pickens, "did you hear ol' Waidelich say there would be a job for me if Cities took us over?"

"I wasn't there, Boone, but I heard about that," said Metz.

"You know what the job is? He's going to offer me the position of Southwest district geologist, based in Ulysses." Metz laughed. "You can quote me on that, Tim."

Friday, June 11, New York

Every day he was in New York, Boone Pickens tried to find some time for running. He would usually rise at six o'clock, run several miles along the periphery of Central Park, and then return to the suite in time for a working breakfast with Lovejoy, Stillwell, and a few of the other Mesa strategists.

On this Friday morning, breakfast was over and Pickens, Stillwell, and

Lovejoy were all sitting around the coffee table, chatting about nothing of any great importance. The *Journal* and the *Times* were stacked on a corner of the table, and the latest batch of Granny Smith apples was piled high in a bowl.

The others were all dressed in suits, but Pickens had yet to get out of his postrunning clothes—a monogrammed white bathrobe and slippers. That casual attire, along with his generally relaxed air, made him seem more like a character on *Love Boat* than a man in search of $1 billion. But he had been deep into it for three days now. Around nine-thirty the group broke up. Pickens took a shower, got into a business suit, and headed downstairs to the other Waldorf suite Mesa was using, where he was scheduled to meet with a potential partner.

It was while he was attending this meeting that the bad news came over the Dow Jones wire: the Cities Service offer had drawn 45 percent of Mesa's stock in a proration pool. In every merger fight, the proration date is a kind of preliminary deadline that gives each side some idea of who is ahead so far. A creation of federal securities law, it comes ten days from the start of the tender offer, and the stock that is tendered in time to make the proration pool gets certain advantages over stock that comes in later. For that reason, Wall Street professionals always tender their stock in the proration pool if they are going to tender at all, and thus on the date the pool closes, a fair indication can be gleaned as to which way Wall Street is playing the deal. Pickens had hoped the number would be a lot lower than it was; some analysts had been telling him that it might be as low as 25 or 30 percent of the stock. Now he had to face the fact that if Cities raised its offer—and everyone on Wall Street assumed it would; that's why they had jumped into the pool in the first place—it would surely attract another 5 percent of Mesa, and maybe a lot more. Cities still had the four-day time advantage; it still had the financial advantage of being able easily to afford to buy the Mesa stock it got. And now there was no doubt that Cities was going to get enough stock to buy Mesa. It was still ahead in this game.

When Pickens returned from the meeting, he hung up his jacket and headed for the phones. He didn't talk much about the proration number; there was too much else to do. The pace of the deal had picked up over the past few days, and there was a sense of urgency that hadn't been there a week before. Time that was not spent looking for potential partners was time wasted. There was a much more clearly defined sense of purpose now.

Sitting at the desk opposite Bush, Pickens turned one of the phones around in his direction and went to work. His first call was to Charles Koch of Koch Industries, a huge, privately held company with petroleum interests.

"How would you like to get in the game here?" Pickens asked when Koch came on the line. "This is the Dome-Conoco deal. There is no doubt that we're going to get over 50 percent of their stock. The question is paying for it; we need to have financing for the 31 percent at $45 a share, which comes out to $1.1 billion.

"There are two ways we can go with this thing," Pickens continued. "One is we could take one partner. One partner could do this deal for $550 million and margin their position"—that is, use the first $550 million as collateral to borrow an additional $550 million—"for the remainder. Then you would own 30 percent of Cities' assets, and you're buying oil for about $5.50 a barrel. That makes it an extremely attractive situation. The second version goes like this: We could bring in several partners to raise the $550 million. They would buy Mesa preferred stock, we would leverage it, and pay for 50 percent of Cities. We would give the preferred a good dividend until it was redeemed, give you an agreed-upon discount of Cities reserves on the order of $5 or $6 a barrel."

Pickens paused for a minute, listening to Koch's reply, and then plunged back in again. "If you want to pick up a sweet deal, this is it. We have to do this quickly, though. If you are interested—and I strongly urge you to take several hours to look it over because it's such a beautiful deal—I would like to show you the deal up here on Saturday morning."

Koch was indeed interested. "Who's working on this with you?" he asked.

"We've got Joe Flom at Skadden, Arps, and Bob Lovejoy over at Davis, Polk, and a whole covey of lawyers at Baker and Botts. Hell," said Pickens, "I don't even want to know what the lawyers' bill is going to be."

Koch said he would talk to his people and get back to Pickens.

"You won't see a better stack of assets that you can get your hands on as cheaply," said Pickens.

With that call, Pickens was in gear. He immediately dialed J. Hugh Liedtke's number in Houston—Liedtke is the chief executive officer of Pennzoil. He wasn't in. "Tell him to call Boone Pickens," Pickens told Liedtke's secretary. "Tell him he's really gonna want to talk to me."

He asked Bush to order him some soup for lunch and went back to the phones.

When room service arrived, Pickens took a few sips of his soup, but then he was back on the phone, talking to Stephen C. Mahood, a Sedco executive vice president. The speaker phone was on.

"I think you can double your money in six months," said Pickens after explaining the deal.

Mahood was skeptical. "What happens if for some reason you can't get from 51 percent of Cities to 100 percent because of legal hang-ups or whatever?"

"All our lawyers tell us that is really unlikely," said James, "so what you're really looking at is putting up money for preferred stock and, six to nine months later, getting properties on an attractive basis. The key thing to know is that you don't put up your money until you know the 51 percent is there, so it's sitting there waiting to be grabbed."

There was a long silence. "Who do you have in the deal with you right now?" Mahood asked finally.

"Well," said Pickens, "we're talking to a lot of people. Sid Bass just left here a little while ago." Sid Bass, along with his father, Perry, has the largest private fortune in Fort Worth. "And there are some others. But if you have any interest, I would say come on up and we're available to you this weekend. I'm not kidding you, this is a sweet deal."

Another, even longer silence. "I'll think it over and call you back." But from the tone of his voice, he didn't sound as though he would.

Pickens made six more phone calls in a row, either to prospective partners or to people whom he thought might have an entrée to prospective partners. Hugh Liedtke called back and Pickens gave him the pitch. Another man Pickens talked to thought he might be able to interest Burlington Northern in the deal.

When he'd finished his flurry of calls, he stood up, stretched, and grimaced. "Boy, do I have a headache."

"Is there anything I can do?" asked Bush.

"Not unless you can order me a new head." Pickens wandered off to the bathroom in search of aspirin, muttering to himself on the way, "Is there anything I'm leaving undone?"

In between all the meetings and phone calls to would-be partners, there was one essential thing Boone Pickens had to take care of: he had to get somebody to carry out Hamilton James' scheme and tender for 10 percent of Mesa. Otherwise Cities would be able to acquire Mesa before Mesa could acquire Cities. In midweek, Pickens had called on an old and trusted friend and asked him to be the ten-percenter. The friend was Tom Brown, the founder and president of Tom Brown, Inc., of Midland. Pickens knew that he was asking Brown to take a chance on his behalf. Tom Brown, Inc., had $217 million in revenues last year; for a company that size, $150 million was a substantial amount of money. Brown would have to borrow it. If Mesa succeeded in taking over Cities, Brown would make some money in the deal;

and indeed, that would be his obvious incentive for getting in. But if the deal for some reason got hung up—in court, for instance—then Brown's $150 million would get hung up too. Nevertheless, when Pickens called him, Brown tentatively agreed to be his ten-percenter.

Late on Friday, Pickens came back to the suite from a meeting to find that Tom Brown had called while he was out. Bob Lovejoy had taken the call, and he wasn't happy. "Boone, what he wants to know is what happens if he has 10 percent of Mesa and then Cities wins. I told him that we'll figure out something. He'll probably want a contract that spells out what we'll do for him while we're still running the board."

"Can we do that?" asked Pickens.

"Well," said Lovejoy, "that gets into that tricky situation. It starts to look like a self-tender. We just can't have a tit for tat in this thing."

"What it comes down to," added Stillwell, "is that he's just gonna have to take your word for it as a good oilman and a good friend."

"Okay," said Pickens, "let's get him on the phone. I'll talk to him."

A moment later, Brown was on the other end of the line. "Hey, Boone," he bellowed over the speaker, "what's the timing on this thing?" Everyone in the room smiled. The ten-percenter was not going to be a problem.

Tuesday, June 15, Houston

Boone Pickens stood at the podium at the Albert Thomas Convention Center in downtown Houston and eyed the crowd uneasily. These were his people out there—prosperous, conservative Texas Republicans who believed, as Pickens did, in the virtues of free enterprise, the evils of government regulations, and the need for Governor Bill Clements' reelection. The convention center was a sea of dinner jackets and shimmering satin gowns. Ronald Reagan was there as the honored guest. Walter Mischer, the Houston developer who organized the dinner, had announced earlier that the event had raised over $3.5 million, more than any fundraiser in the history of the republic. That drew a round of applause. The previous record, he added, had been set four years ago when Bill Clements was first running for governor. Another round of applause. Pickens should have been delighted by the success of the dinner and by this audience of like-minded men and women, but instead, he looked as if he wanted to be someplace else. In a warm bed, for instance.

Pickens had come to Houston to be the master of ceremonies at the fundraiser. He is the state chairman of the Clements campaign and had committed himself to doing this months ago. But for the first time since the Cities deal had begun, he seemed worn down. It had been a tiring weekend. Late Friday afternoon, while Pickens was in a meeting at Skadden, Arps, Cities had done what everyone on Wall Street expected: it raised its hostile tender offer to $21 a share. At last, the Cities offer was above the market price of Mesa stock. The move virtually guaranteed that Cities could buy over 50 percent of Mesa, and that made finding new partners even harder.

The weekend had been spent in meetings with prospective partners. All day and well into the night the meetings had gone on, one piling up on top of another. There were so many people in town to hear about the deal that the Mesa players had split into two teams so two presentations could be made at the same time.

Despite the business allure of the deal—a chance to get oil in the ground at $5.50 a barrel doesn't come along every day—finding partners was proving to be a difficult task. The main stumbling block was all the legal what-ifs. What if each side ended up with 51 percent of the other? What if the deal got hung up in court? What if the ten-percenter was ruled out of bounds by a judge?

One of the first people Pickens had talked to about the deal was Edward Hennessey, chief executive officer of the giant Allied Corporation. For several days Hennessey had seemed extremely interested, but then his interest had waned. Pickens believed that the legal risks were what finally cooled Allied off. He also knew for a fact that that was why Sid Bass had dropped out of the deal. "He said he didn't want to risk $300 million on the possibility of them getting us before we get them," he told Stillwell, after receiving word that they were out. Stillwell just shrugged.

On Monday, Pickens had left New York for the first time in two weeks and flown to Los Angeles to call on Armand Hammer of Occidental Petroleum; the time had come for the mountain to go to Muhammad. At that point, Occidental was one of Pickens' best prospects: the company badly wanted some domestic reserves to hedge its operations in volatile foreign countries, and Flom had successfully "sprinkled his holy water on the deal" in a weekend meeting with Hammer. Pickens met most of Monday with a battery of Occidental executives, including Hammer, and although the Doctor was very quiet during the meetings, Pickens was convinced that Occidental still wanted in on the deal. After spending the night in L.A., Pickens had flown to Houston for a Tuesday afternoon meeting with the Clements campaign staff and for the fundraiser. But his mind was already back in New York.

During his turn at the podium, Pickens brought Cities Service into the proceedings. In the hallowed tradition of masters of ceremonies, he began by telling some bad jokes. "I hear Ringling Brothers is thinking of buying Cities Service," he said. "They want to get the clowns that are running that company."

Reagan threw his head back and let out several loud, practiced chortles, but much to Pickens' surprise, few others in the room seemed to know what he was talking about. Pickens tried a second Cities joke. Again, no response, except from the president, who had been to so many of these affairs that he could turn on the laugh track whether he understood the jokes or not. What was going on here? Didn't people read the papers? Weren't they following the biggest deal of the year? For three weeks Pickens had been wholly consumed by the Cities fight, and everyone he came into contact with on Wall Street was nearly as interested in it as he was. He had lost his sense of perspective. He thought what he was doing was just about the biggest thing happening in America at that moment, and he expected everyone else to think so too. But of course they didn't. Pickens hurried through the rest of his remarks, introduced the dignitaries sitting at the head table, and sat down. Then he folded his arms on his chest and slowly, wearily, closed his eyes, as if to shut out the world.

Thursday, June 17, New York

From the start, Boone Pickens had expected that Thursday, June 17, would be the most important day of the deal—and it was, but for a reason entirely different from the one he had in mind. Pickens had looked forward to Thursday because it was Mesa's proration date, the day he would know whether Cities' shareholders had tendered enough stock to him to provide the hook to snare a partner. As it turned out, he did get enough stock, but just barely. The final figure in the Mesa proration pool was 44.5 percent; coupled with the 5 percent Mesa already owned, it gave Mesa 49.5 percent of Cities. It was not quite majority control, but it was so close that the Mesa strategists all felt sure that it was enough to attract a partner; after all, with that much stock in the pool, Mesa could always *buy* a few shares on the open market to push the figure above 50 percent.

However, at one o'clock that afternoon, the proration figure suddenly became completely meaningless. At that moment the news flashed across the Dow Jones wire that an unnamed company had just offered "over $60 a share" for Cities stock. Cities had agreed to the offer. Ever since he had come to New York, Pickens had said that "a white knight is what can beat us in this deal." Now it had happened. For Mesa, the deal was over.

By late that afternoon, the basics of the new deal had been unveiled. The white knight was Gulf Oil, the sixth-largest oil company in America. The price Gulf was paying for Cities Service was $63 a share. Assuming the deal cleared the federal government's antitrust hurdles—something both Cities and Gulf assured their stockholders would happen—Cities was going to cost

Gulf $5 billion, making it the third-largest merger in history. What Pickens hadn't known was that for 48 hours Cities and Gulf had been furiously negotiating; nonetheless, when the announcement was made, he didn't find it completely surprising. He knew the people at Gulf. They liked the idea of acquiring cheap reserves on Wall Street as much as the next guy.

What, in the end, had driven Cities to find a white knight instead of just buying Mesa? On paper, Cities had all the advantages—it was bigger, stronger, and ahead in the timing of its tender offer. And yet, while each Mesa move had been more adlibbed than part of some grand design, when you added them all up, they combined to put great pressure on Cities. The Cities team had learned from its sources about Tom Brown and realized that when he came into the play, Cities' time advantage would be lost. Cities also knew that Pickens was out hunting up partners, and if he found them, Cities' financial advantage would be lost too. Like everyone else on Wall Street, Cities expected hordes of its stockholders to tender their shares to Mesa. Seeing all this, seeing that the company was in danger of being taken over by T. Boone Pickens Jr.—whom Cities' management reviled and who would surely fire them all the moment he had control of the company—Cities' management clearly became desperate for a way out. A white knight, even though it meant Cities would lose its independence, was the safest answer, at least as far as its executives' jobs were concerned.

Of course, it was also possible that Cities had just panicked. There was one piece of evidence that suggested as much. After the ink had dried on the Gulf-Cities pact, it was revealed that on Friday, June 11, the day Cities learned that its tender offer had drawn 45 percent of Mesa's stock, it had renegotiated the agreement with its investment bankers, First Boston and Lehman Brothers. In the original agreement, the investment banks would each have received fees of $2 million; under the new arrangement, Cities agreed to pay each of its investment bankers $1 million for every point its stock was sold above $50 a share. On that day it was suddenly in First Boston's and Lehman Brothers' best interests to sell Cities off to a white knight. "When I heard about that," one analyst said later, "I knew Cities was dead." Why would Cities sign such an agreement right in the heat of battle if it didn't think it was about to lose to Mesa? What was in it for First Boston and Lehman Brothers is less difficult to fathom. Thanks to that last-minute arrangement, they stood to split $26 million in fees from the Gulf-Cities deal.

Now all Pickens wanted was to cut bait and get back to Texas. There were just a few loose ends to tie up. He would have to decide tomorrow what to do with the 5 percent block of Cities stock he owned—whether to deal it back to

Cities, or sell it on the open market, or put it in the Gulf tender offer. And although the Mesa tender offer for Cities had been preempted by Gulf's higher offer, the Cities tender offer for Mesa was still on the table. That would have to be taken care of, too. But in all likelihood, he thought, he would be on the way to Amarillo by noon on Friday.

Thinking that his work in New York was largely finished, Pickens made a reservation at "21" for himself, Bea, and several of the people who had been with him the past three weeks: Stillwell, Lovejoy, Jim Glanville, Joe Roby, and a few others. But before he left the suite for his last dinner in New York, he had a few phone calls to make. He called Amarillo and spoke with several Mesa directors who were awaiting word from him about the events of the day.

"We did agree on something here," Pickens said after explaining the Gulf offer to them. "We all signed it on a pink doily. We agreed that we would not go for any takeover target larger than $1.4 billion, and the second thing is— and I like this part the best—*no partners!*" Everyone laughed. "If the deal can't be done with Mesa, Tom Brown, and Mike Boswell [the president of Sunshine Mining], we're not going to look at it. Tom and Mike are the only ones who have the balls to go for the deal."

"What happens if they keep tendering?" one of the directors asked.

"I don't know," said Pickens. "But they're ready to quit."

"They don't want us," added Stillwell, who was on another extension, "and they never wanted us."

Pickens placed one last call, to Midland, to tell Tom Brown that the deal was over. He was effusive in his thanks. "We'll be back," he said.

"Tell him he gets four days of free legal service from Baker and Botts," said Lovejoy. Everybody laughed.

"And we'll write him a will," chimed in Stillwell.

"Tell him we may still need him," said Roby. But nobody seemed to notice that last remark.

Friday, June 18, New York

On his last day in New York City, Boone Pickens woke up with a hangover. At eight-thirty, when most of his team arrived at the suite, he sat slumped in one of the oversized chairs by the coffee table, his monogrammed shirt open at the collar and his head resting against his right hand. He looked bleary-eyed.

Dinner at "21" had been a semisweet affair; there was no small pride taken in the knowledge that they—little Mesa Petroleum of Amarillo, Texas—had been the force that brought about the third-largest deal in American history. "We put a $5 billion deal in play with no money," Stillwell had boasted several times. But there was also disappointment that the play was over and they had not come away with the brass ring. There had been several rounds of drinks during dinner, and a few bottles of wine, and afterward, Pickens, Stillwell, and Lovejoy had returned to the suite, where they drank whiskey and talked about the deal until three in the morning.

The three men had let their hair down like this because they were sure that Friday would be an easy sign-the-documents-and-get-out-of-town day. And there was every reason to think they were right. The Gulf-Cities agreement was a monster transaction, surely the sort of thing the federal government was going to want to take a closer look at. Liberal senators like Howard Metzenbaum of Ohio were likely to start howling at the thought of a merger of two oil companies that size (in fact, he did); the Federal Trade Commission was bound to want to inspect the deal for antitrust implications. The last thing Gulf and Cities needed was someone else hovering around the edges of their deal, screaming antitrust. That was Mesa's last card: if Cities didn't drop its tender offer for Mesa, Mesa could run to the courts and attempt to break up the Gulf deal, claiming that it violated the antitrust laws. In 1981, when Mobil had tried to take over Marathon Oil, Marathon blocked the Mobil offer by getting an antitrust ruling from a U.S. district judge in its home state of Ohio. There was no reason Mesa couldn't try to get a Texas judge to make a similar ruling. That was the logic arguing for Cities to drop its tender offer, and it was persuasive. But as Pickens was beginning to discover this Friday morning, Bruce Wasserstein had other plans.

Wasserstein, First Boston's takeover specialist, is the acknowledged master of merger mania. He is a short, paunchy 35-year-old who looks like he's sweating even when he's not—one of those people whose glasses are forever sliding down their noses. Like everyone on Wall Street, Wasserstein wears expensive pin-striped suits, but he has enormous difficulty keeping his shirttail tucked in. No one at First Boston, however, is about to tell Wasserstein to tuck in his shirttail; he and Joseph Perella, his codirector in First Boston's mergers and acquisitions department, have turned what was once a lethargic division into the most profitable section First Boston has. They've done it by being the quintessential hardball players; corporations to them are little more than pawns on a chessboard, there to be captured by a clever tactician. At symposia, Wasserstein has been known to make a case that mergers are good for the economy, but it's hard to believe that that's what he thinks about when he's at work. What Wasserstein likes to do is win, and what he especially likes to do is win in a deal that's never been done before. And despite all the arguments against tendering for Mesa, that's the opportunity he saw before him.

Wasserstein had done big deals before; First Boston had had a hand in both the U.S. Steel–Marathon deal (the largest deal in history) and the DuPont-Conoco merger (ranked number two). What he had never done before—what no one had done before—was a deal in which two companies fell at the same time. If he could persuade Gulf to let Cities sweep up Mesa even as Gulf was buying Cities, then he'd have it: the first double merger, one for the record books. The deal had other appeal as well. Gulf would get Mesa's acreage and properties, which, though smaller than Cities', were in prime locations; Cities would get to extract a measure of revenge against Boone Pickens; and Wasserstein would get an additional fee.

Pickens had his first clue that something was amiss soon after the stock market opened. Several analysts called to tell him that an arb rumored to be close to First Boston had been buying Mesa stock. Since Mesa stock was expected to take a big drop once Pickens got out of the deal, that didn't make any sense... unless the arb knew something Pickens didn't. Then, at nine-thirty, an investment banker called to tell Pickens that a First Boston oil analyst from the Denver office had flown in to make a presentation to financial officers of Gulf and Cities that morning. The subject of the presentation: Mesa Petroleum. "Wasserstein's saying this deal will be a cinch," the investment banker told Pickens. "They're saying Mesa is worth $35 a share and that the $21 tender price is a steal. My sense," the banker added, "is that they probably know it's not in their best interest to go after you, but First Boston is trying to exploit the human emotion of people like Waidelich who want to stick it to Boone Pickens."

Pickens was taken aback. "I can't believe they're really serious about this," he said when he got off the phone.

"I believe it, all right," said Joe Flom. "There's a fee in this for First Boston—and a big one."

Pickens knew there was something to that; the deal was now in the hands of the Wall Street merger industry, which has strong imperatives of its own that carry over from one merger battle to the next. When this deal was over, Pickens would go back to Amarillo and run Mesa Petroleum; Flom would stay in New York and work on another merger. Flom and Wasserstein and Martin Lipton (Flom's legal counterpart on the Cities side) were all friends. Flom worked on as many deals with Wasserstein as against him and had lunch with Lipton once a week no matter how gruesome the particular battle they might be fighting. For Boone Pickens and Mesa Petroleum and Charles Waidelich and Cities Service, the past three weeks had been a battle for survival. For Flom and Lipton and Wasserstein, it had been another very lucrative job. This last-minute hitch was a lethal threat to Mesa and blood revenge to Cities, but to the merger pros it was just another day's work.

By now, there were fourteen people in suite 39-F: James and Roby, Lovejoy, Stillwell and other assorted lawyers, several Mesa financial people, and Bea Pickens. The room had become tense; people would pick up the newspaper and glance at it and then put it down, or stare at the floor, or look out the window. When the deal had been in full swing, the sense of isolation that came from being in the suite had added to the feeling of control: it was a place where you could hold your cards close to the vest. Now that isolation was debilitating: there were people out there plotting against you and you had no way of knowing what was going on. You were cut off. Pickens was sitting at the desk, manning the phones himself. He seemed less overtly nervous than the others, but occasionally he would bite his lip. "Boy," he said, "you just know that they can picture this little scene over here and they're loving it."

There was nothing to do at the moment except wait, but Flom did have one idea. "I think you should call Tom Brown," he said. "We ought to have him standing by, just in case."

"Boy, I hate to get him cranked up again," said Pickens, but he realized that Flom was right, so he put in a call to Brown. Brown wasn't in.

Now it was Pickens with an idea. "I think I should call Jimmy Lee," he said. (James E. Lee is the president of Gulf Oil.) "He's a friend. He knows what he's got at stake here. And I'll just tell him, 'We're playing this like it's a battle, and if we have to come after your deal, we'll do it.'"

"What's the downside risk?" asked Flom.

"None," said Lovejoy. "It's a good idea, Boone."

Pickens assumed Lee was in New York, but he didn't know where to find him. So, like anyone else looking for the president of Gulf Oil, he called Pittsburgh and spoke to Lee's secretary. "This is Boone Pickens," he said. "I really need to talk to him." She promised she would pass on the message. Pickens hung up and redialed Tom Brown's number. Still no luck.

"I think he's ducking us, Boone," one of the lawyers said.

Then he called his office and got the latest stock and cattle futures prices. A few analysts called in, and Pickens tried to find out if they had any news about Cities' plans. They didn't. He was getting frustrated. "I would like to get out of New York," he said. "This is just costing us money."

"What can we do to make it tough for them now?" asked Lovejoy.

"We could get some congressional guys to say they want an investigation," suggested Flom.

"I've never asked a politician for help," said Pickens, "and I sure don't want to start now."

"At a minimum, Boone, we've got to stop talking to the press like it's all over and maybe start making some antitrust noises," said Lovejoy.

Just then the phone rang. Thinking it might be Lee, everyone immediately stopped talking so they could hear the conversation. Pickens grabbed the receiver. It was Tom Brown.

"Listen, Tom," Pickens began, "this may not be over. First Boston is trying to go after us. They're saying it's a cinch deal and they should take over Mesa. So we really need your help now. Same deal as before."

Pickens listened quietly for a moment. It was obvious from looking at him that the news he was hearing was not good. "What we might consider doing," he said, "is putting out a press release saying you were lining up financing for us and you're still considering a tender offer."

Flom interrupted. "Can't issue a press release," he said. "You have to make a tender and you have to do it today. Monday's too late."

Pickens relayed this to Brown, after which the conversation ended. "He's gone," he announced to his somber team. "His lead banker is heading for Europe and all his people are dispersing every which way. He doesn't think there's any way he can get it going again."

Pickens frowned. Mesa had just lost its ace in the hole. If Cities wanted to buy Mesa's stock, there was no legal way Mesa could stop it.

It was creeping toward noontime. Still no word about the First Boston meeting. Pickens tried Lee's secretary a second time. She said she had given him the message. The suite was very quiet.

From the back of the room, one member of the Mesa team suddenly broke the ice. "Boone," he said, "maybe you ought to start thinking about a white knight." The unthinkable had just been thought.

Everyone looked up at Pickens to see his reaction. "No!" he said angrily. "We're not going to do that unless we've run out of options, and we're not near that point yet. Hell, I haven't gotten in touch with Jimmy Lee. I've got confidence in Jimmy. Gulf is running this thing, isn't it?"

"It's their money," said Flom.

Pickens calmed down and leaned back in his chair. "Boy," he said, "if I had known they were going to do this, I wouldn't have stayed up so late last night. This thing has gone from a lot of fun to no fun at all real fast."

Just then a phone call came in for Joe Flom. It was Marty Lipton. *At last!* Lipton would no doubt be relaying word from First Boston. Flom trundled off into one of the bedrooms to take the call. His negotiations with Lipton were almost always conducted in deepest secrecy; not even Pickens got to listen in on their talks. It was all part of the mystique of the merger pros: when the deal hung in the balance, they could face each other down in private.

Flom emerged from the bedroom with a new First Boston proposal in hand. The deal was this: to get Cities to drop its tender offer, Mesa had either to sell its block of Cities stock back to Cities for the same price it had paid (about $45 a share) or to sell the stock on the open market at the going price (probably around $55 a share) but pay Cities a $35 million fee for the privilege of doing so. The point of the $35 million fee, it seemed to Pickens and the others, was to embarrass him. Cities wanted to be able to say that it had forced him to pay $35 million to stay independent. In addition, Flom reported, Mesa had to sign something called a standstill agreement, in which it promised not to buy any Cities stock for five years. Cities, on the other hand, would not have to make a similar pledge about Mesa stock.

"Basically," said Flom, "it's a $35 million holdup. The silver lining in the thing is that it means they don't want you. They're looking for some kind of agreement. But they're betting you won't be willing to bet your company for $35 million. And we're betting they're not willing to screw up their deal for $35 million."

Stillwell nodded his agreement. "It's down to another blinking contest."

Flom stood up and got ready to leave the suite. It was lunchtime, and he had a date with Bruce Wasserstein. He explained to Pickens that the lunch had been scheduled a long time ago and that it concerned another matter—no doubt a deal in which the two of them were working the same side of the fence. Before Flom left, Pickens gave him a message to take to Wasserstein: he could live with the standstill agreement but not the $35 million fee. Still, he was a little put out to see Flom leave to have lunch with the enemy at such a critical moment. But he didn't have much time to dwell on it, for ten minutes later Lee called.

"Jimmy," Pickens began, "are you up to speed on this deal? Well, let me tell you what's going on here." Suddenly the only sound in the suite was Boone Pickens' voice.

"They're talking about having a five-year standstill for us while they don't have any such thing. But the big point is, they are asking us to give them $35 million in the deal. I don't know if you are aware of that or not. That's just unwarranted. We're quite willing to endorse your deal, but I can't see $35 million holding up a $5 billion deal."

Pickens listened to Lee's response for a moment and then continued. "You know my personality well enough to know that I'll get in a fight if I have to. So if the $35 million stays, we're going to have to go after your deal with everything we've got. Antitrust and everything else. It's gonna end up costing one helluva lot more than $35 million. Now, I know that won't bother Marty Lipton a bit. He'll like that play."

Again, Lee said something, but the speaker phone was off, so only Pickens could hear him.

"What's happened in this deal, Jimmy," he said after a long pause, "is there are some people over there who are vindictive. And that's unfortunate. What we need in this thing is a cool head like yours who can go in and say, 'Let's get this damn thing over with.' And our relationship goes back long enough that I don't want to get into a big fight with you. I think if you went in there and calmed the waters, it will be over in two hours, and that's all there is to it."

They spoke for a few more minutes and then the phone call was over. Pickens leaned back in his chair and allowed himself a smile. The tension in the room immediately lifted; if Pickens was no longer worried, then neither was anybody else. "He says they're stretching for this deal at $63," Pickens told the group. "He doesn't want to buy Mesa. That's just a wild idea of Wasserstein's."

Fifteen minutes later, Joe Flom called in. He had something to report from lunch: Wasserstein had made a new offer. Mesa could get out of the deal if it sold its block of stock back to Cities for $55 a share and agreed to a five-year standstill. The $35 million fee was no longer part of the deal. "Okay, Joe," said Pickens, "come on over here and we'll talk about it."

Later in the day, Flom let it be known that he thought it was his lunch with Wasserstein that had turned the tide for Mesa; he had "handled" Wasserstein. Pickens was equally convinced that it was his phone call with Jimmy Lee that had caused Cities to back off. Perhaps they were both right.

It took Flom an hour to return from lunch, and by that time the matter was all but decided. Pickens wanted to take the money and run. The new Cities offer was still $8 a share less than the $63 price Gulf was offering to pay for Cities stock. With Mesa owning 4.1 million shares of Cities, the total difference between the two prices was . . . $35 million. On the other hand, at $55 a share, Mesa would still be making a $10-a-share profit over what it had paid for the stock—$45 million in all. Pickens asked one of his financial people to figure out the profit Mesa could show as a result of selling the stock at that price. After a few minutes in consultation with his pocket calculator, the man came up with a figure of $24 million. "Better than a punch in the eye with a sharp stick," said Pickens.

There was another reason Pickens wanted to sell his stock now, rather than wait and tender the stock to Gulf at the higher price. His talk with Lee had convinced him that the Cities-Gulf deal was soft. The more he thought about it, the more he felt that the deal might fall through. If that happened, Cities stock would take a terrible nose dive and Pickens would end up losing money instead of making it. By midafternoon, when Flom got back to the suite, the $55 offer was looking better and better. Flom went into the bedroom and called Lipton, and the deal was done.

The rest of the day was all silk. Roby and James worked on getting Mesa's actual Cities stock certificates from the New York depositories where they were kept—no easy matter since the depositories had by then closed for the weekend. Stillwell and Lovejoy went over to Lipton's office, two blocks from the Waldorf, to hammer out the agreement. And everyone else stayed in the suite, listening to Boone Pickens tell tales of the old days at Mesa Petroleum. By eight-thirty, two limousines were parked outside the building where Lipton had his offices. Boone Pickens sat in the back seat of one of the limousines, with Bea next to him. He was in good spirits, even though he knew that on Monday morning, despite Mesa's profit, Mesa's stock was going to take a big drop. That's what always happened when a deal ended this way. "The first rule in the takeover defense manual is to get your stock price up," he said. "And if you can't get your price up, buy someone else first. So don't worry about ol' Mesa. We'll be back."

Epilogue

On August 6 Gulf Oil announced that it was canceling its merger with Cities Service because of antitrust objections raised by the Federal Trade Commission. Pickens' instinct had been right, and so was his decision to sell the block of Cities stock back to Cities for $55 a share. The next day that stock plunged to the mid-thirties. This event caused great anguish on Wall Street, particularly among the arbitrageurs, all of whom had thought the deal was a lock and had therefore loaded up on Cities stock. There were stories circulating that the Gulf pullout cost Wall Street as much as $400 million. Some people were even saying that the failure of this deal might have a permanent cooling effect on merger mania.

But on August 13 that talk stopped. Occidental Petroleum, which had been in Mesa's camp back in June, stepped in and offered to take over Cities. On August 25 Cities accepted the offer. The new offer averaged $53 a share, which meant Occidental was paying $4 billion to acquire Cities instead of $5 billion, as Gulf would have done. Even at that price, the deal still qualified as the third-biggest merger in history. Bruce Wasserstein was still Cities' merger strategist, but the new deal cut his fee in half. Now it was $6.5 million instead of $13 million. Joe Flom received $1.1 million from Pickens for his efforts and went on to represent Occidental in the new deal.

As for Boone Pickens, his stock did drop, as expected. After he returned to Amarillo, Mesa stock got as low as $12, down from about $18, which was where it had been while the deal was running. Not only that, but half the profit he made on his Cities stock—$12 million out of $24 million—was eaten up by the cost of the month-long circus in New York. "We gave a party," said Pickens, "and it was expensive."

But in July the rumors started up, and so did Mesa's stock. First, Pickens was supposed to be getting ready to make a tender offer for Louisiana Land & Exploration. Then, he was said to be negotiating a merger of some sort with a much larger oil company, Amerada Hess. By the end of the summer, nothing had happened in either case. But Boone Pickens was still looking for a deal. All the analysts said so.

CHAPTER 2

Jobs Agonistes
(Steve, That Is)

W ell, we all know how this turned out, don't we?

I wrote the *Esquire* 1986 profile of Steve Jobs at an unusual moment for him: he was vulnerable. A year and a half earlier, barely 30 years old, he had left Apple, the company he'd co-founded a decade before, after losing a power struggle to John Sculley, the former Pepsi executive he had lured to Apple some years before. He had sold all but one share of his Apple stock. Though he had a girlfriend, he personal life was pretty much nonexistent. He was deep in the middle of rolling out an ambitious new company, called NeXT, which was going to manufacture a new computer, aimed at the academic and research community. It was impossible to know, at the point at which I met him, whether the new company was going to work or not. His attitude toward Apple was deeply ambivalent; most of what came out of his mouth was contemptuous of his old company. But you could also see that he still cared deeply about what went on at Apple. He wanted it to stumble because that would prove how indispensable he was. He wanted it to succeed because it was still his baby. Founding NeXT was partly an act of revenge and partly a form of psychotherapy.

Even as a young man, Jobs always had a deep need to be in control. I saw plenty of that while I was working on this profile; I remember sitting in a meeting at Pixar, which Jobs had just bought from George Lucas, and watching him absolutely eviscerate a Pixar executive who didn't seem to care enough about staying on budget. I also saw it in the way he treated me at times. I was walled off from certain people he didn't want me to talk to. Though I theoretically had "access" at NeXT, he carefully chose the meetings I could attend. In truth, the only person he really wanted me to talk to inside the company was himself. If you read the article carefully, you'll notice that virtually every voice in the piece that is not Jobs' comes from someone who no longer worked for him.

On the other hand, he gave me far more time than I'd ever imagined I'd get when I first went out to Silicon Valley to do this story. And the interviews themselves had a raw quality that I still find startling. He took me to his house one night to show me a photo album that contained pictures of the old days, when he was inventing the Macintosh computer. We had several lengthy dinners, after which we would keep talking as he drove me back to my hotel or to his office. On my last night in Palo Alto, we sat in the parking lot and talked for an hour before I headed back to my hotel.

I wonder now: was I being manipulated? That's a question you always have to ask yourself when you're dealing with Steve Jobs—something I understand now in a way I didn't 20-plus years ago. Perhaps. But as I read over the piece, it is hard to see how. Later, Jobs would become known among business journalists for only making himself available when he had a product to sell; indeed, he would often refuse to pose for a cover shoot unless the photographer agreed to include the new product in the picture. But in this case, the new NeXT computer was still months away from completion, and really, he didn't have anything else to sell. I think I just happened to catch him at a rare moment when he wanted to reflect on his life. I think he was lonely.

A decade later, when Apple bought NeXT for $400 million, I was on the staff of *Fortune* magazine. Far more than his founding of NeXT, Jobs' return to Apple really marked the beginning of his comeback. The NeXT computer turned out to be a flop; by 1993, Jobs had abandoned the hardware to focus on software. And that's what Apple acquired: the NeXT operating system that became the foundation for a new Macintosh operating system. Plus, of course, Apple got Steve Jobs back. By 1998, he was "interim" CEO; by 2000, the "interim" label was dropped.

At *Fortune*, of course, we chronicled Jobs' subsequent triumphs: the creation of the iPod and iTunes; his masterful ability to convince the major music labels to throw in their lot with him; his amazing showmanship and marketing talent; the way he transformed Apple, more or less single-handedly, from a technology also-ran into the coolest, sexiest, hippest consumer electronics company ever. Bill Gates, his erstwhile technology rival, has largely moved on from Microsoft, but Steve Jobs is still at the white hot center of technology.

I never wrote about Apple when I was at *Fortune*, but I saw enough—especially in his dealing with the magazine's other writers and editors—to realize that the days when Jobs might be willing to talk openly about his life were long over. Every corporate executive uses the press to some degree, but few are as blatant about it as Jobs. And no one is as difficult. As its successes mounted, Apple became an astonishingly arrogant company—an attitude, I came to believe, that was a reflection of its leader. Since joining *The New York Times*, I've written columns that touch on that arrogance, several of which I've included in this chapter. Whenever I call Apple now, I either get no response or an e-mail parroting the Apple party line. That's what happens when you write something Steve Jobs doesn't like.

"My self-identity does not revolve around being a businessman," Jobs told me in 1986, "though I recognize that is what I do. I think of myself as someone who builds neat things. I like building neat things. I like making tools that are useful to people." Twenty-two years later, Jobs is still building neat things and making tools that are useful to people. But I can't imagine that he doesn't now view himself as a hard-core businessman. I would love to be in a position again to ask him that question. But I know I never will be.

The Second Coming of Steve Jobs

Esquire, December 1986

You see them everywhere in Silicon Valley. They are young and unattached and usually men. They favor jeans and T-shirts, and they live in $400-a-month apartments. You see them early in the morning, driving up Route 101 toward the squat, ugly buildings that serve as offices in the Valley, and you see them ten or twelve or fourteen hours later, as they straggle, one by one, out of those same buildings late at night. Almost always, their briefcases are bulging with things they want to work on at home, after dinner.

To an outsider, they can seem a little odd, these people who are drawn to Silicon Valley. Certainly they are single-minded. For although the Valley is awash in money, that is not what has drawn them here. Not really. The Valley is filled with natural beauty, but that does not move them either. They are not here to find love or to enjoy their leisure time. They have come here to work, and they are happiest when they are putting in their fourteen hours in front of their computer terminals. Work is what excites them, what fuels them. Those who consider themselves the luckiest are the people who work for the smaller and newer companies, the "start-ups," where 90-hour weeks are common, and where the intensity of the work experience is as powerful and as addicting as any drug. Maybe that's not so odd. We live, after all, in a culture in which an increasingly large number of people view their work in a similar fashion—not just as a part of life, but as the essence of life. It's just that in the Valley everyone is like that.

And even as Silicon Valley represents the apotheosis of the modern work ethic to the rest of the country, so are there people within the Valley who represent it, in even purer form, to those already here. There are monks among the priests. There is Steven P. Jobs.

He sits at the head of a small conference table in a small room on the second floor. He is chairing a staff meeting. Around the table are seven other people, five men and two women, the oldest of whom is forty. They compose his current inner circle, the key members of a team he has been assembling since a year ago last September—ever since he left Apple Computer, the company he began in 1976 when he was 21 years old. The company he had loved.

Now he has a new company to love, and he has named his new company— his life-after-Apple company—NeXT Inc. Though the name reeks of all-too-obvious symbolism, the small *e* signifies nothing in particular. Almost before he knew what his new company was going to do, Jobs spent $100,000 to have Paul Rand, the grand old man of American graphics, design the company logo; Rand came up with the lowercase *e*. This extravagant bit of aesthetic detail is a classic Jobs touch.

It is late July. The NeXT staff has been deep in "start-up" for eight months. They are building a computer. Not just any computer, mind you, but the neatest, greatest, whizziest computer you ever saw. "We're going to take the technology to the next level," says Jobs enthusiastically, immodestly. The schedule is as ambitious as the computer itself, for they are attempting to have it completed by the fall of 1987. Already there is a feeling that time is running short. A manufacturing plant is still not past the planning stages. People—"great people," "people with our kind of values"—still have to be hired by the handful to add to the thirty or so already on board. There are still major technological hurdles to overcome, and a sales force to put in place, and complicated software to write, and a million other things to do. And Jobs is everywhere—advising, pushing, berating, encouraging. This new computer has become his primary focus, to the exclusion of everything else, including his personal life. What there is of it.

By nature and inclination, Jobs is one of those who have to dominate any room they're in, and so it is here. It's not quite right to say he is sitting through this staff meeting, because Jobs doesn't much sit through anything; one of the ways he dominates is through sheer movement. One moment he's kneeling in his chair, the next minute he's slouching in it; the next he has leaped out of his chair entirely and is scribbling on the blackboard directly behind him. He is full of mannerisms. He bites his nails. He stares with unnerving earnestness at whoever is speaking. His hands, which are slightly and inexplicably yellow, are in constant motion: pushing back his hair, propping up his chin, buried snugly under his armpits. When he hears something that intrigues him, he curls his head toward his shoulder, leans forward, and allows a slight smile to cross his lips. When he hears something he dislikes, he squints to register his disapproval. He would not be a good poker player. His speech is also mannered, full of slangy phrases. "If we could pull this off," he is saying enthusiastically, "it would be *really, really neat!*" "The original idea was good," he is saying about some failed project at Apple. "I don't know what happened. I guess somebody there *bozoed out.*" Around the room there are knowing smirks. To *bozo* is a favorite Jobs verb, but where he once used it mainly to describe some bit of stupidity perpetrated by, say, IBM, he now uses it just as often when he's talking about Apple.

Back in May of 1985, Jobs lost a power struggle to Apple president John Sculley. It was awkward, bitter, and very public. In what was labeled a reorganization, Jobs had been humiliatingly dismissed as head of the Macintosh computer division. Four months later, Jobs walked.

Now, more than a year later, he insists that he has managed to put Apple behind him. Surely, this is wishful thinking. Apple had always been a reflection of Jobs' personality, a mirror of his eccentricities and passions. He used to talk, for instance, about making Apple an "insanely great" place to work, but he wasn't talking about irresistible perks or liberal benefits. Instead, he was talking about creating an environment where you would work harder and longer than you'd ever worked in your life, under the most grinding of deadline pressure, with more responsibility than you ever thought you could handle, never taking vacations, rarely getting even a weekend off... and you wouldn't care! You'd love it! You'd get to the point where you couldn't live without the work and the responsibility and the grinding deadline pressure. All of the people in this room had known such feelings about work—feelings that were exhilarating and personal and even intimate—and they'd known them while working for Steve Jobs. They all shared a private history of their work together at Apple. It was their bond, and no one who was not there could ever fully understand it.

With personal computers so ubiquitous today, you tend to forget that the industry is still barely ten years old; the Apple II, the machine that began it all, was unleashed upon an unsuspecting world in 1977. You forget, that is, until you sit in a room full of people who have built them and realize how young they are. Jobs himself is only thirty-one. If anything, he looks younger.

He is lithe and wiry. He is wearing faded jeans (no belt), a white cotton shirt (perfectly pressed), and a pair of brown suede wing-tipped shoes. There is a bounce to his step that betrays a certain youthful cockiness; the quarterback of your high school football team used to walk that way. His thin, handsome face does not even appear to need a daily shave. And that impression of eternal youth is reinforced by some guileless, almost childlike traits: By the way, for instance, he can't resist showing off his brutal, withering intelligence whenever he's around someone he doesn't think measures up. Or by his almost willful lack of tact. Or by his inability to hide his boredom when he is forced to endure something that doesn't interest him, like a sixth grader who can't wait for class to end.

Which, as it happens, is how he's acting now. Dan'l Lewin, NeXT's director of marketing, has just handed out a complicated diagram outlining his various responsibilities and lines of authority. When Jobs gets his copy his eyes begin to glaze. As Lewin attempts to explain, somewhat convolutedly, what it all means, Jobs fidgets. He rocks back and forth in his chair. He rolls his eyes. He squints. About a minute into Lewin's tortured explanation, Jobs can endure no more. "I think these charts are bullshit," he interrupts. "Just bullshit." Lewin stumbles momentarily, then tries to recover, but Jobs won't relent. Finally, Lewin tries to retrieve all the copies of his diagram. "What are you doing?" Jobs asks pointedly as Lewin tries to pull his away.

"If you think it's bullshit, there's no point in talking about it." Others in the room try to assuage Lewin's hurt feelings, but not Jobs. His mind is already elsewhere. "Can we do something *really* important?" he is asking. "Can we get that electric outlet fixed?"

The meeting drones on. A finance man comes into the room to report the details of a just-completed negotiation. "You did a really, really great job on this," says Jobs when he has finished. (The day before, Jobs had told the man, "This deal is crap.") The man leaves and the discussion turns to other matters. Jobs prods Bud Tribble, a thin, diffident man who is heading his software team, to hire more people. He talks about people in the Valley he'd like to steal away and discusses potential employees who've been in for interviews. As he speaks, he visibly perks up; his mind is engaged again. "We've got to start thinking about middle managers, even now!" he urges his staff. Then an exhortation: "We're not just building a computer, we're building a company!" And after the meeting has broken up, a final, dazed thought: "I'd forgotten how hard it is to start up a company." There is a hint of joy in his voice.

The last time Steven Jobs started a company, he had no idea how hard it would be. How could he? When he and Steve Wozniak founded Apple, Jobs was practically a teenager, a college dropout still living through what he calls "my existential phase."

In college, Jobs had found himself attracted to Eastern philosophy and had also become interested in the power of diets, devouring such books as *The Mucusless Diet Healing System* by a nineteenth-century Prussian named Arnold Ehret. Those interests remained strong even after he returned to the Santa Clara Valley, where he had grown up. He became a fruitarian and lectured his friends on the evils of bagels. Jobs let his hair grow long, smoked dope, and frequently went without shoes. He joined a farm commune, but quickly became disillusioned and wound up back in the Valley.

Jobs wanted to go to India but couldn't afford passage. To earn money, he began doing bits of work for Nolan Bushnell's Atari Corp., helping to build video games. Jobs was no engineer, but he was very quick and very smart—and very difficult. Even then, he was blunt to the point of tactlessness, and that, combined with his unwillingness to shower regularly, caused most Atari employees to find him insufferable. But Bushnell, who is something of an eccentric himself, thought Jobs was valuable to have around, and kept throwing him work. The arrangement suited Jobs perfectly. When he needed money, Bushnell provided him the means to earn it; when he didn't, he could cut loose from Atari for a spell and go do something else. It was the one time in his life he thought about work the way an assembly-line worker might: simply as a means to put money in his pocket.

In the summer of 1974, Jobs finally made it to India, where he did all the things a young, impressionable seeker of truth does in such a place. He attended religious festivals and visited monasteries. He had his head shaved by a guru. He came down with dysentery and returned to California in the fall. Yet the fascination with spiritualism did not fade; Jobs now says he was so serious about it that after India he contemplated going to Japan to join a monastery, if only for the experience. "There is a great tradition in that kind of life," he says. "It offers another kind of training, another way of thinking."

Meanwhile, Jobs had another side, perhaps best typified by his friendship with Steve Wozniak. Woz, as everyone called him, didn't give a hoot about mucusless diets or monasteries, and when Jobs was around Woz, which was often, he didn't spend much time talking about such things. It was a waste of breath. What Wozniak cared about passionately, and what he could talk about endlessly, were digital electronics and computers. He was "the hacker," to use his own description of himself, whose goal in life was to become an engineer for Hewlett-Packard, where he could get paid for doing what he loved. Although Woz was also a college dropout, by 1973 he had achieved his goal, only to find it disappointing. He was assigned to work on calculators, not computers.

Although Wozniak was five years older than Jobs, they were best friends. In the intervening years, they have had their differences, but Wozniak can still say with considerable fondness, "We had great times together." They were both a little out of the mainstream, and they both had an abiding interest in electronics and computers. To be sure, Jobs' interest was never quite as abiding or as single-minded as Wozniak's. But he had done the science-fair bit in high school, had worked in electronic-supply shops, and had spent a summer at Hewlett-Packard. One of the "great times" Wozniak and Jobs had together was building electronic "blue boxes," those infamous devices that allowed you to use the telephone without paying. Jobs was the one who decided they should sell the boxes, which they did haphazardly for about a year.

At around the same time Jobs was trying to decide whether or not to run off to a monastery, his friend Wozniak was attempting to build a small computer. The invention of the microprocessor had made such a machine theoretically possible, and Wozniak and his hacker friends had all become obsessed with the idea of creating one. It was all they did, all the time. They met informally at the Homebrew Computer Club, where they shared information and showed off their latest designs. None of the people in the Homebrew Computer Club had any real sense that microcomputers had much value outside the universe of the hacker. They did it mainly as a hobby, to prove to themselves and each other that such a thing could be done. Of course, none of the big computer companies like Hewlett-Packard had any sense of that, either, which is why none of them were trying to build one. Hewlett-Packard, in fact, turned Wozniak down when he showed the company one of his circuit boards and asked to pursue his hobby for the company. It was still a world of mainframes—big, lumbering machines.

The one person who had some inkling that these smaller machines might have some kind of broader appeal—vague though that inkling was, unarticulated though it largely remained—was Steve Jobs. Somehow he got it, when almost no one else did.

And so his other side, his computer side, began to exert its tug on him. He found himself spending more and more time with Wozniak. They would talk for hours about the technical issues Woz was trying to solve, discussing the kinds of choices Woz was making. What kind of microprocessor should the computer have? What sort of memory device should it use? Jobs was inexorably drawn to Wozniak's machine. By the early part of 1976, he was pestering Wozniak about starting a little company so they could sell the circuit boards Woz was designing. And after that... well, you know what happened after that. You know the legend of Jobs and Wozniak. How they started out in Jobs' garage. How they worked day and night to create the Apple II. How they became modern-day folk heroes.

Jobs says today that at some point early on he had to make a conscious choice: the East or Apple. More recently, he adds, he has come to believe that there was far less difference between the two life choices than appeared to him at the time. "Ultimately," he claims, "it was the same thing." That remark seems more than a little facile, especially when the man saying it is barreling down the freeway in his Mercedes coupe, playing a new compact disc by the Rolling Stones. But certainly there is one way in which the analogy is absolutely true. Jobs' commitment to building the Apple II—to his work—was as all-consuming as any commitment he would have had to make in a monastery. In a sense, he had found his monastery in his garage.

Was it his age that allowed him to work with such maniacal intensity? Sure, that was part of it. If you ask Jobs about the difference between then and now, the first thing he'll say is, "Well, I can't stay up four nights in a row like I used to."

Was it the cocoonlike atmosphere of the garage where he and Wozniak were isolated with their dreams? Sure, that was part of it too; the excitement in the garage was palpable, and anyone who spent any time around Jobs in those days felt some of it rub off. The simple satisfaction of building something was an important part of it: the satisfaction a good carpenter knows. And so was the thought of making money, especially for Wozniak, whose devotion to work was never like Jobs'. Wozniak has always been quite direct: once building the Apple computer was no longer his hobby but his means of employment, his main motivation was money.

But with Jobs, there was always something more, something that ties into the larger culture. Although he was working himself to exhaustion, his approach to work was extremely narcissistic—it was a form of self-expression, of pleasure. His loyalty was not to some faceless corporation but to himself; Jobs likes to say that he is one of those people who wakes up in the morning, looks in the mirror, and says: "Am I doing what I want to do?" Fundamentally, his sense of who he was, which he had been searching for all along, became a function of what he did.

Few people in the country took things to the extreme Jobs did. But during the period when he was in the garage, the young professional class was embracing many of these same ideas about work. Work was no longer supposed to be *work*, it was supposed to be fun. It was supposed to have some larger purpose. It was supposed to offer a form of self-identity. And if it didn't offer those elements—if you woke up one morning and couldn't say to yourself that you were doing what you wanted to be doing—well, then you quit. Your father's loyalty may have been to the company or perhaps to the family he had to provide for. But your loyalty was to yourself, in a manner that had once been the style mainly of artists and ballplayers.

In Silicon Valley, the company most people wanted to work for, pre-Jobs, was Hewlett-Packard. At HP, people were well treated and well paid, and the company was renowned for never laying anyone off, which provided comforting security to anyone who was even remotely competent. But it was—and is—a very large corporation, with more than eighty thousand people, and while you can do good work there, you're also part of a huge bureaucracy. In return for the loyalty the company shows you, it expects the same kind of loyalty. Pre-Jobs, that was about what people thought they had a right to expect from their employers.

In the Jobs era, the young engineers streaming into the Valley had a different set of expectations, and they gravitated to companies like Apple. One former Apple executive remembers the first time he spoke to Jobs about working there. "I said, 'Steve, I really want to come work at Apple, but I don't want to do anything regular. Can you help me find something really, really neat to do?'" Nobody at Apple was ever willing to do anything "regular." Everybody wanted to do something "really, really neat." The implicit promise at Apple was that everybody would discover, while giving themselves up entirely to their really neat projects, the same feelings of pleasure and worth and all the rest of it that Jobs had felt when he was building the Apple II. They all wanted that magical experience. Not least of all Steve Jobs himself.

"The hardest thing," Steve Jobs is saying, "is trying to have a personal life as well as a work life." Well, yes. It is late on a Tuesday afternoon, and Jobs is behind the wheel of his car, en route to a meeting in San Francisco that will start in an hour. The meeting, it seems obvious, could have been better timed. Jobs' girlfriend, whom he's been seeing for two years, will be returning to Silicon Valley in, oh, three hours or so. The two of them had spent a rare weekend water-skiing—something Jobs says he hasn't done since he was a teenager—and though he returned on Sunday to get back to NeXT, she stayed behind for a few days. Before he left, he told her they would have dinner together the night she got back. Now, of course, those plans are out the window.

Late that afternoon, Jobs spent a few minutes at his Macintosh writing her a page-long note explaining why he wouldn't be home when she arrived.

"I miss you terribly," he wrote. Then he raced to his house, a huge old mansion in the hills of the Valley, to drop off the note.

A small thing, perhaps. Or perhaps not. The rumblings around the NeXT office are that Jobs' girlfriend thinks he spends too much time working, and that as a result they don't have "a life together." After spending a few days with Jobs, you find yourself sympathizing with her. The very next day, Jobs committed himself to attend what would surely be a lengthy board meeting of Pixar (a computer-graphics company he had bought from George Lucas) in San Francisco on Saturday. He had previously made plans to leave town Sunday for meetings in Minneapolis with his new ad agency. So there went the weekend. It *is* hard to have a personal life and a work life; it's especially hard when all the compromises come on the personal side, but that's the way it's always been with Steven Jobs.

Why? He is worth, after all, $150 million or so. When he left Apple there was no adventure he could not have tried. Yet he wound up forming a company in which he is re-creating as closely as possible the life he knew before: the life of not just work but nonstop work, no-other-life work. Why is this the path he chose?

On the way up to San Francisco, Jobs is musing on this and other matters. "Whenever you do any one thing intensely over a period of time," he says, "you have to give up other lives you could be living." He gives a shrug that implies that this is a small price. "You have to have a real single-minded kind of tunnel vision if you want to get anything significant accomplished," Again, the same it's-worth-it shrug. "Especially if the desire is not to be a businessman, but to be a creative person...."

But isn't he a businessman?

"My self-identity does not revolve around being a businessman, though I recognize that is what I do. I think of myself more as a person who builds neat things. I like building neat things. I like making tools that are useful to people. I like working with very bright people. I like interacting in the world of ideas, though somehow those ideas have to be tied to some physical reality. One of the things I like the most is dropping a new idea on a bunch of incredibly smart and talented people and then letting them work it out themselves. I like all of that very, very much." There is a note of excitement in his voice. "I've had lots of girlfriends," he adds. "But the greatest high in my life was the day we introduced the Macintosh."

And Apple?

"Apple," he says slowly, searching for the right analogy, "Apple is like an intense love affair with a girl you really, really like, and then she decides to drop you and go out with someone who's not so neat." Lewin, who is sitting next to Jobs, immediately chuckles at the seeming absurdity of the comparison, and that makes Jobs chuckle too. But Jobs truly did love Apple; in a weird way it seems right that he should compare it to a passionate affair.

Mostly he speaks about Apple with more sorrow than anger. There was a time when he thought he would always be connected to it—taking sabbaticals from time to time, but always coming back. Coming home. He clearly regrets that that possibility no longer exists. He will not say anything at all about Sculley, nor will Sculley speak publicly about Jobs; not long ago the Apple president, under contract to write his autobiography, simply could not bring himself to "tell all" about how he bested Jobs. But both men are obviously saddened by their falling out. One mutual friend recently bumped into a limo driver who occasionally drives both men. "Whenever Sculley or his wife gets in the car," the driver said, "the first thing they ask is, 'How's Steve?'"

We have almost arrived in San Francisco. "I think I have five more great products in me," Jobs says, and then goes off on a long, rambling discourse on the joys of working on computers at this particular moment in history. He compares it to what it must have been like to work for Henry Ford when the automobile was still in its infancy and the technological boundaries were there to be broken. "It must have been the most incredible feeling," he says, "to know that this was going to change America. And it did!" He grins suddenly. "If we can create the kind of company I think we can, it will give me an *extreme* amount of pleasure."

After the meeting in San Francisco, Jobs and a party of about ten other people went out to dinner. Someone at the table mentioned some films that Jobs had expressed an interest in seeing. The man mentioned that he might be able to bring them by that Friday night and show them in Jobs' living room. Jobs was immediately enthusiastic about the idea, and within the next minute everyone at the table had been invited to Jobs' house for a party on Friday night. "One thing, Steve," the man asked, as they continued discussing plans for the screening, "I don't remember if you have curtains in your living room. Do you?"

The question stopped Jobs in his tracks. He thought about it for a minute. He had been living in the house for two years. "I don't know," he said.

In 1981, at age 26, Jobs was in the odd position of having nothing to do at his own company. He was fantastically rich by then; Apple had gone public the year before. He was chairman of the board. *Time* magazine was preparing to put him on its cover. And of course the company itself had become one of the great American success stories. By 1981, its revenues were close to $331 million, heading toward $1 billion and beyond, and the Apple II was still the best-known, biggest-selling computer in the world. As the company grew, so did its legend: Jobs' garage became Apple's log cabin.

One thing Jobs never had, not for a day in his life, was control of Apple. Yes, he set the tone, and yes, his input carried considerable weight, but the task of actually running the place always fell to other people—to Sculley most recently, and before that to Mike Markkula, Apple's original chief executive officer, and Michael Scott, its original president. Both men had come on board in the garage days, when Jobs realized he needed some executives around him who knew a thing or two about business. For a long time, the arrangement worked well. Jobs was the brash visionary; Markkula and Scott made the company run. Jobs put his singular imprint on the company's products; Markkula and Scott got the products out the door.

Around 1980, with the Apple II selling well and the company more or less humming along prosperously, Apple decided to create a new computer, one that could get a foothold in the increasingly important office market. It was called the Lisa project. The importance of the Lisa project guaranteed that the new division was where the action was going to be. All the best engineers in the world would want to help build the machine; all the best marketing people in the world would want to sell it. And Steve Jobs wanted to be in charge of it. Much to his surprise, however, Markkula and Scott turned him down. Their grounds were that he was too young and inexperienced to manage an organization as large and complex as the Lisa division was bound to become. "I was hurt," Jobs said. "There's no getting around it."

For the previous five years Jobs had always been at the center of things at Apple. Now he was being pushed to the side. He never seriously considered leaving Apple, but he was floundering, searching for a way to fill the void in his life.

At first, he tried to assume the role of minister-without-portfolio inside the company. He would attend an Apple II marketing meeting, and in typical Jobs fashion, within ten minutes of his arrival he would be telling the group that their marketing plans were dogshit. That didn't go over too well. Or he would drop in unannounced at the Lisa division and spend an afternoon looking over the shoulders of the engineers and managers, trying to get people to listen to his ideas. They wouldn't listen. The Lisa division was run by a former Hewlett-Packard man who brought in other people from HP to build the machine, and as the Lisa design became more grandiose and expensive, Jobs became increasingly agitated over the shape it was taking. He thought the people from the big company had brought their big-company mentality with them—their bells-and-whistles, screw-the-cost mentality. Lisa, Jobs was convinced, was not going to save Apple. She might well destroy it. Meanwhile, many at Apple felt, in the words of someone who was there, that "Steve was a royal pain in the butt."

He decided to build the computer that would save Apple from itself. He was the only one who could do it. All he needed was some way to get started without anyone realizing what he was up to. And then he saw it: a small project that had been stumbling along for a few years without being taken very seriously by management. Could he go run *that?* he asked Scott and Markkula. Yes, they said, by all means. Go. Good luck. See you later. And so, off he went to run this little thing called the Macintosh division. To save Apple. To change the world.

With the Macintosh project, Steve Jobs was attempting to recapture those glorious days when he and Woz were alone, dreaming their dream, in the garage. "The metaphysical garage," Jobs called the Mac project. He even moved the Mac group into its own "garage," a building away from the rest of Apple, and fostered a culture in which the Mac people thought they were somehow divorced from the company that paid their salaries. Although the Mac group was the one division run by the chairman of the board, the people in the group felt like renegades; a pirate's flag flew above their building. And since the Apple II really did change the world, the Macintosh would have to do the same. "Very few of us were even thirty years old," says Mike Murray, Macintosh's former director of marketing. "We all felt as though we had missed the civil rights movement. We had missed Vietnam. What we had was the Macintosh."

Hundred-hour weeks—that's 8:00 A.M. to 10:00 P.M., Sunday through Saturday—were not unusual. People were working so hard they forgot to eat lunch. They were working so hard they forgot to eat breakfast *and* lunch. But did anyone complain about all the work? Of course not! They loved it. They were living the dream. They were doing what they had come to Silicon Valley to do.

There were, of course, drawbacks to having a hundred or so twenty-six-year-olds working fourteen-hour days. One was that a lot of mistakes were made, which then had to be corrected. Another was that nobody could step back and get a little perspective. Especially Jobs. You'd arrive in the morning and Jobs would give you Plan A, and you'd slave over it all day, and then at 7:00 P.M., he'd come by your cubicle to tell you that Plan A had been discarded and here was Plan B (and could you stay late tonight to work on it?).

And when the Macintosh finally did come out, the people who had worked so hard on it for so long—in many cases, two and a half years—

finally took a moment to look up from their desks, and some of them didn't like what they saw. As they had gotten sucked deeper and deeper into the Mac project, other parts of their lives that had once been extremely important had been lost. Marriages had broken up. Friendships had dissolved. People who had poured every ounce of emotional energy into the expectation that the Macintosh would one day change the world started to realize that that wasn't going to happen at all. They became disillusioned. They wondered why they had worked so hard. Slowly, some of the original members of the Mac group began to leave Apple. The drug had lost its kick.

For Jobs, the Mac experience also came at a price, though of a different sort. Even after the machine had been introduced, there was still a tremendous amount of work to be done: software had to be written for it, and a printer had to be built, just for starters. And because there was a computer on the market, the Mac group was under far more time pressure to put out these products than it had been to build the Mac itself. Jobs tried to rally his troops for their next assault, but it couldn't be done. They were too burned out. As a result, they started missing deadlines with regularity, which was more than a little annoying to people who had bought Macintosh computers and were now waiting for some software.

Apple eventually merged the Lisa division with the Mac division, which meant that Jobs had more than a thousand employees working for him. Still, he couldn't change his style. He prodded and cajoled and presumed that everyone would put in ninety-hour weeks. It didn't work. Yet Jobs could not bring himself to concede that he was now running a normal corporate division in which people had to live normal lives. He couldn't let go of the metaphysical garage. By the spring of 1985, Apple was about to announce its first quarterly loss ever. Apple's board of directors, and even its president, John Sculley, who had once deferred almost instinctively to Jobs, now wanted him out. In the ensuing three-week power struggle, Jobs never really had a chance. The Macintosh may have saved Apple—especially when Lisa turned out to be an expensive fiasco. But it also brought down the man who created it.

One night, in his cavernous, sparsely furnished living room, Jobs was talking about his experience building the Macintosh—an experience he views as one of the highlights of his life. He interrupted himself to retrieve what turned out to be several photograph albums. Then he knelt on the floor, propped the albums against a footrest, and began flipping through them.

The albums were filled with pictures taken at several large parties Jobs had thrown for the Mac group. "This was our Christmas party," he said excitedly as he leafed through the largest of the albums. "It was *so great*! I hired seventy-five members of the San Francisco Symphony to play for us. A lot of these people are wearing tuxes for the first time. We subsidized tuxedoes for the manufacturing people because we wanted everybody to be able to come. It was really important for everybody to feel like they were part of the team."

He began pointing out some of the people in the pictures. "There's Woz," he said. Though he was grinning broadly, Wozniak looked distinctly uncomfortable in his tuxedo. "We always invited Woz to our parties." He flipped to another page: "There's Bud!" He pointed to the tiny figure of Bud Tribble, dancing in the background of one of the pictures. "Bud is so incredibly smart. Did you know that after he left Apple he went to med school?"

In practically every picture, Jobs spotted someone whom he now recalled with genuine fondness. "This is Rod Holt. He was one of the unsung heroes of Mac. After it was over, he went sailing for a year. He hasn't worked since. This is Debbie Coleman, the financial controller for the Mac group. She's still at Apple, but she's really a good person." And finally: "This is ———— ————. That's his wife next to him. He'd been married to her forever, and she was a real drip. Just hopeless." He pointed to another woman, a member of the Mac group, posing for a different picture. "See her? ———— became totally infatuated with her. He wanted to marry her on the spot. They started having this affair." One night, Jobs continued, the man's wife asked him if anything was wrong. Half-jokingly, she suggested that maybe he wanted to leave her. He looked up at her and replied, "Yes, I do."

"It was great," said Jobs of this bit of Macintosh matchmaking. "Unfortunately, the new relationship didn't last. Oh, well," he shrugged. "Such is life."

It was all coming back to him now. "The greatest day of my life," he said, looking up from the album, "was the day we introduced the Macintosh." He knew the date precisely—January 23, 1984—and he could recall the scene vividly. Apple was going to unveil the computer at the company's annual stockholders' meeting, which was held each year in the Flint Center, the finest and largest auditorium in Cupertino. Jobs had been up until 3:00 that morning, trying to get the kinks out of the program the Mac group had written especially for this event. He was tired and a little discouraged; all night long, the program kept breaking down.

But then the meeting started, and the curtains opened, and there stood a Macintosh computer, alone, on a pedestal. Behind it, in giant letters, was the word MACINTOSH. Jobs walked over to the computer, took it out of its case, and stuck in a small floppy disk. The theme from *Chariots of Fire* began playing. Then silence. The Macintosh began speaking. *Speaking!* "Hello," it said.

"I'm the Macintosh. I'm really glad to get out of that bag." The room erupted.

For the next half-hour the Macintosh went through its dazzling paces, and when the demonstration was over, everyone stood and cheered for a full five minutes. Jobs, standing on the stage next to his creation, was overcome. Tears began to well up in his eyes. "I looked out at the first four rows," he recalled, "where most of the Mac team was sitting, and I could see tears in their eyes, too. It struck me as so unbelievable that these incredibly great people had come together to make this collective work of art.

"It was such an intense experience," he went on. "What I felt that day was beyond anything I could put into words." He stopped for a moment and searched for the words. "I think I know what it must be like to watch the birth of your child," he said finally. Pause. Frown. He snapped the album shut.

"But that's over," he sighed.

One day in late August of 1985, Steve Jobs had lunch with Paul Berg, Stanford's Nobel Prize–winning biochemist. For most of the previous four months, ever since the Sculley reorganization, Jobs had had nothing to do, and he had hated it. He tried to fill the time by reading and traveling. That didn't help. He toyed with the idea of going back to school, or even getting into politics. (He reportedly asked Regis McKenna, a Silicon Valley publicist, "Do we have to go through that political bullshit to get elected governor?") But neither prospect satisfied him. What he needed was the one thing Apple could no longer provide: work. "It was a very difficult time for me," he says of his brief, forced attempt at a more leisurely life. "I was incredibly depressed." Then came the lunch with Berg. It took place in a coffee shop in Palo Alto. It lasted two and a half hours.

Remember that lunch. If NeXT becomes successful, the lunch with Berg will take its place alongside the garage in the Jobs iconography. The way Jobs tells the story, the restless, underemployed Apple founder was talking to the Nobel laureate about recombinant DNA, which he had been reading up on. Why, he asked Berg, weren't people speeding up the lengthy, arduous, DNA experiments by simulating them on a computer? Because, came the reply, any hardware powerful enough to simulate such experiments cost close to $100,000. And the software didn't exist. Jobs immediately became enthused; suddenly he knew what he had to do. He had to build the computer that Berg—and every other scientist and professor and student in America—was waiting for. He was the only one who could do it. He had purpose again.

Within weeks of that lunch, Jobs left Apple, taking his core of loyalists with him. Within days of his departure, he was talking excitedly to the press about his new dream: to build the first personal computer specifically designed for universities—a machine for learning, not for crunching numbers or writing memos, a machine at least three times faster, ten times more powerful than any personal computer ever built.

Jobs gave a speech to a group called Educom, which consists of key administrators who buy computers for major universities. "We're gonna build products for you guys!" Jobs explained. "Just tell us what you want!" He put up $7 million of his own money to start NeXT, and rented office space, small, cramped quarters at first—"to get back to the purity of the garage"—and then larger offices as NeXT grew. He became obsessed with building his computer. Work was fun again.

Mike Murray says that in conversations he's had with Jobs recently, Jobs always says, "I'm doing better now." By that, Jobs means that he is doing better at managing his new organization, that he has a better understanding of the fact that most people simply cannot work all the time, even if they think they can. "I don't want people at NeXT working more than sixty hours a week," he says. "If I see someone working too late, I tell them to go home. This is a marathon," he adds, "not a sprint."

But you wonder. You wonder what will happen as the pressure grows and the deadline approaches. You wonder if the people at NeXT, most of whom are fueled by work almost as much as Jobs himself, will really be able to click it off at 6:00 P.M. And you wonder about Jobs, too. To change his work habits, Jobs would have to change his very nature—the deepest, strongest part of himself. And that he cannot do.

There is unquestionably something extremely admirable about Jobs' obsession with work. People who accomplish great things almost always live outside the boundaries that hem the rest of us in. They can be rude and oblivious to the feelings of others because they don't have time to worry about people's feelings. It takes their eye off the ball. They are maniacal about details most of us would ignore because they sense that such details will mean the difference between success and failure. They give up their personal life because it seems trivial next to what they are trying to get done. They are driven human beings.

But is it really enough to love your work to the exclusion of all else? It is hard to know how to react to someone who says, in all seriousness, that the introduction of a computer can compare emotionally to the birth of a child. You react, finally, by feeling a little sorry for him.

Jobs, however, will brook no such suggestion. "I'm happier than I've been in a long time," he insists. He is in his car, driving back to NeXT. It is late at night. "I remember many late nights coming out of the Mac building," he is saying, "when I would have the most incredibly powerful feelings about my life. Just exhilarating feelings about my life. I feel some of that now with NeXT. I can't explain it. I don't really understand it. But I'm comfortable with it." And maybe in his inability to explain lies the explanation. It is always difficult to articulate your compulsions, and Steve Jobs is, quite simply, compelled to work. There was never any other choice.

Good Luck with That Broken iPod

The New York Times, February 4, 2006

My iPod died.

It happened right after Christmas—a Christmas, I hasten to add, in which I gave my wife the new video iPod, making it the latest of the half-dozen iPods my family has bought since Apple began selling them in October 2001. We also own five Apple computers, and have become pathetically loyal because of our reliance on the iPod. To the extent that Apple is using the iPod to drive sales of other Apple products, the Nocera family is proof that the strategy works; we've probably spent more than $10,000 on Apple hardware since the iPod first came out. Alas, at least three of the iPods were replacements for ones that broke.

This time, though, I decided to get my iPod fixed. After all, it wasn't even two years old and had cost around $300. Like all iPods, it came with a one-year warranty. Although Apple sells an additional year of protection for $59, I declined the extended warranty because the cost struck me as awfully high—a fifth of the purchase price of the device itself.

Anecdotal evidence—such as chat boards filled with outraged howls from owners of dead iPods—strongly suggests that you can write the rest of this story yourself. You start by thinking: "I'll just call Apple!" But it's so hard to find the customer support number on Apple's Web site that you suspect the company has purposely hidden it.

Eventually, you find the number and make the call. Although the tech support guy quickly diagnoses your problem—a hard drive gone bad—he really has only one suggestion: throw it away and buy a new one. "Since it is out of warranty," he says, "there's nothing we can do."

You're a little stunned. But you're not ready to give up. On the Apple site, there's a form you can fill out to send the iPod back to Apple and get it fixed.

But you do a double-take when you see the price. Apple is going to charge you $250, plus tax, to fix your iPod. There is no mistaking the message: Apple has zero interest in fixing a machine it was quite happy to sell you not so long ago.

Now you're reeling. You're furious. But what choice do you have? You can't turn to a competitor's product, not if you want to keep using Apple's proprietary iTunes software, where you've stored all the music you love, including songs purchased directly from the iTunes Music Store, which you'll lose if you leave the iTunes environment. So you grit your teeth and buy a new iPod. Of course since it's a newer machine, it has that cool video capability. But you're still angry.

You've read recently that Apple has sold 42 million iPods in less than four and a half years. Thanks to the iPod, Apple just reported its most profitable quarter ever. But you wonder: how many of those 42 million units have gone to people who feel, as you do, that you've just been taken to the cleaners by Apple? You also wonder: Why do iPods seem to break so frequently? And why is Apple so willing to tick off people who spend thousands of dollars on Apple products by refusing to deal with broken iPods?

Or at least that's what I wondered as I went through the five stages of iPod grief.

Customer support is the ugly stepchild of the consumer electronics business. Companies like Dell and Palm and Apple have customer support centers not because they want to but because they have to. Computers, personal digital assistants, and other digital devices are complicated machines. They break down much more frequently than, say, old analog televisions. And because there is no modern equivalent of the TV repairman, consumers expect the companies themselves to deal with problems when they arise.

But customer support is expensive for gadget makers. "A phone call costs a company 75 cents a minute," said the well-known writer and technology investor Andrew Kessler. "An hour call is $45." As prices have dropped sharply for computers and other digital devices, keeping those phone calls to a minimum has become supremely important to consumer electronics companies that want to maintain their margins and profitability.

That's why all the big tech companies try to force customers to use their Web sites to figure out problems themselves. It's why so many of them bury the customer support phone number. And it's also why, when you do call, companies like Dell teach its support staff to diagnose computer problems over the phone, and then talk you through some fairly complicated repairs. With its machines so inexpensive, Dell simply can't afford to allow too many customers to ship the computer back to the company to be fixed.

Consumers, though, don't really understand this. As much as they like being able to buy computers for less than $1,000, they don't realize that one of the trade-offs is minimal tech support. Nor do the companies spell this out; instead, they pretend that their service is terrific. Thus, there is a gap between what customers expect from companies that sell them complicated digital machines, and what companies feel they need do to ensure that those machines make money.

With the iPod, Apple has taken this gap and turned it into a chasm. On the one hand, because the price of an iPod is far lower than the price of a computer, Apple has even more incentive to keep people from calling; one long phone call turns a profitable iPod into an unprofitable one. Nor does it make economic sense to repair even the iPods under warranty. Instead, Apple simply ships you a new one.

On the other hand, an iPod is a very fragile device. The basic iPods are built around a hard drive, a device so sensitive that "if it takes one shot, that will pretty much kill it," according to Rob Enderle of the Enderle Group, a technology consulting firm. Its screen cracks easily. Its battery wears down—and can't be easily replaced because an iPod can't be opened up by mere mortals. All of these were conscious design choices Apple made, some of which have to do with keeping the cost down, while others were done largely for aesthetic reasons. But given how much wear and tear an iPod takes—the core market is teenagers, for crying out loud—is it any wonder that they break? "If you get two or three years out of a portable device," Mr. Enderle said, "you're probably doing pretty well."

Which Apple doesn't tell you. Indeed, it doesn't say anything about how long you should expect your iPod to last. And so consumers buy it with the expectation that they'll put all their music on it and they'll carry it around for a good long time. And when that doesn't happen, they feel betrayed.

Steven Williams, a lawyer who sued Apple a few years ago over the failed battery problem, told me that he was amazed to discover, as the litigation got underway, that Apple seemed to feel, as he put it, "that everyone knew iPods were only good for a year or two." Thanks in part to the lawsuit, the battery issue is one of the few Apple will now deal with: if your iPod dies because of the battery you can send it back and get a new one for a mere $65.95, plus tax. Of course, you then lose all your music.

"Apple has been willing to alienate a certain percentage of its customer base forever," said Chip Gliedman, a vice president with Forrester Research, the technology research firm. Why? Because Apple is an extraordinarily arrogant company. "Apple thinks it is special," is how Mr. Gliedman put it.

At this particular moment in its history, of course, Apple *is* special, and it can get away with being arrogant. It has a product that everyone wants, and for which there is no serious competition.

But it seems to me that Apple is on a dangerous course. Yes, it has strong incentives to minimize tech support, but to say "Not Our Problem" whenever an iPod dies is to run the serious risk of losing its customers' loyalty. "I believe that the iPod is one of the most brilliant platforms ever devised," said Larry Keeley, who runs Doblin Inc., an innovation strategy firm. But, he added, he has long predicted that the "maintenance issue," as he called it, would be the product's Achilles' heel. "Consumers are just not conditioned to believe that a $300 or $400 device is disposable." Mr. Keeley, whose daughters all have iPods, has come to believe that their natural life "is just a hair longer than the warranty," and that Apple's level of service is "somewhere between sullen and insulting."

And, he warns, the day will come when the iPod has a real competitor. "There will be competing platforms, and they'll get robust, and other companies will figure out how to crack iTunes," he said. At which point, Apple will reap what it is now sowing.

A final note. You'll notice there is no Apple spokesman defending the iPod or Apple's customer support in this column. When I called Apple, wanting to know, among other things, how long Apple believes an iPod should last, I got a nice young woman from the PR department. She said she'd try to find someone at the company to talk to me. That was on Wednesday.

I'm still waiting.

Weighing Jobs' Role in a Scandal

The New York Times, April 28, 2007

In late June 2001, *Fortune* magazine put Steven P. Jobs on its cover. This, I realize, is not exactly breaking news; the magazine has put Mr. Jobs on its cover with shameless regularity.

This time, though, it was different. The headline read "The Great Executive Pay Heist," and Apple's legendary chief executive was showcased not because he had some slick new product to peddle, but because in January 2000 he had been granted 10 million stock options. *Fortune* valued the grant, disclosed in Apple's 2001 proxy statement, at $872 million, making it "by far" the largest option grant ever. (The stock split in June 2000, giving Mr. Jobs 20 million options.)

The reason I remember that cover is because I worked on it. As a *Fortune* editor, I was part of a team that put together a package of articles for that issue about the "highway robbery"—to use our phrase—that executive compensation had become. I also recall being quite happy with the cover. What a delicious surprise to discover that Mr. Jobs, who had ostentatiously taken only $1 in salary since returning to Apple in 1997, had a stock option package bigger than those of such well-known greedheads as Sanford Weill of Citigroup or Michael Eisner of Disney.

Mr. Jobs, however, was not so happy. He railed about the "unfairness" of the cover. And he wrote a snarky letter to the editor, claiming that because Apple's stock had fallen by almost $20 a share since the options grant was made, they weren't worth $872 million—"they are worth zero." Of course, that is not how options are valued, but never mind. In a tone dripping with sarcasm, Mr. Jobs offered to sell *Fortune* the options for half their supposed $872 million value.

What we didn't know at the time is that the article so infuriated Mr. Jobs that he began agitating to have the options package cancelled. The options were so far underwater that he felt it wasn't worth the bad press to hold onto them.

Did that mean that Mr. Jobs was willing to go back to his $1-a-year salary? Hardly. So at the same time, he and the board began negotiating a new package—7.5 million stock options this time, at a price of $17.83. Those options were agreed to by the board in late August 2001—barely two months after the *Fortune* cover story—but the final negotiations with Mr. Jobs weren't completed until mid-December. And though those options also never paid off for him, and were finally replaced in 2003 by a huge restricted stock grant, they have had enormous consequences. They were one of two big options grants that ultimately embroiled Apple and its iconic leader in the options backdating scandal. Among other things, an Apple underling created fictitious board minutes, two of Mr. Jobs' closest associates were forced out of the company and then faced charges brought by the Securities and Exchange Commission, and Mr. Jobs' own actions and ethics were brought into question. Rarely have so many avoidable problems been created by one man's obsession with his own image. Then again, this *is* Steve Jobs we're talking about.

This has been quite the week for Apple shareholders. The company announced an incredible quarter, with profits up 88 percent, blowing past analysts' estimates. Its stock pushed above $100 a share for the first time ever.

And then there was this week's options backdating news: The SEC brought formal charges against Apple's former general counsel, Nancy

Heinen, and its former chief financial officer Fred Anderson. (Mr. Anderson settled the charges against him for $3.5 million without admitting or denying guilt, while Ms. Heinen's lawyers vow to fight the charges.) These were the two executives the Apple board has been pointing the finger at ever since it completed its internal investigation last fall.

The SEC seemed to agree: its body language this week strongly suggested that it had zero interest in pursuing Mr. Jobs. The agency's position seems to be that the CFO and general counsel are the ones who are supposed to insure that options are handled correctly, and therefore both Mr. Jobs and the Apple board are off the hook.

But almost immediately upon settling the charges, Mr. Anderson pointed the finger right back at his old boss. Mr. Anderson had been involved in an options grant that Mr. Jobs made to his executive team in early 2001—it was the second big grant under scrutiny—and he claimed that he told Mr. Jobs there might have to be an accounting charge if the options weren't handled correctly. There is not much doubt that Mr. Anderson made this statement because he felt unfairly scapegoated by Apple and Mr. Jobs.

With all the finger-pointing, it is difficult to parse whether Mr. Anderson, a wealthy, widely-respected figure in Silicon Valley, did something worthy of government sanction. I made a lot of phone calls this week, but I never did get a good read on it. What is clear, however, is that Mr. Jobs does not deserve the free ride he's been getting from the Apple board, the company's investors, and government regulators.

I am not saying Mr. Jobs committed a crime. What I am saying is that it is pretty obvious by now that he was extremely involved in both of the options grants that have become such problems. So it is hard to see how he doesn't deserve his share of the blame for what happened.

Let's start with the "executive team" grant in early 2001 that Mr. Anderson was involved in. At the time, Mr. Jobs was under pressure to make large grants to key executives to keep them from leaving. (Remember: this was the tail end of the dotcom bubble.) The board gave him free rein to hand out options as he saw fit. The directors approved the grants—a total of 4.8 million options—on January 2.

So far, so good. But then Ms. Heinen suggested the date be changed to later in January to move it past the company's MacWorld event. She didn't want it to appear as though the Apple executives were taking options in anticipation of a stock bump. Mr. Jobs agreed. At the end of January, after some back and forth, he chose January 17 as the new date, according to an e-mail Ms. Heinen sent around at the time. On the seventeenth, the price was higher than on January 2, so there was no benefit to the executives. The board, in turn, approved the January 17 options on February 7. By then, though, Apple's stock price had indeed bumped up, by $3.94 more than the January 17 strike price. Which meant, of course, the options had been back-dated, and should have been disclosed and expensed. Neither happened.

There are lots of people in Silicon Valley who strongly believe that this sequence of events is hardly worth a parking ticket, much less a full-fledged SEC investigation. But the SEC clearly viewed it seriously enough to charge Mr. Anderson with securities violations.

So why not Mr. Jobs? He's the one who made the grants in the first place. He was clearly involved in choosing the new date—two weeks after it had come and gone. And as chairman of the board, he knew—or should have known—that the grants weren't finalized until February 7. To conclude that Mr. Anderson did something wrong but not Mr. Jobs requires some serious mental gymnastics.

Now let's look at the other grant: the 7.5 million options to Mr. Jobs himself. This was the case in which one of Ms. Heinen's subordinates drew up fictitious board minutes to make it appear that the Apple board had approved the grant in October when the real date was December. (The underling says she was instructed to do so by her boss, which Ms. Heinen denies.) That, certainly, you can't blame on Steve Jobs.

What you can blame him for is creating an atmosphere in which these things could happen in the first place. Consider, first, Mr. Jobs' desire to replace the 20 million options with the 7.5 million options. What he was really trying to do was reprice his options without actually admitting that—because repricing would entail an accounting expense. To avoid the expense, he was supposed to wait six months and a day after the cancellation of the first package before Apple gave him the new package.

But he was Steve Jobs, by God—and he wasn't about to go optionless for six months and a day. The Apple directors would later claim that they didn't want him to go optionless either—because then he would have an incentive to drive down the stock price until he got his new options package. (Have you ever heard a nuttier rationale?) In any case, he held onto the 20 million options while negotiating for a better vesting schedule for the 7.5 million; those negotiations had a lot to do with why the package was backdated. If he had been willing to accept a normal vesting schedule—he wound up getting a quarter of his options vested immediately—the whole problem would have been avoided. Instead, the negotiations went on so long that they bumped into a new fiscal year, and caused all kinds of problems for people like Nancy Heinen. (In 2003 both packages were cancelled and replaced with a huge restricted stock grant.)

You get the strong impression that nobody was willing to say no to Mr. Jobs, a notoriously difficult and abrasive chief executive. One imagines the trepidation of the compensation committee members—or Nancy Heinen— telling him that he couldn't get a low option price because the stock had risen during the negotiations. So instead, they found a date in October that approximated the stock price in August—and an underling created phony board minutes.

What is particularly galling is the double standard. You hear from lots of sophisticated investors that it would be terrible if Mr. Jobs were forced out at Apple. How, they say, will that help Apple shareholders? But lots of other CEOs have lost their jobs because of options backdating, and several have even been indicted. However indispensable he may be, there is something terribly corrosive about the notion that Mr. Jobs can't be touched because he's Steve Jobs.

If the SEC is coming to the view that options backdating is just a peccadillo, as Silicon Valley has been claiming all along, it should say so. But if it still believes this is serious stuff, then it shouldn't be making excuses for Steve Jobs, as it appears to be doing.

As for Mr. Jobs, as hard as he's worked to convey the image of an above-the-fray visionary, that's not quite the reality, is it? A few days ago, I stumbled across this quote from him, circa 1985: "I'm at a stage where I don't have to do things just to get by. But then I've always been that way, because I've never really cared about money," he said.

Yeah, right.

CHAPTER 3

The Ga-Ga Years

I turned in the first draft of this story on October 15, 1987. It was a Thursday. I was living by then in the small college town of Northampton, Mass., where I was the executive editor of *New England Monthly*, a wonderful, if short-lived, magazine that had been founded by two friends of mine from *Texas Monthly*. I was also freelancing for *Esquire* to make some extra money. All year long, I had been shuttling back and forth to Boston to write a story about Fidelity Investments for *Esquire*. My goal was to use Fidelity, which had become the country's largest mutual fund complex, as a way of exploring the 1980s bull market.

To my mind, what made this bull market particularly compelling was that it was the first time large numbers of ordinary Americans had money in the market. The stock market, long the province of the rich, was being democratized. Certainly I could see that in my own financial behavior. In the late 1970s, like many Americans, I had moved my money from a regulated bank savings account to something entirely new, an unregulated money market fund—it was the only sensible thing to do in that era of raging inflation. Then, once the bull was in full force, I had taken the next step: moving money from the money market account into mutual funds. In the 1980s, for most Americans, mutual funds were the investment vehicle of choice.

A large part of the reason the country was turning to mutual funds was the roaring success of Fidelity, particularly the Magellan Fund, which was then managed by Peter Lynch, whose dazzling track record made him a kind of Pied Piper of middle-class money. But it wasn't only Lynch. Behind the scenes, Fidelity's owner, an inscrutable billionaire named Ned Johnson, was proving to have an extraordinary instinct for understanding what would attract middle-class money. Despite his Boston Brahmin roots, Johnson had a deep understanding of this democratization process—indeed, he was one of a handful of figures in the financial services industry who was making it happen. That was the story I was trying to capture: what had Fidelity done that made investing so appealing to novice investors like me? And, more broadly, what had happened in the larger culture that has caused us to feel we needed to be in the market?

Toward the end of my reporting, it was pretty clear that the market was getting out of hand. As I recount in the story, that August I sat in a meeting of Fidelity fund managers; their nervousness was palpable. Nonetheless, the story I turned in that Thursday made the assumption that the bull market would continue for the foreseeable future. Four days later—Monday, October 19—the stock market crashed. On Black Monday, as it was almost immediately labeled, the Dow Jones Industrial Average lost 23 percent of its value, making it the single worst day in the history of the stock market. So much for the bull market.

In the short term, it was pretty obvious what I had to do: race back to Boston, gather some "scenes" of the calamity, and rewrite the story. Over the long term, though, the Crash of '87 would inform my work for the next two decades. I became deeply interested in what made the stock market tick, a subject I would return to again and again. The story *Esquire* published, in February 1988, also served as an early outline for a book I wound up writing in 1994 about the democratization of money. Although the book profiled a handful of financial innovators—such as Charles Schwab, and Dee Hock, who put together Visa, the credit-card company—Fidelity remained front and center, and the rise of the mutual fund industry was one of the book's major themes. Nine months after the book was published, Netscape went public, an event that began the Internet boom, and changed everything for the individual investors, not necessarily for the good. It would also begin to change my own thinking about the ability of small investors to invest wisely—a subject about which I am far less sanguine than I was 20 years ago.

As you'll see from the story, Fidelity was happy to cooperate with me, and I remained on good terms with the company throughout the six-year process of writing the book. Ned Johnson gave me several extended interviews, which was not something he did often. But in the late 1990s, when I was at *Fortune*, the company stumbled badly, and a colleague and I wrote a cover story about its problems. Because of my history with the company, I was the one who interviewed Fidelity executives for that story. Johnson himself declined to be interviewed, but I bumped into him one day during my interviews, and he went on an expletive-filled rant, denouncing *Fortune* for wasting its time digging for dirt about his company.

After the story was published, Johnson extracted his revenge, pulling all of Fidelity's advertising from *Fortune*. It never again advertised in the pages of the magazine. Once, years later, a top advertising executive at Time Inc. negotiated an advertising contract for *Fortune* with several top Fidelity executives, including Johnson's daughter Abby. After the terms were drawn up, the contract was left on Johnson's desk for his signature. As I hear the story, when he walked in the next morning and saw the contract, he picked it up, looked at it, and threw it in the trash.

The Ga-Ga Years

Esquire, February 1988

January 28, 1987. Dow Jones Opening Average: 2163.39

It's 10:00 in the morning, and the Dow has already risen 18 points. Amazing. Like everyone else, I've become transfixed by the astonishing upward spiral of the Dow, up almost 250 points since New Year's Day, four and a half years into the greatest bull market in history. Usually, though, I try to wait at least until the evening news. Today, I am standing in a posh storefront in Manhattan, at the corner of Fifty-first Street and Park Avenue, a vantage point from which it would take a supreme act of will *not* to keep track of the Dow's every tick. This is the New York beachhead of Fidelity Investments, the giant Boston-based mutual-fund company that manages more money for more people than anyone else in the world.

It's quite a spectacle here at Fifty-first and Park. Right now I'm staring up at an electronic board that resembles one of those overhead scoreboards you find in modern arenas. Only instead of scores, it is spewing out the current value of Fidelity's Select funds—high-risk mutual funds that invest in only one industry. A light-show for the 1980s. Amber numbers flicker across the screen, disappear, and then blip back up again. Every hour the numbers are updated. Hourly pricing, a Fidelity exclusive, has almost no real purpose: it is little more than a dazzling prop. At the bottom of the board flashes the most dazzling prop of all: the Dow itself. Which, by the way, has just gone up another 6 points.

If money is the new sex—and isn't that what everyone is saying these

days?—then this place is the whorehouse. The scent of the market is powerful here, intoxicating. Stretching across a long expanse of pink marble wall is
one of those digital tapes that announce block trades. Does anyone here have
the slightest idea how to read the thing? So why are we all staring at it so
shamelessly? Above the tape, a mural depicts pleasant scenes from the bull
market. Multiracial investment bankers peering at Quotron machines. That
sort of thing.

All around me I can see the blandishments of money, the seduction of
wealth, the lure of financial security. A recorded voice entices: "Choosing an
investment should be as easy as watching TV." The aisles are lined with fund
prospectuses. "Fidelity Magellan," it says in front of one big stack, "one of
America's most popular funds." "Municipal bonds," it purrs a few aisles
over. "They're not just for the wealthy anymore." I leaf through a few prospectuses. Is it my imagination, or is there a certain furtiveness to this act,
like the way men thumb through *Penthouse* at an airport newsstand?

I see a woman outside, her face pressed hard against the window. She is a
meter maid, young and black, and to judge from her expression, this place
might just as well be Tiffany's. "She comes by every day," whispers a Fidelity
saleswoman. "She really wants to make an investment, you can tell." Just
then, the woman steps haltingly through the revolving door. Once inside,
she looks ga-ga at all she sees. This strikes me as the only appropriate response
in the face of such irresistible come-ons. If the bull-market late 1960s were
the Go-Go Years, then surely these are the Ga-Ga Years.

The lunch hour approaches. The Dow is up 30 points. The place begins to
fill up. Many come to transact business, but just as many are here for the
same reason I am: to browse, to gawk, to stare ga-ga at the Dow as it makes
its relentless climb upward. I watch a young man named Jeff Goddard, one
of a dozen Fidelity "reps" working the room. He is earnest and cherubic and
24 years old. People tug at him, wanting information. A middle-aged man in
a driver's uniform pulls out a pamphlet and waves it at Jeff. He is holding a
prospectus for a bond fund. "They're offering 12½ percent. Can you do better than that?"

"Our highest is 10 percent," admits Jeff. The driver snorts audibly and
walks out. Another man takes his place. "Jeff, remember me? I'm ready if
you are!" The man writes out several checks to put into Fidelity mutual
funds. Next to him, a woman in tattered jeans who might be, oh, 19 years old
is doing likewise. She writes three checks in all, each for—am I seeing this
right?—$50,000. Behind her, a woman in a mink coat says loudly, "I want to
put another $65,000 in my account. Can I sit down with someone?"

I wander over to a bank of computers to punch up a few stock quotes but become distracted by a couple standing next to me. Complete strangers, they are deeply engrossed in conversation. The man looks like Robin Williams, only 20 years older; the woman is that classic type, the "little old lady" who dabbles in the market. In any other setting, it would be impossible to guess that these two are part of the Ga-Ga Years. Yet this is what I hear them say:

She: "My biggest mistake was selling my Carter-Wallace. You know, because of the AIDS thing. Sold it over a year ago."

He: "I hear Pan Am is supposed to be sold."

She: "A Philip Morris man said to me, 'Helen, you will never go wrong investing in Philip Morris.'" She sighs. "But I didn't."

He nods in sympathy. "Philip Morris is the finest of the tobacco companies." Then he asks, "Why don't you consolidate?"

She: "Oh, I couldn't. I love to play with my stocks. I have over $1,000 in newsletters."

They dawdle for most of the afternoon, talking, comparing investment notes, calling up stock quotes. Finally, they walk out together. They are friends now. They met at Fidelity. They have the market in common.

So did we all.

It seems so long ago, doesn't it—those days of ga-ga, when the market looked as if it would never stop rising? Black Monday, it is safe to say, will mark the end of the Ga-Ga Years. And what images will remain? After the Go-Go Years of the 1960s, the names that stuck were Gerry Tsai and Bernie Cornfeld. This time, the symbols will undoubtedly include Drexel Burnham and Boone Pickens and Ivan Boesky. And Fidelity. Just as Drexel will stand for the rise of the junk bond, and Boesky for the wages of greed, so will Fidelity conjure up the return of the equity mutual fund.

Fidelity was everywhere. You couldn't open a newspaper without seeing a Fidelity ad. You couldn't pick up the phone without knowing that Fidelity was ready to respond. At its peak, Fidelity had $85 billion in assets, making it a larger investor of people's money than even Merrill Lynch. It had the most funds—more than one hundred—and in Magellan, the largest fund, too, run by the most famous portfolio manager, Peter Lynch. Fidelity became such an icon of the Ga-Ga Years that on Black Monday reporters scrambled not to the stock exchange to get reactions but to Fidelity.

The last time mutual funds were hot, at the height of the Go-Go Years, 3 percent of American households had money in them. This time around, more than half the households in America had some stake in one—if not an equity mutual fund then at least a money-market fund. That one fact, I think, indicates a sea change in the way people thought about their money during the Ga-Ga Years. Almost alone, Fidelity understood people's evolving feelings about money, and played to those feelings. That was, and is, its secret.

I spent much of last year hanging around Fidelity, seeing in this exercise both a means of coming to terms with the Ga-Ga Years and a way to get at the modern history of money in which Fidelity played such a crucial role. I was at Fidelity when the Dow made some of its great gains. I was there when the crash came, too. Fidelity was always moderately enthusiastic about my endeavor, allowing me considerable access, though never so enthusiastic as to give me free rein of the place. This, I was told, was the way things were there, the way Mr. Johnson wanted it. Edward Johnson III, a reserved and somewhat eccentric Boston Brahmin, had run Fidelity since 1972 and was universally credited with being the genius behind the company's rise. As I began my trip, I wanted to learn more about him, too. Not least, I wanted to know how he saw the Ga-Ga Years coming and got there first.

The History of Money: A Preamble

Gerry Tsai began his career at Fidelity—he not only got his start there but became famous there: the first portfolio manager to get the press of a rock star. It was a different world then, a world in which the middle class still squirreled its money away in bank savings accounts, and small mutual-fund companies such as Fidelity were easily dwarfed by a superstar fund manager. Fidelity was also run by a different Mr. Johnson—Edward Johnson II, who left behind a career as a fairly substantial Boston lawyer when he bought Fidelity and its two small funds in the 1940s.

Johnson was a Boston Brahmin in a profession dominated by Boston Brahmins. But though he was one of them by virtue of class and bearing, he had nothing but scorn for the way they approached money management. Before Johnson, investment management was an overwhelmingly defensive profession, dedicated to preserving capital. Johnson hated the idea that the goal was to avoid losing money instead of making money. He hated the fact that mutual funds were managed by committees, which dithered instead of buying and selling. He believed that mutual funds should be managed by one person, using his own instincts and knowledge to trade stocks. And of course he was right. By the early 1960s, Johnson had created an entirely new species, the fund manager, and charged it with one simple (and radical) mission: to beat the market by as much as possible. Fidelity was the first company to sell not its cachet (for it had none) but the performance of its funds.

Because Johnson believed that money management was too important to be left to Brahmin money managers, he wasn't afraid to hire Gerry Tsai, a young, untested immigrant from Shanghai, as a stock analyst in the early 1950s. When Tsai began running a fund in 1957, he became the embodiment of Johnson's theories. Tsai's fund was called Fidelity Capital, and it was, as John Brooks would later write, "the company's first frankly speculative...fund."

No one had ever run a fund the way Tsai did. He bought all the glamour stocks of the day: Polaroid, Xerox, the conglomerates with their bloated P/E ratios. The turnover in his portfolio was dizzying: 120 percent in 1965 alone. That same year, Capital Fund gained an unheard-of 50 percent. Tsai's performance made him famous, and his fame brought him customers; by the mid-1960s, he was managing well over $1 billion.

And then he was gone. Legend has it that the departure was precipitated by a meeting with Mr. Johnson, in which the younger man asked about succession, and the older man replied that he expected his son to take over when he retired. Edward Johnson III, known as Ned, was running Fidelity's Trend Fund and (it was much noted afterward) outperforming the master as often as not.

Tsai moved to New York to start a new fund, called the Manhattan Fund, hoping to raise $25 million. But so many people wanted to bottle the Tsai magic that when his new fund began life, in February 1966, it had an incredible $247 million. And of course that's when Tsai's touch deserted him. In 1968 the bottom fell out of the Manhattan Fund, and Tsai's humiliating fall from grace became the parable for the Go-Go Years. Shortly thereafter, the bottom dropped out of the Dow itself, and everyone got a similar comeuppance. But Tsai went first, and loudest, and for that he would be forever remembered.

Fidelity itself was hardly immune to the market downturn. Mutual funds can never gain while the broader market is losing; the best a portfolio manager can do is lose less than the market. But during the Go-Go Years, funds had been spectacularly hyped; now, as profits turned to losses, people felt burned, and they began doing exactly what you'd expect: redeeming their mutual-fund shares with a vengeance and putting their money back into the bank, where (they now thought) it should probably have been all along.

The result was that when Johnson II finally handed the baton to Johnson III in 1972, Fidelity was in trouble. The Dow, which had once stood near 1,000, was closing in on 600. Some of Johnson's first acts as boss included firing people he had worked with for years. It wasn't enough. He needed something else, something more dramatic to reverse Fidelity's course. And then he saw it. A man named Bruce Bent, operating out of a tiny office in New York, had invented a strange new fund. It was called the money-market fund, and its creation marked the start of the modern history of money.

March 5, 1987. Dow Jones Average: 2276.43

"The idea first came to me in the summer of 1969," Bruce Bent is saying. It is late on a brisk afternoon in March, and the market has closed for the day. (Up 20 points today! More than 300 on the year!) We're sitting in Bent's corner office on the thirty-fifth floor of a slightly seedy Manhattan office building. He is a trim, handsome man, 50 years old now, with a face like Jack Kemp's—a face enhanced by the first few creases of age. Yet there is a certain prophet-without-honor quality about him. The carpet is faded. The furniture is old—not antique old but 1950s old. Bent's company, called the Reserve Fund, only handles money-market funds, which puts it at one remove from the bull market. While I was waiting in the lobby, I took a look at Bent's prospectus. His funds have only $2.7 billion in assets—peanuts compared to even a small mutual-fund company. If this bothers him, he hides it well.

"It was the summer of 1969," he begins again, smiling as he recalls the time he changed the world. "My partner and I had started our own investment firm. We didn't have any capital, and I was stuck on one question: How do you get money to come to you? Well, the answer was plain as day. *You had to pay higher interest rates than anyone else!*"

In those days, bank savings accounts were limited to 5¼ percent because of something called Regulation Q, a government-imposed ceiling on the interest a depositor could earn. Banks loved Regulation Q because it meant they took in money at an artificially low rate and then turned around and loaned that same money at whatever the market would bear. Bent wanted to find a way around Regulation Q, which he did by inventing the money-market fund. A money-market fund uses "deposits" from investors to make extremely short-term loans to corporations or the government. Like a bank, a money fund could charge market interest rates for those loans. But since it wasn't a bank (no Regulation Q!), it could also grant those same rates to its investors. The fund itself would make money by charging a management fee. Like all great leaps forward, it was both simple and elegant—or at least that's what everyone said once they began stealing Bent's idea.

"In February 1970," Bent says, returning to his story, "we filed with the SEC. The guy said, 'I think we're going to have a problem with this thing.' For the next year and a half we went back and forth with them on it. They just didn't get it. Finally, in November 1971, they let us go ahead. I'm sure they only let us do it because they thought it was going to die."

Can you guess what comes next? Our prophet is rebuffed at every turn. Bent pitches his fund to corporations as an efficient way to manage cash. They show him the door. He talks up the idea among brokers. They yawn. Meanwhile, Bent is trying to support a wife and two small children on zero income. "On bad days, I ate franks," he recalls giddily. "On good days, I ate in the J.C. Penney cafeteria. I took out a home-improvement loan and used it to buy food. I started having trouble handling it, to tell you the truth. My wife, thank God, she understood I had this vision."

On January 7, 1973—more than a year after the SEC gave its approval— Bent got a big break. A *New York Times* reporter, after months of badgering, wrote a short article about the fund. "The next day we got a hundred phone calls," says Bent. "By the end of the year we had $100 million in assets. People I knew on Wall Street would send their mothers to me. Little old ladies would say to me, 'My son told me you have a good thing.' Then they'd say, 'I'm nervous and I don't want to lose my money.'"

And, as we all know by now, they didn't. Money-market funds turned out to be great investments for little old ladies, for unless the fund manager was stupid beyond belief, the principal was never at risk. Only the interest fluctuated. However, since most of us didn't have sons working on Wall Street, it took a long time to figure that out.

It did not, however, take the mutual-fund industry long to see what the money funds were: salvation itself. Here was the means to win back some of those dwindling assets.

"And then," says Bent, finishing his story, "Ned Johnson figured out how to let people write checks against a money-market fund. That really added value."

The History of Money: The Early Years

Do you remember 1974? Do you remember any of your friends investing in money-market funds? I do. I remember exactly one couple. I thought they were out of their minds. So did all their other friends.

Actually, the mutual-fund industry thought Ned Johnson was pretty crazy back then too, what with this check-writing nuttiness. Check writing violated the principle the industry held closest to its heart: make it simple to get into a fund but hard to get out of one. But somehow Johnson saw what no one else did. The money fund wasn't just a temporary stopgap; rather, it marked the beginning of a new era, an era in which people would have options for their hard-earned money. To get people to hand their money to Fidelity, Johnson realized that he would have to treat the buyers of Fidelity "products" the same way McDonald's treated the buyers of hamburgers. Like *customers*. This was his revelation.

Ned Johnson's check-writing feature was the second great invention in the modern history of money. The addition of checks gave the impression that money-market funds were like banks—they felt *safe*. People who invested in them could still think of themselves as savers. In effect, Johnson had begun to blur the distinction between investor and saver.

Fidelity's money-market fund opened for business on June 12, 1974, and was an immediate hit. It was called the Fidelity Daily Income Trust, or FIDIT. Its logo was a frog (fidit, ribit—get it?), and Johnson began scattering frog images about his office. This only reinforced his image as an eccentric, which was then approaching legendary proportions.

He looked a little like Wallace Shawn in those days, vaguely nerdy, with an air of distraction that could rival the most absentminded professor. Whatever big picture he saw remained trapped within the confines of his own mind, escaping from time to time only in little wisps of sentences that came seemingly out of the blue. To the uninitiated, talking to him could be a disconcerting experience, and within Fidelity there developed one school of thought that said Ned Johnson wasn't really a genius at all. He was a flake.

Certainly what he was doing to Fidelity seemed flaky, even to the people on the inside. *Especially* to the people on the inside. Check writing wasn't the half of it. Here was this company still starved for cash, and the boss was spending millions upon millions of dollars. And on what? Well, there were all the fancy new computers Fidelity suddenly had. Now, no one was saying that Fidelity didn't need computers. But the computers Johnson bought were so full of bells and whistles they seemed all out of proportion to Fidelity's needs. Another thing: advertising. Johnson decided Fidelity should do its own selling and began advertising in *The Wall Street Journal*—slick ads with headlines and a sales pitch. The budget was $30,000 a month—shocking!

And the telephones! Fidelity employed six "reps" who worked in an awful windowless room answering calls at random. The six had been hired after Fidelity started running its ads and quickly discovered—and my, wasn't *this* interesting—that people would phone in with questions. Well, six wouldn't do at all! No sirree. Overnight, Fidelity had as sophisticated a system as an airline.

Are you getting the picture here? Ned Johnson remade Fidelity. It became completely self-sufficient, with its own systems company and its own service company, and eventually, its own taxi company. This last, it was said, was the result of Johnson's eccentric inability to flag down cabs during the Boston rush hour. By 1978, Fidelity had gone from being a company that could monitor phone calls weekly to one that could monitor them hourly. But *why?*

Do you remember 1978? You should; that was the year you started to think about your money again. Not that you had much choice; inflation was approaching double digits and interest rates were already there. Both were gnawing away at your standard of living. By then, though, the revolution had come. The money revolution. As you looked around, you suddenly realized that there were ways to outsmart inflation. If you owned a house you felt great. Houses were great inflation beaters. You hired an accountant for the first time, and he told you to borrow as much as you could against your Mastercharge, where the interest was fixed by law, and put that money in a money-market account earning a few percentage points more. And you did it. And it was a real kick: you were making money on the spread. And then there was the night you woke up with a start and realized what an absolute idiot you'd been to keep your savings in the bank, where Regulation Q and inflation were robbing you. This was a truly terrible moment. You felt a little panicky, and your palms were sweaty, and you vowed that the very next day you would switch to a money-market account, the way all your friends were doing.

Do you remember that moment? That is the moment Ned Johnson had been planning for.

May 14, 1987. Dow Jones Average: 2329.68

"Fidelity investments. This is Wendell Weaver. How may I help you?"

Wendell Weaver, who is 23 years old, who is wearing a pair of oversize glasses that make him look like a character out of a Jeff MacNelly sketchbook, who exudes a naive wholesomeness and frothy effervescence that would do Jimmy Stewart proud—Wendell Weaver is sitting in a tiny cubicle on the eighth floor of a banal Dallas high-rise answering the phones. He is joined, on this hot Texas night, by 27 other phone reps manning similar stations along a long, open room. Wendell sits erect, his gangly frame on red alert as he awaits the next call. They come with some frequency.

"Let's see," he says into the receiver, glancing over at a sheet filled with the day's closing prices. "Magellan, up .15. Puritan, down 1. Overseas Fund down .59 to 40.88. Looks like there was some profit taking in the Japanese market." Next call: "Yes, sir. The Ginnie Mae Fund has been taking some substantial losses. Why? Well, when interest rates go up, bond prices go down." Next call: "The price of the yen? Just a minute." He pulls out his copy of *The Wall Street Journal* and rattles off the price of the yen. The calls stop coming for a minute, and he glances at his watch. It's a little after midnight. Welcome to the graveyard shift at Fidelity.

It's May. The Dow is still going up, though it's had a few little tumbles lately—those triple witching hours are murder. No one seems too worried, though. Certainly, there is no sense of worry here on the eighth floor. Off in the distance, I can see downtown Dallas, giving off the illusion of quiet that big cities often emit at night. Things are quiet in here, too, despite the low buzz of telephone talk.

If the portfolio managers in Boston are the beating heart of Fidelity, then this phone operation in Dallas is the belly of the beast. When Ned Johnson put those six people in that little room, the phone became the company's weapon of choice. People who want to switch from one fund to another can do so by picking up the phone. They can call to make stock trades through Fidelity's discount brokerage. They can call just for the hell of it, twenty-four hours a day, seven days a week.

And Lord knows, they do. In a way, the Fidelity phone centers—there are similar setups in Boston and Salt Lake City—are the belly of the Ga-Ga Years, too. Especially at night. Why, I wondered, were people calling Fidelity instead of going to bed? In February 1986, when Fidelity began answering the phones all night, it didn't even bother doing market research. It just *knew*.

Neither Wendell nor anyone else in Dallas can ever recall the phones shutting down completely, except on the day the space shuttle blew up. Then, as the shock wore off, the lines were suddenly jammed, the callers all asking the same warped question: "*What's it going to mean for the market?*" Here in the middle of the bull market, one can see how firmly the ga-ga mentality has taken hold. Wendell detects a certain frantic tone from callers lately, as people who know nothing about the market try to climb aboard, worried that the train is leaving the station. "I spend a lot of time explaining what a dividend is," is how he puts it.

I had come to Dallas because I was simply curious about what people asked about their money at 2:00 in the morning. But nothing at Fidelity is ever so simple as that. Most of the afternoon was devoted to an extravagant tour of the entire Dallas operation. It was, as Fidelity tours always are, impressive. Most of Fidelity's mailings are done from Dallas; in the huge mail room, I saw a figure written on a blackboard for the number of mailings sent out in the first four months of 1987: 8,358,146. Then on to the phone operation: two enormous aisles filled with more than two hundred little phone cubbies.

More than six hundred people answering the phone in Dallas. More than a thousand phone lines open during peak hours. If one center is overloaded with calls, the system transfers calls to another location. And on, and on.

By the time Wendell came on duty at 11:00 P.M., the day's market headline was obvious. So jaded had everyone become by big gains that the Dow's rise on this day, a "mere" 7 points, was a snore. Instead, most callers wanted to talk about the *Japanese* market, which had dropped 172 points, a fact of passionate concern to the many shareholders of a fund called Fidelity Overseas. Overseas was the number-one fund in the country in 1986, due in no small part to its Japanese holding. As a result of that record, it now has some hundred thousand shareholders, most of whom seem to be on the other end of the phone tonight.

At 1:00 in the morning an anxious shareholder calls to say that he has $36,000 in Overseas and what should he do? Wendell gives him a by-now practiced speech. "It's not nearly as bad as two weeks ago," he says. "There's some profit taking. And they're trying to stabilize the dollar. You're still looking at a 34-percent gain since the beginning of the year." Then, a note of caution: "There is some instability in the foreign markets. You need to be aware of that."

It seems a little strange to me that this 23-year-old kid, not long out of the University of Texas, is discussing the market with doctors and lawyers making ten times the $20,000 or so he makes. Or maybe it's not so strange. The doctors and lawyers can't see Wendell after all; they can only hear him. They hear his reassuring voice offering, in some weird way, comfort. "People want me to say it's okay," admits Wendell. But do you know what the whole thing reminds me of? It reminds me of the phone-sex business, in which women in curlers iron their husbands' shirts while talking dirty to some desperate soul in a hotel room.

One-thirty: a sudden upsurge in calls as Salt Lake City closes down, leaving only Dallas open. Wendell takes one from Fresno. A woman wants to close out her position in Magellan. New Mexico calls; a potential customer wants information about rolling over an IRA. At 3:00 Alabama calls, wanting to talk about the downturn in the Japanese market. After Alabama hangs up, Wendell tells me that he could hear the man eating breakfast.

"I talk to people with toast in their mouth every day," he says.

The History of Money: The Middle Years

Early in 1980 there occurred one of those small, seemingly ho-hum events that later turn out to be fraught with significance. The event was the announcement by Time Inc. that Marshall Loeb had been named managing editor of *Money* magazine; its importance, in terms of the Ga-Ga Years, was that by some happy accident, Time Inc. had managed to put precisely the right man in the right spot at the right moment.

Loeb, a nattily dressed man who resembles nothing so much as a leprechaun, was on the fast track at Time, while *Money* was the company's most snakebit publication, having done nothing but lose millions in its eight-year existence. Loeb's mandate, plainly, was to turn things around, which he did in classic golden-boy fashion, doubling the circulation within two years. He did it by openly and shamelessly selling money as the new sex.

Nineteen-eighty: time for another trip in the wayback machine. Interest rates have come down just a bit, but oddly, no one seems to be happy about it. Why is this? It's because, thanks to the money-market fund, we've become a nation of interest-rate junkies, where little old ladies move their money around to feel the thrill of an extra quarter of a point.

Nineteen-eighty was also the year the banks tried to put the clamps on the money funds, having finally realized that Regulation Q was killing them. Congress was so flooded with outraged mail that the banks never had a chance. The secret was out. Only suckers put their money in savings accounts.

As interest rates declined, the fund pushers showed us their other wares. We were interested now. We were curious. As we looked for ways to keep making double-digit gains, we saw...

"*Choices!*" Marshall Loeb practically leaps off his couch in the Time-Life Building, where he now edits *Fortune*. "Just *think* of all the choices you had by then," he exclaims. "You had bond funds. You had tax-free bond funds. You had money-market funds. You had *tax-free* money funds."

You also had Merrill Lynch's Cash Management Account. You had the new Select funds from Fidelity. On the horizon, you had a little retirement idea called an IRA, ready to explode. And of course you had the bull market. When the market took off in August 1982, it became the new fix. Money streamed into stocks, and into their surrogate, the mutual fund. This influx dwarfed anything that had come before because so many more people were thinking about money now. Here was the moment that the transformation from saver to investor—begun by Bent, nurtured by Johnson, championed by Loeb—was complete.

Loeb believes that money became, in his words, "the most discussed topic among consenting adults," as two-income couples began talking about their money over dinner; it was only a matter of time before those private conversations became cocktail-party talk. My own belief is that Loeb had a microphone in the saltshaker, so sure was his feel for those conversations. "*Money* did good journalism," Loeb insists defensively. But who was buying it for the journalism? People were buying it for the fantasy—for the sex.

No one was more ga-ga during the Ga-Ga Years than Loeb. His trademark was his cover, where he regularly put a wholesome young couple next to a headline that read: HOW TO TURN $50,000 INTO $250,000 IN JUST FIVE YEARS. What was this conceit if not the equivalent of *Playboy*'s centerfold? That you had as much chance of getting rich by following the example of the *Money* centerfold as you did of sleeping with a Playmate scarcely seemed to matter. People bought the magazine, took it home, and drooled.

Inevitably Loeb's magazine began intersecting regularly with Johnson's company. The first and most revealing incident came in April 1983, when *Money* chose a wholesome young Fidelity fund manager named Michael Kassen for its cover. The headline read: HOW TO MAKE MONEY IN MUTUAL FUNDS. Underneath that: THEY'RE THE SUREST, SAFEST WAY TO INVEST IN A SURGING MARKET. And finally, the clincher: KASSEN, THIRTY, RUNS A TECHNOLOGY FUND THAT HAS JUMPED 131 PERCENT SINCE AUGUST. A hundred and thirty-one percent! Wow!

Kassen's appearance in *Money* marked a kind of coming out for Fidelity. Ever since Tsai had left, portfolio managers had been forbidden to talk to the press, the lone exception made for Peter Lynch, who was allowed guest appearances on Louis Rukeyser's television show, *Wall Street Week*. That Johnson would now allow Kassen to speak freely to a *Money* reporter about his stock choices, allow him to spend five hours in the freezing cold being photographed in his tennis togs, allow him to talk about his upbringing in Cleveland and his affinity for squash—all of this spoke volumes about how the world had changed. Fund companies needed every little edge now. In this new world, Johnson's decision to open Fidelity to the press, however distasteful personally, was a given.

What was not a given was *Money*'s choice of Kassen to represent the "safety" and "sureness" of the mutual fund. Despite his undeniable talent for picking stocks, he was, in fact, probably the worst choice imaginable. His fund was anything *but* safe. It was called Fidelity Select Technology, and it did not invest broadly in the market like most funds, but only in one segment: high technology.

During the Ga-Ga Years, every modern investment company was also an entertainment company, and with its Select funds Fidelity was playing deliberately to the entertainment side of the market. It always assumed that the constituency for the Selects would be the most active amateurs, people who enjoyed guessing which industries were poised to go up, people who could afford to guess wrong. This caveat, however, never made its way into the *Money* article.

Kassen wound up feeling a little embarrassed by the publicity, but for Fidelity the experience exceeded its fondest hopes. When the article hit the newsstands in April, Kassen's fund was already an established hit, with a little more than $200 million. By *July*, it was closing in on $650 million. Millions of dollars were poured into the fund every day, thousands of checks for $3,000 and $4,000. "It was like watching time-lapse photography of a flower," Kassen recalls. "Surreal."

And then—*poof!*—the joyride was over. In August, technology stocks crashed, and so did Kassen's fund. He was working furiously now, trying to keep his head above water. And by any objective measure, he succeeded brilliantly. "Technology stocks were down 20 percent," he recalls, "and I was only down 10 percent."

Unfortunately, this was not much consolation to all the people who had first learned of his walk-on-water mutual fund from *Money* magazine. As Select Technology fell back during the second half of 1983, a lot of people discovered something about mutual funds they hadn't quite comprehended before. They were not necessarily "sure." To be an investor, rather than a saver, meant accepting risks; and funds like Kassen's, geared to make the quick, spectacular gain, also involved the most risk. But the lesson had not been learned from *Money* magazine. It had been learned with cold, hard cash.

July 28, 1987. Dow Jones Average: 2493.94

"Quite a paper this morning," says Peter Lynch, shaking his head in mock wonder. He is leaning back in the chair of his small corner office, leafing through *The Wall Street Journal*. Lynch, who is rumored to make $3 million a year managing Fidelity's Magellan Fund, is wearing a light-blue seersucker suit, slightly worn and in desperate need of dry cleaning. It is eight in the morning. Late July: as the bull market closes in on its fifth anniversary, the gains keep coming—up more than 500 points so far this year. Incredible.

"Did you see what Boone did today?" Lynch asks. Pickens has announced plans to buy a $15-million stake in the giant airplane manufacturer Boeing. "I've got twenty thousand shares of Boeing," he says—a position worth a little more than a million dollars; pocket change for the $11-billion Magellan fund. Like most portfolio managers, Lynch tends to refer to himself when he means his fund. "Someone forgot to tell that whole sector there's a bull market going on," he shrugs.

As Lynch makes his way through the paper, he finds a story on almost every page that affects his life. He groans over a report that American Express intends to buy back some of its shares. "Look at this." He shows me a printout that lists the previous day's performance of Magellan's 1,700 stocks. At the top of the sheet, written in pen and underlined for emphasis, are the words "Buy AmEx." "I wrote it on the way in this morning. If only they had waited a month."

"Yup," says Lynch, shaking his head again. "It's quite a paper today."

Peter Lynch may be the most famous portfolio manager of the Ga-Ga Years, but he's not famous the way Gerry Tsai was twenty years ago. There is nothing flamboyant about him, nothing exotic, nothing larger-than-life. He is forty-three years old, tall and thin, his hair completely white, with classic Irish features. The only thing that sets him apart is this: for ten years now, he has been the best mutual-fund manager alive.

Of all the smart moves Ned Johnson made in the 1970s, the smartest may have been giving Magellan to Lynch. When he did so, back in 1977, Magellan was a nice little $22-million fund, and Lynch was head of research. Ten years and $11 billion later, Lynch could lay claim to one of the most fabulous statistics of the Ga-Ga Years: if you had put $10,000 into Magellan on the day he took it over, you'd have made $175,000.

The result of Lynch's performance is that Magellan was a symbol of the Ga-Ga Years even before they were over: a few years ago, it was an answer on the game show *Jeopardy*. Just in the time I've been hanging around Fidelity, the fund has grown by $3 billion, as people scramble to get in before it's too late. It is the greatest marketing tool Fidelity has ever had, a powerful magnet pulling people into the company, making it the single biggest mutual fund in America. "Around Fidelity," says one former marketing aide, "Peter Lynch is God."

Well, maybe not *God*. But as the man who manages the franchise fund, his influence on the other portfolio managers is enormous. His lack of flash is part of the ethos of the equity shop. The suspender quotient is low here. Nor is there any flamboyance in the way Lynch and his colleagues buy and sell stocks. There is no worse sin at Fidelity than buying something simply because it is "hot." Back when everybody was in technology stocks, Lynch was a guest on *Wall Street Week*, and Rukeyser asked him which high-tech companies he was buying. None, he replied; they weren't his kind of deal.

On this day in late July, fifteen companies will visit Fidelity; Lynch will see as many as he can. Frank Lorenzo touted Texas Air at breakfast. The officers of a small company in which Magellan holds a large position are scheduled for lunch. An oil analyst is coming by. A huge foreign conglomerate. When you have 1,700 stocks in your portfolio, your job can be defined rather simply: you have to know everything about everything.

At ten o'clock, Lynch goes to his first meeting. "I bought a lot of your stock," he begins in a surprisingly soft voice. "Thanks for making me some money." Although there are a dozen people in the room, Lynch asks almost all the questions. He rubs his forehead with his free hand: a little tic. As everyone settles into their chairs, the CEO says, "We've had a good quarter, which we're reporting in three days. As you are valued shareholders, we'll trust you…" Lynch cuts him off. "We don't want to know that stuff," he says. "Just tell us about the company."

Lynch dashes out of the meeting and heads back to his office. Rummaging around his desk, he yells out to one of his assistants, "Do you know where my Ford file is?" Ford Motor Company is Magellan's largest holding, with some eight million shares—an $800 million position. When Lynch first started buying it heavily a few years ago, Ford was just beginning to show signs of turning around. Now, of course, it is making more money than General Motors.

Everything seems to be happening at once. The phone rings—it's a company he's been trying to reach. The oil analyst has just arrived. A young Fidelity hand pops in to announce some second-quarter results. Lynch's secretary reminds him about the lunch. In the middle of this low-level chaos, Lynch suddenly looks at me and says, "You know, the last two and a half years have been the worst in the last twenty." What's he talking about? The last two years have been *great*. Sensing my disbelief, he adds: "Eighty percent of the pros have lost in this market."

Well, sure. But to me, all that proves is the difference between the way Lynch thinks about money and the way the rest of us do. His goal is to beat the S&P 500, while ours is to make more money than we could make in a bank or a money-market fund. Because of its enormous size, Magellan can no longer beat the market the way it once could; Lynch himself advises people looking for big gains to try another fund. But they don't. Magellan is where people want their money in the Ga-Ga Years. And when they look up later and see that he's made them 20 percent, they are very happy. Who cares if he hasn't beaten the S&P 500?

Though most of the time, he has. "I'm just a little behind it right now," he says. So far this year, the S&P 500 is up 33.8 percent. Magellan is just a shade behind, up 32.2 percent. So I take it back. Maybe the guy is God.

Late in the afternoon Lynch turns his attention to me again. He has a few standard speeches for the press, and now I get one of them. "Economics to me," he says, "is when a company had seven losing divisions and now it only has five. I don't know how long this bull market will last. We had the worst recession since the Depression in 1982. Nobody told me. What I'm trying to do here is find out: is Zayre getting better? That's how you make money over the long haul."

He has another standard speech, about the worth of mutual funds, and the time has come for me to hear it as well. In the past few months, the mutual-fund backlash has been gaining ground. Magellan has been criticized for its high management fee. The industry has been criticized for peddling funds without explaining the risks, not unlike the excesses of the Sixties. But the worst cut of all came in May from the novelist Michael M. Thomas, who predicted a crash of the bull market triggered by the mutual funds. "When mutual-fund shareholders hit the panic button, and start clamoring for redemptions of their shares," he wrote in *The Nation*, "the funds have no legal recourse but to come up with the money, and that could trigger a selling panic."

Has Lynch heard the criticism? I have no doubt. "My mother used to say, 'Never play the market because you'll lose it all,'" he tells me now, with more passion than I've heard from him all day. "But people don't have any choice anymore. They've been pushed into the market. I'm happy to beat the market by 4 or 5 percent. Last year I was up 23.7 percent, or whatever the hell I was up last year. That's after the management fee, after the commissions—after everything." His voice is rising. "*This is a very efficient method for the public*," he says with finality. He gives me a steely look that says, "This is not a point you want to argue with." Not today, anyway.

August 13, 1987. Dow Jones Average: 2669.32

The whole thing is starting to get a little weird. The Dow was down today, 11 points, but it's been going up so far and so fast—up 44 yesterday; up 43 the day before, a new record every day—that there is a lot of nervous talk that we're due for a big correction. Or worse. Surely it can't go on forever. One of these days I'm going to start worrying about it.

Right now, though, I've got other things on my mind. I'm sitting in the office of Ned Johnson. Johnson, I've been told, does not grant many interviews, and there was some question as to whether I'd be granted one. But at long last the moment has arrived.

Johnson's office is full of perfect Brahmin touches—tasteful painting, discreet antiques—and also, I notice, the odd frog here and there; he likes to keep a few reminders of the old days. I spot a Quotron machine by his desk. Although Johnson hasn't managed a portfolio in years, I've heard he still loves the market. A few years ago, when Gerry Tsai joined American Can Company, Johnson called the person who manages his holdings and said: "I worked next to Tsai for five years. Buy twenty thousand shares of American Can."

He does not look like Wallace Shawn anymore. At 57, his hairline is long gone, but over the years his face has gotten thinner and longer, more dignified. There is still that sense about him that though his body may be here, his mind is a million miles away. He is wearing an expensive tie, but when he crosses his legs, I can see that his shoes need new soles.

After some preliminary chitchat, I start the interview. "Mr. Johnson," I begin, "how did you come up with the idea of adding the check to the money-market fund?"

He seems instantly uncomfortable. "Oh, I don't know," he replies with a sigh. "Ideas bubble up and down, and the ones that keep coming back up usually have the most merit." That's it. That's the whole answer.

Oh boy, I'm thinking. He's not going to make this easy. One more try. "Sir, what compelled you to do what you did in the 1970s? What did you see that no one else saw?"

This time he gives a helpless shrug. "I just assumed the equity market would eventually come back. It always has before."

Do you know how I'm feeling here? I'm feeling like Dorothy in *The Wizard of Oz*, and I've just pulled back the curtain. *This* is the insight that changed the world? That the equity market was going to come back?

We talk for an hour, but the interview never really gets off the ground. Finally, I thank him for his time and flip my notebook shut. And then a funny thing happens. Ned Johnson becomes comfortable again. The act of closing the notebook has somehow freed him to talk. I can see it now: the wisps of sentences, the flash of ideas. I'm not saying I see genius, not in a ten-minute conversation, or even that I have any better understanding of where this very private man learned to see the future. But I am willing to concede now that he is capable of such a feat.

Just before I leave, I pop one last question. I ask him how long he thinks the bull market will last. But immediately Johnson reverts to his previous Dalai Lama–like pose. "How do you ever know when you've reached the top?" he replies elliptically. "Each crash is a little different from the one before it." He stares off into space. "They're all a little different," he repeats.

The History of Money: The Late Years

How do you know when you've reached the top? It's mid-August now, and the question is being asked with increasing frequency. I saw Marshall Loeb on television the other night pooh-poohing the bears. Then I saw Elaine

Garzarelli of Shearson Lehman Brothers on CNN, making it sound as if collapse is imminent. It's hard to know what to think anymore.

And what is Fidelity saying about the market—Fidelity with its hundred delicious options for making money? Fidelity isn't saying anything. Fidelity believes that its job is simply to provide the choices. "There are huge attitudinal changes in this country," Rodger Lawson told me in August. Lawson heads Fidelity's giant marketing operation, and he was outlining Fidelity's official world view. "People want control," he said. "They want to make their own decisions."

But I'm not so sure. I think back to my night with Wendell Weaver, listening to callers practically plead for help. And I recall, too, an investing seminar I attended in Cambridge early in the summer, well before the bull market started to get the jitters. The most memorable speaker that day was a charismatic man named Dick Fabian, described by the master of ceremonies as "the father of mutual-fund switching." Flailing his arms like an evangelist preaching salvation, Fabian had proclaimed that everybody should be able to attain "20-percent-annualized-compounded-growth-with-no-downside-risk-as-measured-over-a-five-year-period." He kept repeating these words over and over like a mantra, until they hypnotized.

When Fabian left the podium, he was blocked by a mass of people who had raced to the front of the hall and had surrounded him. To watch these people crowded around Fabian, to see the longing in their eyes, to listen to the desperate quality of their questions, was to realize that they did not feel freed by the new financial marketplace. They felt paralyzed by it. They were drowning in an ocean of choice, and they wanted Fabian to throw them the life preserver. *They wanted him to tell them what to do.* This, I think, is what people most crave as the Dow approaches 2,700. But it is the one thing Fidelity won't provide.

On the eve of the fifth anniversary of the bull market, a balmy day in August in which the market had opened 44 points up (again!), I sat in on a meeting of a group of Fidelity portfolio managers. More than 16 people jammed into a small conference room, all members of the "income-growth" group, which consists of more conservative funds than pure growth funds such as Magellan.

Leading the meeting was Bruce Johnstone, who manages both this group and his own huge fund, Equity-Income, which had returned 600 percent in ten years and bulged with $4.5 billion worth of conservative money. As he stood at the front of the conference table, Johnstone held five different colored markers with which he kept notes on a board behind him.

Short, balding, quick to laugh, Johnstone so overflows with guileless enthusiasm that he can get away with saying things like, "I can't *believe* I've been so *lucky* to work with a genius like Ned. It's been *great!*"

The meeting was a freewheeling discussion of the market: where it had been, where it was going, what was on people's minds. "Salomon Brothers is predicting 6½ percent inflation for 1988," a young analyst began. Johnstone winced skeptically. "Gee whiz, that sounds high," he replied finally. "Where are wages going up?" Everyone clamored to answer at once. "New York just settled with its union workers—three years, 18 percent raise," someone said. "Autoworkers, steelworkers, and mine workers all have contracts coming up this year," added someone else. "The auto companies have made a snootful of money," chimed in a third voice. "What can Ford possibly tell its workers?"

Eventually the discussion turned to the mood of the investing public. Someone mentioned that the *Boston Herald*, the local Murdoch paper, had begun carrying a stock market game. I'd noticed that, too. What could it mean, I wondered, when the lure of the Ga-Ga Years had become so pervasive that Rupert Murdoch could use it as a circulation booster? Maybe it meant the end was near.

Certainly most of the people in this room felt that way. "You simply cannot justify this market on the fundamentals," I heard Francis Cabour say vehemently. Cabour is a legendarily conservative portfolio manager who is always predicting doom. But today everyone agreed, Johnstone included. "Four or five months ago, we thought we were in the ninth inning," he said. "Now it looks like we're in extra innings." Everyone laughed, but it was a nervous laughter—the kind that means the joke has hit home. I looked around the room at this handful of fund managers, all furiously working the bull market for every last dime, and the thing I noticed most was the complete lack of euphoria, that giddy sense of jumping in head first that had characterized the Go-Go Years, or the Roaring Twenties, for that matter. And it suddenly occurred to me that these portfolio managers were feeling what I was feeling—whatever everyone was feeling. In the last few months, as the Dow made some of its most majestic gains, there was none of the joy that usually accompanies such gains. We watched the Dow in awe, not understanding, and not really believing either. We were just ga-ga.

In five years, the Dow has risen 2,000 points, and everybody is supposed to have had such a great time. And it *has* been fun. It's been exciting. So why isn't anyone smiling? I think it's because although we've become investors, in our heart of hearts, we wish we were still savers. We wish we didn't have to worry about whether to stay in or get out. We wish we didn't have to learn about the effect of interest rates on bonds, or the difference between a growth and an income fund. We wish the world were simple again.

As the meeting drew to a close, a young woman, newly hired and not yet in sync with the rhythms of Fidelity, asked for a straw poll on how long the bull market might last. It was an embarrassing moment. People looked in the other direction, or waved her request away. I thought: here I am among some of the smartest money managers in the world, and not one of them is willing to look the bull market square in the eye. They are too nervous, just like the rest of us.

October 20, 1987. Dow Jones Average: 1738.74

Is this how it ends? Not with a whimper but with a bang—a huge, amazing, horrifying bang? Yesterday was Black Monday: the Dow Jones lost 508 points, 22 percent of its value, on a staggering 604 million shares. The worst day ever. A year's worth of gains wiped out. Those tremors I felt in that meeting with Johnstone have suddenly turned into a terrifying earthquake.

And here I am right back where I started, at a Fidelity investment center, in Boston this time. I am transfixed by the Dow again, just as I was that January day in New York. Now, as then, I am staring at that magical Select scoreboard, which in Boston is placed in the window so people can see it as they walk by. Except no one is walking by. They *can't* walk by. They stop, and they stare, their mouths hanging open. They—we—look like zombies, unmoving and uncomprehending.

It is a strange and frightening scene. The crowd has grown so large that it has spilled onto the street, blocking traffic. Truck drivers honk their horns angrily. I hear someone say, "It just dropped another 2 points in two minutes. It's all over now." I see a tourist taking a picture of the Select board—something to show his grandchildren in fifty years? I hear someone else say, "I thought it would recover today. Wishful thinking." It seems, somehow, a fitting end to the Ga-Ga Years, if indeed this is the end. What can be more ga-ga than the greatest crash in history?

I had driven into Boston early yesterday on other business, but by 8:30 this morning, I was in Fidelity's public-relations office. "We're not doing any selling on the phones," the press guy told me. "We're strictly trying to reassure people." Eighty thousand people had called over the weekend, after the market dropped more than 100 points on Friday. Top officials met all weekend and met again after Monday's huge loss. At one meeting, Johnson, surveying the wreckage, concluded that there were a lot of great stock buys out there. Oh, that Ned Johnson.

Fidelity, of course, was hit hard by Black Monday. By the end of the week, its $85 billion in assets will shrink to $76.7 billion, and the company will consider it a victory just to keep that much money in the "Fidelity family"— much of it now residing in money-market funds. Although no one will give out redemption figures, it is clear that shareholders were bailing out like crazy, and that mutual funds played at least some role in creating Black Monday, just as Michael Thomas had predicted. On Wednesday, *The Boston Globe* will describe Magellan as a $7.7 billion fund.

And yet, and yet. Virtually every Fidelity equity fund beat the market on Black Monday. Beat it by a lot. Magellan was down 17 percent, compared with the Dow's 22 percent. Balanced, the fund Cabour now manages, was down only 6 percent. To paraphrase that famous 1960s slogan: Are mutual funds part of the problem or part of the solution? Who can say anymore?

The market opened 200 points up this Tuesday morning, but by the time I get to the investment center, around 11:30, most of the gain is gone. As it drops the crowd keeps growing, making the street ever more impenetrable to traffic. Who has time to worry about traffic? Every time the Dow makes another downward blip, there are audible groans.

At 12:30, with the market down 20 points, the police arrive. They want Fidelity to shut off the Select board so that people will get out of the street. Fidelity complies—and everyone moves twenty feet to stare at the block trade tape in the other window. Fidelity shuts that off, too. No one moves. People are now staring at two blank screens. An old man on a bicycle rides by and asks, in a thick foreign accent, "How's the New York?" Down 20, I tell him. "I hear up 50," he says.

I go inside and walk down a flight of stairs where the Quotron machines are. There must be twenty people crowded around the two machines. The hard core in this group first got here early yesterday. They look dazed and tired as they stare at the Dow. It reminds me of a poker game at 4:30 in the morning—you're sick of playing, and the games all seem stale, and you want to quit. But you can't. You're too deep into it. Clearly no one here will leave before four o'clock, when the market closes. When I go back upstairs a half hour later, the Dow is up 90 points.

Upstairs, I notice another cluster of people. They are waiting patiently on the phone to get through to a Fidelity rep. "I want to buy some IBM," says a man who, judging by the splotches of white paint on his work clothes, appears to be a house painter. IBM closed yesterday at 103, down nearly 32 points. "I'll never get another chance like this." I'm thinking: Ned Johnson strikes again.

I wander back downstairs. "Where's the Dow?" I ask. "Up 10," someone says. "It was just up 90," I say.

"That was ten minutes ago," comes the reply. "Where have you been?" Everyone laughs, myself included. But it's all too crazy. I can't take it anymore. About two o'clock, with the Dow creeping up again, I leave Fidelity and retrieve my car from the parking garage. For most of the drive home, I resist the impulse to find out how the market is doing. But then four arrives, and the market closes, and the impulse is too strong to resist. "For those of you who haven't heard," the announcer says, "the stock market closed up a record 102 points." Good God: 102 points! Now what do I do?

CHAPTER 4

Michael Milken, Mitigated (Well, a Bit)

I n my experience, whenever booms turns to busts, the culture undertakes a search for scapegoats. There are two reasons for this. The first is that it is so hard for us to acknowledge that the fault for our losses lies with us—that we lost our heads during the boom times, and now we have to pay the price. So instead we blame, for instance, the analysts who touted Internet stocks, or the brokers who talked us into buying this or that high-flying, "once-in-a-lifetime" stock. Post–bull market lawsuits almost always revolve around placing blame elsewhere—sometimes with justification, but mostly not.

The second reason is that it is not just you and me who lose our heads during a bubble. So do the big boys. Bankers make crazy loans. Deal makers make insane deals. Analysts do indeed tout stocks they shouldn't (which doesn't mean you should have listened to them!). And rich guys working on Wall Street get greedy and cross lines they shouldn't cross.

Michael Milken, clearly, was one of those rich guys who crossed lines he shouldn't have crossed. I've never doubted that. As I say in this article, he was greedy beyond all reason. He ultimately pled guilty to violating securities laws, and spent two years in jail. But when I phrase it like that, it sounds so *small*, doesn't it? And yet, during the time Milken was being pursued by investigators and prosecutors—with then–U.S. Attorney Rudy Guiliani leading the charge—he was portrayed as a master criminal, the leader of a vast insider trading conspiracy that enriched himself at the expense of, well, who exactly? That was never made clear. Yet it never dimmed the hysteria.

At the time I wrote this column, in late 1992, Milken was still the subject of a polarizing debate between his defenders and his accusers. Giuliani, for instance, said publicly that Milken should have to serve more time because of his lack of cooperation with the government. His supporters said he'd been railroaded by the defenders of the status quo. That kind of fervor has since dissipated, in no small part because Milken himself has kept a pretty low profile.

But it's not the only reason. Since leaving prison, Milken has spent enormous amounts of money and energy trying to find a cure for prostate cancer, a disease with which he was diagnosed shortly after being freed. In 2000, Giuliani, by then New York's mayor, was also diagnosed with prostate cancer. He invited Milken to Gracie Mansion, where they discussed treatment options. He told *The New York Times* that Milken had been "very kind and generous to me." And then he called on President Clinton to pardon the man he used to characterize as the embodiment of Wall Street evil.

Michael Milken, Mitigated (Well, a Bit)

GQ, December 1992

"What is your daily routine?" the interviewer asks America's most famous white-collar prisoner.

"I get up early in the morning, between four A.M. and five A.M. depending on how restless I'm feeling," replies Michael Milken. "Breakfast is at six A.M. Currently most of my day consists of my job—tutoring....I tutor some inmates before they go to work in the morning. And some of the others like to study after ten P.M. at night. So I generally don't get into bed until sometime between 11:30 P.M. and 1:30 A.M." Well, Michael Milken never did need much sleep.

The food is okay, he says. He walks to get exercise. Before he was a tutor, he was a janitor: "waxing the floors, washing windows, taking out the trash." Unlike Ivan Boesky, whose "confessions" are the reason Milken is in prison, he does not pay other inmates to do his assigned work. He still follows the junk-bond market he largely created at Drexel Burnham Lambert—a market that has rebounded tremendously in the past year—and he and his family are still worth, according to court documents, close to $500 million, even after handing over more than $1 billion to the government to settle the various criminal and civil cases brought against him. Not that it's doing him much good at the moment. In his mid-1980s heyday, Milken spent practically every minute of every working day on the phone; now he is limited to a few short calls, using a pay phone from which he can only call collect. Still, he does what he can: When Chrysler was stumbling last year, he called Lee Iacocca, collect, to give him a pep talk.

So it goes for Michael Milken as his prison sentence winds down—a sentence that will most likely end this March, after his original, ten-year prison term was reduced this past summer by Judge Kimba Wood. Though he still faces three years of community service, the worst is about to be over; when he gets out, he will have spent two years in prison. From the interview I've just quoted, which was conducted by a sympathetic British journalist named Fenton Bailey, one gets the distinct (and surprising) impression that Milken is not consumed by bitterness, except toward the press, which he never understood and which he blames for casting him as the villain of his own life story. Even with his lawyers and "handlers," who did such a miserable job on his behalf, he tends to let bygones be bygones: They did the best they could under the circumstances, he tells friends. Mostly, he seems sad. And perplexed, as if he still can't quite comprehend how he wound up where he is.

On the eve of his release from prison, I find myself perplexed. Even after all this time, the dust refuses to settle on the Milken affair. It all seemed simpler somehow, five years ago, when the rumors swirled about his then-impending indictment, with *The Wall Street Journal* publishing stories cataloguing his misdeeds and *Barron's* accusing him of operating a junk-bond daisy chain from his office in Beverly Hills, from which he destroyed the nation's S&Ls and wreaked havoc on America's corporate balance sheets. Those few writers who rose to Milken's defense early in the game—the author Edward Jay Epstein comes to mind—were scorned as "naive" or "bought." One paradox of the Milken case is that it was easier to turn a deaf ear to his protestations of innocence *before* he was forced to plead guilty to six felonies.

Since that day in 1990 when Milken admitted to committing six crimes, a lot has happened, most of it unsettling to those of us predisposed to believe that Milken was at the center of "the greatest criminal conspiracy the financial world has ever known," to borrow a memorable line from James Stewart's *Den of Thieves*. For starters, the felonies themselves, while serious enough, didn't remotely prove that Milken was the greatest financial criminal of the month, much less of all time. Where was the insider trading he was supposed to have been engaged in? Where was the evidence of the evil conspiracy he was supposed to have been at the heart of?

Even as Milken was being carted off to prison, the case laid out by such critics as Stewart and Ben Stein (who wrote most of the *Barron's* articles)— not to mention the prosecutors themselves—began to slowly crumble. Or so it seems to me. First came an unusual presentencing hearing, in which Judge

Wood gave the prosecutors a chance to put the "real" Milken crimes on display, so that we could all see the extent of the conspiracy. Their failure in that hearing was stunning. Then came the judicial repudiation of the methods used by the U.S. attorney's office to make their Wall Street cases, as one guilty verdict after another was overturned on appeal. Boesky's credibility as a witness was so damaged that prosecutors went to considerable lengths to avoid putting him on the stand. Gradually, the suspicion took hold that when Boesky convinced the prosecutors that Milken was the greater criminal (and that Boesky should be given a lighter sentence for turning Milken in), he had pulled off one of the greatest con jobs in history.

Meanwhile, in the wake of *Den of Thieves* has come a series of books that take an aggressively revisionist stance toward Milken's guilt, like Jesse Kornbluth's *Highly Confident* and Fenton Bailey's more recent *Fall From Grace*. We began hearing about the government's harassment of Milken's family—how the Feds showed up to "interrogate" his 92-year-old grandfather; how his children who have epilepsy began to have more-serious seizures as the weight of the case bore down on the family; and, most of all, how Milken's brother, Lowell, who appears to have had nothing to do with junk-bond transactions, was indicted by the government solely to put pressure on Milken. I don't know about you, but I found myself revolted by such tactics. And finally, there was the sentence reduction, which Judge Wood granted despite Milken's essential refusal to help the government put anybody else in jail (the way he was supposed to), and which strongly implied that Wood, too, had come to see Milken's crimes in a more benign light.

I say all this, I confess, with no small trepidation. To show the slightest sympathy for Milken, or to express any doubt at all about the "true" nature of his crimes, is to open yourself to the same accusations that were hurled at Ed Epstein. It means, somehow, that you've been "captured" by the "Milken PR machine." "[T]here are a number of well-known journalists in this country who are simply on [Milken's] payroll," Ben Stein has alleged, without a shred of proof.

Also, this whole exercise puts me in the queasy position of edging away from the side peopled with reporters I admire greatly—not only Stewart, but *The New Yorker*'s Connie Bruck, who has been a major Milken critic. But what can I do? I have questions about the Milken affair that nag at me, and neither the Milken critics nor the Milken apologists have answers that ring true. Some things, I guess, you just have to find out for yourself.

There are two enormous red herrings, I'm now convinced, that confound every effort to come to terms with who Milken really is and with what he really did. The first is the allegation that he was the central figure in a grand conspiracy to defraud America's financial markets. With apologies to Stewart, it just ain't so. Stein's accusation that junk bonds were a daisy chain is nuts; the robustness of the junk market today should give the lie to that canard. Although America's S&Ls bought large quantities of Milken-issued junk bonds—as they were legally entitled to do—Milken was not the reason behind the collapse of the nation's S&Ls, even though he has been blamed for it. Anyone who knows anything about the S&L crisis knows that real-estate deals—both sleazy and legitimate—were the root cause.

On and on the list goes. Whatever insider trading took place between Milken and his clients was neither systematic nor flagrant, as it has been described. (Cases in which Milken is supposed to have tipped Boesky to deals have proved particularly shaky.) "Thousands of workers lost their jobs [as a result of Milken's junk bonds]," writes Stewart, "companies loaded up with debt to pay for deals, profits were sacrificed to pay interest costs on the borrowings, and even so, many companies were forced into bankruptcies or restructurings. Bondholders and shareholders lost many millions more." All true enough—though it is also true that many companies were *created* as a result of Milken's junk bonds. But while there were many people who were deeply offended by hostile takeovers and junk bonds and all the rest of it—including Milken's infamous $550 million salary in 1986—none of these things counts as evidence of a conspiracy. If Milken is in prison because he created the financial device that made the Eighties possible, he shouldn't be there. Hostile takeovers and junk-bond financings may have been morally dubious, but they weren't criminal. There's a big difference.

The second red herring appears at the other extreme—the one that says that Milken's fatal flaw was his saintliness. "He took care of people" is how Kornbluth puts it. Out of this impulse came his many charitable contributions, his time spent with ghetto kids, blah, blah, blah. According to this view, it was this same impulse that caused Milken to commit the petty crimes to which he pleaded guilty. When his clients asked him to park stock, which is against the rules, or to help them create short-term tax losses or to prop up the price of an equity for a day—which is *really* against the rules—he just couldn't say no.

This tack, too, is a crock. "Mike said no plenty of times," scoffs one former Drexel hand. When he parked stock or created tax losses for clients, he did so either because it was such standard Wall Street practice that he never gave it a second thought or because there was something in it for him. When he did a favor for a client, the client then owed him a favor; that was the unwritten code. Wall Street is a business in which people shade the truth a lot—for instance, making a newly issued junk bond sound hot when it isn't—and Milken himself had no problem doing that. Certainly, his conscience never held him back.

Once you stop seeing Milken as either Attila the Hun or Saint Francis of Assisi, he starts to come into somewhat clearer focus. The focus is never completely clear, to be sure, because there is much about him that is enigmatic and contradictory. As a result, no one—not his former Drexel partners, not the buyers of his junk bonds, *especially* not the government—can say absolutely that he knew everything Milken did. In coming to terms with him, I've found it helps to admit that up front, too.

When you start asking around, the picture of Drexel's Beverly Hills office in its glory days looks something like this: It's an extremely aggressive place, of course, but not just in terms of roping in deals and making money. It's also aggressive in its stance toward securities regulations. New employees notice this right away; most are startled at first to see how blasé their boss is about walking right up to the edge of the regulatory line. Milken views the line as fuzzy, in any case, and he doesn't have much respect for fuzzy lines. There are regulations limiting the size of the spread on stock transactions. Do these regulations also apply to junk-bond transactions, which are not specifically mentioned in the regulatory language? No, Milken concludes. Thus, when he is brokering a junk-bond trade—buying an issue from one client and selling it to another—he sets a spread that others might find unconscionable. Nowhere is it written that he can't. One new employee discovers that the bulk of the very first bond issue he handles winds up in the private partnerships Milken reserves for himself and his most favored staff members. It isn't illegal, the man says now, but "it didn't pass my smell test." If Milken, according to his lawyers, is not breaking the letter of the law, he is perfectly willing to break its spirit.

Everybody likes Milken, but most feel slightly uneasy about him. He's brilliant and naive, focused and opaque. There will be five meetings going on at once, in five conference rooms; Milken will spend five minutes in each and somehow come up with the solutions they've spent hours searching for. He's like a chess champion playing twenty amateurs at once. On the other hand, sometimes when you ask him a question, you get an eye-glazing sermon in response. He is the family man to end all family men, yet no one spends more time at the office. He goes out for lunch once a year, when he takes his wife out on their anniversary. He has an idiot-savant quality about him, people say, a feeling that he is at sea outside the world of the trading room.

One thing is sure: he is greedy beyond belief. There is no question about it, in spite of his modest home and lifestyle. This trait has been widely viewed as another of the great paradoxes of Milken, but anyone who works in the Drexel office realizes that there is nothing paradoxical about it at all. Milken is one of those people for whom money is the way to keep score, even if he has no interest in spending it. "His greed is a character issue," says one Drexel source, "not a money issue." He has a way of justifying what other people would view as unjustifiable—the classic example being his $550 million salary. ("In his mind," says this same source, "he had created so much that he was entitled to it.") He made a deal with Drexel: he and his office would get one of every three dollars they generated for the firm. To Milken's way of thinking, a deal is a deal. You don't change it just because it creates a windfall.

He is also greedy for market share. Along with his refusal to carry a more finely tuned moral compass, it is his biggest lapse in judgment. He wants to be the biggest and the best in everything he gets involved in. He wants to do every deal. He wants to humiliate every competitor. He wants every last penny he feels he and the firm deserve. If there is anything that pushes him over the line, it is this hunger to do everything.

Did Milken do things he shouldn't have done? Somewhat to my surprise, most of the former Drexel people I talked to said yes. Yet they hem and haw when you ask them what it was, exactly, that he did wrong. No, they insist, he did not have captive clients whom he manipulated at will. (This allegation is the basis of Stein's daisy-chain theory.) On the other hand, they concede, he did have junk-bond buyers, like Fred Carr, chairman of the troubled Executive Life, who wouldn't hire a research staff because he preferred to have Milken tell him what to do. Similarly, was it Milken's fault that any number of S&L operators were, as one former competitor put it, "dumb as rocks," not knowing the difference between a good bond and a bad one—and not bothering to find out? When a Drexel salesman heard that the corporate-finance department was buying a stock—for what reason, he didn't know—and then advised a client wanting to sell that same stock that he might be better off holding on to it, was that an example of insider trading? Or was it something more innocent? When a manager of a junk-bond mutual fund got a piece of a Milken-led deal, was that a bribe? Or was it an example of doing favors for friends and supporters? Virtually every example of a Milken "crime" comes down to these kinds of hazy judgments.

And nothing illustrates that better than his dealings with Boesky, which should be seen, I think, as the logical consequences of Milken's desires and appetites. He got involved with Boesky in the first place because of his insatiable desire to dominate markets. He already ruled the world of high-yield bonds; now he wanted to rule the world of equities. Boesky was his wedge into the equity market. That Boesky was widely viewed as a shady character was of no concern to him; there was no place in his brain to integrate such an "irrelevant" fact. A week before he issued junk bonds to raise a $660 million takeover fund for Boesky—a deal in which he was also (typically) an investor—he was sent a message by someone in a position to know that the Wall Street arb he was dealing with did not do business on the up-and-up. "I'm a big boy," he replied dismissively. "I know what I'm doing."

Milken's lack of an ethical compass was very much in evidence in his Boesky dealings. By both underwriting and investing in Boesky's fund, Milken was placing himself in the middle of a nasty conflict of interest. In effect, he was investing in an arbitrageur while also playing a key role in the very takeover plays that were an arb's stock-in-trade. When he then tried to "help" Boesky, it was surely because his own money and reputation—that is to say, his own self-interest—were also at stake.

Finally, at the same time he was earning that staggering $550 million salary, he was also billing Boesky a paltry $5.3 million for "investment-banking services." It was the discovery of this bill, as much as any other thing, that put Milken in prison, for despite his denials, the government was convinced that those services included insider tips and other illegal acts. But why would Milken bother billing such a comparatively puny sum, especially since Boesky was such a pain in the neck about paying? *Because Boesky owed it to him.* To Milken, that's all that mattered: If you owed something, you had to pay it. The people I talked to, most of whom worked side by side with Milken for years, all insist that Milken and his staff did a huge amount of legitimate research for Boesky. Given their financial interest in seeing Boesky succeed, I don't doubt it. But what I find more instructive is that they were also willing to assume that buried in that $5.3 million bill lay at least some wrongdoing by Milken. Not insider trading, perhaps, but *something.*

"I really like Mike," one former Drexel employee told me, "but he deserved to do some time. He was totally out of control at the end." "Ninety-five percent of what we did was totally aboveboard," said another Drexel source. Then he corrected himself: "Make that 98 percent."

That still leaves anywhere between 2 percent and 5 percent that wasn't. Even in the grand scheme of things, that's an awful lot of wrongdoing. The line may have been fuzzy, the things he did may have been standard operating procedure on Wall Street, but still . . . wrong is wrong. After my own foray into Milken's former world, I wind up agreeing that he deserved to do some time, not because he made it possible for nobodies to threaten big companies with hostile takeovers or because, to borrow Michael Lewis' wonderful line, he was caught "loitering in the vicinity of the S&L crisis." Not, in other words, because he became the symbol for everything that went wrong in the 1980s. Rather, he deserved jail time for a simpler, more persuasive reason: he broke some laws. That's not as sexy a reason for putting him away as is being at the center of a conspiracy, nor is it satisfying to those Milken true believers who continue to think of him as a martyr to high yields. But I think it's what's true.

There was a time, early in the investigation, when Milken was offered the chance to plead to one felony, with a $100 million fine and a maximum two-year prison term, meaning, with parole, he would have been out of jail within six months. To my mind, that was the punishment that would have fit the crime. It also would have avoided much of what came later—the elevation of Milken to a whipping boy who had to be punished for how the 1980s had turned out. But he couldn't do it. He couldn't look himself in the mirror and concede he had done things that deserved punishment. From everything I've read, he still can't. As he prepares to emerge from prison, and begin the process of rehabilitating his reputation, I'm wondering if he ever will. What I'm also wondering is whether the rest of us will ever be able to see him in more-dispassionate terms. If we're ever going to come to grips with what really happened during the Decade of Greed, we need to start trying.

CHAPTER 5

Charlie Merrill and His Stock

When you start out on a business story—or, in this case, a book—you really have no idea which of your main characters are going to turn out to be memorable and which are going to be dull as dishwater. The businessperson with the transformative idea; the one who loves to make breathtaking deals; the entrepreneur who starts the next Google—their business accomplishments alone don't guarantee that their lives will make for enjoyable reading. Often, in fact, it's just the opposite: highly successful businesspeople are often so single-minded and unidimensional that breathing life into them is a surprisingly difficult task. Which is another way of saying: thank goodness for Charlie Merrill!

I discovered Merrill when I set out to write *A Piece of the Action*, my 1994 book about the democratization of money. In 1914, Merrill founded the firm that eventually became the nation's largest brokerage house, Merrill Lynch, and though I had not originally expected my history of Americans and their money to go back that far, I soon realized I simply couldn't leave him out. There were two reasons for this. The first was that, in a business sense, he was a man ahead of his time: in an age when Wall Street was largely rigged on behalf of wealthy insiders—when, indeed, it usually turned away money from small investors—Merrill was the first major Wall Street figure to push for the middle class to invest in stocks and bonds. This was his crusade, and though his efforts brought Merrill Lynch itself enormous success, it's fair to say that, during his lifetime, his message never really took hold beyond his own firm and its clients.

In 1953, toward the end of his life, he delivered a speech to his firm that reflected bitterly on his industry's refusal to pay him heed. "If the average man had invested a set sum of money every year since 1937 . . . and reinvested his dividends every year, he would have done considerably better than if he put the same amount of money out at ordinary…compound interest," he said. But, he added, "you could tell that story to nine out of ten men in our line of business, and they wouldn't even listen to you, much less believe it." Thirty years later, you could hear Merrill's echo as people like Charles Schwab and Peter Lynch talked about the importance of ordinary Americans investing in the stock market. By then, though, circumstances were such that the country was ready to listen. Though they may not have realized it, Schwab and Lynch were Merrill's spiritual descendants.

The second reason I had to include him is that he was by far the most colorful financier I'd ever come across. During the course of my research, I met a man who had written an in-house history of Merrill Lynch, and he generously handed me three huge loose-leaf bound volumes that recounted Merrill's life. They had been commissioned by Merrill's daughter, Dorothy Magowan, but had never been published. (One of the volumes appeared to be a condensed version of the other two.) For my purposes they were pure gold. Merrill's womanizing; his difficulties with his children, especially his two sons; his three marriages; his bold business strokes; his mawkish letters; his enormous appetites—it was all there. (No wonder Dorothy Magowan had decided not to have them published!) I was astounded. And then it turned out that his daughter was the longtime doyenne of San Francisco, and his grandson Peter owned the San Francisco Giants, and his son James was a great American poet, and his other son Charles was the founder of a very liberal private school in Boston, and…and…and…You get the picture. I could scarcely believe I had been handed such rich material.

I wound up writing only half a chapter about Merrill, which helps explain why my fascination with him—and his family—remained unabated after the book was done. I was even toying with the idea of writing a Merrill biography. So when I was I searching for an article I could write for GQ that would help plug the book, I gravitated toward Charlie Merrill and his family.

In the story that ensued, I relied on that wealth of material I had culled from those unpublished biographies—you'll see them quoted liberally. But I also wound up interviewing a number of his heirs, including his two sons, a handful of grandchildren, and one great-grandchild. To this day, I'll never quite understand why they all talked to me, and so freely at that; I was asking them questions that were very close to the bone—about their own relationship to the money they inherited from Merrill, and how it affected their lives and their relations with each other. Even by the time I had finished a draft of the article, at least one Merrill—his oldest son, Charles—had second thoughts, and refused to be photographed. After the article came out, however, James Merrill, who had never been bashful about talking (or writing) about his father, wrote me a nice note. Sadly, four months later he died, a month before his 70th birthday.

The ease with which I had been able to land interviews with the different generations of Merrills gave me a false sense of the effort required to report about wealthy families. Not long after this story came out, I proposed a story to *The New Yorker* about the descendants of R. J. Reynolds, the founder of the tobacco giant. I knew that one of his grandchildren, Patrick, had become an anti-smoking crusader, and I assumed he would be a willing participant. Instead, he wrote me an angry letter, denouncing the press in general and me in particular. I tried to find other Reynolds who might be willing to talk about the family, but got nowhere. I gave up the project, with a new realization of how lucky I'd gotten with the Merrills. The next time I wrote about a wealthy family, I did so with a much healthier respect for the effort it would take.

That family was the Bancrofts, the descendants of Clarence Barron—and the longtime owners of *The Wall Street Journal*.

Charlie Merrill and His Stock

GQ, October 1994

In America, our kings are self-made. Born into unremarkable circum-stances, they somehow shed their past and remake themselves into Great Men. They are driven by talent, yes, and usually a singularly shrewd idea, but even more by a fierce and unyielding hunger—for money, for esteem, for success, for all of it. They build companies, and sometimes entire industries, from scratch. They force others to adapt to their vision of how things should work—of how things should *be*. And over time, as we come to see clearly the outlines of their accomplishment, we celebrate them, not so much for the particulars of the accomplishment as for the mere fact of it—for the way their lives embody every mythic thing we believe about America. John D. Rockefeller, Henry Ford, Joseph P. Kennedy: These are the kind of men I'm talking about, the men who become American patriarchs—patriarchs of their industries, of their companies, of their employees.

And, not least, of their families. So powerful is their grip during their lives that when books are finally written about them, it is made to seem as if the family history did not really begin until they had decided to grace this earth with their presence. More often than not, their families tend to see it like this too; though they know him in a completely different way, they are as much under the patriarch's thumb as are any of his executives. But then death arrives, as it must even for Great Men, and the descendants are left with the task of loosening his once-iron grip. Most spend at least some part of their lives reacting to—or against—the life the patriarch led. And if it's easy enough to say that the story of a particular kind of American family begins with the rise of its patriarch, one is left with a more difficult, and interesting, question: Where does that story finally end?

The patriarch of one enduring American family was a short, blustery, flamboyant man named Charles Edward Merrill. An incorrigible womanizer ("getting my batteries recharged" was his euphemism for philandering), a domineering father and a genuinely great businessman, Charlie Merrill was also about as pure an example of the self-made king as one could imagine. Born in October 1885, in tiny Green Cove Springs, Florida, the son of a good-hearted but poor rural doctor, Merrill died almost exactly 71 years later, in October 1956, in the bedroom of his palatial home in Southampton, Long Island—one of three such estates he owned by then. At the moment of his death, he was one of the wealthiest men in the country. His decision, as laid out in his will, to put more than $35 million in a charitable trust, to be given away by his heirs, made the front page of *The New York Times*. His funeral was attended by more than 700 people, who included not only his many business associates but also two of his three ex-wives.

Of course, his three children were there, too. His younger son, James Merrill ("Jimmy," his family calls him), had just finished a novel—a thinly disguised account of his father's last years as an invalid, entitled *The Seraglio*—and was at the beginning of a career that would see him become one of the country's most celebrated poets. His other son, Charles, had returned from Paris to be at his father's deathbed; living abroad, he was trying, unsuccessfully, to become a novelist himself. Within two years he would return to America to found an unapologetically elite (and exceedingly liberal) private school in Boston, called the Commonwealth School. He would also sit on the board of the charitable trust his father had established—where he would battle with his more conservative relatives in his efforts to fund the left-wing causes he favored. Accompanying Merrill's daughter, Doris, was her husband, Robert A. Magowan, who the year before had been installed as the chairman of Safeway Stores, the Oakland, California–based supermarket chain the elder Merrill had played a critical role in founding; Magowan would also sit on the board of the trust, where his main activity would be crossing swords with Merrill's older son, Charles. And of Merrill's ten grandchildren, also in attendance, several were a decade away from becoming

Sixties radicals, while another, Peter Magowan, would succeed his father as the CEO of Safeway before taking over the ownership of the San Francisco Giants. Some 38 years after that funeral, all of these descendants, with the exception of Robert Magowan, are still alive (the oldest of them, Doris Merrill Magowan, is 80), and many are still grappling, in one way or another, with the insistent fact of their lineage.

But who *was* Charlie Merrill that he should have cut such a swath? The short answer is that he was the Merrill in Merrill Lynch, the firm he founded and which became in his lifetime the largest brokerage house the world had ever seen. He first hung out his shingle in 1914, at the age of 28, and though he struggled in the beginning (of course!), in less than two years, he was a millionaire.

What makes Merrill an important historical figure is not merely that he was a poor boy who got rich. Merrill had ideas and insights that were both right and prescient. For instance, he was one of the very few Wall Street titans who saw the Great Crash coming and said so, loudly. More enduringly, he was among the first to realize that Wall Street shouldn't be content simply to underwrite the stocks of big, well-established companies. Rather, he backed emerging companies that traditional Wall Street firms scorned, chief among them chain stores. As much as any single thing, Merrill's backing allowed chain stores to blossom in this country, and he believed in them deeply. Always, when his firm underwrote a stock offering for a chain store, he bought warrants, convertible into stock, for his own account. The warrants, far more than the underwriting revenues, were what brought him wealth.

Most of all, Charlie Merrill was the first reputable Wall Street figure to seriously attempt to draw the middle class into the stock market. He is the man who coined the phrase "bringing Wall Street to Main Street," and everything his firm did, especially after World War II, as the middle class began to prosper, was aimed at enticing "the modest sums of the thrifty" (as Merrill used to put it) into the market. Today, with a staggering $7.6 trillion in stocks, bonds, and mutual funds—and with much of that money coming from the middle class—one can appreciate the prescience of his vision.

Oddly, Merrill has never been the subject of a published biography. This omission strikes one now as an egregious oversight, and not just because of his business accomplishments. Merrill was a deeply memorable character; the small glimpses one gets of him in James Merrill's writings make one yearn for more. Here he is, for example, preparing for an audience with Pope Pius XII in the early Fifties: "First calling the concierge to make sure the Pope had no monopoly on white raiment, he appeared in snowy, double-breasted swank. A gold bill-clip shaped like a dollar sign held his blue silk tie conspicuously in place. 'Hey, Charlie, great!' cried Neddy [a relative]. 'His Holiness'll kiss *your* hand when he sees that.'" Here he is discovering that his younger son is having a homosexual affair with an Amherst professor—and contemplating, fleetingly, having the man killed. Quickly, though, he calms down, and soon, wrote James Merrill, "the situation had begun to modulate toward comedy: my father was thinking of hiring a prostitute to seduce me into the paradise of sex with women."

Charlie Merrill had a southerner's gift for storytelling. He had wonderful, improbable tales of his early days in New York, when he and his pal Eddie Lynch (the Lynch of Merrill Lynch) would work all day and carouse all night, crashing society parties and seducing rich girls away from their dates. He was a prideful man, who remembered every slight he had ever endured, who was also capable of writing long, overwrought letters filled with raw sentimentality. He was the sort of man who would walk around his mansion turning off the lights to save energy but would impulsively hand over a hefty check to someone with a preposterous sob story. He wore the best clothes, ate the richest food, bought the most expensive gifts, lived in the most luxurious homes: he could never resist indulging his enormous appetites.

His largest appetite, though, was for women. So well-known was Merrill's philandering that once, when a woman seeking money for an abortion approached his long-suffering secretary, she handed it over without even consulting Merrill, who was away on business. When Merrill returned and his secretary informed him of what she had done, he thanked her for taking care of the matter, then added, "It may interest you to know, though, I haven't seen the lady for two years." His divorces were grist for the gossip columns, what with his wives' allegations of unfaithfulness and "cruelty" and the like, and once he was divorced, it was his habit to remarry almost immediately, vowing, this time, to stay on the straight and narrow. But he never could.

Even when he was old and sick, Merrill was still chasing women; he actually bought his third home, in Barbados, to be closer to a woman of whom he was enamored, though he soon found himself drawn to another woman instead, the wife of a close friend of his. After a series of heart attacks in his late fifties and the onset of a crippling struggle with angina, his days in Southampton revolved around a daily bridge game with a handful of women who vied for his attention. He was at the center of their universe, which is exactly where he wanted to be.

Or, perhaps more accurately, where he *needed* to be. For in many ways, this is the point about self-made kings like Charlie Merrill: They have an almost unselfconscious assumption that the world revolves around them—

and because of their wealth and power and overwhelming personality, it usually does.

"I thought of him a little like Louis IX: this small man who had everyone terrified," recalled his son Charles recently, from the remove of many decades. "One of my major aims [as a child] was to keep out of his turf."

Charles Merrill, who is 74 years old, speaks slowly, almost shyly. If the father was a boisterous teller of tales, this does not appear to be a quality inherited by his son. Then again, it is hard to think of any qualities father and son do share, with the exception of a sheer, willful stubbornness. Whereas Charlie Merrill reveled in business and deals, Charles has viewed business as little more than a necessary evil. Whereas the father was a Wall Street Republican, this son was on the far left of the political spectrum; during the Sixties, nothing pleased him more than seeing his students—and his own children—take part in the civil rights movement or protest the Vietnam War. And whereas Charlie Merrill took a deep and abiding pleasure in spending his money, this son has found no such joy in the money he inherited, most of which is in the form of trusts set up for him when he was a child and from which he has drawn millions of dollars during his life. "My undeserved chance" he once called his inheritance.

On the day I visited him, Charles Merrill was wearing plain khaki pants and an inexpensive short-sleeved shirt. We met in the study of his New Hampshire farmhouse, where he spends a good deal of his time; having retired from Commonwealth School, in 1981, he has taken up his pen again. He has written a handful of small books, which were scattered about the sturdy, unadorned room, and was trying to find a publisher for an enormous work he has written about his involvement in Eastern Europe, a part of the world that has been a lifelong passion. Merrill's farm is beautiful, but the homestead itself is extremely plain, lacking any hint of the ostentation the Old Man favored. This is no accident. For there is nothing more obvious about Charles Merrill than that he has tried to live his life as a kind of rebuke to his father—even though his father's money has, in essence, funded this rebuke.

As a young man, Merrill fought constantly with his father; James Merrill would later recall his half brother's "breathtaking repertoire of shock tactics, diversionary movements, positions secured by verbal barbed wire, and so forth, [that] kept the old man on the defensive...." He would have nothing to do with his father's wish that he one day join the firm. The thing Charles most noticed when he visited the firm as a child was the way everyone was seated behind cages—"like zoo animals." And he freely admits that he first focused his attention on Eastern Europe and began traveling there because it was an interest his father would never share.

His politics likewise began as a form of rebellion. He remembers, with particular horror, Sunday-night dinners on Long Island during the Depression, when Merrill and a handful of his Wall Street cronies would discuss the events of the day. How narrow those men were! How filled with anti-Semitism! How little they cared about the great mass of Americans whom Roosevelt was trying to help with his New Deal programs! The worst fight Charles ever had with his father was over his plan to work on a "Christian socialist collective farm" after his junior year in college: "I told him I was fighting international fascism by working with the humble poor," he told me. Always he was acutely aware of his social class and his privileged existence. Always, it made him uneasy.

He even made a halfhearted stab at getting rid of his inheritance. Upon returning from Europe after World War II, Charles went to see the accountant who handled his trusts. He told the man that he was deeply troubled by the devastation he had seen overseas and wanted to give his inheritance to CARE. "I can see your point," the man replied, "but I could not authorize this without discussing it with your father, and I know he would be very upset." In the end, Charles did not force the issue. And, of course, that money is what made it possible for him to write five unpublished novels, to live in Paris for several years, to befriend Hungarian and Polish intellectuals, and, eventually, to found Commonwealth School. The money, he now confesses, was a "blessing."

It was a blessing for Jimmy, too; as the *Oxford Companion to Twentieth Century Poetry* puts it, "Merrill's freedom from financial pressures has meant that he has been able to live how and where he pleases, a privilege almost unique among modern poets." This is an assessment with which James has no quarrel. And yet as a young man, he also fantasized about renouncing his inheritance, provoking a wounded letter from his father, dripping with the self-pity the Old Man so often resorted to when someone refused to bend to his will. It wasn't that Jimmy objected to money. Rather, he feared that the money would turn him into a dilettante.

So when I said to James that the arc of his life—that of the great artist who emerges from the family of a great industrialist—is a common theme in America, he arched his eyebrows slightly and replied, "Oh, really? Who else is there?"

This conversation took place over a long, pleasant lunch on Manhattan's Upper East Side, at a restaurant around the corner from Merrill's tastefully appointed apartment. While he was dressed casually, there was no mistaking him for other than a man of means; he wears his inheritance comfortably. Though only 69, he seems older than Charles somehow, especially in his face, which is heavily lined. Yet one cannot look into that face and fail to see how beautiful he once was—how gay men in Greece and Rome and New York and everywhere else Merrill has lived must have found him impossibly alluring. It didn't hurt either that, like his father, he was flamboyant, brilliant, and promiscuous. His was just a different kind of flamboyance; a different kind of brilliance; a different kind of promiscuity.

In a way, James Merrill wears his life comfortably, too. Over lunch, he talked easily about such matters as his father, his family, and his homosexuality. This did not come as a complete surprise, for some of Merrill's best poetry has been autobiographical in nature. One of his finest poems, entitled "The Broken Home," is about the dissolution of his parents' marriage. Another, "18 West 11th Street," is about the apartment where he lived with his parents as a child—and which was accidentally blown up in 1970 by Weathermen who were building bombs in the basement. His most celebrated poem, the 17,000-line epic *The Changing Light at Sandover*, chronicles years of Ouija-board sessions that he and his longtime lover David Jackson conducted in the dining room of their home in Stonington, Connecticut. Merrill was out of the closet long before most gay men in America. More accurately, he simply ignored the closet, carving out an existence in which there was no need for it. Is it too much to say that the Old Man's money helped make this circumstance possible? I think not.

His real problem, growing up, was simply that he was Charlie Merrill's boy. The lurid newspaper accounts of his parents' divorce haunted him for years. Mention of his father's relentless womanizing crops up frequently in his poems. As a young man, he cringed whenever someone asked him if he was related to the founder of Merrill Lynch. Even his father's kindnesses could feel oppressive. After satisfying himself that his son had "professional" talent as a poet—an opinion he solicited from the president of Amherst College—Merrill had a small book of James' youthful poems privately published. *Jim's Book*, it was titled. For its author, the collection was a source of short-lived pride, followed by a deep and much-longer-lasting embarrassment.

In the spring of 1950, James Merrill moved to Europe—to "places where the family name cut no ice, the Firm had no branch office, and I might if need be, like the Duke of Mantua in *Rigoletto*, pass myself off as a poor student," he wrote. He stayed there for two and a half years, during which time he underwent psychotherapy, fell in and out of love a half-dozen times, and began to fashion his life as a writer and an aesthete. It was there that the weight of being Charlie Merrill's son began to lift. Even so, upon his return, he began to write *The Seraglio*, a book whose protagonist is quite blatantly based on his father and that is filled with tart and unflattering portraits of most of the rest of the family as well. Reading it now, one gets the impression that *The Seraglio* was something James Merrill needed to get out of his system. When he was finished, he sent the book to his father, but the Old Man was too sick to read much of it. According to one observer, however, "the family and Merrill's old friends were outraged by the book, which they considered a cruel, distorted picture of a dying man." One family member noted that when it came out, Jimmy's half sister, Doris, wouldn't speak to him for a year and a half.

In the summer of 1935, Doris Merrill married Robert A. Magowan. In doing so, she gave her father the one thing he didn't have: a son (or at least a son-in-law) who would follow the Old Man off the cliff, if that's what he should ask. Unlike her brothers, Doris had grown up worshiping her father, and she chose a husband who felt likewise. Bob Magowan didn't have to be strong-armed into joining the firm; he was *thrilled* to become a part of Merrill Lynch. So devoted was he to Merrill that he named his second son Merrill Lynch Magowan. When Charlie Merrill wanted him to go to San Francisco to learn about the food business at Safeway, Magowan saluted and went. When Merrill wanted him back in New York at Merrill Lynch, back he came. After World War II, he became Merrill Lynch's head of sales, set up a training school for brokers, acted as a business confidant to Merrill, did a hundred different things that needed doing. He was good at these tasks, and he would surely have one day run Merrill Lynch if Merrill hadn't sent him back to San Francisco in 1956 to run Safeway, a position he relinquished in 1971. (He remained on the board until 1979.) He was good at running Safeway too; it was during his tenure that the company made significant strides toward becoming the largest grocery chain in the country. Still, whenever he was asked the secret of his success, he always made the same self-deprecating remark: "Decisiveness," he would reply. "I decided to marry the boss's daughter."

One reason he found his father-in-law so admirable was that he saw in the Old Man's past a mirror of his own upbringing. Magowan had grown up poor in Chester, Pennsylvania, and had spent his early career with his shoulder to the wheel, trying to make something happen. Also, the two men shared a number of surface similarities: a lack of height, a volcanic temper, athletic abilities (Merrill had been a semipro baseball player; Magowan was a fine tennis player), and a gruff but incisive manner. "Bob Magowan was such a close carbon copy of Merrill that people often were amused by the resemblance," one writer commented.

But he wasn't, really. He was Merrill without the personal charm, and Merrill without the business genius. As a businessman, Magowan "was good at getting a team together and pointing them in the right direction," his oldest son, Robin, told me. "My grandfather believed that my father had no larger vision." He lacked as well the Old Man's charisma, the Old Man's generosity, and the Old Man's courtliness. One of Magowan's sons recalled that words such as "pinko" and "kike" and "fairy" were a regular part of his dinner-table vocabulary. He sent notes to his executives on stationery adorned with a smiling ram if the memo was one of praise or a scowling ram if it conveyed criticism ("R.A.M." being his initials). Once, after receiving a smiling ram, a young executive went in to thank Magowan, only to be told "There are only a few inches between a pat on the back and a kick in the ass." Charlie Merrill would never have said anything like that.

There was another important difference between the two men. Merrill, for all his flaws as a father, knew enough to stop fighting when the battle was lost. But that was never true of Bob Magowan. All his life, he would try to impose his will on his five sons. When, as was frequently the case, they objected, he would rail and rage, engaging in feuds with them. The story Peter Magowan has always told about his decision to join Safeway was that he applied directly to the Washington, D.C., district manager without telling his father because, as he put it, "I wanted to try and do it on my own without my father orchestrating my career." But one of his brothers has a somewhat different explanation: The reason Peter didn't broach the issue with his father was that, at the time, they weren't on speaking terms. In fact, Bob Magowan was frequently not on speaking terms with one or another of his sons.

Magowan's battles with his fourth son, Stephen, who is gay, were said to be particularly awful (Stephen declined to be interviewed for this article), but all of his sons have stories about their fights with him. Some of these fights were about matters of genuine importance—which is not the same as saying that Magowan's objections were legitimate. More than once, for instance, he feuded with his sons over their choice of wives. But at least as often, he would pick fights over things that didn't matter a whit. Merrill Magowan vividly recalled how angry his father would get when the two of them played tennis and Merrill didn't play well: "He'd start scowling, and the worse I played the madder he got, until by the end of the match he wasn't speaking to me." Merrill, who wound up spending twenty years at Merrill Lynch, searching for a route to the top, served on the board of Safeway during his father's tenure as chairman. He was stunned to discover that his father acted as a conciliator when his executives disagreed about something. "He would say, 'Joe, can you live with this? Bob, how about if you tried it this way?'" said Merrill Magowan. "He *never* acted like that with his family." When Merrill decided to name one of his sons Douglas Robert instead of Robert Douglas, Bob Magowan was so incensed at not having his name come first that he boycotted the baptism.

The Magowans lived the kind of life that Charlie Merrill had always assumed his heirs would lead. Added to the millions Doris had inherited from her father was a great deal of money Bob Magowan made himself; he left an estate worth around $20 million. They owned homes in Southampton and Palm Beach, which were fully staffed at all times. They had a gorgeous house in San Francisco. Several of their children attended private school in Switzerland. The family went on extravagant shopping sprees in Europe. Once, reported Robin Magowan, his mother had a swimming pool moved fifty feet so she wouldn't have to walk around it to get to the garden. Some of that sense of entitlement has rubbed off on even their most rebellious children: "A Magowan doesn't know if he likes something," one family friend reportedly once said, "unless he buys it."

It is Robin Magowan's belief that for a long time—until his father came down with Legionnaires' disease and learned, late in life, to smell the roses— Bob Magowan was consumed by his money. Given Robin's jaundiced view of the family, it is hard to gauge how true this is. What is certainly true is that Bob Magowan tried to use money as a weapon in his efforts to control his children. As his sons got older, Bob parceled out living allowances to them and was forever threatening to cut them off for one sin or another—the main sin being their refusal to chart a life course that met with his approval. Even from the grave, he couldn't let go. After he died, in 1985, the family discovered that Magowan had decided not to give Robin and Stephen—the two sons whose life choices he disapproved of—control of their inheritance. "I was disinherited," said Robin with some bitterness. That's an exaggeration; the money was actually put in trust. But whenever he's wanted access to any of it, Robin has had to talk to the trustees, one of whom is his brother Merrill. It was one final humiliation inflicted on him by his father.

Robin Magowan is now 58 years old. A tall, thin, handsome man, he spoke to me from a rocking chair on the porch of his Connecticut farmhouse. He hasn't been living there long; it was only a few years ago that he moved back to America from Europe, where he had spent the better part of seventeen years. He had homes in both England and France, and when I asked him how, if he was kept on a short leash for so long, he was able to afford them, he shrugged. "Whenever we wanted to buy a house, money would materialize," he said. His speech was slow and sometimes hard to follow, like that of someone who has overcome a stutter, which he has. Sometimes, as he talked about what it was like to be the oldest grandson of Charlie Merrill and the oldest son of Bob Magowan, he began to rock back and forth and his eyes took on a distant look: he seemed to be talking more to himself than to me. And maybe he was. For Robin Magowan has spent most of his life talking to himself about being a Merrill and a Magowan. This is a subject that has consumed him.

He was christened Robert A. Magowan, Jr., and on the day he was born, his grandfather set up a trust fund in his name. "A silver yoke was given me," he would later write, "and I've been lugging it around ever since." All his life he would feel pinned down by the sheer weight of the family history, the family wealth, the family expectations, the family everything. The chief expectation was that he would follow his father into the business—whether Safeway or Merrill Lynch hardly mattered. To the delight of both his father and his grandfather, he worked a summer in the Merrill Lynch research department, and when he was in college, he once took a summer job at Safeway, searching for sites for new stores.

It was while Robin was at Harvard that he began to harbor thoughts about taking a different path—and the budding career of his uncle Jimmy, only ten years older, seemed to suggest a possible alternative. "[Jimmy] was the most important person in my life," Robin said, but when I repeated this to James Merrill, he seemed to shrink away slightly, as if this were a responsibility he had never meant to assume. But there it was: Uncle Jimmy was a student of Proust rather than of Wall Street; he was getting published and garnering critical acclaim; and what's more, he was a great deal of fun to be around, as Robin discovered when he began spending more time with James. One night during college, when he was 19, Robin took some Dexedrine and dashed off about five pages of stream-of-consciousness prose. He concluded at that moment that he would be a writer too—a sentiment, he related, that James encouraged. In his euphoria, he wrote several long, detailed letters to his parents explaining what had happened to him that night and how his life had suddenly been transformed.

This, of course, was a terrible mistake, as Robin soon realized. "What have we ever said or done," his father wrote back, "to merit such treatment?" When it became clear that Robin was serious about his change of course, his father dropped the other shoe. "This is a direct declaration that I will not finance any adventures that do not meet my approval," he wrote sternly. "And if I don't pay for them, I don't know who else will—with the possible exception of one of your uncles. If they do that, they risk an estrangement from which I think they would shrink." "My father," Robin said with a sigh, "couldn't believe I had any talent."

In fact, Robin Magowan does have talent. I am not equipped to judge his poetry, but he has written several fine travel books and a number of quite serviceable books about bicycling, in which he got interested while living in Europe. What he does not possess, however, is the kind of transcendent talent that characterizes his uncle's work and with which very few writers are blessed. Even if he had possessed that kind of talent, following his uncle's example would have been difficult, for like every other serious poet in America, James Merrill has never made a living from his writing alone. His great good fortune is that he's never had to. "Jimmy set up his life perfectly," said Robin, a touch of envy in his voice—but it wasn't just money that made that possible. Merrill "set up his life," in part, by breaking free of his family—by becoming James Merrill the poet, rather than James Merrill the son of the founder of Merrill Lynch. This is a step Robin has never been able to take.

Robin Magowan taught English, first at the University of Washington and then, in the late 1960s, at Berkeley. He smoked dope and played soccer, a game he enjoyed much more than the tennis he had been force-fed as a child. He dabbled halfheartedly in radical politics. He wrote poems like crazy. He sired children and had affairs. He divorced his first wife and took up with a freshman student who became his second wife. (The marriage didn't last long.) Appropriately enough, the bed he slept in each night was one he had inherited from his womanizing grandfather, and one day he brought into that bed a woman named Nancy Ling Perry. Robin believes that this affair "was to propel me out of the dynastic labyrinth." In fact, it ensured that he would never break free.

The name Nancy Ling Perry rings a faint bell, does it not? She was a member of the Symbionese Liberation Army, the group of radicals who first gunned down the superintendent of Oakland schools and a few months later kidnapped Patricia Hearst. Some eighteen months before she committed her first terrorist act, Ling Perry was taking mescaline and having sex with Robin Magowan. Even after their six-month affair ended and she went underground, she did not completely lose touch with him; shortly before everything happened, she hit him up for money. His name was listed as the reference on the lease application for the apartment where Patricia Hearst was first held. And after the superintendent was killed but before the Hearst kidnapping, police got hold of a list of possible kidnap victims. On it was Bob Magowan.

Robin believes that he was also among the possible kidnap targets. Soon after the list was uncovered, a friend of Robin's received a note from Ling Perry asking where she could get in touch with him. But he was in France, leisurely working his way back toward the States from a trip to India. It was while in France that he read about the Hearst kidnapping—and realized that Ling Perry must be involved. And it was while in France that he read about Ling Perry's death in a wild shootout with the FBI. Through his father's secretary, he got word that he was probably better off staying abroad, at least for the time being. He wound up staying for the next 17 years, and he began what would become his life's work. Not yet 40 years old, Magowan started writing his autobiography—which has been his way of trying to come to terms with his father and his family and his affair with Ling Perry. This is what he has been doing, draft after obsessive draft, ever since. Twenty years later, he's still at it.

"When I turned 21," recalled Catherine Merrill, "I came into an inheritance from my grandfather—somewhere between $200,000 and $300,000. My father, because of his complex about money, never gave me one word of advice as to what to do with that money. Whenever I asked my parents what I should do with my money, they said 'This is your grandfather's will. It has nothing to do with us.'"

Catherine Merrill is the first of the younger Charles Merrill's five children. She is 51, a small, attractive woman, a sculptor and a potter who lives in a decidedly working-class section of San Francisco with her 24-year-old daughter. When I met her this past summer, she had just moved to San Francisco from Hawaii, where she had lived since 1981. Though she had once been a Sixties radical, her choice of neighborhood was predicated mainly on necessity: what money she had, she wanted to put into her studio. Once she was working again, she would think about moving to another place. In the meantime, she needed to conserve. This she had learned the hard way.

"We grew up in an unreal world," she said. Her father tried to impose a middle-class existence on his family—and yet they lived in Paris for several years. The obvious contradictions were ignored. "There were vibes in our household about what you could and could not use money for," she remembered. "Spending on travel or books was okay, but not on extra cars or swimming pools." There were silly deprivations; the Merrills never had a television set in their home. And then the family would go to visit their grandfather or their cousins in Southampton, and they would see, all around them, money being spent without guilt or shame. And it was...*confusing.* "In some ways," Catherine Merrill reflected, "I was envious of the Magowans. They are what they are." She added, "Most people grow up with a father who wants to make money and make his family life better. My father's goal was to give it away."

And so, when she was handed that lump sum, she did what she thought would make her father happy: she began giving it away. In New York, she was working as a substitute teacher, performing with a theater group, doing illustrations for *The Nation*, involving herself in various protests. She gave money to the theater and to a recovery program for addicts, as well as to many less-worthy causes. "People would hit on me," she said, "and I was susceptible. I was vulnerable."

She moved to San Francisco in 1967, and a few years later, deciding that the protest movement was becoming, as she put it, "brutal and troubling," she moved to Mendocino, where she bought a home, set up a pottery studio and had a daughter. At this point, she began to realize that her inheritance, which she had once thought of as unimaginably large, was in fact finite. Within ten years, it was gone.

Here was the crucial difference between her father's money and her own. His was a renewable resource; the principal in his trust fund would always generate income. Hers did no such thing: when it was gone, it was gone. By the time she understood this, it was too late. She had also found that her money was a destructive force in her relationships. Men she had gotten involved with would quit their jobs or suddenly become spendthrift when they found out whose granddaughter she was. And "friends would find out I was a Merrill and suddenly they would act differently. I was always left feeling that I was a party of one," she told me.

So, just as James Merrill had once moved to Europe to evade the weight of his last name, Catherine moved to Hawaii for the same reason. She had used the last of her inheritance to help set up her then-husband in the restaurant business; when they sold the business, the proceeds enabled them to get to Hawaii. Then they were on their own.

Catherine Merrill clearly views the move as the best thing she ever did. It was in Hawaii that she discovered she could earn a living as an artist and survive without a husband (she got divorced while living there). It was there, she believes, that she shed the effects of her upbringing. But for a while, early on, it looked as if that would never be the case. "At first," she said, "we were not pulling it off, and we were very poor." She reacted to her lack of money angrily, confronting her parents, writing letters to her siblings, complaining bitterly about her relative poverty in a family of such obvious means. She felt, in effect, damaged by her father's unwillingness to accept straightforwardly that he was a wealthy man. "We feel inferior to the Magowans," she told her horrified parents. "There was a lot of pain at the time," she admitted to me, "but ultimately it was a good thing. We're closer now as a result." And having aired her family grudges, she was ready, at last, to move on.

"I've finally waded through all of this," she said. "I'm happy about my life. I'm finally not neurotic about money." Indeed, one of the reasons she moved back to San Francisco was that she felt it was time to become a Merrill again; one of her favorite people, she said, is her aunt, Doris Magowan, and she wants to be able to spend time with her. I mentioned to her something her father had told me earlier: his children must feel, he had said, as if they are standing under an avalanche. That avalanche is the money they will inherit when he dies—far, far more than the amounts they got from their grandfather when they were born.

She laughed. "An avalanche?" she said. "No, I don't feel that way. I'm ready. I'll know what to do with it this time."

So where *does* it all end, finally?

Here is Bruce Merrill, 46, one of Catherine's younger brothers: "For the most part," he wrote to me, "the connection between myself and my grandfather has been one which I have tried to avoid, or downplay." His inheritance, he added, has allowed him to be an "independent scholar," though he ruefully conceded that "it has also allowed me to pay a price for such extravagance: that after an embarrassing number of years, I still have not been able to gather up my labors properly."

Here is Stephen Magowan, a 50-year-old playwright who, like his older brother Robin, writes obsessively about his family. Most recently, after surviving a bout with cancer, he has been working on a movie script with Robin's son James (named after James Merrill, of course). It has nothing to do with any Magowan- or Merrill-related theme. Most family members view this as a healthy thing.

Here is Merrill Lynch Magowan, 56, Bob Magowan's second son, who can unthinkingly disparage Robin and Stephen—"my nonworking brothers," he calls them—yet has his own set of regrets, starting with his name, which he says is "more of a curse than a blessing." In a 20-year career at Merrill Lynch, he never found a path that could take him to the top; his greatest accomplishment was starting and running a successful branch in Carmel, California. Eventually, he left the firm and set up as an independent money manager, in which capacity he has done quite well. And yet not long ago, he got involved in a venture with two of his sons: they bought a company that farmed and sold Norwegian salmon, and tried to run it. The experience was miserable for all concerned. Merrill Magowan is on the hook for some $6 million, since he personally guaranteed some of the company's loans. He grimaced when he talked to me about it. "My net worth used to be bigger than Peter's," he said. "But that was before the LBO...."

Here is Peter Magowan, 52, some five years after the Safeway LBO that made him his own, independent fortune—an LBO that was highly controversial because it meant that Safeway had to lay off thousands of workers and sell hundreds of stores, and yet it was something Peter felt he had to do because the company was under assault from corporate raiders...and he had the family to think of. "I did feel it was a family issue, in part," he said from his current office, at Candlestick Park. "I'm glad my father never had to see what happened."

In Boulder, Colorado, I met one more Magowan: Felix Magowan, Robin's oldest son. I met him in the office where he publishes a group of successful bicycling magazines. He is 31, gregarious, funny, and handsome in a California way, and though deeply interested in his family, he seems somehow divorced from it—or at least not tortured by it.

He told me his story: After his parents divorced, his mother got child support from his father, but it wasn't much, and essentially he grew up a lower-middle-class kid. "My first bike was bought at a police auction," he recalled without the slightest trace of bitterness. "The phones would get turned off sometimes. The usual middle-class stuff."

He gets along famously with his father, though he didn't see him all that often after Robin moved to Europe. He did, however, see a good deal of his grandfather, who became "a surrogate father." He spent time in Southampton, received the occasional expensive present—and yet there was no angst about not having access to all the money he saw around him. He worked at Safeway as a bag boy and stock clerk and was actually quite interested in the grocery business but decided to steer away from it. In his early twenties, he and a friend bought a bicycling-magazine business with $125,000 borrowed from Robert Magowan's estate. When that money ran out, he wisely decided not to go back to the family. Instead, he put together a plan that allowed him to raise $500,000 from outside investors. He was on his way.

Felix loves his family, clearly. He is connected to it. Yet somehow he is unaffected by it all—by his father's tortured rumblings and his grandfather's brutal expectations and his great-grandfather's wealth and business legacy. It seems odd to think that the Magowan who had his phones shut off when he was a kid turned out to be the lucky one in the end. But maybe that's what it takes for the story to end. Maybe that's what is required for the ghostly pull of the patriarch to fade at last.

CHAPTER 6

Lawyers from Hell

I grew up in a liberal household in a liberal state, Rhode Island. My parents, both high school teachers, were committed Democrats, and one of my brothers helped elect Edward Kennedy's son, Patrick, to the Rhode Island state senate and then worked for him for a number of years. (Patrick Kennedy is now a congressman from Rhode Island.) Even now, after decades of covering business—decades during which I've become a fervent believer in free markets—I still have certain liberal tendencies: I don't believe that all government regulation is idiotic, nor do I think that lower taxes are always a panacea. But there is one issue where I stand proudly with *The Wall Street Journal* editorial page. I think the plaintiffs' bar is the legal equivalent of a plague of locusts. My first story for *Fortune*, "Fatal Litigation," is the reason why.

I had started at *Fortune* in early May 1995, and was searching for a saga I could dig into. In mid-May, an item in *The Wall Street Journal* caught my eye. It said that Dow Corning, the country's leading manufacturer of silicone breast implants, had filed for bankruptcy protection. The reason, according to the company, was that it had become so buried in lawsuits claiming that the implants caused autoimmune disease that it was losing its ability to function as a growing concern.

I knew nothing at that point about Dow Corning, silicone breast implants, or the controversy surrounding the implants. I had always assumed that plaintiffs' lawyers were the good guys who fought for justice and brought evil corporations to heel. They redressed wrongs by transferring money from companies that deserved to be punished to customers who have been taken advantage of.

Yet the deeper I looked into the circumstances surrounding the Dow Corning bankruptcy, the more dubious I became of that assumption. Here was a situation where Food and Drug Administration commissioner David Kessler had, in effect, set off a panic by banning silicone breast implants without any real proof that they caused disease. He had made what amounted to a political judgment after receiving leaked Dow Corning documents from a plaintiffs' lawyer; in so doing, he had overruled a scientific panel set up by his own FDA to explore whether silicone breast implants should be taken off the market. The Kessler ban, in turn, had generated tens of thousands of lawsuits. In court, the plaintiffs' lawyers used friendly jurisdictions, dubious expert witnesses, a handful of ambiguous internal documents, and sympathetic clients to evade the one fact that should have reigned supreme: the scientific evidence linking breast implants to autoimmune disease simply didn't exist. Instead, the breast implant companies were paying millions of dollars to settle cases, were losing multimillion-dollar judgments in court (especially in Harris County, Texas, were much of this story takes place), and were desperately looking for a way to negotiate a multibillion-dollar "master settlement" to put the problem behind them. In other words, the science didn't really matter. The dynamics of the mass tort itself were bringing these companies to their knees.

Obviously, companies do things they shouldn't, and when that happens, they ought to be punished—though I'm no longer convinced that plaintiffs' lawsuits are the most sensible way to exact that punishment. But this story helped show me that the plaintiffs' bar has a business model—it needs a steady stream of mass torts to generate cases and money. I no longer automatically assume that just because a big company is being sued that it has done anything wrong. Sometimes it most assuredly has. But sometimes it hasn't.

Bill Lerach, who until recently was one of the most feared plaintiffs' lawyer in the country, is a prime example. On the one hand, he got rich suing companies, especially tech companies, who announced bad news, causing their stock price to drop. Then, rather than uncovering actual wrongdoing—since usually there was no wrongdoing—he would torture the companies until they settled with him. On the other hand, he also extracted over $7 billion from the banks that aided the Enron fraud—a genuinely good outcome. *The New York Times* column about Lerach that I include in this chapter was written at a time when the news had just broken that he was under a Justice Department investigation. Since then he has pleaded guilty to one count of obstructing justice and has been sentenced to two years in prison.

As for Dow Corning, it wouldn't emerge from bankruptcy until 2004. By then, there was widespread agreement in the scientific community that silicone breast implants didn't cause disease. Nonetheless, Dow Corning had to put well over $2 billion into a fund for women who claimed that breast implants had caused their autoimmune disease. That money is still being paid out today.

Fatal Litigation

Fortune, October 16 and 30, 1995

I.

It usually begins slowly, almost imperceptibly, the first faint gust of wind that signals the coming storm. Somewhere in America, a plaintiffs' lawyer files a lawsuit alleging that a familiar and widely used product harmed his client. Then, somewhere else, a second plaintiffs' lawyer files a similar suit. A third is filed, then a fourth, until there are dozens of parallel "tort" claims across the country, all making the same accusation about the same product. Yet as long as these remain individual suits in individual jurisdictions, crawling along at their own pace, they don't necessarily pose a mortal threat to the product's manufacturer. They have no broader context, no larger meaning. Which is to say, the perception has not yet taken hold among the nation's plaintiffs' lawyers that there is in these cases—or more precisely, in the *accumulation* of these cases—a tremendous opportunity to bring a company down, and to make a killing in the process.

Thus does Richard Mithoff, a lawyer based in Houston, recall the first case he ever brought against a manufacturer of silicone breast implants, a product that over a million women have used in the 30-plus years they've been on the market. This was 18 years ago, when Mithoff was still a young associate with the legendary plaintiffs' attorney Joe Jamail. His client had undergone a series of operations after her implants had ruptured, and Mithoff was suing the manufacturer, Dow Corning. Mithoff wasn't claiming that the silicone gel from the implant had caused "autoimmune" disease; such frightening allegations were still years away. He was simply saying that the ruptures and subsequent operations had caused his client pain and suffering, for which she should be compensated. A jury awarded her $170,000. "Back in 1977, we thought $170,000 was a lot of money," says Mithoff. And then he starts to laugh.

Eleven years later, when the winds had gotten considerably stronger, Rick Laminack took on his first breast-implant client. Laminack was also a young Houston attorney working for a Texas legend, the flamboyant and wildly successful John O'Quinn; he, too, had no feel for the brewing storm—or his own future role in bringing it about. "One day a woman came into our office with a jar containing two ruptured implants and a dozen letters from other lawyers turning her down," recalls Laminack. "Because she was a friend of a friend, I got corralled into taking her case. So we sued the plastic surgeon, and as an afterthought, we sued the manufacturer"—a subsidiary of Bristol-Myers, the giant pharmaceutical company. He shrugs, and almost in spite of himself, a wicked smile forms. "And that's how we got into it."

Today, seven years after Laminack took that first case, no one can doubt that the storm has arrived with a fury. There aren't merely dozens of breast-implant lawsuits anymore, there are thousands of them—nay, tens of thousands. It has become one of the most fearsome waves of mass litigation ever to hit corporate America. Mithoff's first target, Dow Corning, has been laid waste by the litigation, driven into bankruptcy by the sheer impossibility of trying to defend itself against that many lawsuits. And its ordeal is not over. The plaintiffs' lawyers who pushed it into bankruptcy court are now trying to move in for the kill; they talk boldly about taking the company over completely.

Laminack's first target, now known as Bristol-Myers Squibb, has spent the better part of the past three years begging for mercy, settling cases as they've come up and offering to pay huge sums of money to be rid of the lawsuits. The two other main defendants, Baxter Healthcare and 3M, have also been trying to settle the litigation, to no avail. In all, the defendants have offered more than $4 billion to the plaintiffs. Four billion dollars, and it's not even close to being enough.

Typhoons of litigation like this one have come to be known as "mass torts," and there is no more terrifying phrase in corporate law. It is well known, and largely accepted, that companies will often make a business judgment to settle lawsuits that have little merit, simply to be done with them. A mass tort is the ultimate abuse of this idea. The dynamics of a mass tort *demand* that companies try to settle litigation—regardless of the merits—if they want to continue in business. The volume of lawsuits, their oppressive weight, is what brings companies to their knees. This is no exaggeration; just ask any major asbestos defendant, almost every one of which has been vaporized by litigation. Or ask Peter Angelos, the Baltimore lawyer who feasted on asbestos cases and became wealthy enough to put together the syndicate that bought the Orioles for $173 million.

Over the past decade, as mass torts have grown in size and scope and audacity, they've become a kind of beast that needs periodic feeding. More and more plaintiffs' lawyers have come to see mass torts as an essential part of their business, and they are no longer willing to wait for such cases to land on their doorstep. There are now scores of lawyers—lawyers whose collective pockets are deeper than the companies they're suing and who don't blink twice at pushing a company into bankruptcy if it can't meet their demands—who actively hunt for products they can build a mass tort around. Today it's breast implants. Tomorrow it will be the contraceptive device Norplant. The day after, it will be something else.

And if the evidence of the product's harm is largely nonexistent? That offers little protection. For the single most stunning fact about the breast-implant mass tort is this: *There has yet to be published a single peer-reviewed study that supports the central allegation behind the lawsuits*—that silicone breast implants cause disease. It's not proof the plaintiffs' lawyers need, it's numbers. That's the cruel calculation behind a mass tort.

How can the plaintiffs' bar demand billions of dollars in damages with no proof that what they are claiming is true? How does such a tempest get created? How is it that companies can be destroyed while lawyers reap millions? What perverse logic governs these unnatural disasters? Answers to these questions lie in the extraordinary experience of Dow Corning, the case in which mass torts came of age. Dow Corning did not play its hand as well as it might have, it's true. But really, once the plaintiffs' bar had the company in its sights, it never had a chance.

Once a set of ordinary lawsuits mutates into a mass tort, it's the big boys who run the show—the high-priced lawyers with their resources and staying power and capacity to gather the thousands of clients who will give them leverage. But in the beginning, when there is merely one sick client convinced that a company's product has caused her illness, the big boys tend to stay away. There's too much risk in being the first to try to build a complex product-liability case, and that's especially true of lawsuits that aim to prove a connection between a popular drug or medical device and a disease. For one thing, in this early stage, it is the company that plays Goliath to the plaintiff's David—throwing up legal roadblocks, deploying squads of lawyers, and generally doing its best to grind down the other side. There's also a serious financial risk for the plaintiff's lawyer. It is he, after all, who fronts the legal expenses—expenses that can easily run into the hundreds of thousands of dollars—with no guarantee of a paycheck at the end of the road. Indeed, one of the chief tactics companies use in attempting to squash such lawsuits is to simply try to outlast the plaintiff's lawyer until he goes broke.

The kind of lawyer willing to tackle such a case in its virgin state tends to be a true believer, a zealot on a mission. He completely buys into the notion that his client has been grievously injured by a heartless corporation, and he's out for justice, the financial risk be damned. And if he doesn't yet have the proof, well, he thinks, it's just a matter of time. After all, evidence of A.H. Robins' problems with the Dalkon Shield intrauterine device wasn't exactly handed to plaintiffs on a silver platter. It is cases like that one that sustain the true believer, that fire his imagination. Rarely does he realize that he's laying the foundation for a mass tort. But that's what he's doing.

In the breast-implant litigation, the truest of true believers is a San Francisco lawyer named Dan Bolton. "There is no doubt in my mind," he says firmly, "that silicone breast implants cause autoimmune disease." He could not be more sincere in his belief that breast implants can have terrible effects—that the silicone gel in the implants somehow causes a breakdown in a woman's immune system, resulting in everything from achy joints and fatigue to such classic autoimmune diseases as lupus and scleroderma. That a flurry of recent studies have cast grave doubt on this theory does not move him. Like many lawyers in the breast-implant case, he views his clients' anecdotal evidence—they had breast implants, after all, and they also have an autoimmune disease of one sort or another—as far more compelling than any scientific study. And his belief that Dow Corning made and marketed a product that it knew could cause such problems is, if anything, even more firmly held. "Dan Bolton," says one defense lawyer, "*hates* Dow Corning."

Like all the other lawyers in the early days, Bolton fell into his first breast-implant case more or less by accident. In 1982 a woman named Maria Stern walked into a small plaintiffs' firm in San Francisco, complaining of a ruptured implant. She also suffered from chronic fatigue and joint pains. Her doctors, unable to fix on the cause of her symptoms, told her that the leakage of silicone gel into her body might be at the root of the problem. Though no scientific literature supported this theory, her doctors thought that it might at least be a possibility.

Stern wanted to sue Dow Corning, which had made her implant, not just for manufacturing a defective product but for selling her something that had made her ill. No one had ever made that allegation before—at least not in a lawsuit—and the lawyer she went to see immediately understood the inherent difficulty in pursuing such a case. Nonetheless, he took Stern on as a client, and threw the case to Bolton, whom he had recently hired out of law school.

Though he didn't realize it at first, Bolton had two great advantages in gunning for this particular product. The first was that, even though they were put into the human body, silicone breast implants, like all medical devices at the time, were only loosely regulated. Even though they'd been on the market since 1964, they had never been put through the kind of premarket wringer that the Food and Drug Administration requires for, say, new pharmaceuticals.

Bolton's second advantage was, to put it bluntly, that he was going up against Dow Corning. Founded in 1943 by Dow Chemical and Corning (then known as Corning Glass Works)—which remain its sole shareholders—its only mission has been to find new applications for silicone, which is derived from silicon and is one of the most useful substances ever created. This it had done with great success, generating $2.2 billion in annual sales by 1994 and churning out some 8,700 silicone products. Its medical-devices division alone makes everything from pacemaker parts to shunts for relieving water on the brain. (Breast implants occupied a small and not especially profitable corner of the company.) Over time the company culture had instilled in its employees an almost childlike awe at the wonders of silicone.

Perhaps because it had to report to only two sympathetic shareholders, it was an insular, even naive company. Its Midland, Michigan, headquarters was filled with cheery Midwesterners who had never had to face down the threat of sustained litigation, let alone a bout of bad publicity. In this, it could not have been more different from its co-founder and neighbor, the much larger Dow Chemical, which had been toughened up over the years by exposure to both. Dow Corning was an innocent in a dangerous world.

This was perhaps never better illustrated than when Bolton finally got the court to agree—after the usual lengthy struggle with the company's lawyers—to his demand to visit Dow Corning and search for documents. For a lawyer with a theory he can't prove, this "discovery" phase of litigation can be a crucial fishing expedition. Ordered by the court in 1984 to give Bolton access to certain documents, Dow Corning actually bought him the airline ticket—first class, no less—and paid for his hotel room. That week, Dan Bolton found his case.

To this day, Bolton can remember his growing excitement as he realized what a treasure trove Dow Corning had opened up for him. In the 20 years it had been manufacturing silicone breast implants, Dow Corning had compiled thousands upon thousands of memos relating to every aspect of the product—including the question of whether the gel could cause an immune reaction. Many of those memos were written in language so strong as to border on the inflammatory. Bolton found a 1983 memo, for instance, that concluded: "As Product Steward...I must strongly urge that Bill's group be given an approval to design and conduct the necessary work to validate that these gels are safe...only inferential data exists to substantiate the long-term safety of these gels for human implant applications." Another 1983 memo said, "However, I want to emphasize that to my knowledge we have no valid long-term implant data to substantiate the safety of gels for long-term implant use." To Bolton, these were "classic smoking-gun-type documents. I was amazed."

He also stumbled upon a raging controversy within the company during the 1970s over a side effect called "contracture"—in which the tissue around the implant could harden—as well as over "bleed." Gel bleed was a phenomenon well known among plastic surgeons in which minuscule amounts of gel escaped through the implant shell. The controversy resulted from the fact that a number of plastic surgeons, feeling that Dow Corning implants both bled excessively and caused an unacceptably high rate of contracture, had stopped buying implants from the company. The salesmen were beside themselves about the loss of business, and the internal memos they wrote to their higher-ups provided Bolton with yet more ammunition. "Several of our customers," wrote the author of the most damning such memo, "asked me what we were doing. I assured them, with crossed fingers, that Dow Corning too had a 'contracture/gel migration' study under way. This apparently satisfied them for the moment but one of these days they will be asking us for the results of our studies."

Bolton was delighted. "With all our little goodies, we felt like Santa Claus," he recalls now. "We came back very, very up about the case."

One could argue, as Dow Corning later did, that these documents represented an ongoing internal debate, and that for every scientist who worried about the effect of implants on the immune system, there were others who were equally convinced of their safety. One could offer various innocent explanations for things that were in the documents. And one could point out that while the "Dow documents" (as they later became known) weren't exactly reassuring about the safety of breast implants, they didn't show them to be unsafe either. On the central question of the lawsuit—did silicone breast implants cause an immune reaction in women?—they were silent.

What Bolton understood, however, was that none of this mattered. In the hands of a good plaintiffs' lawyer, the 800 pages of documents he came back with would make Dow Corning appear negligent while obscuring the fact that the central allegation remained unproven. Combined with the other elements he had put together—an ex-employee who had agreed to testify against Dow Corning; a handful of "experts" he had found who were willing to theorize that silicone affected the immune system; the sympathy that Stern herself was likely to arouse in a jury—the Dow documents gave Bolton the upper hand. Even Dow Corning could see that; in the spring of 1985, just before the trial was set to begin, it offered to settle. Bolton said no.

That July his bet paid off when a jury awarded Maria Stern $1.7 million. Of that, $1.5 million was punitive damages, meaning that the jury believed Dow Corning had done bad things that deserved serious punishment. (The company and Stern settled the case for less while it was on appeal, a very common outcome.)

Bolton had shown the way: You could allege in court that silicone breast implants caused disease, and you could win a lot of money.

To Bolton's surprise, though, the Stern verdict did not create much of a stir. It was the legal equivalent of a tree falling in the forest: if no one heard it, did it really make any noise? After the trial, the court ordered Bolton to return the Dow documents to Dow Corning and forbade him to talk about what was in them. In the plaintiffs' bar, the belief endured that these were difficult cases and, Stern notwithstanding, not especially remunerative. That's because so much of the award was in punitive damages, which quite often get reduced or thrown out on appeal.

For any complicated lawsuit to sprout into a mass tort, something more is needed than a victory or two against a company. There has to be a climate of fear surrounding the product, and a group of angry users who want to make the company suffer as they themselves have suffered. Once potential claimants are on the verge of a stampede, then a big jury award can set it in motion.

Which is why, as important as the Stern case was, Bolton's second big breast-implant trial six years later was infinitely more so. It wasn't that the facts were especially different; Bolton's new client, a woman named Mariann Hopkins, had a ruptured implant and a history of joint pain, fatigue, and weight loss. And Bolton tried the case in much the same way he'd tried the Stern case, relying on the Dow documents (which he'd retrieved from Dow Corning), his "experts," and so on. But the *context* was different. And that changed everything.

By then, there had been an increasingly loud drumbeat of publicity, as reporters began to pick up on the charges that breast implants caused disease. Television magazine shows are particularly powerful purveyors of fear about products; to this day, everyone on both sides of the breast-implant litigation remembers a broadcast by Connie Chung in late 1990 about the breast-implant allegations. The show had a tremendous ripple effect, as women with implants started up support groups to share information and to vent their anger at the makers of breast implants. It was a tremendously emotional issue—how could it not be?—and there were instances when women with implants panicked upon hearing the allegations. In one infamous case, a woman tried to cut her own implants out with a razor. Meanwhile, Sidney Wolfe, who runs Ralph Nader's Health Research Group, was loudly calling for breast implants to be banned and selling litigation documents to plaintiffs' attorneys for $750.

Added to this volatile mix was one other element, perhaps the most crucial of all in creating the atmosphere for this mass tort: the federal government began to bear down hard on breast implants. Having finally concluded that implants needed to be strictly regulated, the FDA was in the process of applying to them the same tough standards it applies to drugs. The process wasn't going well for Dow Corning, because it hadn't done enough science. And FDA Commissioner David Kessler appeared to be in no mood to cut the company any slack; according to an FDA source, he was continually pushing the FDA staff to finish up its breast-implant investigation quickly.

In November 1991, a scientific panel convened by the FDA held a widely publicized hearing on breast implants, which turned into a contentious, highly charged affair. Although the panel ultimately concluded that implants should remain on the market, its decision was barely noticed. For by that time the Hopkins jury had reached a verdict. In mid-December 1991, a jury awarded Mariann Hopkins not the $1.7 million Maria Stern had gotten but $7.34 million, of which $6.5 million was punitive damages. Suddenly there wasn't a plaintiffs' lawyer in the country who didn't understand the rare opportunity in breast implants.

And Dan Bolton still had one last card to play. Enraged by Dow Corning's continued insistence that breast implants were safe, he decided that Kessler should see the Dow documents. Violating a court order that they be kept under seal, he managed to get them to Kessler, who was reportedly appalled. On January 6, 1992, the FDA commissioner, claiming that the documents contained information "that has increased our concern about the safety of [implants]," announced a temporary moratorium on their use (though, oddly enough, he said they could still be used for women who needed them for reconstructive surgery after breast cancer). "We owe it to the American people to see to it that these questions are thoroughly investigated," he added.

In a less litigious society, a government official would be able to say out loud that a medical device needed further study, and that's what would happen: there would be further study. Instead, Kessler's call for an implant moratorium became the spark that finally lit the blaze. Within weeks, 100 lawsuits had become 1,000 lawsuits. The stampede had begun.

Among the handful of people who instantly understood the enormous ramifications of Kessler's decision for Dow Corning, two in particular stood out. One was Keith McKennon, a former president of Dow Chemical U.S.A. During his career, McKennon had been Dow Chemical's point man for several mass torts; he also sat on Dow Corning's board. McKennon was thus the most logical person to see the smaller company through the crisis. Afflicted with cancer, on the verge of retirement, but deeply loyal to the two companies, McKennon reluctantly agreed to become Dow Corning's CEO. His tenure began a month after the moratorium.

The second man was a well-known Cincinnati attorney named Stanley Chesley, whose tactics in big-time tort litigation have made him both rich and infamous. Three weeks after Kessler's announcement, Chesley filed papers in his hometown with U.S. District Judge Carl Rubin asking that he certify breast-implant recipients (and their husbands!) as a "class."

Turning major tort cases into class-action suits—lawsuits he largely controlled as the lead attorney for the class and that virtually guaranteed him millions of dollars in fees once they were settled—was how Stan Chesley made a living. Created by an act of Congress, class-action suits were initially intended to allow large numbers of people to redress a fundamentally similar "harm," such as price rigging, or civil rights violations. Chesley, however, was the first to adapt class-action suits to complicated tort cases; in so doing, one legal publication later wrote, he "revolutionized tort law." In a Chesley class action, the money damages were potentially huge, while the harms suffered by the "class" of victims were often not even remotely similar. This latter is a particularly important point, for it allowed Chesley, and other class-action specialists who followed him, to create—and then settle—mass torts that included both plaintiffs who were so sick they were confined to wheelchairs and others whose symptoms were so minor they were barely detectable.

For Chesley, the light bulb went on in 1977, when, after a fire at a Kentucky supper club killed 165 people, he acceded to Judge Rubin's request that all the plaintiffs be declared a class. "Although I originally opposed the class certification," he says now, "it turned out to be an incredibly effective device." Because the club had minimal insurance—and because its records were destroyed, making it impossible to know who manufactured the aluminum wire that might have started the fire—other lawyers viewed the case as a loser. But Chesley devised a theory that *all* aluminum wire manufacturers were liable for making a faulty product, so it didn't matter whose wire was in the supper club. Chesley's theory generated an astonishing 1,100 defendants, the great bulk of whom had nothing whatsoever to do with the fire. But because the victims had been declared a class—and the companies therefore faced only one lawsuit instead of several hundred—many found it easier to settle than to fight. Chesley ultimately generated $50 million in settlements, of which some $6 million went to his firm. From that point forward, turning big disasters into class-action lawsuits, and then settling them before a trial ever took place, became Chesley's preferred method.

Though they had never met in person, McKennon and Chesley went way back. Like battle-hardened generals on opposite sides of a war, they had squared off in several previous mass torts. In fact, in their intertwined history one could find the seeds of the mass-tort phenomenon, for their first battle, in 1983, turned out to be the one that started it all: the Agent Orange case.

Looking back now, what is astonishing about the Agent Orange class action is the extent to which all the vital precedents it set appear to have been accidental. It was never meant to be the instigator of all the subsequent mass torts; on the contrary, it was supposed to *discourage* mass litigation. For instance, the very decision to certify a class of Vietnam veterans—who, you'll remember, were claiming that they had been made ill by the defoliant during the war—was a stunning precedent. If Chesley's disaster cases had stretched the definition of a class action, this distorted it beyond recognition—while opening up a whole new area for plaintiffs' lawyers, who had never before been able to get class-action status for people with such varied symptoms, or even for people who were claiming a product caused disease. Yet the judge who ruled over the case, Jack B. Weinstein, was motivated in part by the most prosaic of reasons. He feared that if he didn't allow the class, Agent Orange cases would clog the courts for years, just like asbestos cases, which had never achieved class-action status and had become the black hole of the American legal system.

Weinstein strong-armed both the plaintiffs and the companies that had manufactured Agent Orange—chief among them Dow Chemical—to begin settlement talks. Again, his motives were mundane. If the companies and the plaintiffs fought a duel to the death, *his* court would be tied up for years. Amazingly, though, he was pushing for a settlement despite his vocal belief that the Agent Orange veterans had a weak case. Indeed, to show how weak he thought it was—and to keep the plaintiffs from bolting from the settlement process—he summarily threw out several cases brought by lawyers whose clients had "opted out" of the class to bring their own, individual lawsuits. No proof of causation, he ruled—meaning that, in his judgment, they had failed to prove a link between Agent Orange and their illnesses. It was all very Machiavellian, and it worked. In the end, the defendants paid $180 million to settle the lawsuits, in return for which the plaintiffs agreed that no veteran would ever be able to bring another Agent Orange suit. Here was the real breakthrough: the companies were paying millions of dollars to the plaintiffs even though there was no hard evidence that Agent Orange caused disease.

And what did McKennon think of this astonishing settlement? Actually, he thought it was fine; like everyone else, he missed the larger picture. To him, it was simple: Dow Chemical, faced with a potential multibillion-dollar liability, had erased the litigation with barely a scratch on its balance sheet. "The harsh reality," he shrugs, "is that if there is a critical mass of lawsuits, you're going to wind up paying some money."

Instead, it was the plaintiffs' lawyers who were irate. The settlement completely shortchanged their clients, they charged; the most a veteran could collect—no matter how disabled—was only $12,000. And it shortchanged the lawyers as well, for in perhaps the deepest cut of all, Weinstein allowed the plaintiffs' attorneys to take only 7.5 percent of the settlement instead of the 30 percent to 40 percent they usually command. (Once again, the judge was doing so to discourage future mass litigation.) The plaintiffs' lawyers knew exactly whom to blame: Chesley, who had been invited into the litigation specifically to negotiate a settlement. Out of the Agent Orange case came a perception that when Stan Chesley got control of a class-action suit, he would negotiate a quick settlement, selling everybody's clients down the river while ensuring himself a fat fee. (In Agent Orange, Chesley's firm was awarded $525,000 for less than a year's work.) Over the years other lawyers have called him everything from "an economic broker" to "the ultimate grotesque, exaggerated perversion of what it means to be a lawyer."

Chesley calls his critics jealous, but even his own description of what he does makes him sound more a broker than a lawyer. "In this kind of business," he boasts, "you have to be resolution-oriented. Companies involved in mass torts are looking for resolution."

Do companies understand what Chesley's up to? Of course they do, which is why they are often willing to negotiate right from the start if they see him sitting at the table. They too want resolution, after all, as does Wall Street, which will often push up a company's stock when a piece of thorny litigation is settled, even if it's for hundreds of millions of dollars. More often than not, it's his fellow plaintiffs' lawyers Chesley winds up fighting. These lawyers, who see themselves as trial lawyers rather than class-action specialists, believe that a company's need to "resolve" litigation is simply not their problem. To them, the implicit Chesley exchange—resolution in return for a hefty but nonrecurring sum of money—is anathema. For that matter, so is Chesley himself.

Dow Corning was a company in shock when McKennon arrived in early 1992. Feeling under siege, its employees hunkered down in their isolated headquarters, embittered and paralyzed by the lawsuits.

McKennon's first order of business was to erase the bunker mentality. He courted the press, appearing conciliatory. Even at the height of the Agent Orange battle, McKennon had always felt some measure of sympathy for the veterans, who were convinced that Agent Orange had made them sick. Women with breast implants had the same kind of conviction, McKennon knew, and he wanted the company to acknowledge that their anger was real. One of his first moves was to take Dow Corning completely out of the breast-implant business, an action that dismayed many Dow Corning employees, who saw it as an implicit admission of guilt. But McKennon knew it had to be done, if only to send a signal to women that this was not an uncaring company. He also hired from Dow Chemical a scientist named Ralph Cook and charged him with doing something Dow Corning should have begun years before. Cook was given the task of using Dow Corning's money to seed the broad, complex epidemiology that was required if the medical questions surrounding silicone breast implants were ever going to be answered. "I said publicly that we were willing to go wherever the science took us. And I meant it," McKennon says. "If there was a flaw in my assessment," he adds ruefully, "it was in not realizing that no matter how definitive the science, the other side wasn't going to believe it."

Finally, Dow Corning began retaining lawyers with mass-tort experience, including an animated, cigar-chomping Washington attorney named Kenneth Feinberg, who had been Weinstein's special master in the Agent Orange case and had etched out a career negotiating mass torts ever since. The demand for Feinberg's specialized services is such that he commands around $200,000 a month when he gets involved in a case—with a seven-figure bonus if there's a settlement. Needless to say, this gives Feinberg as strong an interest in "resolution" as it gives Chesley, with whom he had negotiated some half-dozen mass torts. Despite being on opposite sides of the table, the two men speak admiringly of each other—"Stan Chesley is a genius at what he does," says Feinberg—and one suspects that, like enemy fighter pilots, they prefer each other's company to the people in their own camps. McKennon's hope was that the two men could work their special magic and settle the litigation quickly.

Now in paperback, the acclaimed *New York Times* bestseller by Joe Nocera and Bethany McLean

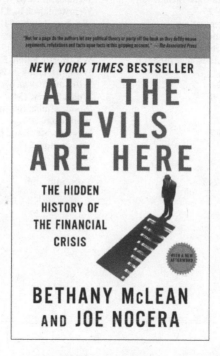

"The best business book of 2010"
—*Huffington Post*

Portfolio / Penguin
A member of Penguin Group (USA) Inc.
www.penguin.com

PO #: 4500346511

What McKennon missed, however, were the hard feelings toward Chesley among other lawyers. There was simply no way that Chesley's many enemies in the plaintiffs' bar were going to allow him to corner the market in the breast-implant litigation. Even as Judge Rubin certified Chesley's class, the trial lawyers began lobbying to have the case taken away from Rubin, whom they viewed as a Chesley ally. It quickly turned into a civil war between the trial lawyers and the class-action lawyers; meetings of the attorneys who had a piece of the mass tort invariably degenerated into shouting matches between pro-Chesley and anti-Chesley factions.

Ultimately, the federal class action was taken away from Rubin, primarily because of the revolt among the trial lawyers. There is now so much mass litigation in this country that there exists a panel of federal judges that does nothing but decide whether a particular group of similar cases has become so unwieldy that it needs to be "consolidated" in one courtroom. This is called the "multidistrict litigation" panel, or MDL. Since there were now thousands of breast-implant cases being filed all over the country, there wasn't much doubt that they needed to be consolidated. But instead of Rubin, the MDL panel chose to give the cases to a highly respected federal judge in Birmingham, Alabama, named Sam C. Pointer Jr. It was then up to Pointer to decide which of the many plaintiffs' lawyers should be named to the all-important plaintiffs' steering committee. In any mass tort, it is those lawyers who essentially run the case and who reap the biggest fees when it's settled.

Had the class action stayed with Rubin, it was a foregone conclusion that Chesley would have run the steering committee; now Chesley had to angle for a spot like everyone else. But Chesley could angle with the best of them. Hearing a rumor that Pointer was enamored of computer technology, Chesley vowed to underwrite a state-of-the-art computer facility that would give all the parties easy access to the many documents and depositions that were collected; eventually the depository would hold nine million documents, all of them indexed and on CD-ROMs, at a cost to Chesley of close to $1 million.

In the end, Pointer, ever the careful jurist, balanced the steering committee with representatives of both factions. Not only did Chesley make it onto the committee, but he was also named its co-chairman. The other co-chairman was an Atlanta lawyer named Ralph Knowles—"an old-fashioned fender-bender type," sniffs Feinberg—who had emerged as a big Chesley critic. "This is not my idea of practicing law," Knowles says of the mass tort he found himself in. But with almost 200 breast-implant clients, he was in too deep to cede the field to someone else. Besides, somebody had to keep an eye on Chesley.

If Chesley understood this, he did not acknowledge it. After the hearing, he boldly proclaimed that all the bad feelings of the previous few months had vanished. "I see a very united front on the plaintiffs' side," he told the press. "There is one enemy," Chesley added. "The defendants."

Despite Pointer's attempt to be inclusive, there was a gaping hole in the plaintiffs' steering committee, and everybody knew it. No plaintiffs' lawyers from Texas were on it. This was no small thing, for once the stampede began, Texas quickly became breast-implant central; one out of every four lawsuits was filed in the state. Rick Laminack and his boss, John O'Quinn, had filed 78 lawsuits just during the week the moratorium was announced, and already had more breast-implant clients than any other law firm in the country. Another Houston attorney, Mike Gallagher, whose toll-free phone number was being deluged by potential breast-implant clients, was building a roster that would soon exceed 1,000 plaintiffs. Richard Mithoff, who'd had that first Dow Corning case back in 1977, had also gotten back in the breast-implant business. He had more than 400 clients.

And their absence from the plaintiffs' steering committee was no oversight. They had no intention of playing in Chesley's game and were purposely staying as far from Pointer's court as they possibly could. They had their own game to play. They were accumulating clients not to participate in some national settlement process, which they openly mocked, but to prepare large numbers of cases to take to trial in state court. The state court system was their refuge. As long as they could keep their cases in Harris County, the jurisdiction that encompasses Houston, and away from the federal judiciary, they would be able to get trial dates. Generating huge numbers of clients and then pushing their cases through the Texas court system, one after another, like quarters in a slot machine, that was the essence of their strategy. While Chesley's strategy lay in the consolidation of cases, which he could then settle en masse, the Harris County lawyers found their opportunity in the opposite approach: *preventing* consolidation (at least of their cases) and then using the implicit threat of 2,000 separate trials to extract money from big companies. That's how big-time trial lawyers like O'Quinn played mass torts.

There were tremendous advantages that came with this approach. One was the economy of scale that came with having hundreds, and even thousands, of more or less similar cases. There was also the potential domino effect should they win even one high-profile case, which would make companies think twice about risking another trial rather than settling future cases as they came up. On the other hand, a big win for the defendants didn't

get them all that much: There were still 1,999 cases stacked up right behind it. This was a strategy of attrition, and it worked just fine. Even as Chesley awaits his first dime from the breast-implant litigation, John O'Quinn has grossed around $100 million in settlements from his breast-implant work. He keeps 40 percent.

Lawyers, it almost goes without saying, have big egos, but few have egos as big as O'Quinn's. A tall fellow with craggy, Marlboro-man features, he has a smile that is both disarming and ever so slightly malicious. In the years he has been practicing law in Houston, he has become a legend—something he himself is the first to point out. He likes to tell the story of how he won $8.5 million in damages for the death of a *bull*. ("A friend of mine had a paraplegic case against Exxon...at the same time. I told him, 'I'll get more for my dead bull than you'll get for your paraplegic,' and I did.") He is said to have lost only once in his entire career, and many of his victories have brought breathtaking damages: $650 million in one case, $517 million in another, $109 million in a third. He is regularly compared to the most famous of all Harris County trial lawyers, Joe Jamail, who won what may well be the most spectacular judgment of all time: Pennzoil's $11 billion victory over Texaco.

Even the scandals O'Quinn has been embroiled in have a larger-than-life quality. In 1989, when the State Bar of Texas tried to have him disbarred on grounds of improper client solicitation and fee splitting, O'Quinn responded by hiring seven of the best-known criminal lawyers in the state, whom he labeled "The Magnificent Seven." (He got off with a slap on the wrist.) Another time, he was accused of having an affair with a juror. He admitted to the romance but insisted that it had not begun until the trial had been concluded. This admission cost him his marriage but saved his career.

That O'Quinn believes his own myth seems beyond question; at staff meetings, he regularly declares that he has been "blessed by God to help the little guy." But there is another part of his success that he doesn't talk much about. O'Quinn and the rest of the Harris County plaintiffs' bar operate in a county, and a state, where the deck is stacked in their favor. Texas is a plaintiffs' mecca. In Texas judgments are higher than they are practically anywhere else in the country—"the Texas premium," some lawyers call it—and the standards for evidence are far more favorable to the plaintiffs. In Texas people who've never so much as set foot in the state are able to try lawsuits in state court, using rationales that would be laughable in other jurisdictions. And in Texas it is much easier for plaintiffs' lawyers to get large numbers of cases scheduled for trial than it is in most other places—cases in which the defense doesn't even know which of the many plaintiffs they will face in

court until just days before the trial. "They control the docket," complains Dow Corning's general counsel, James Jenkins.

Finally, and most important, Texas state judges must stand for election if they want to keep their seat. Not surprisingly, the most prodigious campaign contributors in the state are the plaintiffs' lawyers. O'Quinn donated $183,000 between 1990 and 1994 just to statewide political candidates—a figure that doesn't even include his contributions to judicial candidates. A Harris County judge named Carolyn Johnson received $6,250 from O'Quinn in the fall of 1993—just months after she had become a judge and had been handed one of O'Quinn's big breast-implant cases. It was her largest individual contribution. And as for judges who are not considered pro-plaintiff—and there are some—the plaintiffs' bar is not above quietly working for their defeat.

Texas's pro-plaintiff reputation is widely known among corporate lawyers, and the standard strategy for dealing with it is to get cases filed in Texas "removed" to federal court. In most other states, in fact, breast-implant cases were being removed regularly to Judge Pointer's court in Birmingham—that was how consolidation worked. But the defense quickly learned that they could not remove the Texas cases. The rules governing removal state that if one party resides in the state, then the case can stay in state court. The Texas "party" O'Quinn and the other Harris County lawyers found was neither plastic surgeons nor companies. Rather, they were the *inventors* of breast implants, Dr. Thomas Cronin and Dr. Frank Gerow, both Houstonians, and both dead. Amazingly, their estates constituted a legitimate party to the litigation.

In no small part because he has been able to apply his considerable talent in this most pro-plaintiff of jurisdictions, O'Quinn is today worth somewhere around $500 million. His reputation is so fearsome that many companies will settle quietly with him—for far more than they would settle with other lawyers—rather than face him in court. And his law firm is structured in such a way as to maximize his income. Although there are three other names on the door (including Laminack's), the firm is not remotely a partnership. It is, as O'Quinn himself describes it, "a benevolent monarchy." The other lawyers in the firm are paid a salary, plus a percentage of the income they generate—O'Quinn has called this giving them "a piece of what they kill." He alone decides what that piece is; he gets the rest.

For Dow Corning and the other defendants, the consolidation of breast-implant cases at the federal level was a mixed blessing. Consolidation saves companies millions of dollars, and even more in man-hours, because depo-

sitions (to cite one obvious example) have to be taken only once instead of hundreds of times. But consolidation also helps the plaintiffs. New attorneys can jump in knowing that a huge amount of work has already been done—instantly becoming, in Chesley's words, "armed warriors." Dozens, and even hundreds, of cases can be filed for the price of a single filing fee. Inevitably, the consolidation of litigation creates more litigation. Thus did 1,000 breast-implant lawsuits mushroom into 5,000 and then 10,000. The process had begun to feed on itself, as it always does.

The emergence of the Harris County strategy, on the other hand, was an unmitigated disaster for the companies. Lawyers like O'Quinn could get trial dates quickly. And any Texas trial, with its frightening prospect of Texas-size damages, had the potential to greatly raise the stakes. In effect, the companies found themselves caught in a kind of legal pincer movement, one at the federal level and another at the state level. Of the two, Harris County was by far the more dangerous.

O'Quinn and Laminack began building up their client base, which would eventually reach an astounding 2,500 plaintiffs. They did so partly by gobbling up referrals from lesser-known lawyers, who would get a small percentage of the "kill" once the case was settled, and partly by attaching themselves, barnacle-like, to some of the breast-implant support groups. Like most big plaintiffs' firms, they also relied on advertising. Naturally, O'Quinn's ad stood out from the pack. Under a photograph of a well-endowed woman ran the headline: ARE DREAM BREASTS TO DIE FOR? Then they began preparing cases for trial, taking depositions and doing discovery, all the while sneering at the slower pace of lawyers on the federal track. Sure enough, by the fall of 1992, Laminack and O'Quinn had a case ready to try, against Bristol-Myers Squibb. On the eve of the trial, it was settled. O'Quinn and Laminack were up and running.

Chesley and Knowles were up and running too. Though their own case preparation was moving at a snail's pace, behind the scenes the two men were engaged in secret negotiations with Feinberg. By late 1992, these negotiations included not only those three men, but negotiators for Baxter and Bristol-Myers Squibb as well. As the negotiations progressed, Chesley and Knowles, the former antagonists, struck up a friendship that became firmer every day. Of course, neither the fact that negotiations were already under way nor the news of the Chesley-Knowles alliance was likely to bring joy to the other lawyers in the case. And sure enough, when word of the negotiations began to leak out in the spring of 1993, the trial lawyers erupted.

Once more there were angry meetings among the plaintiffs' lawyers, only this time there were 200 lawyers in the room instead of 50. Once again, the

class-action lawyers and the trial lawyers hurled insults at each other. The climactic meeting was held in Pointer's courtroom in April 1993. A sheepish Knowles—the man who was supposed to be looking after the interests of the trial lawyers—admitted that he had gone along with a request for secrecy, but he insisted that Dow Corning, not Chesley, had imposed that condition. He also insisted, however, that he and Chesley were not giving away the store; in fact, he said, it was Chesley who had changed his ways. "Ralph calmed troubled waters," says one lawyer who was there. Still, the other lawyers were adamant that the negotiating committee be broadened, and Pointer agreed. He quickly named three additional lawyers to negotiate with the companies. One of them, surprisingly, was Mike Gallagher, of Harris County, Texas.

Why would Gallagher, a trial lawyer with all the advantages he had in Harris County, get involved in the federal case? One answer was that with so many cases in Texas, he felt it important that "their" plaintiffs be represented at the negotiating table. He also got involved because he was sure he could negotiate a better deal for plaintiffs than Chesley could. He turned out to be right: eventually he negotiated a deal so rich that it was bound to implode. But in the meantime, he became the Chesley watchdog.

After their first case was settled, O'Quinn and Laminack had immediately begun working up their second, also against Bristol-Myers Squibb. That was how they operated: finish one, start the next, keep the pressure on. Their second client, however, was not exactly a dream plaintiff. Her name was Pamela Johnson, and she was 45 years old, with a ruptured implant and the usual symptoms of fatigue and joint pain. She had had implants put in for purely cosmetic reasons, which juries tended to frown on. She smoked a pack of cigarettes a day. She'd received her implants when she was 29 but didn't receive any medical treatment until she was in her 40s. She hadn't lost much time at work, despite her illness, which O'Quinn described as like having "a bad case of the flu all the time." O'Quinn's own research showed that juries were not likely to work up much sympathy for her. Perhaps that's why Bristol-Myers decided that instead of settling, it would try the Pamela Johnson case.

The case was shown on Court TV, and it became the best single advertisement O'Quinn has ever had. During breaks in the trial, the Court TV anchors would take calls from viewers—invariably implant recipients looking for some free advice. More than once, the anchors responded by referring the caller to O'Quinn's office. Viewers could also see O'Quinn in action, as he skewered Bristol-Myers with its own internal documents, gently guided Johnson through her testimony, and delivered his fire-and-brimstone closing argument.

And they could see the result. Two days before Christmas 1992, the jury awarded Pamela Johnson a staggering $25 million. *That* was Texas-style damages! Never mind that the case was settled while on appeal for considerably less. The $25 million was the number that stuck in the public mind. It was a number that created huge expectations among the thousands of women who had filed lawsuits. It put tremendous pressure on those negotiating the global settlement, who now had to cope with those expectations. And it guaranteed a whole new round of publicity. Immediately, the stampede started up again. Within a matter of months, the number of breast-implant lawsuits nationwide had doubled. And so had John O'Quinn's clientele.

II.

Ever since the mass tort had begun, in January 1992, the complex legal maneuverings had been dominated by Chesley and O'Quinn. From his position as co-chairman of the plaintiffs' steering committee, Chesley was running what might be thought of as the Big Case. O'Quinn's strategy, meanwhile, rested on his ability to push his huge caseload through the system and force companies to either try them or settle them.

O'Quinn's $25 million verdict in the Pamela Johnson case had caused Bristol-Myers to run up a white flag. Bristol-Myers never again tried a breast-implant suit, but settled them whenever trial dates were set—for a sum rumored, in Texas, to be $1 million a case. Of course, a verdict like that also strengthened the bargaining position of those working on the Big Case. So well did these strategies reinforce each other that one could be forgiven for wondering whether the lawyers were acting in concert. They weren't; there was too much bad blood between them.

In the months after the big Bristol-Myers verdict, though, Chesley and O'Quinn began to share center stage with two other attorneys. The first was Mike Gallagher, the Houston lawyer who had decided that he needed to participate in the goings-on in Pointer's courtroom. Having practically forced his way onto Chesley's negotiating committee, he began slowly taking command of the negotiations. By turns blunt and coy, funny and angry, Gallagher was the kind of negotiator who would joyously drink you under the table by night even as he was demanding your first-born by day. To his considerable financial detriment, Gallagher spent the next year negotiating alongside Chesley instead of following O'Quinn's lucrative strategy in Harris County.

The second man was a natty, disarming, whip-smart attorney named David Bernick, a 38-year-old "national litigator" for the rough-and-tumble

Chicago firm of Kirkland & Ellis. Bernick was Dow Corning's lawyer. Along with Kenneth Feinberg, who was handling the settlement negotiations, he had been retained back in 1992, after the mass tort had gotten under way. Bernick, though young, had already built a reputation as someone who could win complex product-liablity cases. His best-known victory had come some five years before, when he had defended a product called Sarabond, a mortar additive that allegedly weakened brick structures and corroded steel. By the time Bernick got involved, the manufacturer, Dow Chemical, had lost the only two lawsuits that had been tried and had spent more than $100 million in settlements. Bernick's first trial, however, resulted in a verdict for the company so convincing that no Sarabond case was ever tried again.

Though he had never taken more than basic science courses in school, Bernick had a gift for science. Perhaps even more than his trial skills, that was what he brought to cases like the breast-implant lawsuits. He also had a talent for explaining complex scientific issues to nonscientists in a way that was understandable without being patronizing. "My basic premise," he says, "is that jurors can understand science if you take the time to explain it to them." Though Bernick knew he had to be able to defend the company's actions, to mute the plantiffs' cries of negligence, he saw his primary goal as something else: refocusing the lawsuits on the allegation that had created this mass tort in the first place. Did breast implants cause disease, or did they not?

As is often true in a mass tort, science was the plaintiffs' Achilles' heel. When you got right down to it, all they had was a theory. The theory said that the silicone gel somehow caused a breakdown in a woman's immune system, making her susceptible to autoimmune symptoms. The strongest evidence in support of this theory, of course, was the plaintiffs themselves— women who had both implants and a disease. What the lawyers didn't have was any serious science—things like controlled studies—to support their claim of a link between the two.

Until Bernick arrived on the scene, they had managed to fudge this pretty well. Dan Bolton, the lawyer who had won the first important breast-implant case, had dug up several "experts" who genuinely believed that silicone gel implants were harmful—people like Pierre Blais, a chemist who formerly worked for the Canadian government. Like virtually all the plaintiffs' experts, however, Blais had never conducted a study to test his theory, nor had he attempted the kind of epidemiology that could discover whether women with breast implants had any greater incidence of autoimmune illness than the rest of the population.

As spring approached summer and Bernick prepared to try his first case, he concentrated on three things: showing that Dow Corning's internal story

was more honorable than the plaintiffs alleged; laying out mainstream science's belief that silicone breast implants were safe; and gathering the ammunition he needed to shoot holes in the other side's expert testimony.

That trial took place in Colorado in May and June of 1993; when it was over, Bernick's grateful client could claim its first victory. Although there were complaints afterward that Bernick had conducted a campaign of "character assassination" against the plaintiff, a former stripper, the people he actually went after were the experts. Blais got off easy; he was merely neutralized. Several others weren't so lucky. A doctor named Andrew Campbell, who ran a chronic-fatigue clinic in Houston where he had "diagnosed" hundreds of clients referred to him by various attorneys, was forced to admit that his résumé had been doctored and that he had never published a research paper in his life. So devastating was Bernick's cross-examination of Campbell that his career as an expert witness abruptly ended.

Bernick's Colorado victory was the first good news in a year and a half for Dow Corning. It also gave the defendants their first bit of bargaining leverage in the global settlement talks: Now it was the plaintiffs who needed to think twice about trying these cases forever. And the Harris County lawyers realized something else: when the moment came, as it surely would, that John O'Quinn found himself up against David Bernick, it was going to be something to see.

As encouraging as Bernick's victory was for the defendants, it couldn't undo the perverse logic of any mass tort—that the final leverage lies in the numbers. Thus, its major effect was to intensify negotiations toward a settlement in the Big Case, which was still Dow Corning's best hope of getting out alive. Kenneth Feinberg immediately began pushing hard for a deal with Chesley. The two men were old hands at this; they had sat across the table in most of the big settlements to date. But this one would be different. Gallagher, a trial lawyer suspicious of their relationship, was determined not to permit the kind of cozy agreement that so often enriches attorneys at the expense of everyone else.

Thus, Gallagher insisted that the plaintiffs be given not one but two separate opportunities to "opt out" of any broad settlement and bring their own cases if they thought the money wasn't enough. He also began demanding that the plaintiffs not be required to prove "causation." In other words, no woman would have to show a link between her implants and her ailments to be eligible for damages. What's more, he wanted women to be able to participate in the settlement even when their symptoms did not amount to a recognizable disease. His rationale was rooted in Agent Orange. "In Agent

Orange," he recalls bitterly, "the veterans got screwed because of so-called science. A lot of them were really sick, but their symptoms didn't add up to a known disease." He continued: "Silicone implants don't cause lupus so much as they cause something *like* lupus. A lot of my clients may not have lupus, but they can't walk up the stairs." Though you won't find it in any medical textbook, the plaintiffs' experts were calling this loose collection of symptoms "breast adjuvancy disease"; thanks to Gallagher, the phrase was eventually embedded in the settlement language.

At one point Feinberg tried to reopen the proof-of-illness issue. Gallagher slammed his fist on the table in anger. "I worked out a claims process," he shouted, "where the claim goes in one end and a check comes out the other end. And we're not going to change that!"

And of course all the plaintiffs' negotiators were insisting on gigantic sums of money. Gallagher once said that the hardest thing about being a plaintiffs' lawyer was "keeping a straight face the first time you ask for a million dollars." Now he and the others were asking for billions, and they weren't laughing. For months, the two sides haggled over the sum—not only how much it would come to but how the settlement fund would be structured. In the end, the three defendants engaged in the negotiations agreed to pay around $4.75 billion over 30 years, 25 percent of which would go to the lawyers. As incredible as that sum was, the only reason it wasn't any higher was that Feinberg told the plaintiffs that Dow Corning had reached its financial limit; by pushing for more, he implied, they might push the company into bankruptcy. Since bankruptcy halts litigation, it was the one thing the plaintiffs' negotiators wanted to avoid at all costs.

Then the question became: how much would each company kick in? This took another seven months to decide, as the companies fought furiously with each other, all their built-up resentment at their plight finally exploding in an orgy of mutual recrimination. All the while, Ralph Knowles, another plaintiffs' negotiator, openly threatened "massive litigation" if they didn't stop dawdling and agree to terms.

When the settlement was finally made official in the spring of 1994, it was revealed that Dow Corning would pay $2 billion and the others would pay the rest. The amount itself had been reduced to a little under $4 billion; the assumption was that a fourth defendant, 3M, would come in and make up the difference. Within two months 3M did come in, bringing the total amount to $4.25 billion. Wouldn't you know it: 3M entered into the settlement just weeks after going to trial against John O'Quinn. The judge was Carolyn Johnson. Three plaintiffs won a $27.9 million verdict. O'Quinn had struck again.

. . .

What is hard to understand, even now, is how anybody could have believed that such a deal could possibly work. Under the terms, individual claimants would be eligible for sums that ranged from $200,000 to $2 million, depending on their ages and the severity of their symptoms. But the money was supposed to last 30 years; only $1.2 billion would be available for current claims. So even using that lowest figure of $200,000, the fund would cover only 6,000 women. There were *already* three times that number of lawsuits pending. Even the negotiators assumed that number could rise to 60,000 potential claimants.

Worse, no one could say for sure that "only" 60,000 women would join the settlement class. In fact, by the time the numbers were in—and it took close to a year—there weren't 60,000 women but an almost unbelievable 480,000. They were drawn on the one hand by the prospect of the six- and seven-figure sums that were being advertised, and on the other by the fear that it was now or never. Even women who suffered no symptoms were driven to get "on the grid," as it was called, in case they became ill later on.

Then there was the John O'Quinn problem. A mass tort settlement won't make lawsuits go away unless the vast majority of plaintiffs abandon their lawsuits and take the money. With O'Quinn's success in Harris County, why would he ever advise his clients to do that? Far better for them to "opt out" of the settlement so that they could continue bringing cases in state court. Since the Harris County bar as a whole had around 6,000 cases, and most of those cases were likely to be opt-outs, the defendants still faced a tremendous amount of litigation. It was quite possibly the worst mass tort settlement ever negotiated.

Ah, but what a glorious time it was to be a breast-implant lawyer in Texas! Those spring and summer months of 1994—the opt-out period, as it was called—that was when a Harris County plaintiffs lawyer could *really* make some money.

Just picture, for a moment, the pressure on those who had negotiated the settlement. Here they were racing around the country, trying to persuade several hundred lawyers to commit their clients to the settlement by the opt-out deadline. Always, their pitch was the same: If too many women opted out, the companies would walk. Then they'd all be back where they had started—except that it would be worse because Dow Corning, in all likelihood, would file for bankruptcy. The threat of bankruptcy was Dow Corning's leverage.

The last thing any of the negotiators wanted during those months was a multimillion verdict coming out of Harris County. Which, of course, is exactly why every plaintiffs lawyer in Houston was lining up trial dates as

fast as he could get them. As cases came up, defendants had no choice but to settle them. One source close to the O'Quinn firm says they were bringing in upwards of $13 million a month during that stretch, a figure O'Quinn dismisses. ("It's too low," he joked to one writer.)

Finally, that June, as Dow Corning realized that Harris County had become a bottomless pit, Feinberg made an extraordinary secret trip to Houston. There he met with Rick Laminack, who was O'Quinn's breast-implant point man, and Richard Mithoff, who had his own large caseload, to plead for a temporary truce. The two men had 34 cases scheduled for trial over the next two months against Dow Corning. Feinberg told the lawyers that the company would settle all 34 cases—for a sum that reportedly topped the $1 million per case that had become the Harris County benchmark— but the money could not change hands until *after* the opt-out deadline. The Harris County lawyers agreed to the deal.

But in late August, after the deadline, Feinberg returned to Houston bearing a different message. Dow Corning had decided that it wasn't going to settle the cases after all, he bluntly told Laminack and Mithoff. There had simply been too many opt-outs, Feinberg continued—most of which were in Harris County. The company just didn't have the money to keep settling individual lawsuits indefinitely. "I've never been lied to like I was lied to by Dow Corning," Laminack later fumed. But that's when he knew that Dow Corning's eventual bankruptcy was probably inevitable.

All that summer and into the fall, women around the country streamed into law offices either to join the global settlement—or to opt out of it, on the assumption that they would get so little from the settlement that that they would still do better in court. Both developments were equally disastrous. Yet it took months before the participants finally conceded the obvious: their settlement was hopeless.

Why hadn't they seen it coming? One school of thought says that Feinberg, with a seven-figure bonus at stake, simply willed himself into believing the terms made sense. This Feinberg vehemently denies: "No one expected 480,000 claims," he says, "and no one expected all those opt-outs in Harris County. O'Quinn wrecked this settlement." The other person who received much of the blame was Gallagher. With his insistence on "claims coming in one end and a check coming out the other," he was largely responsible for the loose medical standards that brought so many women into the class. And he knows it. "I was wrong," he says contritely.

In terms of sheer destructive power, this mass tort was proving to be mightier than even the plaintiffs had ever dreamed. The pincer movement that

had begun years before—Chesley's Big Case in federal court; O'Quinn's guerrilla actions in Harris County—was closing in on the defendant companies. The problem was, their armies had grown so large, and their greed so uncontrolled, that there simply wasn't enough loot to go around. They needed a deeper pocket. They needed to rope Dow Chemical into the case. And for that, they needed each other.

Dow Chemical, of course, had co-founded Dow Corning in 1943; it and the other co-founder, Corning Inc., remained Dow Corning's only shareholders. With $20 billion in annual revenue, Dow Chemical was a truly deep pocket—larger than Corning and ten times the size of Dow Corning. It was also, ever since the Agent Orange litigation, the most hated company in America among plaintiffs' lawyers. That Dow Chemical had never made a breast implant in its history did not bother the plaintiffs' lawyers in the least. The way they saw it, Dow Chemical was as culpable for Dow Corning's missteps as Bristol-Myers, Baxter, and 3M were for the breast-implant subsidiaries they had once owned. But Judge Pointer disagreed, ruling that since Dow Corning was not a subsidiary but an independent company, its founders were not responsible for its legal problems.

The plaintiffs' lawyers had no intention of accepting Pointer's ruling as the final word. Convinced that Dow Chemical was in this thing up to its elbows and that Dow Corning was, in effect, sacrificing itself to shield its larger neighbor—Chesley was calling Dow Corning "the Manchurian candidate"—they set about a new round of discovery with one aim: to establish a strong enough connection between Dow Corning and Dow Chemical to cause Pointer to change his mind.

There was no finesse involved in this attempt. They simply sat Dow Corning and Dow Chemical people down in a small room, turned on a videocamera, and questioned them for days at a time. What did they learn? First, they learned that before Dow Corning set up its own toxicology lab in the early 1970s, Dow Chemical used to do some of its silicone toxicology work. They also discovered that Dow Chemical once controlled a small company in Italy that marketed breast implants abroad. And finally, they came across some joint Dow Chemical–Dow Corning studies from the mid-1980s exploring the possibility of developing silicones for insecticides. And that was it. Even Bolton, by then watching the big boys skeptically from the sidelines, was bemused at how slender a reed this was on which to hang a potential multibillion liability. "That's a tough sell," he remarked, shaking his head in wonder.

The big boys, though, had exactly what they wanted. They raced back to Pointer's courtroom, laid out their new "evidence," and then asked him to

stick Dow Chemical back into the case. Stunningly, Pointer reversed. "[U]nder the substantive law of at least some states—though not necessarily all states—the evidence would create a jury question in federal court," he wrote. As ever, though, one state hadn't waited for Pointer. In the fall of 1994, well before Pointer's decision, a Texas judge had concluded that the evidence was sufficient to make Dow Chemical a defendant. And John O'Quinn was preparing to try just such a case.

Dow Chemical's first reaction upon learning of the Texas ruling was to sue Dow Corning. The suit was really a legal maneuver to obtain Dow Corning's help. After all, Dow Chemical didn't have a clue about how to defend a silicone breast implant. It needed quick access to the things Dow Corning knew, and more to the point, it needed David Bernick. In all, seven lawyers would be representing the four principals at the trial; in addition to the two companies, there were also two different plaintiffs. But everyone knew that this was about Bernick and O'Quinn.

O'Quinn scoured Harris County for the perfect plaintiff, eventually choosing someone not from his own 2,500-client roster but from that of a lawyer named Edward Blizzard. O'Quinn's choice was Gladys Laas, a sweet, matronly 57-year-old woman who had received breast implants after an operation to remove fibrocystic tissue. "She's a wonderful person," attests Blizzard. "Deeply religious, with a good, solid work history. She had been a nurse at St. Luke's." But she could no longer work because of her pain. Her once happy and productive life had degenerated into a spiral of suffering and anguish. "John," adds Blizzard, "was very impressed with her." The other plaintiff, a client of Mithoff's, was no less sympathetic. Jenny Ladner, a 35-year-old doctor and mother of three, was about to leave the Army to go into private practice. She had lupus. The two plaintiffs were asking for $29 million in damages.

The trial began last November and instantly became the kind of event that people want to see. Among those who could be found in attendance was the Houston mayor's wife, Elyse Lanier, who sat on the University of Houston's board of regents with O'Quinn—and had breast implants.

The stars in this theater were determined to live up to their billing. Here was O'Quinn, with his fiery rhetoric, calling on the jury to punish the evil Dow entities: "Dow Corning violated the sacred rules that you don't sell a product to be put in the human body until you have first done the testing and proven it to be safe," he railed. "This case is not that much about science and chemistry," he said at another point. "This case is about ethics." And here was Bernick, throwing it right back at him: "In all the closing argu-

ments that you have heard today from the plaintiffs, where did you hear reference to one...study where they said...'Let me tell you about this piece of data'? Not once. Why?" He concluded sarcastically, "I guess because this case is about ethics, not science and chemistry."

In fact, in the months before the trial, several important epidemiological studies examining the link between implants and disease had been completed. Though their sample populations were too small to be definitive, they strongly backed the companies' position. One study, by a group of researchers at the Mayo Clinic, had been published in the *New England Journal of Medicine*. A second study, by researchers at Harvard, had not yet been published, though an abstract was being circulated. Bernick, of course, wanted to be able to tell the jury about the studies; O'Quinn wanted them kept away from the jury. The judge ultimately ruled the jury could be told about the Mayo Clinic study, but not the Harvard one, because it hadn't yet been published.

Mostly, though, the trial revolved around the testimony of the "experts" O'Quinn had brought in to attest to the dangers of breast implants. Campbell and Blais were gone, of course; they had been damaged too badly in the Colorado trial. O'Quinn had a whole new crop of experts, but Bernick was ready for them. Harris Busch, a professor at Baylor College of Medicine who was a critic of breast implants, spent parts of five days on the stand. During that time he admitted that the first time he had ever criticized implants was at a convention of plaintiffs' lawyers, and that there had never been a controlled study showing a connection between implants and disease. Another scientist, Nir Kossovsky from UCLA, who had supposedly come up with a way to test for an immune reaction, was forced to acknowledge that in his study of 250 women with breast implants—all of whom claimed to be ill—only two "tested" positive to immune reaction.

And so it went. O'Quinn would put an expert on the stand, and Bernick would poke holes in his testimony. Which would cause O'Quinn to put yet another expert on the stand, and they'd start all over again. This went on for months—yet in all that time, the one expert O'Quinn would not put on the stand was the man who had actually diagnosed Gladys Laas. His name was Bernard Patten, and he too was a doctor at the Baylor College of Medicine. By his own account, he had examined more than 1,000 women—women who had been fed to him by plaintiffs' lawyers all over Harris County. So when it came time for the defense to put on its case, Bernick simply read to the jury from Patten's deposition. It was devastating. He had believed that implants had caused autoimmune disease since 1988 but hadn't said anything for three years. His one paper on the subject, which he called his "disquisition," was

intended, he said, "to be a virtuoso demonstration of my knowledge of classical antiquity and oratorical techniques." And he said he had never told any of his patients that their implants had caused their disease.

By the time the testimony had ended, there was no doubt that Bernick had damaged the O'Quinn mystique. Just before the closing arguments, O'Quinn came down with a severe case of shingles. The trial was delayed until he recovered; the jury didn't get to deliberate until February, some three months after the trial had started.

When it emerged several weeks later, it rendered the single most confusing verdict in the entire history of the breast-implant litigation. In the case of Jenny Ladner, it found that the two companies were innocent of any wrongdoing. She got nothing. In the Gladys Laas case, the jury concluded that Dow Corning had not acted negligently, had not made a defective product, had not misrepresented the implants, and had not acted with "conscious indifference." It did not award Laas any punitive damages. As each question was answered by the jury, the plaintiffs' team seemed to sag under the weight of their growing defeat. But then, on the last question, the jury found Dow Corning guilty of a "deceptive trade practice," and awarded Laas and her husband $5.2 million in actual damages. In addition, the jury found that while Dow Chemical had not "conspired" with Dow Corning, it should nonetheless pay 20 percent of the damages to the Laases.

Even O'Quinn knew that the verdict was problematic. "Dave," he said quietly to Bernick after the jury foreman had finished speaking, "it don't make any sense."

Publicly, of course, O'Quinn spun a different tale. The next day, on CNN, he was asked point-blank about the jury's rejection of the charges against Dow Chemical. "They are clearly implicated," he retorted. "And I believe [the judge] will uphold that." But he was wrong. Dow Chemical's assessment was soon thrown out, when the judge found it inconsistent with the jury's other findings. And for the same reason, it seemed likely that the judgment against Dow Corning would be thrown out on appeal as well: it didn't square with the rest of the verdict.

But this vindication never came. Even before the Laas appeal could be argued, Dow Corning finally succumbed to the stark calculus of the mass tort: It filed for Chapter 11 bankruptcy protection. Despite the prospects for a reversal, it just couldn't wait any longer. At that moment all litigation was frozen, including the Laas case.

At a bankruptcy hearing a few days after the filing, Dow Corning President Gary Anderson tried to explain what had led the company to take this drastic step. It had already spent over $400 million in "costs and legal liabili-

ties." And despite its $2 billion commitment to the global settlement, there was no end in sight. "As we enter the summer," said Anderson, "we will face 75 cases, with over 200 plaintiffs represented. And it is going to be physically impossible for our corporation to deal with that." It was "ironic," he added, that this was happening now, just as "the science we talked about is beginning to come in [and] beginning to say there is no connection between the implants and the immune-system diseases that are alleged here."

And it was ironic. But so was this: because of the bankruptcy, the $5.2 million judgment awarded to the Laases still stood. Which meant that Gladys Laas and her husband held a liability that made them, in theory, Dow Corning's 20th-largest creditor.

Dow Corning filed for bankruptcy on May 15, 1995. Over the intervening months, the breast-implant mass tort has gotten no closer to being resolved. For most of this past summer, the non–Dow Corning defendants were engaged in marathon negotiations with the plaintiffs' steering committee to salvage what they could of the settlement. Pointer set two deadlines; both were missed. The third deadline, set for the end of September, would have been missed as well except that Pointer essentially pushed the plaintiffs' negotiators aside and struck his own deal with the companies. Under the revised terms, the three companies will pay anywhere between $10,000 and $100,000 to be rid of those cases at "the bottom end of the grid"—the cases that Gallagher's demands had brought into the settlement. That could well add up to $3 billion—a huge sum just to clear away the weakest cases. Those whose symptoms are more severe will be eligible for sums that could go as high as $1 million, but they have to pass much tougher medical criteria. It is a foregone conclusion that most of these women will opt out and keep suing. This could well mean that an additional 50,000 lawsuits will be filed.

Though it received far less publicity than the settlement talks, Dow Chemical was also engaged in a mammoth struggle this past summer. After Dow Corning's bankruptcy, numerous lawyers around the country refiled their Dow Corning lawsuits as Dow Chemical lawsuits. Suddenly Dow Chemical found itself on the receiving end of thousands of breast-implant suits. It first attempted to have the suits frozen, arguing that they could not be separated from the Dow Corning bankruptcy. By the end of the summer, though, it seemed clear that it was going to have to go to trial in at least some states. Its first trial began in Reno on October 2. Meanwhile, in Texas, the company is still fighting to keep cases in federal court rather than state court. If it loses that fight, it knows exactly what will happen next. O'Quinn and Laminack alone have 800 cases waiting for Dow Chemical.

As for Dow Corning, it's difficult to say at this point how or when it will emerge from bankruptcy. In some ways, bankruptcy gives the company some control over its destiny. The lawsuits have stopped. It has some breathing room. And it can deal with its problems before one judge, rather than piecemeal in courts all over the country.

Still, bankruptcy has hardly allowed Dow Corning to elude the plaintiffs' lawyers. In any bankruptcy, the creditors will have a large say in how events play out—and its main creditors are the plaintiffs. The plaintiffs' lawyers talk boldly about forcing the sale of the company, with the proceeds going to the plaintiffs. That, of course, is exactly what happened to A.H. Robins, the maker of the Dalkon Shield.

Dow Corning, for its part, is pushing for a "common issue" trial, which would allow a judge to set some kind of value for breast-implant cases—and determine the company's liability for the litigation. Bernick, of course, would try the case for Dow Corning, and who knows? Maybe, after hearing the evidence, the judge will rule that its liability is small, and Dow Corning can emerge relatively unscathed. In any case, the company and its opponents face months, and perhaps years, of legal wrangling.

In the meantime, the company's current CEO, Richard Hazleton, has tried to rally support in Washington, describing the plaintiffs' bar as "Litigation Inc.," and calling on Congress to pass a tort reform bill. Although breast implants have become Exhibit A for Republicans who want a tort reform measure, the bills currently under discussion would actually help the mass tort industry. Their centerpiece is a provision that would cap the size of outsize awards (think McDonald's coffee) that seem to assault common sense. With such a cap, though, lawyers out to make an old-fashioned killing will have to do it by accumulating many cases instead—in other words, by fomenting mass torts.

The one thing Dow Corning continues to have in its favor is the science. The Harvard study has since been published, and it too fails to show a link between silicone breast implants and disease. And an even bigger Harvard study is said to be only a few months away. FDA Commissioner David Kessler recently told Congress: "We now have, for the first time, a reasonable assurance that silicone-gel implants do not cause a large increase in... disease in women." So far, though, he has refused to lift his "temporary" moratorium, which, of course, triggered the mass tort in the first place. Nearly four years after Kessler's decree, the mass tort he helped create is not even close to ending.

Early one morning this past summer, with all the complexities of the breast-implant litigation swirling around him, Rick Laminack took time out from

an interview to consult privately with one of his associates. It turned out that the associate was in a meeting with lawyers from 3M, trying to settle some upcoming cases. When the interviewer expressed surprise that settlements were continuing, even after the Dow Corning bankruptcy, Laminack broke into a sardonic grin. "There are settlement talks going on in here every day," he said. His associate quipped, "Gotta pay the bills, you know." As the two lawyers swaggered out of the room, they both chuckled at the younger man's remark.

Months before, a plaintiffs' lawyer had been asked if there was anything to stop O'Quinn and Laminack from bringing breast-implant lawsuits forever. He thought for a minute. "No," he replied finally. "There isn't."

The Lawyer Companies Love to Hate

The New York Times, July 2, 2006

Sitting in the back of a town car this past Wednesday, as his driver pulled away from the federal courthouse and headed toward his hotel in midtown Manhattan, William S. Lerach reached for a ringing cell phone in the pocket of his natty suit. How had his day gone, asked the person on the other end. "We went two for two," said Mr. Lerach, the most aggressive, feared, and controversial plaintiffs' lawyer in the land. "It was a good day."

No, he didn't mean he'd won two cases—but what he'd won was almost as important. In two hearings, Lerach Coughlin Stoia Geller Rudman & Robbins, Mr. Lerach's San Diego–based firm, had been named lead counsel. For Mr. Lerach—indeed, for every big-time lawyer who makes his living suing companies on behalf of an aggrieved "class" of shareholders—being named lead counsel is the key to everything. The lead counsel controls the case. He negotiates the fees. And best of all, the lead counsel takes most of the lawyer's cut: 20 percent to 30 percent of whatever he ultimately extracts from the big bad corporation.

Of course you can't become lead counsel in a securities fraud case unless you're representing some shareholders who have been hurt by a company's misdeeds. And it now appears that Mr. Lerach's courting of shareholder plaintiffs has landed him in hot water with the Justice Department.

Late last week, a federal grand jury indicted Seymour M. Lazar, who had long been—how to put this nicely?—a regular in the stable of Mr. Lerach's former firm, Milberg Weiss Bershad Hynes & Lerach. (Last year, Mr. Lerach

and Melvin I. Weiss, a co-founder of Milberg Weiss, split the firm in two. Mr. Weiss's firm, based in New York, is now known as Milberg Weiss Bershad & Schulman.) The government contends that over the years, Mr. Lazar received some $2.4 million in kickbacks from Milberg Weiss for lending his name to literally dozens of stockholder class-action lawsuits brought by the firm. Mr. Lazar's lawyer maintains that his actions were "ethical and appropriate." While neither has been charged, both Mr. Lerach and Milberg Weiss have denied any wrongdoing. Typically, though, Mr. Lerach's camp has been the more aggressive in pushing back.

The people in Mr. Lerach's camp have been quick to cast the investigation as politically motivated, an example of a probusiness Republican administration going after a scourge of corporate wrongdoing—and a big contributor to the Democrats to boot. Besides, doesn't Mr. Lerach currently have a shareholder suit against Halliburton, one that even points the finger at its former chief executive, Vice President Dick Cheney? Hasn't he extracted so far $4.7 billion for the beleaguered shareholders of Enron, the company once run by President Bush's old friend "Kenny Boy"?

Mr. Lerach's lawyer, John Keker, said in a statement that "Bill Lerach has done more to protect shareholders than this SEC and the Department of Justice combined"—and made ominous references to Mr. Lerach's "powerful enemies."

While I have no way of knowing whether Mr. Lerach is innocent of the charges he may soon face—or whether the investigation is politically inspired—I do know that Mr. Lerach is hardly a candidate for canonization. For much of his career, he made his living playing a dirty game.

He would watch for the stocks of companies to drop, especially volatile high-technology stocks that missed their earnings estimate, and then he would round up a small shareholder like Mr. Lazar and race to the courthouse to be first in line to file a suit seeking class-action status. And then, usually with little else to go on, he would essentially torture the company with discovery motions and deposition requests and legal filings until it finally settled to make him go away.

And he was so gleeful about it! And so taunting! And so vindictive! He sued 3Com five times. Intel, too. He would tell executives of the companies he was suing, "I'm going to take away every penny you own." Once when Alan Shugart, the CEO of Seagate Technology, which was being sued by Mr. Lerach, started a campaign against "abusive litigation," Mr. Lerach sent him a note that said, "Dear Al: More is coming." John Doerr, the Silicon Valley venture capitalist, has called Mr. Lerach "a cunning economic terrorist."

In 1995, Congress passed the Private Securities Litigation Reform Act, whose purpose, in part, was to put Mr. Lerach out of business. Under the new law, in order to be named lead counsel, it no longer mattered if you arrived at the courthouse first with a suit; what mattered was whether your client was a big shareholder who had lost a lot of money. The law also made it much more difficult to sue companies simply because they reported bad news and their stock prices went down. Plaintiffs' pleadings had to have some, you know, facts.

For a while Mr. Lerach floundered. Other firms quickly forged alliances with big pension funds and stopped filing frivolous lawsuits, searching instead for actual fraud. Mr. Lerach, meanwhile, had his own troubles to deal with, especially a lawsuit brought by an expert witness who testified for the defense in shareholder lawsuits, and who asserted that Mr. Lerach had tried to litigate him out of business. Milberg Weiss wound up paying $50 million to settle the case.

But Mr. Lerach eventually figured out how to make his way in this new environment. Which is why, when Enron came along, a real fraud by any reckoning, he could claim the University of California Regents as his client, and land the coveted lead counsel spot.

If Mr. Lerach's pre-1995 behavior shows him at his worst, the Enron case shows him at his best. Put aside his flamboyant histrionics—Mr. Lerach surrounded by cameras, holding a box of "the shredded evidence," as he called it. Focus instead on his legal tactics. The money Mr. Lerach has won for shareholders has come largely from the banks and investment banks—including Citicorp and J. P. Morgan Chase, which recently settled with Mr. Lerach for $4.2 billion combined—that did Enron's bidding. (And there are more banks that will probably be settling with Mr. Lerach in the not-too-distant future.)

Yet he has won this money despite a clear-cut 1994 Supreme Court decision that banks cannot be held liable for aiding and abetting a securities fraud—something they clearly did in the Enron fraud. Knowing this, Mr. Lerach cleverly wrote a 500-page complaint that never once used the words "aiding" or "abetting," but asserted instead that the banks and Enron had "schemed" together to defraud investors.

Larry E. Ribstein, a law professor at the University of Illinois, called Mr. Lerach's brief "a masterpiece: he made the most convincing case that could be made." By the time all the banks he's suing have settled, Mr. Lerach will have probably generated upward of $6 billion for shareholders, and he'll keep 8 percent of that. (He cut his usual fees to get the case.)

In his town car, I asked Mr. Lerach about the effect of the 1995 law. His

answer was not surprising. "I think the law contributed to the scandals," he said flatly. "When the new law was passed, some very fine cases got thrown out. That emboldened executives."

To which I say, "Baloney." The 1995 law did exactly what it was supposed to do. It made it much more difficult to win the kind of lawsuits that used to be Mr. Lerach's stock and trade: the ones that were never about corporate wrongdoing, but were about cost-benefit analysis. Much of the fraud now being prosecuted took place because we were in a bubble, and greed overtook fear. And strangely, the law wound up helping Mr. Lerach, because when the big cases like Enron came along, he had one of the few plaintiffs' firms with the money and talent and wherewithal to run with them. He finally got to play the good guy for real.

And yet I couldn't help noticing that even now, Mr. Lerach's firm files a lot of lawsuits that seem to be based on not much more than some bad news and a big drop in the stock price. Eastman Kodak, OfficeMax, DreamWorks SKG and dozens more companies are facing that kind of lawsuit from him. He also has a new version of the small shareholders he used to have in his hip pocket: various plumbers' and pipe fitters' unions in places like Tennessee and Kentucky.

Mr. Lerach gave an unapologetic shrug when I asked him about these suits. "We like to have a lot of cases," he said. "That's our business model. It keeps you sharp. It's good training for your young lawyers." He described some of his competitors in the plaintiffs' bar, the ones who stick to big institutional clients and only file lawsuits against the likes of American International Group and WorldCom as "living off the low-hanging fruit."

With that, Mr. Lerach hopped out of the car and walked into the hotel. The old dog knows some new tricks. He really does. His problem now is that he can't stop using the old ones.

CHAPTER 7

How the Bancrofts Blew It

One day in late 1996, John Huey, who had hired me at *Fortune*, attended a dinner with Bill Gates. There were maybe a half dozen other top business editors at the dinner, and at some point somebody asked Gates a question about Dow Jones, the company that owned *The Wall Street Journal*. For most newspaper companies, the threat to their profits posed by the Internet was still well into the future, but Dow Jones was in a different, and altogether tougher, spot: it was a financial data company as much as a newspaper company, and it was being eaten alive by the competitors like Bloomberg, Reuters, and Thomson. Its stock had dropped 40 percent over the previous decade.

Gates gave a long, detailed response—so detailed, in fact, that Huey's antennae went up. "He knows way too much about Dow Jones," I remember him saying again and again over the next few days. Why had Gates learned so much about Dow Jones' predicament? Was Microsoft thinking about making an offer for the company? Or maybe Gates was consulting with his good friend Warren Buffett, who sat on the board of The Washington Post Co. and owned the *Buffalo News*. Huey didn't know the answer, but he smelled a story.

I have worked for many terrific editors in my career, but few could see around corners the way John Huey could. That was his gift. In this case, we never did find out how Gates had acquired his deep knowledge of Dow Jones. But, boy, was there a story!

The story, of course, was that two members of the Bancroft family— Elisabeth Goth, then 32, and William Cox III, then 41—had begun a campaign to persuade the rest of their family to start demanding better results from Dow Jones management. For the Bancrofts, this was an unprecedented event; in nearly a century of ownership, the family had always prided itself on backing management, and otherwise staying out of the way. This was

true even of the family members who sat on the company's board. It was also a family that abhorred publicity. It proved enormously difficult to get any Bancrofts to talk about their internal divisions—even Elisabeth wouldn't talk to us for fear that her family would retaliate. On the Friday night we were closing the story, she finally authorized one of her advisers to give us a background interview—and thank goodness. At least half the details about her odyssey came from that interview.

As it happens, John Huey conducted that interview and then fed me the details to weave into the narrative. There were times when it felt as though half the *Fortune* staff was working on this story. I was used to doing stories on my own, taking months if necessary. This was a very different experience, a story that was pulled together quickly, and that resulted from an old-fashioned team effort of the sort Time Inc., *Fortune*'s publisher, used to be famous for. It was surprisingly satisfying.

You read this story now—with Dow Jones and *The Wall Street Journal* having passed into the hands of Rupert Murdoch—and you don't know whether to laugh or cry. Elisabeth was right to be worried about her family's reaction to the publication of our story; led by their trustee, Roy Hammer, the Bancrofts responded by giving her and her cousin William the cold shoulder for years. But instead of scorning the two young Bancrofts, the others should have thanked them for sending up a warning signal they could have—and should have—heeded. Murdoch wouldn't arrive on the scene for another decade. In that time, nothing changed. The stock was still a laggard. The company was still troubled. The competition from Bloomberg et al. was fiercer than ever. And the Bancrofts had never budged from the view that demanding results from management was an act of disloyalty.

I spoke to Elisabeth frequently after Murdoch made his bid for the company in early 2007. At first, she was as leery of him as the rest of her family. But in time, she came to the view that there really wasn't any choice. The company could no longer go it alone, no other media company was willing to match or top Murdoch's offer, and the Bancrofts, through their negligence, had forfeited their right to own Dow Jones. As Elisabeth told me in the *Times* column I wrote after the Bancrofts finally voted to sell to Murdoch, the Bancroft family dynamics—dynamics our *Fortune* story had first exposed—made it impossible for them to be good stewards of a company, and a newspaper, they all so clearly loved.

Disgruntled Heiress Leads
Revolt at Dow Jones

Fortune, February 3, 1997

The world of business didn't take much note last May of the death, from lung cancer, of 55-year-old Bettina Bancroft in Los Angeles. Perhaps it should have. Ms. Bancroft, you see, was one of nine great-grandchildren of Clarence W. Barron, the portly Boston journalist who, in 1902, persuaded his wife, Jessie, to buy *The Wall Street Journal* and the Dow Jones News Service with a $2,500 down payment. Barron died in 1928, leaving behind what would eventually become a ton of Dow Jones & Co. stock tied up in various trusts for his descendants.

Bettina Bancroft was a vivacious woman, given to wearing ostrich plume dresses, who entertained grandly at her Hollywood Hills mansion, dined often at hot spots like Spago, and charmed most who came within her circle. Her passion was horses; a world champion in five-gaited riding, she also bred Morgan horses on her farm in Rancho Santa Fe, California.

She had another passion, though. Like the rest of her generation of Barron heirs and heiresses, she was a loyal supporter of *The Wall Street Journal* and of the management team that ran Dow Jones. Along with the other three family members who sat on the company's board, she unfailingly backed management—even during this past decade, when a string of disastrous business decisions has produced dwindling profit margins, a return on equity that is less than half what it was ten years ago, and a stock—recently around 36, down from its 1987 high of 56$\frac{1}{4}$—that has missed the greatest bull market in history. Always, Bettina Bancroft voted the way management asked, hewing to the long-held family view that Dow Jones was akin to "a quasi-public trust"—as it was once phrased in a proxy statement—rather than the publicly held company it was.

Now Bettina is dead, and suddenly the torch has passed, for the first time, to a member of the next generation of heirs: her 32-year-old daughter, Elisabeth "Lizzie" Goth. Lizzie Goth isn't just another great-great-grandchild of Barron. In the first place, her Dow Jones stake is perhaps the largest of any member of her generation. At her mother's death, she received outright about 700,000 shares of stock, currently worth around $23 million. And she remains the beneficiary of hundreds of millions of dollars' worth of Dow Jones shares, still held in trusts, most of which won't be distributed until the last member of her mother's generation dies.

Soon after her mother died, Lizzie went to her money manager for an assessment of her Dow Jones holdings. His report was grim. At that point, according to a confidant, "she woke up and said, 'I care. This is my fortune. This is my asset. Now what do I do?'"

That question has launched Lizzie Goth on a seven-month quest in search of answers. Her travels have included visits with the likes of Warren Buffett; Nancy Peretsman, a media investment banker at Allen & Co.; Tom Murphy, former CEO of Cap Cities/ABC; and Ira Millstein, the corporate governance crusader who helped the GM board oust CEO Robert Stempel. In those visits, she has pursued three fundamental issues. First, is her $23 million stake in Dow Jones worth holding on to? Second, given the fact that she could have hundreds of millions of dollars' worth of the stock tied up in trust for decades, what can be done to get the share price moving in the right direction? And finally, when you have this kind of performance problem, whom do you hold accountable?

Innocent as her quest may have been in the beginning, it has angered a number of her relatives, chilled company management, and opened the first fissure in what could be the coziest partnership between a family and a publicly held company in America. Ultimately this fissure could have a profound effect on the company's management or its ownership, or both. As one source close to the action puts it: "The process has begun of trying to figure out what can be done about this company."

For a long time—for decades, really—the astonishingly passive relationship between the company and the family that owned it worked well enough. Although family members have always sat on the Dow Jones board, their essential belief was that good journalism was best left to good journalists—and that the highest goal of the company was to produce the best journalism possible. So unlike almost all other prominent newspaper-owning families—the Sulzbergers of *The New York Times*, the Grahams of *The Washington Post*, the Knights and the Ridders, the Scrippses and the Howards—the descendants of Clarence Barron have pretty much stayed out of the affairs of Dow Jones and *The Wall Street Journal*, content to collect dividends, rubber-stamp management requests, and bask in the reflected glory that came with owning an American institution. The only time anyone remembers that tradition being broken was at a board meeting some years ago when a Dow Jones executive outlined his plan to purchase a small community newspaper in New England. The late Jessie Cox, one of Clarence Barron's two granddaughters and a feisty, profane sportswoman, objected vociferously. That paper, she said, had written something scurrilous about one of her horses.

Another tradition embraced by the family has also worked for the better part of a century: always giving the top job at Dow Jones to a journalist—which, as a practical matter, has meant someone who has risen through the ranks of *The Wall Street Journal.* The current CEO, Peter Kann, made his mark as a Pulitzer Prize–winning foreign correspondent, while his predecessor, Warren Phillips, distinguished himself first as a foreign correspondent and then as managing editor of the paper. The late Barney Kilgore, the CEO generally credited as the visionary who shaped the modern *Journal,* was also managing editor.

There can be no doubt that this tradition has a lot to do with why *The Wall Street Journal* became one of the tiny handful of truly great newspapers in America. Over the years it has gained a deserved reputation as a uniquely literate, fearless, and enterprising paper, one that no serious businessperson could do without. In the decades of economic expansion following World War II it gained great prosperity as well, prosperity that peaked in the 1980s, when the appetite for business news reached something like a frenzy. In good times and bad, the people running Dow Jones put their journalistic mission front and center, even if it sometimes stood in the way of profits. In this, of course, the Bancroft heirs fully concurred. To this day, Peter Kann writes an annual letter to readers of the *Journal* in which he trumpets not the overall performance of the company—something just about any other CEO would do—but the journalistic feats performed by the *Journal*'s crack reporting staff.

Even after Dow Jones took its stock public in 1963, little changed in the relationship between family and company. The family held the vast majority of the stock, much of it in trust, and a handful of family members sat on the Dow Jones board, approving whatever management asked them to approve. In 1986, the family took a drastic step to ensure its continuing control of the company: Following the example of several other newspaper families, including the Grahams and the Sulzbergers, it added a second class of stock, called Class B, that had ten times the voting power of the common stock. And here was the kicker: whenever anyone sold any Class B stock, those shares would lose their magical voting powers and turn into common stock.

Among other things, this arrangement allowed family members to sell common shares from time to time, retaining control of the company through their Class B shares. It has worked: the family now owns slightly less than half the common stock, but it still controls some 70 percent of the Class B shares.

The arrangement had two other consequences, neither of which was viewed unhappily by either management or the family. First, at a time when hostile takeovers were in vogue, it was the ultimate defense. If someone were

to make a hostile bid for the company, the family would have the voting power to reject it, no matter how attractive it might be to nonfamily shareholders. The family made no apology for this: The creation of the second class of stock, a proxy read, "is in the best interests of the Company... because the retention of control by the Bancroft family is the most likely means of assuring the continued independence and integrity of *The Wall Street Journal* and the Company's other publications."

Even after the 1980s turned into the 1990s and hostile takeovers gave way to a more respectable kind of shareholder activism, Dow Jones remained the company that couldn't be touched. "It pops up on our screen all the time as a terribly underperforming company," says Bob Monks, who founded the shareholder rights group LENS (and who grew up in Cohasset, Massachusetts, down the street from several members of the Bancroft family). "But the stock situation makes it impossible to do anything about it. So we just go on to other, more productive things."

Second, the existence of the Class B shares makes it vastly more difficult even for a family member to threaten the cozy arrangement that exists between family and management. Why? Because the single most potent weapon a disgruntled heir has—the threat of selling a big block of stock to an outsider—is taken away. What outsider in his right mind would buy stock that loses most of its voting power the moment he gets his hands on it? No, a disgruntled heir would have to find some other way to shake up the company. She'd have to be tough, she'd have to be tenacious, and she'd have to be persistent.

Which, it turns out, is a fairly good description of Lizzie Goth, according to people who know her. (*Fortune* has never laid eyes on her or spoken to her.) At the age of 32, she is already a champion equestrienne, just as her mother was. This past November, for instance, at Madison Square Garden, she took first place in the American Saddlebred Three-Gaited Stake—this despite missing the first half of the show season because she was in the middle of a divorce. Also, like her mother, she is a strikingly attractive and vivacious woman—"a beautiful blonde who looks like a model," says a show horse aficionado.

She is said to be disarmingly candid, and to present herself as somewhat naive. Upon meeting investment experts, she is likely to begin by saying, Hi, I'm a large shareholder in a company I don't know much about. You guys are professionals. Help me.

At one such meeting, for example, she was told that Dow Jones is far from a star performer. "Is that because there is something wrong with the business they're in?" she asked. "No," she was told, "this isn't something terrible you want to get out of. This is one of the great franchises in the world."

. . .

And so it is. The problem has been that over the past decade, during the tenure of both Warren Phillips, who became CEO of Dow Jones in 1975, and then Peter Kann, whose stewardship began in 1991, Dow Jones has failed to cash in on its great franchise—and this in an age when brand management in the media business has never been more crucial. In a sense, that's the underlying story of Dow Jones in the modern media era. Back when the definition of a good newspaper company simply meant producing and distributing a good newspaper, Dow Jones was a superstar. But the more the world changed around it, the more Dow Jones seemed to lose its way. "They have been very slow at the switch and very risk-averse," says former Dow Jones executive vice president Bill Dunn. And as it flailed about, Wall Street began treating it with contempt. Over the past decade, for instance, Dow Jones has become the worst-performing stock in the S&P 500 publishing index. One particularly telling comparison is with Reuters, a company with which Dow Jones competes in the global electronic news business. Ten years ago, the two companies had roughly the same market capitalization, around $3.5 billion. Today, Reuters' market cap is more than $20 billion—while Dow Jones is still stuck at around $3.5 billion.

In fact, the only figure connected to the stock price that has gone up substantially in the past ten years is the amount Dow Jones has paid out in dividends: from $53.6 million in 1986, the payments rose to more than $90 million in 1996—about 50 percent of net income, a large proportion, though certainly satisfying to the Bancroft family.

And if the company's professional managers have been directly responsible for its sad decline, the family has hardly been blameless. By tradition, a block of board seats has been reserved for Bancroft family members, and no board members have been as resolute in their unquestioning support of management as the family directors.

Because of the byzantine web of Bancroft family trusts, not even Elisabeth Goth knows exactly how much she has at stake in the future of Dow Jones. But with several hundred million dollars in those trusts, she knows one thing for sure: she's left an awful lot of money on the table during the past decade's bull market. So you can hardly blame her for seeking advice on how to go about getting a better return on her investment. Even before she set out, she knew she had one ally inside the family—a cousin who had been grousing loudly about the performance of Dow Jones for years. His name is William Cox III.

Billy Cox, 41, is in a markedly different position from Lizzie Goth. For starters, he is one of the few Bancroft heirs who work for Dow Jones; his

title is management director, Dow Jones Global Indexes. His father, Bill Cox Jr., a board member, is also a longtime employee. The elder Cox, son of the late Jessie Cox (she of the horse maligned by the newspaper), is a jovial, beloved figure at Dow Jones and a man extraordinarily devoted to the company.

Within the family—and the company—Billy is regarded as something of a loose cannon, in no small part because of his willingness to speak his mind about Dow Jones no matter who happens to be within earshot. "The last ten years speak for themselves," he told *Fortune*. "In all honesty, if I were a portfolio manager, I would have to have been a fool to have this stock in my portfolio over that period." Over the years, Lizzie had heard him sound off at various family functions. So she enlisted her cousin in her quest.

Billy, who considers himself a value investor (and says he's done well at it), happened to read a paragraph in Warren Buffett's 1993 Berkshire Hathaway annual report that mentioned Dow Jones and Hershey Foods as examples of companies with controlling owners not involved in management. Through a contact in Chicago, he arranged for a meeting with Buffett, the Yoda of value investors, and traveled with Lizzie last June to Omaha to seek his counsel.

"It was a fact-finding mission to get his thoughts on what might be done to improve shareholder value and return on equity," says Billy. And what did Buffett have to say? "He said, 'Your company is really in the right place at the right time. It has all the ingredients to be a dynamite content company.'" And, the younger Cox says, Buffett had some ideas on how that might be accomplished. Among other things, Buffett brought up the name of his close friend Tom Murphy, the man who had built and run Cap Cities/ABC, with Buffett as the most important investor. His main piece of advice, though, was simply that Billy and Lizzie had some standing in the affairs of Dow Jones, and that they shouldn't be afraid to use it to prod the company to do something about its stock price. "Act like owners," Buffett said. Toward that end, he suggested that they sound out Murphy about the possibility of his taking on an important role at the company.

Shortly afterward, they made the next stop on their journey: a trip to an investment banker, in this case the folks at Allen & Co., famous for the annual summer media conference in Sun Valley, Idaho, at which important things sometimes happen—things like Disney's Michael Eisner sitting down with Buffett and Murphy and proposing to buy Cap Cities/ABC. Lizzie's money manager, Brian McNally, was a social friend of an investment banker at Allen & Co. named Nancy Peretsman.

Peretsman hosted a meeting for the two cousins, which turned into a

series of meetings. She knew little about Dow Jones, and so took the opportunity to learn a few things. And rather than offer Buffett-like advice, she took a "just the facts, ma'am" approach, laying out for Billy and Lizzie the performance of the stock price, the return on equity, the declining profit margins, the market cap: the whole horror show. Then she looked at the holders of Dow Jones stock other than the family and pointed out to the two heirs that few of the institutional investors that one would normally expect to find in a high-quality media company were present. But there was one highly interesting name on the list, George Soros.

Lizzie and Billy listened raptly and asked lots of questions. Mostly, they wanted to know: what else should they do? Where else should they seek advice? As it happened, Peretsman's husband, an investment banker at Morgan Stanley, knew somebody they might want to meet. That was Ira Millstein. So off they went again.

Millstein, 70, an engaging, aggressive corporate lawyer with New York's Weil Gotshal & Manges, has made a crusade in recent years of forcing corporate boards to begin taking seriously their role as the shareholders' watchdog. He got the chance to put this principle into practice, to spectacular effect, in 1992, when he advised the General Motors board in its ouster of CEO Robert Stempel. Millstein, who was neither a director nor an employee of GM, had developed a relationship with GM's outside directors in the 1980s when he was brought in to advise them on their feud with Ross Perot. When the directors felt that Stempel wasn't acting quickly enough to stem GM's losses and boost its market share, they came to Millstein, who worked closely with them as they first replaced Stempel as chairman, and then, six months later, pushed him out of the company altogether.

After hearing out Lizzie and Billy, Millstein quickly signed on. Dow Jones was exactly the kind of company Millstein rails against: a bigtime underperformer with a rubber-stamp board. Soon after that meeting, Millstein headed to Boston to see a lawyer named Roy A. Hammer, an important behind-the-scenes figure because he serves as trustee for many of the family trusts. Millstein told Hammer that he was representing Elisabeth and that he was "not there to cause trouble." But he did want to focus on the issue of fiduciary responsibility. He also asked for an opportunity to speak to the family directly. That meeting took place on December 18, and Millstein talked about corporate governance and Dow Jones's performance. The meeting, recalls Billy, was very well attended.

The split in the family's ranks was becoming more pronounced. On the one hand, there were relatives who were furious with Lizzie. "Some of the family was screaming at her, telling her to shut up and go back to California," says someone close to the situation. The family members who sat on the Dow Jones board rallied around the company. In an interview with *Fortune*, family board member Martha Robes went so far as to deny that a rift even existed. "I think Lizzie is very much behind the company," Robes said. "But she's listening to a lot of outsiders...who are getting her all wound up."

But Lizzie remained undeterred, and truth to tell, other family members found themselves increasingly interested in what she was doing. Lizzie invited several cousins of her generation to attend one of the informational meetings with Nancy Peretsman. When it was over, one Bancroft heir muttered, "I knew things were bad, but I didn't know they were *this* bad."

So how bad is it?

To hear Dow Jones executives tell it, you'd think there is just a little glitch in the works from time to time—nothing to worry about really. In an interview with *Fortune*, Kann expressed nothing but optimism about where Dow Jones is positioned in the increasingly competitive media marketplace. *The Wall Street Journal*, he said, has become a global newspaper during his tenure as CEO, a franchise "that has been expanded and leveraged." The paper's Web site has become "the most successful public site on the Web." The *Journal* had "its highest revenues in history last year," Kann said. His No. 2 man, Ken Burenga, added, "The *Journal* booked more ads in October than *Money* magazine will book for the entire year." Kann again: "It's unfair to view *The Wall Street Journal* as a problem."

Yes, Kann and Burenga conceded, the stock price took a hit in late 1996, but that was because of a slowdown in business in the Telerate division. They insisted they were on top of things. Burenga himself was running Telerate, at least for now. They had a plan. In their view, in fact, the market has not treated Dow Jones stock fairly: "I think part of our problem is that we're too candid," said Kann.

This, of course, is quite likely the same sort of explanation Kann has been giving to the Dow Jones board as the company has underperformed. But as Lizzie was learning from her advisers, management's explanations tend to go up in smoke the closer you look at them. There is a reason Dow Jones's stock price is stuck in the 30s and its market cap is one-sixth the size of Reuters'. The company's problems are serious.

Look at the litany of mistakes Dow Jones management has made over the years—selling its stake in Continental Cablevision in the 1980s; losing out to NBC for the Financial News Network; passing on the chance to control business news at CNN; and so on. Those mistakes probably cost Dow Jones billions of dollars.

It's "unfair" to see *The Wall Street Journal* as a problem? On the contrary, it's unreasonable to see it any other way. Yes, its revenues are at historic highs, but its profit picture tells a different story. In the midst of a financial services boom, the *Journal* has suffered declining profit margins: pretax margins in the early 1980s sometimes ran to almost 30 percent; in the past eight years, they've seldom exceeded 15 percent.

Expansion into other media? Yes, the *Journal* has a popular Web site, but in television it has invested hundreds of millions of dollars over the years, with nothing to show for it but losses—between $40 million and $50 million in this past year alone. And then there's the real noose around the company's neck: Telerate.

Telerate is in the business of providing sophisticated, real-time data to Wall Street professionals. On the face of it, that sounds like a good business for Dow Jones to be in—a natural way to extend the franchise. Certainly, that is what the company thought when it purchased Telerate, something it did piecemeal between 1985 and 1989, at a cost that eventually added up to $1.6 billion, making it by far the most expensive acquisition in the company's history.

Telerate and certain other businesses that Dow Jones lumps together as "financial information services" are today a big part of the company, producing revenues that in 1995 were $960 million and close to being as large as the *Journal*'s. That year, the information businesses also earned $197 million in pretax operating profits, though how much of that is Telerate's isn't clear. Kann says only that Telerate has been consistently profitable.

Plainly, though, Telerate's problems go way beyond its immediate profits, whatever those are. This operation is a sponge for money. Said Kann in the 1991 annual report: "Telerate is a business that requires continuing investment—in some cases to meet the competition and in other cases to leap ahead of it—and Dow Jones is making those investments."

Critics charge that one reason Telerate has floundered is that Dow Jones replaced most of the entrepreneurs who built the company with risk-averse middle managers, including several journalists. Today its terminals are outmoded, and the kind of simple, real-time information they provide seems out of a different era when compared with Bloomberg terminals, which offer historical comparisons—and a great deal besides—at the press of a button. And Telerate in recent years has been squeezed both from above—as Reuters continues to widen its commanding lead in this market—and from below, where Bloomberg, Telerate's newest competitor, has been making tremendous inroads.

"Telerate?" scoffs a Wall Street money manager. "I ripped my terminals out two years ago. I don't know anybody who uses Telerate anymore.

Bloomberg is so much better it's ridiculous." Adds a former high-ranking Dow Jones executive: "Once Bloomberg gets up and running overseas, where Telerate now does most of its business, they'll blow right past Telerate."

"Everyone knows what the problem is at Dow Jones," says an investment banker who specializes in media deals. "They have a market cap of around $3.5 billion and $1.6 billion tied up in Telerate. If they had to sell it tomorrow it's very doubtful they could get $1.6 billion, and there is some question as to whether they could get anything at all." This investment banker went on to say that what really spooks Wall Street about Telerate is the specter of Quotron—the once dominant maker of stock quote terminals that was driven out of business when newer, better technology passed it by. Citicorp, which had bought Quotron, ultimately wound up writing off $500 million.

This past year, Kann and Burenga were finally forced to confront the problems at Telerate. Carl Valenti (a current board member), who had been running the division, was pushed aside and Burenga himself took over the operation. And Kann conceded at a Paine Webber conference in December that Telerate was the reason Dow Jones's 1996 earnings would be 5 percent lower than its 1995 earnings. He terms the earnings drop "mildly disappointing."

Naturally, the analysts at the meeting pressed Kann about what he was doing to turn Telerate around. He insisted that the company has a strategic plan to fix the problem but that he wasn't ready to unveil it. In the interview with *Fortune*, both Kann and Burenga expressed confidence that they could fix Telerate. "We have a focused strategy that we are beginning to promulgate throughout the company," Burenga said. "We're going to update our infrastructure to deliver content faster. We're going to be making the investment we need to make. We're going to be expanding the kinds of data we offer."

But how much will that cost? That was something neither Kann nor Burenga was prepared to say. When told that *Fortune* had heard that Kann had presented the board with a figure of $700 million as part of his master plan, Kann denied it. "We've discussed with the board various levels of investments," he said. "This is still in the discussion stage. We've been talking about a wide range of figures at this stage."

Not coincidentally, in the period since Kann is said to have proposed the $700 million investment to the board, Elisabeth Goth has stepped up her schedule of meetings with family members to discuss the company's activities.

The rumored $700 million in further Telerate investment exemplifies everything Lizzie believes is wrong about the way Dow Jones and its board oper-

ate. Consider: we are now entering proxy season. She knows full well that at least four board members will probably be resigning their seats—including disgraced former Mexican President Carlos Salinas and family board member Martha Robes. In other words, management is trying to push through this plan before any new, possibly more independent board members can weigh in with questions or objections.

"How can they ask board members to approve something this significant when they aren't going to be around to be held accountable for it?" asks one person sympathetic to Elisabeth Goth's cause. It's a good question. And then there are others. Where do they get the $700 million? The balance sheet doesn't show it to be available. Will they borrow it? Will they issue stock, at a time when the company's shares are so low? "Okay, you borrow $700 million for Telerate and it doesn't work? Then what's the stock worth?" asks the same person.

Understand this about Elisabeth Goth, says this source: "Her mission is single-minded and uncomplicated. She is interested in seeing her only real asset, her stock, appreciate. At no time have I ever heard Lizzie say anything radical like, 'This company should be sold.'" So what is her plan? Right now, following the advice of Ira Millstein and others, she wants to see a management that is held accountable for its actions reporting to a board that feels accountable for the company's performance. And the only way that can happen, she feels, is for a group of knowledgeable, skeptical, respectable businesspeople to replace the retiring board members.

Roy Hammer has encouraged her to "be constructive" and become involved in the affairs of the board. He has encouraged her to offer suggestions for new board members. She is said to have suggested Tom Murphy, but at age 71, he has passed the mandatory retirement age for Dow Jones board members, so he isn't eligible. But this is what really separates Lizzie Goth from the pack: When she was approached about the possibility of taking one of the family board seats, she replied, "Why would you want me? I don't know anything about business. What we need is people who do." So much for co-opting this shareholder.

Right now, lists of candidates for the board are being compiled, probably by every faction. No doubt management has its ideas; current board members have theirs; and yes, Elisabeth has hers. *Fortune* hasn't learned who is on any of these lists, but nominations are due very soon, and it will quickly become apparent who's winning the first round of this struggle.

The struggle right now is not between good and evil but between a cozy board, thick with family members, and the idea—for it's no more than an idea at this point—of a tougher, more independent board with real

authority: a modern, professional board of directors. This, of course, would spell huge change for the way the company is managed. Dow Jones would no longer be a quasi-public trust coddled by a protective family, but a modern-day company, playing by modern-day rules.

One recent afternoon, the four members of the Bancroft family who sit on the Dow Jones board, along with Roy Hammer, placed a conference call to *Fortune*. The purpose of the call was to answer questions we had been posing to both management and family representatives about the recent activities of Lizzie, as well as some of the fiduciary issues raised by Ira Millstein in his meetings with Hammer and the family. The message they conveyed was unequivocal: They remained firm in their total support for, and confidence in, Peter Kann and his management team.

"They have a plan, and it's a good one," said Christopher Bancroft, 45, when asked specifically about the troubles at Telerate. Chimed in Bill Cox Jr.: "I support Dow Jones management 100 percent." The family members were dismissive of Lizzie's potential to effect change, calling her voting strength "insignificant." And Hammer said categorically that he has no fiduciary responsibility to any shareholders of the company other than those whose trusts he oversees. "The *Journal* is the finest business publication in the world," said Bill Cox Jr. as the conversation was winding down. "It is not for sale at any price."

He's right on one level: The *Journal* and Dow Jones are not for sale, and no one has suggested otherwise, including Lizzie Goth. She doesn't want to sell the company; she just wants to reform it. But on another level, Cox and the other family directors are dreaming if they believe Dow Jones can remain as it was before Lizzie began asking her naive questions. Suppose someone did put an offer on the table, an offer for, say, $65 a share. Would Lizzie's generation really stand by idly and allow their elders to turn it aside? Thanks to Lizzie, it seems unlikely. At the least, Roy Hammer would face a far more difficult dilemma than he would have even a year ago. Somehow everything's different now. And it's never going to go back to the way it used to be. "This is the first chink in the armor," says someone closely connected to the company who owns a chunk of the common stock. The once heretical thought—that Dow Jones and *The Wall Street Journal* could one day pass out of the hands of the Bancroft family—is no longer so unthinkable. No matter what else happens from here on, that is what Lizzie Goth has wrought.

A Family's Benign Neglect at Dow Jones

The New York Times, August 4, 2007

"The primary reason I was in favor of the deal," said Elisabeth Goth Chelberg on Wednesday, "is because I did not think that family ownership was ever going to be in the best interest of the company." She paused for a second, and then offered a small, sad correction. "I mean *this* family ownership."

"I just didn't realize that they were so disorganized," said Rupert Murdoch on Thursday. He shook his head in wonder. "I thought we would have a rational series of meetings. They didn't want that."

Ms. Chelberg is a striking 43-year-old woman who lives half time in Prague, where her husband is an entrepreneur, and half time near Lexington, Ky., where she raises show horses that she rides, with immense success, in competitions all over the world. Rupert Murdoch, of course, is a 76-year-old, Australian-born captain of industry who has spent his adult life single-mindedly building the News Corporation into a dominant global media company.

In other words, it would be hard to find an unlikelier pair of allies. But Ms. Chelberg is also a Bancroft, and over the last three months, as her family flagellated itself over whether to sell its beloved *Wall Street Journal* to Mr. Murdoch, Ms. Chelberg never wavered. Yes, her family had owned the *Journal*'s publisher, Dow Jones, for 105 years, and yes, it was a source of immense pride. But her fundamental belief was that her family had long since forfeited the right to own the asset. Benign neglect does not true ownership make.

Ms. Chelberg did not have a vote in the sale to Mr. Murdoch; her 800,000 shares were held in a trust controlled by her uncle, Christopher Bancroft, who fiercely opposed selling to Mr. Murdoch, fearing that he would destroy the paper's editorial independence. But she played a big role nonetheless. Indeed, it is not too much to say that this all started with her, 10 years ago. And what she started, Mr. Murdoch finished, as enough family members finally agreed to sell to him early this week. As the dust began to settle, I went to see them both.

"I really went to a lot of trouble 10 years ago," Ms. Chelberg said with a laugh as we sat at her dining room table in Kentucky. She had dug up some papers for me. One was a January 1997 letter to her family, imploring them to "act

as the owners we are." Several were legal bills: $73,000 in January 1997, $94,000 in April. "That went on for two years," she said with a grimace.

Ms. Chelberg was 33 then, single, a recovering alcoholic whose mother, Bettina Bancroft, had died the year before, leaving her an inheritance. Virtually all of it was in Dow Jones stock, some of which was in trust and some of which she owned outright. Not knowing a thing about the company—not really knowing anything about business—Ms. Chelberg decided she needed to understand this asset she now owned. As she wrote in that same 1997 letter, "I was very disturbed to discover that my investment in what I had been taught to consider an unassailable company had diminished in value—by approximately 40 percent from its 1987 peak to its recent levels."

Her search to understand what was wrong at Dow Jones caused her to seek out Warren E. Buffett, among others. She learned how other media companies had surpassed Dow Jones. She came up with a list of possible new board members. Her goal was never to see the company sold; rather it was to rouse her family, to make them realize that simply accepting management's view of the world was not the way to act like owners.

Her attempted wake-up call could have been a turning point for the Bancrofts and the company. In retrospect, she had given her family a 10-year window to grab control of the company, install new management, and give Dow Jones a fighting chance. But instead of being thanked, she and her cousin, William Cox III, who was also talking about management's failures, were scorned and vilified. She wound up selling the shares she owned outright. The shares in trust, however, she was stuck with.

"We were disenfranchised," Ms. Chelberg told me; it was years before she and Mr. Cox could even attend family meetings again. Some years later, several other cousins, including Crawford Hill, who would write a 4,000 word e-mail message supporting Mr. Murdoch, tried to raise many of the same issues. The same thing happened. "We all tried to work within the system, but there was no system to work within," she said.

Last fall, someone representing Mr. Murdoch came to see her and Mr. Cox to discuss the possibility of making a bid for Dow Jones. She didn't take it all that seriously; over the years, suitors had come and gone. So she was shocked in April when CNBC broke the news that Mr. Murdoch had made his audacious $60-a-share bid for the company.

What didn't shock her was what stunned the rest of us: the extent to which the family's dysfunctional nature was placed on vivid and painful display. Christopher Bancroft, who is a board member as well as a trustee, absurdly boycotts a crucial family meeting—and then, even more absurdly, asks Mr. Murdoch to pick up his personal expenses in exchange for abstain-

ing from voting, only to discover that the trust doesn't allow it. Another family board member, Leslie Hill, decides after meeting him that she doesn't like Mr. Murdoch, and refuses to take his phone calls after that. The family keeps asking for Mr. Murdoch to up his offer, failing to understand that he has zero incentive to bid against himself. A family matriarch resigns as a trustee the day before the voting. And on, and on.

Watching the family flail these past few months, one couldn't help agreeing with Ms. Chelberg's assessment: the Bancrofts simply weren't capable of owning Dow Jones. They were barely capable of selling it. "We took from this asset, instead of giving to it," she said, speaking of the hefty dividend that cut into Dow Jones's earnings. She, meanwhile, had spoken again to Mr. Buffett, who told her that Dow Jones would have trouble competing as an independent company. So did other experts she spoke to.

She acknowledges that Mr. Murdoch could wreck the paper. "But that is a risk you would take with any new owner," she said. "He has a tremendous opportunity," she continued, "and I don't think he's going to blow it. He's going to put money in the company, he'll grow the brand, and he can do things through his distribution channels we never could. TV? We lost that chance 20 years ago."

Was she happy Dow Jones had been sold? No, she said, but she had made her peace with it. "Ultimately, my love of *The Wall Street Journal* is what caused me to support the sale."

When I went to see Mr. Murdoch the next day in New York, he succinctly made the point that Ms. Chelberg had been working toward the previous afternoon. "The first road to freedom," he said, "is viability."

What he means, of course, is that a newspaper has a lot better chance of being editorially independent if it makes healthy profits. What he didn't say is that if the Bancrofts had turned down his deal, Dow Jones's steady, inexorable decline would likely have continued. But then, he didn't have to say it. Enough Bancrofts finally understood what their negligence had wrought. That's why they sold him the paper.

We had breakfast in a small private dining room in the News Corporation's Manhattan headquarters. Seeing that I had come tieless, Mr. Murdoch quickly doffed his tie and jacket, leaned back in his chair and happily recounted stories from the deal.

Was there ever a time he thought of pulling the offer? I asked. "Yeah," he replied. "After they sent that letter. It was so insulting." That was the letter in which the Bancrofts hoped to ensure editorial integrity by giving themselves the right to nominate News Corporation directors as well as a special

editorial board for *The Wall Street Journal*. He swiftly rejected it, and eventually the Dow Jones board took over the negotiations that resulted in the creation of a small oversight board to protect the paper's editorial independence.

Mr. Murdoch himself seemed unruffled by the need for such an agreement—or even by the accusations that he runs roughshod over the newspapers he owns. "I'm used to it," he shrugged. He dismissed the idea that he would meddle inappropriately with a quick one-liner: "I won't meddle any more than Arthur Sulzberger does," he joked. (Arthur Sulzberger, Jr. is the chairman of The New York Times Company.)

My own view is that the chances of Mr. Murdoch wrecking the *Journal* are lower than you'd think; he needs a credible *Journal* for his own strategic purposes, and at 76, he surely must be thinking about his legacy. Besides, in the *Journal*'s cantankerous, provocative, deeply conservative editorial page, he already has the opinion page of his dreams, and one that packs enormous political clout.

Which is not to say he isn't going to *change* the *Journal*. "We have lots of decisions to make," he said. "How much should we really spend developing the Saturday paper? What should we do digitally? Should we remain subscription-based on the Web, or should we make it free? How much should we spend beefing up political and international coverage? I want it to be more competitive with *The New York Times*," he added. "But that will be expensive."

He suddenly picked up a *Wall Street Journal* that was lying in front of him, and I could almost see the ink flowing through his veins. "I would like to see real breaking news," he said. "I like A-heds"—the famous less-than-serious feature that often runs down the middle of the front page—"but I don't like a whole page of A-heds."

He scanned the front page up and down. Sometimes his expression suggested deep approval of what he was seeing; but sometimes he frowned, suggesting that he had a different idea of what ought to run on the front page of this great newspaper he would soon own. "I just think the *Journal* needs a little more urgency," he said finally.

Myself, I'll miss the A-heds if Mr. Murdoch decides they should disappear. But I won't view it as the End of Journalism as We Know It, nor will I view it as evidence that Mr. Murdoch is destroying the editorial integrity of *The Wall Street Journal*. Rather, I'll view it as an example of a new boss who has strong views about what people want from a newspaper.

And if the Bancrofts miss the A-heds? They can't say they weren't warned.

CHAPTER 8

Saint Warren of Omaha

B y the late 1990s, Peter Lynch had faded into the sunset—and in a sense, so had mutual funds. Although the industry continued to gain hundreds of billions of dollars in assets, that was mainly because it was the happy beneficiary of a major change in the way companies handled retirement benefits. For decades, the primary retirement vehicle had been the pension plan, which companies managed, and from which retired employees drew monthly stipends. Starting in the 1980s, however, pension plans began to fall by the wayside, and employees were expected to make their own retirement investment decisions, through a new device called a 401(k) plan. The vast majority of such plans offered an assortment of mutual funds as their primary investing options. Thus did the mutual fund industry direct its marketing firepower toward corporate decision makers, instead of individual investors.

And yet this was also a time when individuals were investing with an abandon the country had never seen before. Except that it wasn't in mutual funds; it was in stocks, especially technology stocks, which only seemed to go in one direction: up. In the 1920s, investing was equally frenzied, but it was mainly the "swells" who were in the market; most Americans lacked the means to invest. In the 1990s, though, it was easy to invest in stocks. You didn't even have to use a broker! You could set up an account with an online brokerage and begin trading just like the big boys. And of course that's exactly what thousands of people began doing, many of them even quitting their jobs to do it full time. We had entered the age of the day trader.

Early in his retirement, Peter Lynch had written a series of highly readable investment books—the best known of which was the first, *One Up On Wall Street*—in which he argued that (as *Publishers Weekly* put it) "average investors can beat the Wall Street professionals by using the information

179

gleaned from everyday life." Around 1992 or so, I traveled with him to Chicago, where he was doing a series of appearances to promote his second book, and what I remember most clearly about that trip is that everywhere he went, he was treated like a king. People wanted his autograph, or a word of advice, or just a chance to shake his hand. It occurred to me then that if investing were really as easy as Lynch said it was, he would not be the subject of such adulation. He was an icon for the same reason Michael Jordan was: he could do something the rest of us would love to be able to do—but couldn't.

The same is true, I'm convinced, of Warren Buffett. It is not an accident that he went from being a business celebrity to a full-fledged cultural figure right around the same time stocks were replacing mutual funds as the investing vehicle of choice for the middle class. During the 1990s, we had convinced ourselves that we had the skill to make money in the stock market—just like Buffett! But, really, the only reason our portfolios were climbing is because the bull market was making everyone look like investing geniuses. It usually does.

Still, I've always thought that on some level, we understood that what Buffett did and what we did were very different things—just as we had once implicitly understood that about Lynch, no matter how much he proclaimed that we could beat the Wall Street pros. Buffett has the intelligence, the judgment, and the emotional makeup to be a true value investor, which is a very hard thing to be. We, on the other hand, were chasing high-flying tech stocks. Investors would flock to the Berkshire Hathaway annual meeting—"the capitalist's Woodstock," Buffett likes to call it—to listen to his words of wisdom. And then we would go right on investing the same foolish way we always had. It was bound to catch up to us. And sure enough, it did. By then, though, I had come to the belief, which I hold to this day, that most people simply don't have the makeup—especially emotionally—to be good investors. That's why we'll never be able to follow Warren Buffett's example. And it's why I now view the democratization of money as, at best, a mixed blessing.

Saint Warren of Omaha

Money, July 1998

And then the skies parted for Warren Buffett. No, really. They did. It was the first Saturday in May, Omaha, Nebraska, the beginning of a three-day extravaganza known as the Berkshire Hathaway annual meeting. The

chairman and CEO of Berkshire Hathaway, of course, is Warren Buffett. But what investor doesn't know that already? And who among us hasn't heard how he turned this failing textile company into the vehicle through which he created what is perhaps the best sustained investment performance ever? And how, in the process, he turned his disciples—a.k.a. his shareholders—into millionaires, and transformed himself into the second richest man in America, worth around $34 billion. I mean, is this the greatest investment story ever told, or what?

Buffett uses this yearly event as an excuse to throw a gigantic party for the faithful. On Sunday, there would be a monster cocktail party at Borsheim's, the famous Omaha jewelry store Berkshire Hathaway owns (shareholders are welcome to buy jewelry!), followed by a trip to Buffett's favorite steakhouse, Gorat's, then another huge fete at the Dairy Queen on 108th Street, where Buffett would be on display slurping down a sundae. (Berkshire Hathaway bought the Dairy Queen chain last year.) On Monday would come the annual meeting itself, and some 11,000 Buffett followers would crowd into Omaha's largest arena to soak up the wisdom of their guru and his legendarily laconic sidekick, Charlie Munger, in an all-day session more closely resembling an investment teach-in than a typical corporate annual meeting. The tone of the whole weekend, in fact, would have less to do with gaining insight into the genius that truly sets Buffett apart—something not easily reduced to a sound bite or folksy remark—than with a seductively simple kind of blind faith.

Which was what made Saturday's threatening skies so fascinating. The only shareholder event that day—other than the opportunity to buy furniture (at the employee discount!) at the Buffett-owned Nebraska Furniture Mart—was an Omaha Royals baseball game. Buffett, who owns 25 percent of the team, likes to start the weekend by throwing out the first ball before heading to the upper deck, where, amid a jostling horde of cameramen, he signs autographs and poses for pictures with shareholders until the game ends.

But this year it had been raining all day, the kind of hard, steady downpour that doesn't offer much hope. The weather reports were equally grim. Shareholders, who had been arriving at the Omaha airport from all over the world, began muttering darkly about alternate plans; what would they do if the game was canceled? It was an awful thought. But then the clock struck 5 P.M., and the rain suddenly stopped, and the sun broke through the clouds. Two hours later, when Buffett threw out the first pitch, the field was dry enough to play on and the weather just about perfect. It stayed that way for the duration of the game. And wouldn't you know it? The moment the game

ended and Buffett headed for home, the skies darkened. By the time the stands emptied, the downpour had begun again in earnest.

Among the Buffett faithful, no one seemed the least bit surprised.

Is it too much to call Warren Buffett a modern-day miracle worker? Oh, probably. It's not as if he walks on water, though I suppose one could argue that an investment record like his—an average annual gain of over 30 percent since 1965—is a kind of modern equivalent. He is certainly a living, breathing refutation of the "random walk" theory so beloved by academics— the notion that stock movement is random because all information about the future prospects of a company has already been built into the share price. The academics explain away Buffett by pointing out that in any game of chance someone has to come out on top—it just happens to be him.

But you know that's not true; it's like saying that the reason the ball goes in the basket more often for Michael Jordan has to do with luck, not skill. No, like Jordan, Buffett has something we mere mortals have no real hope of emulating. And hence the real Buffett paradox, which is quite the opposite of the supposed random walk paradox. Just as Jordan is far more likely to ascribe his success to hard work than to his supernatural talent, so too does the greatest investor of our time make investing seem easier than it actually is. Listening to him speak, reading his many writings on investing, absorbing his message, even watching his investment moves over the years, one is far more likely to gain hope than to lose it. How difficult can it be, after all, to buy Coca-Cola and hold it forever—which is at the core of Buffett's methodology? All the fancy trading techniques so beloved by modern Wall Street—the techniques that make it seem as though the big boys have an insurmountable advantage over the rest of us—Buffett eschews. He won't even invest in technology companies—because, he says, he can never hope to fully understand them—preferring to stick with his old standbys: the Washington Post Co., Gillette, Geico, and the rest of them.

And yet I came away from the Berkshire Hathaway weekend utterly convinced that what Buffett does is, in its own way, as unreachable as anything Michael Jordan does. So I take it back: What Buffett has accomplished in the course of his long career—and especially the way he's done it—really is miraculous.

Part of the reason Buffett creates the illusion that he can be emulated is that he himself seems so perfectly ordinary. He is neither strikingly handsome nor particularly charismatic; on the contrary, he seems rumpled most of the time. For a man worth $34 billion, he lives amazingly simply—his house is

the same one he's lived in for decades, for instance, and everyone in Omaha knows where it is. Yes, Bill Gates is his friend, but so are a lot of the people in Omaha he grew up with. Some years ago, *The Wall Street Journal* tried to paint Buffett as a hypocrite because—so the *Journal* alleged—he bought expensive suits and owned a private jet. But the story was a stretch. Buffett has long acknowledged the jet as his one indulgence—the Indefensible, he calls it, with appealing frankness. And as for the expensive suits, if Warren Buffett really is a clotheshorse, it was manifestly not in evidence during the weekend of the annual meeting.

Indeed, rather than hypocrisy, it is the opposite trait that is the most striking thing about Buffett. He comes across as someone refreshingly lacking in guile—someone who says what he thinks, who hasn't a trace of the paranoia that can often afflict corporate bigwigs, who doesn't worry about what the papers will say about him and who tries to accommodate people whenever possible. (In fact, the entire Berkshire Hathaway weekend is, in one sense, a giant attempt to accommodate his shareholders, who hunger for the chance to meet him and ask him questions.) All weekend long, the only times he got squirrelly were when reporters tried to pin him down on where he thought the market was headed. But who can blame him for dodging that loaded question? He is also, by the way, very funny, which is another part of his appeal. "If I taught a class in valuation," he said at one point during the annual meeting, "I would ask the students, for the final exam, to pick an Internet company and tell me how much it's worth." Pause. "Anyone who gave me an answer would flunk."

Then there are his business principles, which are equally appealing—at least in part because they are so at odds with standard operating procedure in corporate America. Buffett believes that investors should be buying a business, not simply a stock. He believes that, as the CEO of a giant holding company (in addition to its famous stockholdings, Berkshire Hathaway owns dozens of businesses outright and employs nearly 40,000 people), his job is to give his managers whatever support they need and otherwise stay out of their way. He isn't hankering to change the tax code so he can pay less. "I'd rather be the one paying the taxes than be the person on the other side, someone who needs help from the government," he says. He believes that stock options mask a true reading of a company's earnings, so he refuses to grant any to Berkshire Hathaway's executives—and freely admits that this means he must find other ways to keep them motivated. He believes that annual reports should be both readable and honest. And on and on.

Buffett's own annual report is nothing if not readable—quite famously so. Recently, a law professor named Lawrence Cunningham compiled some

excerpts into a book, *The Essays of Warren Buffett: Lessons for Corporate America*. The professor showed up in Omaha to hawk his book, and at his booth outside the Borsheim's party, it sold briskly.

And why not? It is an extraordinary document, full of wisdom, humor, and common sense. For the millions of investors who don't come to Omaha, it is by far the best window into the way Buffett's mind works.

Here's a typical nugget: "After 25 years of buying and supervising a great variety of businesses, Charlie and I have not learned how to solve difficult business problems. What we have learned is to avoid them. To the extent we have been successful, it is because we concentrated on identifying one-foot hurdles that we could step over rather than because we acquired any ability to clear seven-footers."

And here is one that strikes me as about as good a one-paragraph summary of Buffett's investment philosophy as you'll ever read: "Whenever Charlie and I buy common stocks...we approach the transaction as if we were buying into a private business. We look at the economic prospects of the business, the people in charge of running it, and the price we must pay. We do not have in mind any time or price for sale. Indeed, we are willing to hold a stock indefinitely so long as we expect the business to increase in intrinsic value at a satisfactory rate. When investing, we view ourselves as business analysts—not as market analysts, not as macroeconomic analysts and not even as security analysts."

This is the essence of what I think of as the Buffett illusion. On the one hand, this paragraph is so steeped in old-fashioned values—largely vanished from trading-obsessed Wall Street—that one can immediately understand why Buffett has followers. How can you not fall for a guy who thinks like that?

On the other hand, the straightforwardness and simplicity of the language suggests that, really, Buffett's investing style just isn't that difficult. It amounts to a four-legged stool: Buffett cares about the future prospects of the business. He wants to know that management has both integrity and drive. He doesn't want to overpay for the stock. And whether the shares go up or down, he won't sell so long as the fundamentals remain the same. Isn't that the way we should all invest? Of course it is.

So why don't we? I think the answer is twofold. First, truly great investing requires a temperament that very few people have. For most of us, it is difficult not to panic when the market tanks, for instance. It is hard not to want to jump on the hot stock, even if we know nothing about the business. The ups and downs of the market are stomach-churning events. The fundamental equanimity required to be a great investor is an extremely rare thing.

Buffett, however, has that trait in spades. He is happy when markets tank because it means he can buy stocks he wants at a cheaper price. Indeed, one of the themes of the annual meeting this year was that this current upmarket, which has most of us rejoicing, is not the kind he prefers—because it makes it hard to find affordable stocks. "These are tough times for us," he kept saying all weekend. And he is never, ever ruffled—which I think is a key to great investing: his judgment seems never to be affected by emotion. At one point during the annual meeting, one of the shareholders asked him what kept him up at night. Buffett thought about that question for a minute, and then he replied: "Nothing."

The second reason we don't invest like Buffett is because his methods are a lot more complicated than they sound. Think about it: When Buffett talks about the "economic prospects" of a potential investment, what he means is that he wants to be able to see where its business will be 10 years from now. If he can see the business remaining dominant for the next decade, he'll consider buying the stock.

The next decade! Can you predict, with any certainty, how many of the companies you own will be dominant players in 10 years? Of course not. But Buffett can—and with a surprising amount of certainty. At a short press conference he gave on Sunday, a reporter asked him and Munger to name their biggest mistakes. "Our biggest mistakes," said Munger, "were things we didn't do, companies we didn't buy." Added Buffett: "The real mistakes were that we didn't do things we knew would work. We could have made billions and billions of dollars." You and I—we may do the best we can in looking into a company, but we don't know. Not like Buffett.

One of the most important reasons for this difference goes almost entirely unacknowledged among those who hope to find in Buffett an easily reproducible investing style. He is a genius when it comes to numbers. "Accounting," he likes to say, "is the language of business." It is a language in which his own fluency is unsurpassed, and which gives him an enormous competitive advantage. Usually, all he needs is a quick glance at a balance sheet to know whether he's interested in buying a company or not—because he finds meaning in numbers that the rest of us don't.

Again and again during the weekend, you could see his own shareholders struggling to get their arms around accounting ideas that are second nature to him. A classic example is "intrinsic value," which is Buffett and Munger's primary way of evaluating the true worth of a company—and which Buffett describes as "the only logical approach to evaluating the relative attractiveness of investments and businesses." He adds, "Intrinsic value can be defined

simply: it is the discounted value of the cash that can be taken out of a business during its remaining life."

Simply? Well, maybe for Buffett and Munger. But it sure isn't simple for the rest of us. Indeed, more than once shareholders asked Buffett to define intrinsic value during the annual meeting; his answer was invariably unsatisfying. It is just not something that can be explained easily, in front of 11,000 people. And besides, Buffett seems to feel that people should be able to figure it out for themselves: when a shareholder asked him what the intrinsic value of Berkshire Hathaway is, he responded by saying that he had provided all the pertinent information in the annual report and that the shareholders should be able to come up with it themselves. As if they could.

Here's the thing, though: over the course of the six hours that Buffett and Munger took questions from their audience during the annual meeting, such moments were largely lost, overshadowed as they were amid the general revelry—amid the jokes and the commonsense explanations and the string of self-deprecating remarks and pearls of wisdom. (My personal favorite: "Time is the enemy of the poor business and the friend of the good business.") Time and again, the Buffett persona overshadowed the Buffett genius.

Then again, it always does.

CHAPTER 9

The Rise and Fall of
Henry Blodget

Michael Milken, meet Henry Blodget.

Every boom needs its villain, and if Milken was the living, breathing embodiment of the 1980s boom, then certainly Henry Blodget played that same role during the tech bubble. As you see in the first of the two articles that comprise this chapter, I was horrified by the Blodget I first met, when he was riding high as the Internet analyst for Merrill Lynch. I thought his approach to stock picking was silly—utterly lacking in the kind of rigor that characterizes serious stock research. When the article was published, Blodget was furious, and left an angry voice message on my voice mail.

But of course it wasn't his shoddy analysis that caused his downfall. It was the fact that he had written e-mails to his colleagues absolutely trashing certain stocks he covered even though he had "buy" ratings on them. Everybody on Wall Street knew why he had done this: those "buy" ratings were intended to please the companies' executives and help generate investment banking business for Merrill. Indeed, the reason everybody knew it was because everyone else was doing it too. All up and down Wall Street, analysts' multimillion-dollar bonuses were tied to how much investment banking business they helped bring in. Few of them, however, were so foolish as to document their hypocrisy—in easily subpoened e-mails, no less!—as Blodget. Once then–New York attorney general Eliot Spitzer got ahold of those e-mails, Blodget was a goner. With the help of those e-mails, Spitzer forced the big investment banks to pay, collectively, over $1 billion in fines, and clean up the research side of the business. (Not surprisingly, the clean-up has brought its own set of problems, but that's a story for another day.)

As you'll see in the *Times* column I've included in this chapter, I've since come to believe that Blodget deserves a little redemption. Yes, what he did

was very wrong, but just as Milken didn't truly deserve to be the focus of so much investor anger, neither does Blodget.

Since being drummed out of the securities business, Blodget has become a writer, and a pretty good one at that. But because he's *Henry Blodget*, everything he writes always has a subtext that he can't shake. What offends me now is that so many people seem to still blame him for the mistakes they made during the bubble—as if a "sell" recommendation from Blodget would have caused them to sell off their Internet stocks and invest in T-bills.

But we know better than that, don't we? What really would have happened is that investors would have tuned him out, as they did to any bearer of bad news back then. In all likelihood, Blodget would have lost his job. And when the bubble finally burst, some other unlucky soul would have had to play the villain.

The Cheerleader

Money, June 1999

God, he's young. That's the first thing you think when you meet Henry Blodget. With his wavy blond hair, athletic frame and intense blue eyes, he looks like a West Coast frat boy who just got out of school. In truth, Blodget is a bit older than he looks—though he's still only 33. In his particular line of work, however, he is a grizzled veteran. His line of work is following Internet stocks, which he currently does for Merrill Lynch. He's been doing it for about four years. Which, as he points out with a wry smile, "is about as long as there have been Internet companies."

Do you know the story of Henry Blodget? Or rather, do you know the story of how he became the Man of the Moment? It took place just this past December, and it was one of those amazing Internet-stock moments that cause people to shake their heads in wonder.

At the time, Blodget was an Internet analyst at CIBC Oppenheimer, a small firm where an analyst has to make a lot of noise to get heard. One of his favorite stocks was Amazon.com, but it was coming under attack, with questions being raised about its business strategy and its stock price, which was—and remains—off the charts. The lead attacker was one Jonathan Cohen of—yes—Merrill Lynch, who was predicting that Amazon's stock price, then about $240 a share, would drop to $50.

So Blodget decided to make some noise. He raised his 12-month target

price for the stock to $400—an action akin to "throwing gasoline on a bon-fire," he now concedes. That day, Amazon rose more than 45 points. Shortly afterward, the stock split three-for-one, and it kept rising into the strato-sphere. Exactly 13 trading days after Blodget's call, the stock hit $134, thus topping his pre-split target. During those wild 13 days, Blodget was trans-formed from a nobody into a star. Soon after, Cohen left Merrill Lynch, where he was replaced by—yes—Henry Blodget.

Cohen was not permitted to talk to me for this story, because his new employer, Wit Capital, is in the quiet period prior to its IPO. But he has told others that his departure from Merrill was amicable—and unrelated to his bearish stance on one of the hottest stocks in the universe. Even so, it is instructive that Blodget replaced him. Let's be honest here: without that $400 call, it is extremely unlikely that Blodget would have been a big enough deal to merit wooing by Merrill Lynch. Yet what did that episode say about Blodget's ability to analyze Internet stocks? Not a thing. After all, if he had had a genuine rationale for his $400 target, he would have downgraded the stock once it hit his number. Instead, he continued to "pound the table" for Amazon, something he does to this day. What he was doing with that call was not analysis; it was cheerleading. Which raises the real question: when it comes to Internet stocks, does anybody really want anything more than that these days?

Perhaps there is a place for some Internet-related cheerleading—or at least some enthusiasm. Internet bears throw up their hands at the out-of-sight market caps of such stocks as eBay, Yahoo!, Amazon, and others. But the naysayers forget that there is a reason these stocks are being run up so dramatically. (And so quickly: wasn't it just months ago that we were mar-veling that Amazon's market cap equaled those of Barnes & Noble and Bor-ders combined? Well, as of mid-April, Amazon's $28 billion valuation was *eight* times the combined market caps of its two big rivals.)

The reason, of course, is that these stocks serve as the tangible proxy for the amazing potential of the Internet; the limitless valuations reflect the new medium's limitless future. Part of Blodget's job is to remind people of that future. As he put it in an "overview" report he wrote shortly after joining Merrill Lynch, "We consider"—Wall Street analysts have a thing for the royal we—"the Internet a global megatrend, along the lines of the printing press, the telephone, the computer and electricity." Surely he is right about that, which means that eventually some of these dot-coms are going to turn out to deserve their "crazy" valuations. Really, they are.

The other admirable thing about Blodget's work is its unflinching use of words like "bubble" and "gold rush." He concedes that there is no real way to

value Internet stocks, and he admits that some of these stocks are moving "out of the solar system." He assumes, first, that even though some companies will wind up justifying their stock prices, many others will not and, second, that when the bubble bursts, there will be "a lot of wreckage." Yet he also insists that "there are good reasons for investors to pay through the nose for the leading Internet companies."

But what are those reasons, Henry? It's when he grapples with that basic question that you begin to see how threadbare his analysis is. When you listen closely, what you hear from Blodget is that the main reason you should be buying Internet stocks is because other people buy them. Which is to say, his analysis is itself part of the bubble.

"Stocks don't go up or down because they have a specific 'value,'" he told me. "They go up and down because investors decide to buy or sell." In other words, the key issue is not whether a company's business model makes sense and will someday generate profits. Rather, it's merely a question of getting while the getting is good. In fact, Blodget goes so far as to say that the real mistake is being made by investors who *don't* throw some money into Internet stocks. After all, he says, the potential loss is finite—it can't exceed the original investment—but the potential gain is practically infinite.

What's more, he is convinced that big market caps alone won't burst the bubble. "We believe," he wrote in that same report, "that the broad-based Internet mania will end when the fundamentals at the leading companies stop improving...." Fundamentals? Now there's a word you don't hear very often in the same sentence with "Internet stocks." But what does the word mean when applied to, say, Amazon, a company fast approaching $1 billion in revenues but nary a cent in profit? Blodget, alas, doesn't have a clue.

"First of all," he said, when I asked him about this, "selling stuff online is a lot harder than it looks. There are subtle barriers to entry." Such as? "Creating a good customer experience. Building a brand and reputation. Back-end fulfillment. If there were no barriers, then all these companies would be the same size. Instead, you have one company, Amazon, with towering market share, and all the others are small."

The problem with this answer is that it doesn't really speak to the fundamentals of Amazon's business; it's more a logical deduction than an act of securities analysis. And indeed, when you push further, you discover that what Blodget really means by "fundamentals" is growth, which is not the same thing at all. As he put it in his first Merrill Lynch report on the company, given that "Amazon.com has blown away expectations since its IPO, it seems reasonable to assume that it might continue to do so." Really? When I

asked Blodget about this line, he shrugged. "It's something you have to take on faith," he said.

That's the real problem with Henry Blodget; his so-called stock analysis is a giant leap of faith. In that same report on Amazon, written in early March, Blodget noted that if one employed a standard Wall Street model with five-year projections for the size of the customer base, revenues per customer and the like, the stock seemed to be worth around $30 a share. He even admitted that those were his own "official" projections. And yet, while the stock then stood at about $130 a share, he had a "long-term buy" on it. So how did Blodget square that circle? He simply assumed that the company would blow away the projections, since, after all, that's what it had always done. Once he made that assumption, he wrote, "suddenly the stock is worth $150." Of course, as I write this column, the stock is closing in on $190. But never mind.

Look, I know it's tough to be an Internet analyst. With the obvious exception of Netscape, which had the misfortune to run into a buzz saw called Microsoft, no brand-name Internet stock has yet rewarded an analyst for downgrading it. But that doesn't excuse the cheerleading that masquerades as analysis. Of course stocks go up when more people are buying them than selling them. But tulips went up too. An analyst's job is not to say, "All aboard the gravy train." It is to make sense of the gravy train, to understand why some companies deserve their multiples and some don't, to prepare for the day when fundamentals once again matter.

And they will, you know, even for Internet companies. By then, Henry Blodget will be a little older. Let's hope he's also a little wiser.

Led into Temptation? Who Wasn't?

The New York Times, September 3, 2005

Before he became an Internet analyst, Henry Blodget wanted to be a writer.

Let me rephrase that. Before he became the living, breathing embodiment of Wall Street wrongdoing during the late, unlamented Internet bubble, Henry Blodget wanted to be a writer. (That's more like it, right?) After living in Japan in his 20s, Mr. Blodget wrote a book about his experiences, which was never published. Later, he eked out a meager living in New York as a freelance writer and copy editor.

So it is hardly a surprise that as he tries to recover from his post-bubble disgrace, the former Merrill Lynch analyst has returned to his first love. In 2003, Mr. Blodget began writing regularly for *Slate*, the online magazine, where he has covered the Martha Stewart trial and the business explosion in China, among other things. Articles under his byline have also appeared in *New York* magazine, *Business 2.0*, and most recently, the Op-Ed page of *The New York Times*.

The *Times* article, which ran on Tuesday, used the 10th anniversary of Netscape's initial public offering to meditate on the nature of booms and busts. It was smart, cogent, well written, and—regarding Mr. Blodget's own travails—disarmingly self-deprecating. It made the worthy point that both the Internet bubble and subsequent bust were of a piece with booms and busts from time immemorial, and that promising new technologies, from railroads to personal computers, are always accompanied by initial flights of crazed enthusiasm, as money chases ideas both good and bad. Eventually, though, the bad ideas go down in flames, along with investors' capital. After which, the smaller handful of good ideas serve as the foundations for entire new industries.

To judge from the handful of letters the newspaper received, however, one of them published yesterday, readers were in no mood to hear sage words about bubbles—or anything else—from Mr. Blodget. They're still too mad at him for losing their money. As one letter writer, an ex-securities analyst herself, put it, "It broke my heart (and investors' wallets) when my former profession was degraded under the watch of Mr. Blodget."

As you'll no doubt recall, it was Mr. Blodget's private e-mail messages disparaging companies he was publicly promoting to investors—companies from which Merrill Lynch was reaping investment banking fees—that pretty much catapulted Eliot Spitzer's career as a Wall Street crusader. For his sins, Mr. Blodget paid a $4 million fine to the Securities and Exchange Commission, and agreed to be banished from Wall Street forever. Though plenty of other analysts were pushing unworthy stocks because of banking fees—so many, in fact, that Mr. Spitzer, the New York attorney general, was able to extract $1.4 billion from the big Wall Street firms and force a series of reforms on the profession—only two were singled out for public humiliation and punishment: Mr. Blodget and the Salomon Smith Barney telecommunications analyst Jack Grubman. If there is a Wall Street version of the Scarlet A, Mr. Blodget wears it.

Myself, I think it's time to give the guy a break.

In sticking up for Henry Blodget, I am not sticking up for what he did. It was wrong, a violation of his responsibility to investors. Nor am I arguing that

his punishment outweighed his crime; after all, he never faced criminal prosecution, he still has money, and frankly, the government did him a favor by banning him from Wall Street. He fell into Wall Street without training or background, and he never belonged there. He was a creature of an environment—and an era—that he never really understood. He was the Internet era's Chauncey Gardiner.

No, what bugs me is the way we, the investing class, continue to embrace the all-too-convenient belief that we were somehow "victimized" by Mr. Blodget's stock picks. Be honest here. Did you buy bubble stocks like eToys or Pets.com because Henry Blodget told you to? Of course you didn't. You bought them because, like everyone else around you, you had taken leave of your senses.

David Denby, a film critic at *The New Yorker* and the author of *American Sucker*, a memoir about how he lost $900,000 playing the market during the bubble, came to know Mr. Blodget during his stock market obsession, and made him a central character in his book. In the early chapters of *American Sucker*, Mr. Denby is enamored of Mr. Blodget, hanging on his every word. By the end of the book, however, the author is thoroughly disenchanted with his former muse.

But when I asked Mr. Denby how much he had relied on Mr. Blodget's stock picks, he replied, "I didn't buy anything on his say-so." Indeed, he largely rejected the analyst's rather sound counsel: "He warned me explicitly to be careful. He said I shouldn't have more than 10 percent of my portfolio in Internet stocks." Mr. Denby, however, looking for the quick killing, instead stuffed his portfolio with New Age stocks and wound up losing his shirt.

Millions of Americans were looking for the quick killing during the bubble, just like Mr. Denby. It wasn't just investment bankers who wanted analysts to upgrade lousy stocks—so did investors. Recall that Mr. Blodget's predecessor at Merrill Lynch actually lost his job because he was bearish on an important Internet stock, Amazon. It is pretty unlikely that investors would have reacted well had Mr. Blodget started downgrading stocks like InfoSpace (that "piece of junk," as he once memorably called it in an e-mail message). We just didn't want to hear it. Our need now to find someone to blame for our own mistakes is one of our worst traits as a culture.

Here's something else Mr. Denby told me: even at the end, when he was thoroughly disillusioned, he still liked Henry Blodget. That is undoubtedly another reason I'm soft on Mr. Blodget. I like him, too. More than that, I admire the way he's handled himself in the aftermath of his humiliation.

Over the last year or so, as he's tried to make the transition from pariah

to writer, I've had lunch with him several times. At Mr. Blodget's insistence, the lunches are always private conversations. (He declined to comment for this column as well.) But I can tell you that Mr. Blodget neither excuses what he did, nor whines about his fate. He doesn't wallow in bitterness. Though he can't talk directly about his experience, he comes across as someone who finally has some perspective on how, and why, he became the hero of the bubble and the villain of the bust. And he's humbled. Contrast that with Mr. Grubman, who still doesn't get it. When asked recently by a magazine writer why he had been brought low by Mr. Spitzer, he replied arrogantly, "When the market collapsed, who were they going to go after but the top dogs."

Recently, *Slate* held a staff retreat, and invited Mr. Spitzer to be the luncheon speaker—before the sheer awkwardness of the situation dawned on Jacob Weisberg, the editor. Nonetheless, Mr. Blodget went to the retreat, listened gamely to the attorney general's remarks, and then had his first-ever conversation with Mr. Spitzer. Mr. Weisberg described the exchange as "extremely gracious."

There is something distinctly American about falling flat on one's face—even doing something very wrong—and then starting over and reinventing yourself for the better. Isn't that what Martha Stewart is doing right now—to the applause of million of Americans? And doesn't that also describe that symbol of 1980s Wall Street wrongdoing, Michael Milken, who spent several years in prison, but is now widely admired for his efforts to fund a cure for prostate cancer? Why shouldn't Henry Blodget be able to do the same?

I happen to know, in fact, that Mr. Blodget has written a memoir of his time as an Internet analyst. It is sitting on a shelf somewhere, but Mr. Blodget cannot publish it because of constraints placed on him by either the government or Merrill Lynch. (Mr. Blodget won't say which.)

I would very much like to read Mr. Blodget's book. My guess is that his book would be vastly superior to the usual "I done wrong" memoir. His experience, not just as an Internet analyst but as a symbol of everything that went awry, has been tempered by time and distance and, I believe, a certain wisdom and maturity. I think he could tell us a good deal not only about what he did, and what Wall Street did, during the bubble, but what many of us did. I think we could come away with lessons about the madness of crowds, and about the nature of human frailty.

But then, I'm biased. I'm rooting for Henry Blodget's redemption.

CHAPTER 10

The Smartest Guys
in the Room

My knowledge of the Enron scandal came not from reporting or writing, but from editing. At *Fortune*, I often edited the work of Bethany McLean, who, in the decade I was at the magazine, rose from junior fact-checker to star writer. Perhaps her best-known article was the short, pointed three-page piece she wrote in March 2000, "Is Enron Overpriced?" which was the first to ask tough questions about how Enron made its money. Alas, she then turned her attention to other subjects, in the classic fashion of the magazine writer searching for new territory to explore. (I have that syndrome as well, but in this case, how I wish, as her editor, that I had pushed her to keep digging on Enron!) Instead, it was *The Wall Street Journal*, seven months later, that exposed the secret partnerships controlled by the company's chief financial officer, Andy Fastow. That disclosure, in turn, triggered Enron bankruptcy that December. Bethany then went back at it, writing a terrific cover story about Enron's astonishing six-week death spiral, which I edited.

Cataclysmic business events like Enron inevitably generate books, and over the next two years, Bethany and her *Fortune* colleague Peter Elkind took an extended leave from the magazine to co-author *The Smartest Guys in the Room*. I was also deeply involved as their in-house editor. They did all the heavy lifting, spending weeks at a time in Houston, ferreting out sources, and piecing together a tough, thorough account of what had gone wrong at Enron. I didn't do a single interview for the book, but the three of us talked often during their reporting—and daily when they were writing—and I became almost as well versed on the subject as they were. I also became a firm believer in the central thesis of the book. As they wrote in the book's epilogue: "Those who want to blame all of Enron's woes on the greedy former CFO claim that Enron was a good business brought down by Andy Fastow.

195

But that was never true. Enron was a bad business that was, for a time, propped up by Andy Fastow."

I wrote a number of columns for *The New York Times* about the trial of Enron's two former top executives, Ken Lay and Jeff Skilling, which took place in Houston in the spring of 2006. Three of those columns comprise this chapter. Throughout the trial, the central claim of Skilling, who is now in prison, and Lay, who died of a heart attack after the trial, was precisely the opposite of our thesis: that Andy Fastow was indeed the true bad guy. If he hadn't been skimming from those partnerships...if he hadn't been so crooked...if he had only put Enron's interests ahead of his own....What they could never explain, however, is why Enron needed those partnerships in the first place. In truth, if Enron had been generating real profits, rather than phony profits that were "reportable" only because the company was so good at gaming the accounting rules, it wouldn't have needed Andy Fastow and his sleazy partnerships.

The trial, I wound up thinking, validated our thesis. As you'll see in the first of these columns, I was worried that the old-fashioned, easy-to-explain nature of Fastow's crimes would overshadow the larger crimes of Enron, namely, that it abused (and often violated) the rules of accounting in order to paint a portrait of a company that simply didn't exist. I expected those larger crimes to be too complicated to explain—which would play into the hands of the defense. But that's not how the trial played out. Remarkably, the prosecution, with the help of Fastow's testimony, made the larger crime seem pretty simple too. When you misuse accounting rules to create fictional profits—and, ultimately, a fictional company—you've committed a crime. On May 25, 2006, when the jurors found Skilling and Lay guilty, they made it clear that they agreed.

A Revenge Fantasy, Except It's Reality

The New York Times, January 28, 2006

The original *Fun With Dick and Jane*, a 1977 comedy that starred George Segal and Jane Fonda, tells the story of a rising aerospace executive who is suddenly laid off, can't find a job, and in desperation turns to bank robbery to keep up with the Joneses in his upscale suburb.

Here and there, the movie has some fun lampooning corporate heartlessness, but that's not really what it's about. On the contrary, when Dick

Harper, the division head played by Mr. Segal, is fired by the company's chief executive (played by Ed McMahon, of all people), the boss is completely sloshed. He's been drinking because he's so depressed at having already laid off 50 people that day. "I have blood on my hands," the CEO moans. For a guy who's busy downsizing, he almost seems sympathetic.

The remake of *Fun with Dick and Jane*, which came out just before Christmas and stars Jim Carrey and Téa Leoni, also tells the story of a rising young executive who unexpectedly loses his job and turns to robbery to sustain his lifestyle. But in the remake, corporate mendacity is front and center. Jim Carrey's Dick Harper works for a company that has the sleek but meaningless name of Globodyne and a business model so convoluted that even he, a communications pro, can't explain it. One day, in the blink of an eye, it implodes, to the shock of not just Mr. Harper but all the company's thousands of employees, who lose their pensions along with their jobs.

In the remake, however, the chief executive, played by Alec Baldwin, is not shedding tears for his underlings. Knowing the company was a house of cards, he has squirreled away $400 million in corporate assets; now he's secretly planning to move the money to an offshore bank account. Thus the real plotline of *Fun With Dick and Jane* is: How will Dick Harper and his wife re-steal the $400 million and give the money to Globodyne's downtrodden employees?

In other words, the movie is an Enron revenge fantasy. Which helps explain, I think, why this decidedly mediocre film has made more than $100 million at the box office so far.

Starting Monday, the real Enron revenge fantasy will begin playing out in a courtroom in Houston, as Enron's former leaders, Kenneth L. Lay and Jeffrey K. Skilling, go on trial for their roles in the highest-profile corporate scandal in more than 70 years. Not since Richard Whitney, a former president of the New York Stock Exchange, got caught stealing from his customers in the 1930s has there been a business scandal that has so repulsed the public, and so captured its imagination.

It has been more than four years since Enron filed for bankruptcy protection, the final act of an astonishing few months in late 2001, during which a company that was widely viewed as an exemplar of the New Economy was exposed as a Potemkin Village and was pretty much vaporized. In modern America, which has the attention span of a gnat, four years is an eternity. Yet our fascination with Enron—our hunger to know what really happened; our thirst to punish those responsible for its demise—hasn't really diminished.

There have been what—a dozen books? Two movies? A handful of

television docudramas? Saturation newspaper coverage? And it's not just Mr. Skilling and Mr. Lay who've become public figures. So has Andrew S. Fastow, the former chief financial officer who has pleaded guilty to various crimes and will be a key witness against his former bosses. Sherron S. Watkins, a once-obscure employee, made the cover of *Time* magazine— co-person of the year in 2002, no less—as the Enron whistle-blower. She now makes a handsome living giving speeches about corporate scandal and governance issues. A whistle-blower! That never happens.

So what is it about Enron? Why is it the scandal we still care about? The one we can't stop thinking about? Let me suggest four reasons.

The most basic reason is that it was first. In the years just before the Enron scandal, the companies that "blew up" were dot-coms like Pets.com and eToys, companies that never made a penny in profits—but never pretended to. They were creatures of the Internet bubble whose demise was inevitable once the bubble burst. Yes, shareholder lawsuits were filed, but no real criminality was involved, just stupidity.

The Enron scandal was the beginning of something else entirely: the unmasking of companies run by executives so desperate to keep their stock prices high they created profits out of whole cloth. To make matters worse, it then turned out that all the insiders—not just the executives themselves, but the directors, the accountants, the lawyers, the investment bankers, and the Wall Street analysts—had either been willing accomplices or had studiously looked the other way. Investors discovered that all of the people who were supposed to look out for their interests had been negligent. Indeed, most had been paid handsomely for their negligence. As investors began to understand the breadth of the corruption, they were genuinely shocked. They still are.

The second reason is a tad bogus: shortly after the bankruptcy, political reporters latched onto Enron, thinking that it had all the makings of a juicy political scandal. What prompted this orgy of journalistic piling-on was the news that Mr. Lay had called several top Bush administration officials, seeking help.

The help, of course, never came. Nonetheless, for a stretch of about a month, starting about three weeks after the bankruptcy, it was all Enron all the time on the front pages of the country's most important newspapers. Even now, politics fuels as least some of the rage directed at Enron. Mr. Lay, after all, was said to be close enough to President Bush to have been bestowed one of his trademark nicknames: Kenny Boy.

But Enron was always a business scandal, not a political scandal. Indeed, the lowest moment in the Enron documentary *The Smartest Guys in the*

Room occurs when the anti-Bush pundit Kevin Phillips makes the absurd claim that the Bush family's ties to Enron are unprecedented in American history. Methinks someone should whisper the words "Lyndon B. Johnson" and "Brown & Root" in Mr. Phillips's ear. (For the record, I have a small financial interest in the movie.)

The third and most compelling reason for our continued interest in Enron, though, is that as scandals go, this one has just about everything. "It's like a good soap opera," said Michael Useem, a professor at the Wharton School of the University of Pennsylvania. "There's greed. There are people whose lives have been ruined. A whistle-blower. A clueless boss. Even a suicide." (J. Clifford Baxter, an Enron executive, killed himself shortly after the bankruptcy.) It has sex, too, but you'll have to read the Enron books to learn about it.

"It is a classic Greek tragedy," said Nancy B. Rapoport, the dean of the University of Houston Law Center. "It's about charismatic people with the fundamental flaw of hubris." Ms. Rapoport added a note that has always seemed to me to be at the heart of our anger toward Enron's executives: a small handful of people got very rich while pretending they were running a real company. Then they sold their shares before the fraud was exposed, leaving everyone else, employees and investors alike, with nothing. "It's a little like the Titanic," she said. "First class made it out pretty much intact. But everyone in third class drowned."

I think there's one final element. The people who ran Enron were gaming the system—and that is infuriating to the rest of us. In recent interviews, Mr. Skilling's lead lawyer, Daniel Petrocelli, has been saying that the defense will argue that most of what transpired at Enron that is now being called fraudulent was, in fact, perfectly legal. Mr. Petrocelli told me that the government was trying to "criminalize" transactions that had long been common practice in the business world.

There is some truth to what he says. Some Enron transactions clearly violated the law, though no one knows right now whether Mr. Skilling and Mr. Lay were aware of the illegality. Far more often, though, Enron didn't break the rules so much as it warped them, bent them to its own twisted purpose. It took financial instruments that had been developed for one legitimate purpose or another and used them, quarter after quarter, for a completely illegitimate purpose: to create the illusion of a healthy, growing company. Enron was anything but.

It is a distinct possibility that this defense will win. Mr. Lay and Mr. Skilling have used their ill-gotten gains from Enron to hire the best criminal lawyers money can buy. They will spend the next four to six months in court

explaining away the tiniest details of transactions so complex they will make the jurors' heads hurt. They will argue that they never knowingly did anything wrong, that panic and hysteria are what brought Enron down. Brace yourself.

The two men who ran the phoniest company in modern history are aiming to game the system one more time.

Mr. Skilling, for the Defense

The New York Times, April 15, 2006

In 1995, Jeffrey K. Skilling was feeling blue. Since joining Enron from McKinsey & Company five years earlier, he had worked nonstop to build Enron Capital and Trade Resources from the ground up. In that time, the division had become Enron's crown jewel, and the once stodgy pipeline company had been transformed into a sleek and modern trading machine. The division's success had made Mr. Skilling a wealthy man.

But that success had come at a price, he testified at his trial this week. His marriage was in serious trouble. "And I wanted to spend time with my kids," he said. To get some balance back into his life, he decided to share the leadership of the trading unit with Ron Burns, an Enron pipeline executive. Mr. Skilling would work two weeks out of every month, focusing solely on strategy, and leave the operational decisions to Mr. Burns.

"It was a screwball idea," Mr. Skilling conceded on the witness stand, responding to the gentle, skillful questioning of his lawyer, Daniel Petrocelli. He's right about that, of course. Although he said in court that Mr. Burns was "a great guy," in truth, Mr. Skilling had contempt for his new partner. As soon as Mr. Burns began making decisions, Mr. Skilling started complaining to his inner circle that "Ron doesn't get it." It wasn't long before Mr. Burns had resigned and Mr. Skilling reclaimed his position as the sole chief executive of Enron Capital and Trade Resources. So much for the blues. So much for the wife and kids. So much for balance.

Two years later, Mr. Skilling's co-defendant, the Enron chairman Kenneth L. Lay, would name Mr. Skilling president of the entire company. The rest, as they say, is history.

Mr. Skilling, of course, stands accused of playing a leading role in the unraveling of Enron, and faces 28 counts of fraud, conspiracy, insider trading, and

making false statements. (Mr. Lay has been charged with six counts.) To the surprise of absolutely no one, he spent the week flatly denying that he had ever done or said anything wrong, and even claimed that Enron was a healthy, growing company that didn't need to commit fraud to generate its glittering earnings.

Those partnerships run by Enron's chief financial officer, Andrew S. Fastow, that existed solely to do deals with Enron? Completely on the up and up! Vetted by the accountants! Not used to gin up phony earnings but to lock in legitimate gains! The attempt to hide huge losses from one failing division by folding it into the highly profitable trading business? It was just a plain vanilla corporate reorganization! The accusation by the former Enron treasurer Ben F. Glisan Jr.—currently serving a five-year prison term—that Mr. Skilling applauded one partnership in particular because it "allowed him to circumvent the accounting rules"? "That's absur..." Mr. Skilling responded angrily, and then caught himself. "That's not true," he said through gritted teeth. Again and again, Mr. Petrocelli would ask Mr. Skilling if he had schemed or deceived or committed fraud. The answer was always the same: "Absolutely not."

In the world according to Jeffrey Skilling, Enron was brought down by two things: the revelation that Mr. Fastow was using his partnerships to make millions while also skimming from the company—actions Mr. Skilling contends he knew nothing about. (The government has asserted that he signed off on a secret side agreement with Mr. Fastow, guaranteeing his profit.) And secondly, he says, Enron was done in by a handful of short sellers, who organized a conspiracy to attack the stock.

Well, what did you expect him to say? Yet in between the cracks of his denials—and embedded in his explanation of how Enron ran its business under his leadership—another question emerged. How in the world could anyone have thought that Mr. Skilling had the skills and the emotional makeup to run a publicly traded corporation? If character is destiny, Enron was doomed the moment he became its president.

Consider: would you trust your company to someone who says in one breath that he needs to step back and save his marriage—and then in the next that he can't let someone else make business decisions? But Mr. Skilling was never a particularly even-keeled executive. He could be filled with euphoria one minute, and wear "dark-colored glasses," to use his own expression, the next. When he quit Enron in August 2001, after only six months as chief executive—one of the events that led to Enron's collapse—he was emotionally distraught in no small part because Enron's stock was falling. But what kind of captain abandons a sinking ship? Afterwards, he fell

into a deep depression and took to the bottle for solace, something he admitted early in his testimony. On Thursday, during the last half-hour on the stand, he sounded overwrought—and even a little unhinged—as he recounted one last time his final days at the company.

For most of the time on the witness stand, Mr. Skilling seemed smaller than life. He often wore a timid, tentative facial expression, a little like a third grader hoping not to be reprimanded by the teacher. But at least once a day he would have momentary meltdowns, and all the bitterness, sarcasm, and self-pity would creep to the surface—only to be tamped back down by Mr. Petrocelli. In the course of answering a question about Mr. Fastow's crimes, for instance, Mr. Skilling took an unprompted swipe at the FBI—an incredibly foolhardy thing to do in front of a jury. When you're on the witness stand, fighting for your life, there is nothing more important than being disciplined in what you say and how you act. Mr. Skilling was no more up to that task than he was to running Enron.

And that was the other thing about listening to Mr. Skilling this week. Again and again, I found myself astounded listening to him describe Enron's business practices. He wants to bring in an outside CEO to run Enron's new (and ill-fated) broadband business, but as soon as his buddy Ken Rice says he'll quit if that happens, Mr. Skilling folds like a cheap suit. Instead, he gives the job to the utterly unqualified Mr. Rice, who doesn't have a clue how to build a broadband business. The traders from one division throw the traders from another division right off the trading floor, and Mr. Skilling does nothing. Mr. Fastow approaches him about setting up a partnership to do business with Enron. He blithely tells Mr. Fastow to work something up and bring it to him—as if this extraordinary concept, so filled with conflicts and so easily abused—is no big deal.

He has a budget meeting with Lou L. Pai, the head of a poorly performing division called Enron Energy Services. The previous year, the division lost $69 million. Mr. Pai is projecting $50 million in profits for the next year, but Mr. Skilling thinks he's being "sandbagged," and tells Mr. Pai he wants $100 million. Why? Not because he knows anything about how the business is actually performing.

Rather, his rationale is based on the fact "we had made a significant investment" and hired hundreds of people and he's decided that he now has to have a return on that investment. It is as if the actual operational details—the blocking and tackling, the execution, the things that make businesses work—are meaningless. He seems to expect profits to magically appear simply because he says they should. I came away from his testimony thinking that, in fact, is how he believes business is conducted.

In the many detailed discussions about all the deals Enron did with Mr. Fastow's partnerships this last week, one thing usually was left out. Rarely did Mr. Skilling try to explain their underlying economic rationale. He acted instead as if Enron's dealings with those partnerships were as common as a thing could be, so ordinary they barely needed explaining. But of course that wasn't remotely true. What was extraordinary about those deals was they had no underlying economic purpose. They only had an accounting purpose. They existed to disguise the truth. If Mr. Skilling understands that fact, then he's a crook. If he doesn't, he's a fool. Either way, he should never have been in charge of Enron.

Being on the witness stand, of course, is a test of character, every bit as much as running a company is a test of character. Next week, Mr. Skilling's character will be tested anew when Mr. Petrocelli cedes the questioning to the federal prosecutor Sean M. Berkowitz for cross-examination. I couldn't help notice that on most breaks, Mr. Berkowitz strode the courthouse hallway with a big grin on his face. I'm not surprised. Given Mr. Skilling's performance this week under the tender gaze of Mr. Petrocelli, I'm taking odds that he cracks next week.

Fastow's Long Walk to Less Time

The New York Times, September 30, 2006

In some deep part of his soul, Andrew S. Fastow, who was given a surprisingly light six-year sentence this week for his role in the Enron debacle, always knew he was guilty of crimes. Not the big crimes, mind you, like his role as Enron's chief financial officer in dreaming up those special-purpose entities he controlled—the ones that generated hundreds of millions of dollars in fake earnings, helping to create the illusion that Enron was a prosperous company.

At Enron, that was something to be proud of. That was how they gamed the system. As Mr. Fastow testified during the trial of his former bosses, Jeffrey K. Skilling and Kenneth L. Lay, when he set up his first special-purpose entity, called LJM, "I thought I was being a hero for Enron."

It was the petty crimes, the skimming operations, the secret guarantees that his partnerships wouldn't lose money: that's where Mr. Fastow knew he was vulnerable. Not long after Enron filed for bankruptcy, he met with several advisers, one of whom recalls his response to a question about whether

all the deals had been proper. Well, he replied, the Southampton deal was a problem.

The Southampton Place partnership originated in a 1999 deal in which Mr. Fastow and his right-hand man Michael Kopper conspired with three British bankers to defraud NatWest bank of Britain of $19 million. It wasn't one of those complicated Enron accounting scams that are impossible to explain. It was the kind of straightforward crime jurors understand.

So why then, knowing what he knew, did it take Mr. Fastow three years after the feds began circling Enron for him to agree to a plea bargain? And why did it take more time still for Mr. Fastow to morph into what the federal prosecutor John Hueston described to me as a man who gave the Enron task force "extraordinary cooperation, unprecedented in my 13 years as a prosecutor"? And why, oh, why, given how long it took him to get there, did he wind up getting a 40 percent reduction in the 10-year sentence he agreed to when he finally decided to help the government put away Mr. Skilling and Mr. Lay?

Lawyers who do white-collar work like to compare defendants facing the possibility of hard time to a patient learning he has a deadly disease. There are stages to go through: denial, depression, anger, acceptance, and, finally, surrender. Mr. Fastow went through all of them.

In the beginning, he still acted as though he were the chief financial officer of Enron—arrogant and prone to hissy fits—but also unwilling to think ill of Mr. Skilling. Mr. Skilling had shepherded Mr. Fastow's career, brought him into the Enron inner circle, and gave him a high-paying job for which he was supremely unqualified; as chief financial officer, he could barely dissect a balance sheet. (According to Mr. Fastow's testimony, Mr. Skilling is also the person who signed off on secret side deals ensuring that LJM would not lose money on its transactions with Enron.)

In addition, like many white-collar defendants, he thought that if he fought the charges with everything he had, then maybe—just maybe—he could wangle his way out of trouble. He felt sure that Mr. Kopper would not turn on him. His plan was to tough it out.

Then came the anger. There's no denying that Mr. Fastow was at the center of the Enron scandal. But the fact that he committed obvious crimes also made him an easy scapegoat for everyone else embroiled in the Enron scandal. Daniel Petrocelli, Mr. Skilling's lawyer, told me that "Fastow and Michael Kopper are the two people who brought Enron down and deserve the stiffest sentences." Mr. Skilling has long insisted that had Mr. Fastow not been committing criminal acts behind his back, Enron would be alive today.

But that wasn't remotely true, and no one knew that better than Mr. Fastow. Though he was making millions on the side, his partnerships were critical for Enron. They created a Potemkin village that made everybody at Enron rich, as the stock rose and their stock options became worth millions. In Mr. Fastow's view, all the Enron executives owed their wealth to him.

Mr. Fastow bitterly resented being the scapegoat. He told people that he had tried to explain to Mr. Skilling and Mr. Lay how bad things were, and that they knew much more about Enron's problems than they were letting on.

In August 2002, Mr. Fastow's chief ally, Mr. Kopper, became the first former Enron executive to plead guilty and agree to cooperate with the government. If anything should have caused Mr. Fastow to realize that the jig was up, that was it; virtually everything Mr. Kopper pleaded to involved Mr. Fastow. And yet, for the next year and a half, he continued to resist.

Meanwhile, a frustrated prosecution was homing in on his wife, Lea Fastow, for filing a false income tax return—a charge also related to the Enron scandal. It is hard to know what happened next. Mr. Fastow's supporters say that Mr. Fastow tried desperately to cut a deal that would allow her to remain unindicted. People in the prosecution insist that it was only after her indictment in March 2003 that Mr. Fastow finally realized, however grudgingly, that he had to start cooperating. Ultimately, under a joint plea agreement, Ms. Fastow served a year in jail—and Mr. Fastow agreed to a 10-year sentence in return for his cooperation.

Even then, though, he didn't come willingly. In the beginning, said Mr. Hueston, the prosecutor who spent the most time with Mr. Fastow, "I saw a bitter, distant arrogant man who showed virtually no remorse." Sometimes Mr. Hueston would be asking him a question, and he would say, "I'm bored and I'm tired."

But over time, that began to change. "You wake up and look at yourself in the mirror, and say, 'I'm a convicted felon,'" said Craig Smyser, one of Mr. Fastow's Houston lawyers. "It is extremely difficult, but it can give you a kind of strength."

Mr. Hueston said that at first Mr. Fastow would become extremely angry whenever his wife's plea agreement came up, but he eventually accepted the fact that "his wrong decisions had dragged his wife into the case." (During the trial, Mr. Fastow testified that he had lied to his wife about the source of the money that was central to the tax return case—and that is why she had filed a false return.)

Mr. Hueston also said that the prosecution "had begun to conclude that if he didn't change he would make a terrible witness at trial."

"But," Mr. Hueston added, "over the course of the two years, he made a remarkable change." Mr. Fastow accepted responsibility for what he did. He acknowledged his crimes. He stopped rationalizing his behavior at Enron. He had reached the final stage: surrender.

Mr. Fastow turned out to be a terrific witness in the Enron trial. In his opening statement, Mr. Petrocelli had said that he would "destroy" Mr. Fastow's testimony, but that never happened. Mr. Fastow's contrition, remorse, and acceptance of his wrongdoing trumped Mr. Petrocelli's every effort to cast him as the ultimate Enron villain. "He had the strength of a humbled man," Mr. Smyser said.

Mr. Petrocelli said that after the verdict at least one juror said that no one had paid any attention to Mr. Fastow's testimony. But even if that's true—and I have my doubts—Mr. Fastow's cooperation was critical in giving the government the deep understanding it gained of how Enron became a house of cards—and the role of Mr. Skilling and Mr. Lay in perpetuating the Enron fraud.

Which still poses the question: did Mr. Fastow deserve a 40 percent reduction in his sentence? Although he didn't say so directly—either in court or in our conversation—it seems clear that Mr. Hueston believed the reduced sentence was deserved.

But there are many people in Houston who are outraged. When Loren Steffy, a columnist at *The Houston Chronicle*, wrote a sympathetic article about Mr. Fastow's sentencing, he was bombarded with reader complaints. "What a travesty!" wrote one.

Others pointed to the notorious case of James Olin, a mid-level Dynegy executive who was originally sentenced to 24 years in prison for his role in one deal—one deal!—that tried to make a $300 million loan look like cash flow. Recently, his sentence was reduced to six years—that is, the same as Mr. Fastow's, who was involved in dozens of such deals, on a much broader scale, with a more much devastating outcome.

It is good that the judicial system has become tougher on white-collar crime. It's overdue, actually. When Mr. Skilling is sentenced next month, he is likely to be facing 20 to 30 years in prison. Bernard J. Ebbers, the 65-year-old former WorldCom chief executive, began serving a 25-year sentence this week.

Mr. Fastow gave the government incalculable assistance, and does indeed seem to be a changed man. Give him credit for both. But it took him a very long time to get to that place.

In the end, he did the crime. And he should have served the time—all 10 years.

The Quantitative, Data-Based, Risk-Massaging Road to Riches

I n the spring of 2005, I left *Fortune* and joined *The New York Times*, where I became a full-time business columnist and part-time magazine writer for *The New York Times Magazine*. These next two chapters contain two profiles I wrote for the magazine. This first one is about Clifford Asness, who manages a successful hedge fund called AQR Capital Management.

At the point I met Cliff Asness, there was enormous curiosity in the culture about hedge funds. Seemingly out of nowhere, they had come to dominate the financial world. Whereas once the talk had been about mutual funds, and then about Internet stocks, now all anyone could talk about was hedge funds. Here was hedge fund manager Eddie Lampert forcing Kmart into the arms of Sears! There was hedge fund manager Jim Chanos, sniffing out Enron before anyone else! Here were hedge fund managers driving up stock prices, buying huge estates in Greenwich and the Hamptons, and making so much money they made CEOs look like paupers. But people also wanted to know about them because, as a group, hedge fund managers were extraordinarily secretive. Partly that was due to SEC rules; to this day, the SEC won't allow hedge funds to publicly disseminate their performance numbers on the grounds that that would constitute marketing, which hedge funds are not allowed to do, at least not to the masses. (A ridiculous rule, by the way.) But it's also because hedge fund managers simply prefer secrecy. Talking to the press can only cause them problems, they believe. Divulging their strategies can only attract new competitors. Indeed, their secrecy caused people to wonder whether they were doing things that would ultimately damage the country's financial system.

In that respect at least, Asness was the world's most unlikely hedge fund

manager. A former academic, he published with abandon. He had no fear of the press—indeed, it was through my former *Fortune* colleague Justin Fox, now a columnist with *Time* magazine, that I first met him. And oh, could he talk! After I joined the *Times*, and learned that the magazine wanted me to find a hedge fund manager to profile, I knew immediately who I wanted to write about. When I approached him, Asness hesitated for about a nanosecond, and then we were off and running.

In the story, I raise the question—which many were raising at the time—about whether we were then in a hedge fund bubble. I'm now fairly convinced that the answer is no. Less than a year after my article was published, the financial world became obsessed with the next big thing—private equity—without the hedge fund balloon ever really bursting. Instead, it's the private equity bubble that burst, and then the subprime mortgage bubble, and then the credit bubble. If hedge funds have damaged the financial system, they've done no worse than much larger, more visible institutions, like Citigroup. Mainly, though, hedge funds have just kept chugging along. True, some have gone out of business, but others have started up. And big institutional investors have continued to gravitate to hedge funds, a trend I noted in my story.

What is clear, however, is that hedge fund returns are not nearly as spectacular as they were even a few years ago. This is largely due to another factor noted in the story: successful hedge fund strategies have attracted imitators, which have made outsized returns much more difficult to attain. Indeed, sometimes it's been worse than that. In the summer of 2007, for instance, there was a scary, but short-lived, crash among market-neutral funds like Asness's, caused by a sudden sell-off by many of his new competitors. AQR took a big hit, as did the other big market-neutral funds, but quickly recovered. After which, Asness did the thing that most separates him from his hedge fund brethren: he gave me an interview and explained what had happened.

The Quantitative, Data-Based, Risk-Massaging Road to Riches

The New York Times Magazine, June 5, 2005

Clifford Asness is probably going to be annoyed when he sees that this article begins with a discussion about how much money he makes, but there's no way around it. Asness is a very successful hedge-fund manager,

and very successful hedge-fund managers make stupendous amounts of money, even by Wall Street's extravagant standards. And in the public mind, their staggering compensation tends to overshadow pretty much everything else. "Filthy Stinking Rich" was *New York* magazine's unambiguous take on the hedge-fund phenomenon some months ago. Last month, in its survey of the best-paid hedge-fund managers, Institutional Investor's *Alpha* magazine reported that the average pay for the top 25 hedge-fund managers was an astounding $251 million in 2004. Asness himself has written, in one of his better lines, that hedge funds "are generally run for rich people in Geneva, Switzerland, by rich people in Greenwich, Conn."

Asness likes to point out that he wrote that sentence before he moved his own hedge fund, AQR Capital Management, to Greenwich, Conn. He started AQR, with three partners, in the spring of 1998, when he was 31 and had just walked away from a high-paying job at Goldman Sachs, where he was one of the firm's brightest young stars. During AQR's first three years, Asness and his partners didn't make much money. But by 2002, the firm was doing well, investors were clamoring to get in, and AQR was managing about $3 billion in assets. (It's up to around $13.5 billion today.) And the partners were getting rich. Asness cracked the *Alpha* list for 2002, taking down a reported $37 million. The next year, the magazine reported, he made $50 million. Asness won't discuss the specifics of his pay, but if you ask him what it's like to have that kind of money, he won't duck the question the way most hedge-fund managers do. Instead, he'll lean back on his couch, scratch his neatly trimmed beard for a minute, and then offer a sheepish smile and an endearing, exaggerated shrug. "To quote Dudley Moore in the movie 'Arthur,'" he'll reply finally, "it doesn't suck."

Cliff Asness says things like that. It is one of the qualities that make him different from his brethren in the hedge-fund community, who tend to shroud themselves in secrecy, as if they're trying to protect some special formula they've devised for making investors—and themselves—money. They don't just shy away from talking about their pay; they shy away from talking about just about anything. Have you ever heard of Stephen Mandel Jr., or Daniel Och, or James Simons? Among hedge fundies, they are three of the most respected names in the business. Yet they studiously avoid having their names in the paper.

Cliff Asness, on the other hand, is an outspoken, exuberant Ph.D. in financial economics who has built a public reputation for his willingness to write and say what's on his mind. In academia, he's known for the witty, biting papers he writes for such publications as *The Financial Analysts Journal*. (One recent title: "Stock Options and the Lying Liars Who Don't Want to

Expense Them.") Among financial journalists, he is known as a cogent and articulate bear—someone who can make a compelling case that stock-market returns over the next few decades will almost certainly be lower than the double-digit returns investors have come to expect as their birthright. And among the hedge-fund cognoscenti, Asness has become known as someone who has been thinking hard thoughts about the future of hedge funds. A hedge fund is nothing more than a private, largely unregulated pool of capital that can buy stocks, sell stocks, or do just about anything else. It is Asness' essential belief that hedge funds—or, rather, some hedge funds—are doing things that are genuinely useful for investors, especially sophisticated institutional investors like pension funds and university endowments. You will not be surprised to learn that Asness includes AQR among the useful hedge funds.

These are strange times for hedge funds. They are, right now, at the abso-lute forefront of the collective financial psyche. Every day, it seems, a half-dozen more young Wall Street hotshots abandon the millions they're making at the big firms like Goldman Sachs or Morgan Stanley and start hedge funds. There are now 8,000 of them, about 40 percent of which have been opened in the last four years, and money is absolutely pouring into them—they're at $1 trillion and counting—as institutions search for ways to gener-ate positive returns in this difficult market. Just as business-school graduates once gravitated to venture capital or private equity or dot-coms, now they all want to work for hedge funds.

Hedge funds have also become a huge force in the market. When hedge funds are enthusiastic about a stock, they have the collective buying power to drive up the price, at least for a while. When they turn on a stock, they can drive the price down. Some hedge-fund managers have become activists, buying up stakes in companies and then demanding change from manage-ment. One hedge fund—Eddie Lampert's ESL Investments—engineered a merger between Kmart and Sears.

There are plenty of people, even in the hedge-fund world, who are con-vinced that we have entered bubble territory. Their secrecy, their power, the incredible amount of money flowing into them, the sense that everybody on Wall Street is trying to start a hedge fund, and of course the staggering riches: it all seems a little crazy and out of control. Hedge funds right now feel a little like mutual funds in the late 1960s, or junk bonds in the 1980s, or dot-coms in the late 1990s. You just assume they are going to get their come-uppance eventually. Isn't that what always happens?

But do you remember what happened after the mutual-fund boom burst? Or after the junk-bond craze? Or even after the dot-com insanity? It turned

out, in every case, that underneath the craziness, something enduring was being created. The modern mutual-fund industry emerged in the wake of the early 1970s mutual-fund crash. Junk bonds today are a critical part of the world's financial scene. Amazon and eBay and lots of other real, profitable companies emerged from the dot-com mania, after all the pretenders were swept away in the rubble of the collapse.

And so it is with hedge funds. There are hedge funds today—big ones, run by serious people—that are creating portfolios that are less risky than either the typical mutual-fund portfolio or the market itself. Certain hedge funds are becoming important tools for institutions that want to diversify their portfolios and become less dependent on the ups and downs of the overall stock market. Hedge-fund managers are convincing institutional investors that they are far better served not seeking outsize returns, because those returns entail taking too much risk.

Cliff Asness uses a highly complex, computer-driven investing strategy. You and I will never be able to invest the way he does. And yes, he's become immoderately wealthy as a result. But if you can get past how much money he makes, you'll find he has something worth listening to. Boiled down, what Asness really does is try to understand the relationship between risk and reward. And in that broad and important sense, there are lessons in what he does for anyone in the market.

Asness is hardly the first hedge-fund manager to employ techniques for managing investment risk; in fact, that concept goes back to the very origins of hedge funds. The man generally credited with coming up with the first such fund was a former *Fortune* magazine writer named Alfred Winslow Jones, who hung out his shingle in 1949 with $100,000 in capital and a new idea about making money in the market. He wanted to invest aggressively while still trying to protect investors' capital. These would seem to be contradictory goals, but here's how he went about it: instead of simply buying stocks and hoping the wind was at his back, Jones also had a certain percentage of his portfolio on the "short" side—that is, he was betting those stocks would go down. In doing so, he was limiting his fund's exposure to the market, or as they say today, he was limiting his "market risk." Since his shorts were likely to make money in a down market, they acted as protection—a hedge!—when his "longs" weren't doing well. Yet because Jones also borrowed money to buy more shares—that was the aggressive part of his strategy—when his stocks went up (as they usually did, for he was a very good stock picker), his returns were much higher than they might otherwise have been, despite having those shorts hedging his portfolio.

Jones was enormously successful; between May 1955 and May 1965, his fund returned 670 percent, according to *Fortune* magazine, nearly twice as much as the best-performing mutual fund. But Jones was also an innovator in other ways. Because he wanted complete freedom to invest as he pleased— and didn't want to deal with regulatory restrictions—he never let more than 100 wealthy investors into any of his funds at any one time; under the rules, this allowed him to avoid registering with the Securities and Exchange Commission, which regulated mutual funds. And he used a fee structure that called for him to get a whopping 20 percent of the profits if he made money. Mutual funds, by contrast, collected fees based on the size of the fund: the more assets under management, the more the fund company made, no matter how well (or poorly) the fund performed.

As hedge funds evolved, Jones's essential structure stuck. Hedge-fund managers made sure their investors were both wealthy and few in number; these days, the rules allow them to have up to 500 "qualified" investors and still avoid most SEC regulation. (The theory is that wealthy investors should be able to look out for themselves and don't need as much government protection as the rest of us.) Of course they all adopted performance fees— usually 20 percent, just like Jones. Hedge funds also became hooked on asset fees, just like their mutual-fund brethren. Today, when a hedge-fund manager says he charges "2 and 20"—and many of them do—he means he is taking a 2 percent asset fee as well as his 20 percent performance fee. To the extent that hedge funds remain the most Darwinian of investment vehicles, it is because most hedge funds simply can't afford to lose money for even a single year: if they do, investors and employees head for the exits, and the funds shut down. But that fee structure of "2 and 20" is what makes the business so potentially lucrative. A $4 billion hedge fund that gains 10 percent in a year and charges 2 and 20 has generated $160 million for itself. A $4 billion hedge fund that charges 2 and 20 and makes *no* money for investors still pockets $80 million thanks to its asset fees.

What got lost over time was the idea that hedge funds were supposed to hedge. That was primarily because of the powerful bull market that began in August 1982 and ended in March 2000. Investors took outsize risks and invariably wound up being rewarded, because the market was going straight up. The bull market forgave a lot of investing mistakes. Hedging seemed unnecessary—even a little silly.

In fact, during the bull market, hedge funds became synonymous not with hedging but with the most extreme forms of investment risk-taking. Think for a moment about the hedge-fund giants who captured the public imagination in the 1980s and early 1990s—George Soros, Julian Robertson,

Michael Steinhardt, and a handful of others. Those men were all swashbucklers who didn't want to control risk—they wanted to embrace it. They ran billions of dollars, and their fame and fortune was based on their willingness to make stunning bets on markets, currencies, stocks, even on entire economies. When they bet right, they made hundreds of millions of dollars; Soros netted more than $1 billion when he made his legendary bet in 1992 against the British pound. And when they bet wrong? On Valentine's Day in 1994, Soros got caught on the wrong side of the yen and lost $600 million in one day. "Making money took courage," says Steinhardt, who is now retired, with no small satisfaction.

Today most people still think of the Soros-Steinhardt-Robertson model when they think of hedge funds. And indeed, there are still hedge funds that make the kind of big "macro" bets the grand old men were so justly famous for. But there are all kinds of other hedge funds as well. There are hedge funds that deal in distressed securities. Others are dedicated to short-selling. Still others deal in the various derivative markets. The main thing hedge funds have in common today is not the way they invest, but their structure—including, of course, those lucrative fees.

Since the end of the bull market, though, the idea of using hedge funds to actually hedge has been making a comeback. Some of the best hedge funds, like Maverick Capital and Lone Pine Capital (the latter is run by the aforementioned Stephen Mandel) use the classic A. W. Jones technique of having a certain percentage of their portfolios on the short side—betting stocks will go down—to limit their market risk. Others search for small inefficiencies in discrete segments of the financial world to eke out small but steady returns. All of them are offering institutional investors ways to generate returns that are less connected to the rise and fall of the market itself than, say, a mutual fund is. And then there's Cliff Asness, who runs something called a "market neutral" fund. Which means that although he's buying and selling stocks, the returns he generates aren't connected to the overall market at all.

One crisp day this past April, Cliff Asness was sitting on a sofa at one end of his large corner office in a nondescript low-rise building in Greenwich. "Sitting," however, doesn't quite do justice to what he was doing. One second he was scrunching into the sofa, the next he was leaning forward intensely, and the second after that, he was gesturing excitedly, as some new, interesting thought entered his head that he had to convey right that instant. He was like an exuberant, well-dressed, overgrown kid, so overflowing with enthusiasms that he couldn't contain himself. Except that the enthusiasm in

question at that particular moment was for the research that had led to one of his earliest published papers, "OAS Models, Expected Returns and a Steep Yield Curve"—which, frankly, made it a little bewildering to be on the receiving end of his monologue. Realizing that I was pretty much lost, Asness finally stopped talking and let out a loud, self-aware cackle. "This is so geeky!" he said finally. Well, yes, it was.

Asness did not emerge from the womb a fully formed geek. Growing up in Roslyn Heights, N.Y., he was an underachiever who played soccer and didn't spend a lot of time engrossed in his studies. Much to everyone's surprise—including his own—he did well on his SATs, which got him into the University of Pennsylvania, from which he graduated with degrees in engineering and economics. It was the mid-1980s by then, and the bull market had begun, but Asness wasn't exactly walking around campus with *The Wall Street Journal* tucked under his arm. "I tacitly assumed I would be applying to law school," he said, following in the footsteps of his father, a trial lawyer. When his father heard of his plans, however, he told his son: "Why do you want to go to law school? You're good at this math stuff. You should do that." It was good advice.

"I think it's a little weird for a 20-year-old to be interested in finance," Asness said, but the academic, "portfolio theory" side of finance—the geeky side—had captured his imagination. By the late 1980s, the field of portfolio theory was undergoing enormous ferment. The long-accepted academic dogma, the so-called efficient-market hypothesis—which states that the stock market is entirely efficient, with all available information already built into stock prices, and thus can't be beaten on any consistent basis—was coming under at least mild assault. Accepted into the Ph.D. program at the University of Chicago's business school, Asness found himself right in the middle of the ferment.

The dominant figure in the University of Chicago's finance department—indeed, one of the dominant figures in all of academic finance—is Eugene Fama. Fama is often described as the father of the efficient-market hypothesis, because in the 1960s and 1970s he wrote a series of elegant papers that laid out the theory with more clarity than anyone else had before, gave it its name, and said, in effect, that it seemed to make a lot of sense. He also said, however, that it needed to be tested. To test it properly—by going back and looking at the historic performance of stock prices—you had to grapple with a series of issues that had yet to be worked out: how should a stock's riskiness be measured? What kind of risk-adjusted returns should a stock have if it were, in fact, acting "efficiently"? And so on. Still, a series of early, crude tests seemed to bear out the theory, and in time, the central idea

behind the efficient-market hypothesis even filtered down to the rest of us. Although Wall Street still makes most of its money convincing people that they can beat the market, it also peddles index funds, which have become popular precisely because people want to be in the market but don't believe they can beat it.

By the time Asness got to Chicago in 1988, academics had begun to come to a better understanding of risk. Most of us think of risk as being related to the volatility of an individual stock—that is, how much it bounces around from Point A to Point B. But new research was measuring how the risk characteristics of an individual stock changes the overall riskiness of an entire portfolio. Fama, along with a younger colleague named Kenneth French, was among those conducting a newer and deeper series of tests. In particular, they were working on a paper comparing the risk-adjusted historic returns of two different types of stocks—value stocks versus growth stocks. (Growth stocks are typically those of companies whose investors are optimistic about their futures. Their stock prices are high relative to their actual corporate earnings and other measures. Value stocks are the opposite—their stock prices are low compared with their earnings because the market is either pessimistic or nervous about their prospects.) A draft of that paper began circulating soon after Asness arrived on campus, and when it was finally published in 1992, under the unassuming title of "The Cross Section of Expected Stock Returns," it created something of a sensation. It essentially showed that if you took a large, diverse portfolio of value stocks, which are cheap, and put it next to an equally large, equally diverse portfolio of growth stocks, which are expensive, the value stocks would outperform the growth stocks *more than the efficient-market hypothesis suggested they should.* Asness describes the results of that paper: "Cheap beats expensive more than it should."

Using a large universe of stocks, going back to 1927, Fama and French showed that if you divided the stocks into thirds, put the cheapest third in the "value basket" and the most expensive third into the "growth basket," the value stocks outperformed the growth stocks in more than two-thirds of the years. This, of course, did not mean you couldn't lose money betting on value over growth—no investment strategy is risk-free. It did mean that if you took this approach, history strongly suggested that the odds would be on your side. What's more, it seemed to make no difference whether the market had a good year or a bad year. The pattern stood up. There were years when the market was down, and cheap beat expensive—and other years when the market was up, and cheap still beat expensive. In other words, this method didn't just reduce market risk, the way A. W. Jones did when he was

devising the first hedge fund. It eliminated it entirely. To use hedge-fund lingo, the pattern was uncorrelated to the market.

By his second year in the Ph.D. program, Asness had become Fama's teaching assistant and had enlisted both Fama and French as his thesis advisers. For his dissertation, Asness had his own idea about testing the efficient market: he would take a look at a popular short-term strategy called momentum investing, in which an investor buys a stock for the simple reason that it is going up. In an early draft, he called it the "fool's strategy." (Most day traders during the Internet bubble were momentum investors, for instance.) "I was nervous telling Fama that I wanted to investigate momentum investing," Asness says now. "But his reply was the best thing he ever said to me: 'Sure you can write it. If the data shows something interesting, then write it.' What Gene really believes in is empirical testing. Go where the data takes you."

And wouldn't you know it? Asness (along with other academics doing similar work) discovered that a large, diverse portfolio of momentum stocks also "worked" more than it should under the efficient-market hypothesis. Nobody can say with any assurance why these things worked. Asness guesses that in both cases, investors, as he puts it, "overextrapolate." There is usually some bad news associated with value stocks—and investors assume there will always be bad news, so they avoid these stocks more than they should. As for momentum, people often get too optimistic about growth stocks and pay too much for them. In the short term, that enthusiasm will often drive the prices higher. But eventually the enthusiasm will wane, and the stocks will come crashing down.

Academics still argue about what these discoveries mean. Fama remains a committed efficient-market man. He says he thinks these findings don't overturn the hypothesis but suggest instead that academic finance needs a better model for measuring risk. Asness, however, came to the view that the market was not perfectly efficient: that human beings thought and acted in ways that created market anomalies. There is now an entire branch of economics that tries to explain the market in terms of the way humans behave—both rationally and not. Asness does not classify himself as a strict behavioralist; "I think the market is reasonably close to efficient," he says, "but there are a lot of little inefficiencies." And in exploiting these inefficiencies a business could be built.

After grad school, Asness landed at Goldman Sachs, where he spent a year and a half trading mortgage-backed securities on the fixed-income desk while finishing his dissertation. Then Goldman asked him to set up a "quantitative research desk." The firm wanted Asness to somehow use the wealth of new research coming out of university finance departments to help it

make money. Asness quickly hired two friends, Robert Krail and John Liew, both of whom he knew at the University of Chicago, and they began building a model that would combine both Fama and French's value insight with Asness' momentum insight.

The computer model they developed—and which, after many refinements, they still use today—grabs a wealth of up-to-the-minute data to identify the cheapest value stocks (Fama and French), but only value stocks that seemed to have started on an upward swing (Asness). They buy a large block—about 200 to 300—of those stocks. Then the model identifies stocks with the opposite characteristics: growth stocks whose rise is stalling. They sell an equally weighted amount of those stocks short. Unlike A. W. Jones, who had only a percentage of his portfolio on the short side, the Asness portfolio is perfectly balanced between longs and shorts. That is what makes his fund "market neutral." It doesn't matter to him whether the market goes up or down. AQR makes money if its basket of value stocks beats its equally weighted basket of growth stocks—the way the history suggests it should two-thirds of the time.

Asness and his colleagues soon discovered that the strategy they had come up with worked not only with stocks but with currencies, commodities, and even entire economies. (Yes, economies. Asness and his team use economic data to sort out "overvalued" versus "undervalued" countries, and then buy—or short—those countries' market indexes, their S&P 500 equivalents.) In time, they developed models that sorted out cheap versus expensive in all kinds of different investments.

In 1995, Asness's group started an internal hedge fund for Goldman partners and a few clients, using the new model. The fund did so well that the firm rolled it out and began to market it. Within two years, Asness and his crew had $7 billion under management. Their run was amazing—barely a down month, and some spectacularly good years. Like A. W. Jones, they borrowed money, using leverage as their way to take on more risk and boost returns; one year they returned more than 100 percent before fees. "Intellectually," Asness says, "I knew we couldn't sustain that kind of performance. It was a lucky period. But I was young and I was arrogant."

And in his youth and his arrogance, he looked around him and saw that other Goldman hands were leaving to start hedge funds and that they were putting themselves in a position to make geometrically more money than he was making. For much of his time at Chicago, his working assumption was that he'd be an academic and make maybe $100,000 a year. At Goldman, by 1997, he was making millions, and he was unhappy. The firm wouldn't leave him alone to do his research and run money; it was always asking him to fly

to Tokyo, or to make a presentation to clients, or to help some in-house port-folio manager whose performance was down. One member of his original group quit to open a hedge fund. "That bugged me," Asness said. "He was doing what we had all invented together." His colleagues kept pushing him to quit and kept meeting secretly to map out plans. Finally, in November 1997, he decided to break from Goldman. He gave notice two days after receiving a big bonus.

The four founders of AQR—Asness, Liew, Krail and an ex-Goldman hand named David Kabiller—set up shop in New York City in March 1998. They immediately set out to rebuild their computer model and to raise money. By August 1998, they had $1 billion committed, which at the time was thought to be the largest sum ever raised for a hedge-fund startup. (Last year, a young former Goldman partner, Eric Mindich, started a hedge fund and raised the current record: more than $3 billion.) That first month, AQR made money. Then came a market event that all of Asness' historical stock research, and all his complex models, hadn't prepared him for—a market that was not just a little bit inefficient, but that was insanely inefficient. The Internet bubble had begun.

Remember earlier in this article, when I quoted Asness' funny line about hedge funds being "run for rich people from Geneva, Switzerland, by rich people from Greenwich, Conn."? There was a time when that was true—when the vast majority of hedge-fund investors were, indeed, rich people trying to get richer. By the time Asness set up AQR, however, that was all changing. Although AQR had a few individuals among its investors—some friends and relatives, mainly—the fund was primarily marketed to large institutions, especially university endowments. The best of the institutional investors were sophisticated, they were demanding, and they insisted on understanding the underlying strategy and having regular conversations with the fund managers.

If an investor had asked George Soros or Michael Steinhardt for that kind of access, he would been given the back of the hedge-fund manager's hand. But the new breed of hedge-fund manager had a different mind-set. From Cliff Asness' point of view, sophisticated investors who understood his com-plex, quantitative approach were exactly the people he wanted as clients. They would understand how his approach fit into their overall portfolios. If he hit a bad patch, he had a far better chance of holding on to a big institu-tion's money than that of a panicky rich person. Most of all, Asness and the other partners at AQR understood that the most forward-thinking of the endowments had themselves become influenced by what was going on inside academic finance and were trying to incorporate some of those ideas into

the way they managed their own money. Indeed, in setting up his "market neutral" hedge fund, Asness was reacting to the changing demands of the marketplace.

Even in the middle of a roaring bull market, these institutions had come to believe, first of all, that they shouldn't be completely reliant on a rising stock market for their returns. After all, someday the market was going to go down. Thus, having a diversified portfolio didn't just mean having a broad mix of stocks and bonds. It also meant going beyond the market and adding "alternative" asset classes. Timber, energy, real estate—these were all assets that could help institutions diversify. And so could hedge funds, so long as they were the right kind of hedge funds. These hedge funds weren't set up to make the kind of huge gains Michael Steinhardt and George Soros made, but that was O.K. They had a different goal. They were trying to manage risk and produce a return that was commensurate with the risks they were taking. Just as important, by adding hedge funds that were uncorrelated to the market—even ones that were moderately risky—they were lowering the risk characteristics of their overall investments.

The institutional money manager who led the way into hedge funds was David Swensen, who took over the Yale endowment in 1985. A former investment banker himself, Swensen had a deep understanding of both portfolio theory and the hedge-fund industry. He and his endowment colleagues got to know which were the best of the lot and sank money into a diverse range of hedge funds. Simultaneously, he cut way down on stocks, despite the bull market. The results are undeniable: over the past decade, Yale has generated annualized returns of 16.8 percent. (The S&P 500, by comparison, generated annualized returns of 10.8 percent during that period.) Seeing these results, other institutions—Notre Dame, Stanford, Princeton among them—began emulating Swensen's hedge-fund strategy.

Which, it turns out, was a good thing for Cliff Asness and AQR. Had he been operating in the old days, when the clients were all wealthy individuals, his firm would never have survived the Internet bubble. His investors would have all cut and run and put their money in some fund that was investing in dot-coms. But the institutions understood what Asness was doing, and even though his fund shrank from that original $1 billion to $400 million over the next 20 months, a surprising number of them stuck by him. What he was doing made intellectual sense, and it would work again so long as the bubble eventually ended. Which had to happen, didn't it?

Not that Asness was sanguine during the bubble. AQR's first year and a half in business was a time when investors completely lost their heads, when dot-coms with neither profits nor revenues had triple-digit stock prices and when millions of investors actually believed that the rules of investing had

changed. It was a period of such utter insanity that it seemed to repudiate the essential mathematics that had always guided the market. That drove Asness completely crazy. He had never lost money for investors over any significant period; indeed, he'd never in his adult life been anything but a superstar. Now his new hedge fund was like a dripping faucet he couldn't turn off: every month, it seemed, it was down another 2 percent. The fundamental insight that drove his model—cheap beats expensive more than it should—simply didn't work during the Internet bubble. Expensive wasn't just beating cheap. It was *crushing* cheap. Outrageously expensive tech stocks just kept getting more expensive. During the height of the dot-com era, the fund fell about 20 percent.

"I snapped during the bubble," Asness concedes today. His partner John Liew looked at the bubble the way a statistician might—it was a hundred-year flood, and there was nothing you could do but wait for it to recede. Intellectually, Asness agreed, but emotionally he could not distance himself from the awful downward slide. He had much of his own money in the fund; many of his investors were people he had known for years; even his father had put a good portion of his retirement money in the fund. The pressure was nearly unbearable. He railed about the stupidity of investors who were driving up the stock prices of tech stocks. One night in the middle of one such diatribe, his wife, Laurel, said, "But Cliff, you always told me you made money when people acted stupidly." Asness stopped talking and looked up at her. He knew she was right. "Now you're whining about it," she continued. "I guess you just want them to be a little stupid."

What Asness didn't do, however, was capitulate to the bubble. "Our belief in the process never wavered," Liew said. "The evidence was that the models we had devised had worked going back to the 1920s." In fact, the bubble gave Asness a cause. "We try to make money by making a lot of little venal trades," Asness said. But fighting the bubble seemed to imbue him with some larger purpose. He began to see himself as on the side of good fighting evil. Bubbles, after all, put investment capital into the hands of company founders who know nothing about how to build companies. They finance lots of terrible ideas. And they hurt investors, who wind up losing money once the giddy ride ends.

Mostly, though, it offended Asness that so many investors were willing to blindly toss aside decades of accumulated market history and data. By early 2000, he began to write a lengthy article exposing what he saw as the fallacies being used to justify crazy stock prices. It was unlike anything Asness had ever written. It was biting, sarcastic, tough-minded, and occasionally even funny. He laid out the math for why even the stock prices of strong companies like Cisco Systems were not sustainable. He called the paper "Bubble Logic."

The draft of "Bubble Logic" that Asness showed me is dated June 1, 2000. As we all now know, the bubble had ended by then; the air began leaking out of it three months earlier. That March was the low point for Asness and his partners at AQR. Feeling that his father had too much money in the fund, Asness—against his father's wishes—tossed him out. ("If I was going to go down," he says now, "I didn't want to take him with me.") But in April, the fund made money, and it gained again in May, and when the year ended, AQR had made back a substantial chunk of its losses. It would be another year before the partners started making hedge-fund-like compensation themselves—that's because it is standard practice for hedge funds to make back all their investors' money before they start tacking on that 20 percent performance fee again—but the ship had righted itself. For months, an early draft of "Bubble Logic" had been circulating among Asness' friends in academia; it was discussed in online forums; it was even quoted here and there in business publications. But it was never published. There was no need to publish it. Asness says that if the bubble had lasted six more months, he would have been out of business. But it didn't. He had outlasted it.

Once the bubble ended, the AQR model went back to working just the way the data say it is supposed to. Over the last five years, the firm's primary hedge fund is up an average of 13.2 percent a year after fees. Those are not George Soros-like numbers, of course, but AQR generates those returns with a little less risk than the overall market. More to the point, when it is added to an institutional portfolio of stocks and bonds, it reduces the overall riskiness of that portfolio. And though it does not seek out new investors, big institutions are banging down the door trying to get in. Why? Because once the Internet bubble ended, the market did go down, a lot. And the institutions that had loaded up on stocks for the past 18 years were suddenly losing money. So they all decided, en masse, to load up on hedge funds, to replicate what Yale was doing.

Hedge funds, it turns out, had a fabulous run during the downturn; while the mutual-fund industry was losing more than $1 trillion, the hedge-fund community was essentially breaking even. The best of the hedge funds made money during the bust. Even CalPERS, the giant California state pension fund, began dabbling in hedge funds a few years ago. The real reason so many new hedge funds are being started these days is that the demand is insatiable. And that demand is coming from institutions. Every big institutional investor in the country—if not the world—wants what Yale has: a truly diversified portfolio that generates decent, positive returns with less risk than the market itself offers. And really, who wouldn't want that?

"David Swensen was so successful, and so eloquent in explaining what he

did that he convinced folks that he had it figured out," says James Chanos, who runs Kynikos Associates, a short-selling hedge fund with more than $2 billion under management. "It looked like he had found the Holy Grail."

But here's the problem: there is no Holy Grail, not when it comes to investing. Or, more precisely, investing Holy Grails are, at best, temporary phenomena. As hedge funds proliferate, for instance, the quality of fund managers is bound to go down, and that will hurt the performance of hedge funds. That's what happened when mutual funds became wildly popular, and it is already happening in hedge-fund land as well. (Hedge-fund returns are down slightly this year, for instance.) Let's face it: even though there are 8,000 hedge funds, are there really 8,000 great hedge-fund managers? Of course not.

There is a second issue as well. You know those little inefficiencies that so many hedge-fund managers are trying to capture? Those strategies work well when there are only a handful of people employing them. But once there are hundreds of fund managers all trying to exploit the same inefficiencies, the anomalies tend to go away. The very fact that all these people are trying to do the same thing makes the market more efficient. As Chanos puts it, "Success breeds imitation, and imitation breeds mediocrity." He adds: "I think a lot of the institutions that are just getting into hedge funds now are going to be extremely disappointed. And there is going to be a gradual recognition that the fees aren't worth it."

Most people I talked to in the hedge-fund world don't believe that the hedge-fund bubble will end in some giant cataclysm that threatens the foundations of the financial system. It is far more likely that the air will gradually come out of the bubble in ways that most of us will barely notice. Hedge funds with mediocre returns will go out of business. A lot of the power hedge funds now have in moving the markets will dissipate. Some scam artists—who always emerge during bubbles of any sort—will be exposed. Some hedge funds that have taken too much risk will crash and burn. New regulations will be put in place. Business-school grads will find the next hot thing to gravitate toward.

And what will be left? There are those, like Chanos, who say they believe that hedge funds will contract over time and that what will be left is a cottage industry of successful funds that don't outlast their founders. But there are others who believe that the hedge funds that are left standing—the funds run by grown-ups who understand how to manage risk, and who position their funds as an alternative asset class for institutions—have a shot at becoming permanent institutions and a normal part of the investing land-

scape. There is, after all, something powerful in these ideas of managing market risk and generating returns that are uncorrelated to the market.

This is not, however, a case in which a big idea eventually filters down to the rest of us. Theoretically, mutual funds could develop market-neutral funds like the one Asness runs; the regulations that limited how much short-selling a mutual fund could engage in were repealed years ago. But the fund industry has historically shied away from shorting stocks. For one thing, there's a strong psychological aversion to short-selling in the investing world. Rather than pumping money into companies to help them grow and prosper, the short-seller is rooting for a company's defeat. It seems somehow un-American, or at least not very *nice*. But other things once viewed as unseemly or un-American, like buying on credit, were quickly adopted by the masses once some smart guy figured out how to sell the idea in an appealing way. The real obstacle to the massification of hedging is that it is hard. What Cliff Asness does requires an immense amount of skill. There just aren't that many people who can do it well. And that's not going to change any time soon.

Of course, if the mutual-fund industry did start rolling out such funds, it would further degrade the ability to make decent returns, because it would mean there would be yet more people trying to execute the same strategies. Around and around it goes.

Asness, of course, is in the camp of those who would like to see hedge funds become a more permanent part of institutional portfolios. But he can see the impediments as well. Last year, he published a lengthy paper on the subject of hedge funds in *The Journal of Portfolio Management*. Titled "An Alternative Future," it was written as a two-part series. In the first part, he laid out all the reasons that hedge funds could wind up achieving the same kind of permanence as mutual funds: the power of the ideas behind them, the attractiveness of using them to diversify institutional portfolios, and so on. In the second part, he laid out all the reasons that it might not happen—at least any time soon—including the real possibility of lower returns in the near term, as well as "those pesky fees," as he put it.

In our various discussions, I pushed him often on the subject, but I could never get him to commit one way or the other. "I'm very schizophrenic on the subject," he said toward the end of one of our talks. "To me, the real question is whether these institutions are rationally going to accept lower returns. Or are they secretly hoping that even if everybody else is getting lower returns, their hedge funds will still be getting the big returns? If it's the latter, we'll have problems." Some things even Cliff Asness doesn't have the data to predict.

CHAPTER 12

If It's Good for Philip Morris, Can It Also Be Good for Public Health?

This story, about a tobacco executive named Steve Parrish, grew out of my longtime fascination with litigation and its consequences. While at *Fortune*, I had watched with amazement as the states' attorneys general had joined forces to bring the once-invincible tobacco industry to its knees. On the one hand, the huge 1998 settlement struck between 46 of the 50 states and the tobacco industry certainly struck me as another example of the breast implant phenomenon: if only one or two states had sued Big Tobacco, rather than almost all of them, it is unlikely that the tobacco companies would have settled.

On the other hand, who could argue with the result? The companies ultimately agreed to hand over hundreds of billions of dollars that would help fund anti-smoking programs. And they agreed to sharply curtail their advertising and marketing.

My original plan was to take a close look at the consequences—both intended and unintended—of that 1998 settlement. But the closer I looked, the more I realized that what had happened during the mid-1990s represented not the triumph I had once thought, but instead one of the great missed opportunities in the history of American public health. It was a tragedy, really: the country had had a chance back then to regulate the single most dangerous consumer product ever devised—and it has whiffed, in no small part because of divisions within the public-health community. The settlement with the states was little more than a consolation prize. As of 2006, when I wrote the story, 400,000 Americans were still dying each year from smoking. Some triumph.

To me, the great revelation as I began my reporting was the discovery that a high-ranking tobacco executive—Parrish—was actually pushing hard for

tobacco to be regulated. He turned out to be a fascinating character, a man who had had a conversion experience during the tobacco wars of the 1990s, yet had remained with Philip Morris (renamed Altria in 2004), where he had led the company's efforts to get Congress to pass a bill regulating tobacco a few years earlier. In this, he was allied with the public-health community— though no one in public health, aside from Matt Myers of the Campaign for Tobacco-Free Kids (who did so gingerly), was willing to admit that out loud. One of the problems with the public-health world, I came to realize, is that it simply could not let go of the past. They could not countenance the idea that they were on the same side as Altria—and I'm convinced that this is at least part of the reason why the 2004 bill eventually died.

As I write this, in the fall of 2007, there is yet another effort to get a bill passed that would place cigarettes under the jurisdiction of the Food and Drug Adminstration. Once again, Parrish is working alongside the public-health community—and once again, no one on the public-health side will acknowledge that obvious fact. And once again, the bill's prospects are extremely uncertain. There is another reason, though, why the bill might not pass. Even though tobacco is as great a scourge as it was in the mid-1990s, the body politic has moved on. And so will Parrish. In the summer of 2007, Altria announced that it was spinning off its two giant tobacco divisions, Philip Morris USA and Philip Morris International. By the time you read this, the Altria holding company will be no more, and Steve Parrish will be retired, bill or no bill.

If It's Good for Philip Morris, Can It Also Be Good for Public Health?

The New York Times Magazine, June 18, 2006

"We don't make widgets," Steve Parrish likes to say, and that acknowledgment strikes me as a good place to start this story. Parrish, whose title is senior vice president for corporate affairs, is a highly paid executive at Altria Group, a New York–based holding company that is the 10th-most-profitable corporation in America. If the name of the company doesn't strike you as terribly familiar, that's because a few years ago the company changed its name. It used to be called Philip Morris, a name that still attaches to two of its holdings, Philip Morris USA and Philip Morris International. (Altria also owns Kraft Foods.) So, yes, let's stipulate right up front: Steve Parrish represents the country's leading tobacco company, whose best-known brand,

Marlboro, is so dominant it accounts for 4 out of every 10 cigarettes smoked in the United States. Last year, Philip Morris USA alone made $4.6 billion in profits. What was it that Warren Buffett once said? "You make a product for a penny, you sell it for a dollar and you sell it to addicts." They most certainly don't make widgets.

Let's stipulate a few other things. First, despite everything—the universal knowledge about the dangers of tobacco, the warnings on cigarette packaging, the antismoking public-service ads—lots of people still smoke, and one of every two long-term smokers will die from the habit. In all, more than 400,000 smokers in the U.S. will succumb this year to heart disease, lung cancer, emphysema, or other diseases because they smoked. Although the trend has gone steadily downward over the past two decades, some 20 percent of the adult population smokes—that's about 48 million people. John Seffrin, CEO of the American Cancer Society, calls tobacco-related diseases "the single-most-preventable cause of death in the world." Who can disagree?

You'll no doubt recall that in the mid-1990s, there was a huge public outcry about the behavior of the tobacco industry, and efforts were made to bring the cigarette companies to heel. State attorneys general sued the big tobacco companies, and private class-action suits were mounted; Congress held hearings excoriating Big Tobacco, while Dr. David Kessler, the commissioner of the Food and Drug Administration at the time, tried to claim regulatory authority over the industry; whistle-blowers leaked damning documents to the press. It was a moment when the cigarette companies were exceedingly vulnerable, and serious reform could have been imposed by the federal government. But that didn't happen. A reform effort failed in Congress, and 46 states and the industry wound up settling their litigation with something called the MSA—the Master Settlement Agreement—which imposed marketing and advertising restrictions on cigarettes, financed an antismoking ad campaign and transferred a staggering sum of money ($206 billion over 25 years) from the big tobacco companies to the state governments. (Four states settled separately for an additional $40 billion.)

And then the body politic moved on. So, a final stipulation: cigarettes aren't going away. Nobody is about to ban tobacco, nor is anybody about to put the cigarette companies out of business, much as they might like to. These days, although Philip Morris USA loses the occasional lawsuit, the litigation threat that once seemed so onerous has become quite manageable. And though the MSA has done some very good things—it's the reason you no longer see cigarette billboards—it has both limits and unintended consequences. For one, it has resulted in the rise of about 100 small cigarette

companies—with names like Liberty Brands and Virginia Brands—that now undercut the big boys on price. And it has given the states a rooting interest in the continued prosperity of the tobacco companies, because they now depend on MSA money to balance their budgets. All the while, cigarettes remain exactly what they've always been: the most dangerous unregulated legal product in the country.

When you talk to Steve Parrish about all of this, though, he doesn't use the language tobacco executives once used. He doesn't talk about "individual choice," nor does he pretend that cigarettes aren't addictive. On the contrary: "Cigarettes are addictive and cause the disease and death of hundreds of thousands of people every year," he said in one of our conversations. "When you set tobacco on fire and inhale it into your lungs, bad things happen." In another conversation, he said, "If fewer people died from smoking, that would be good for Altria's shareholders." He says that it is important to keep kids from starting to smoke and freely concedes that tobacco can never be viewed as just another product because it is so deadly. It can be quite startling the first time you hear him say these things.

Most amazing of all, Parrish says that tobacco needs to be regulated by the Food and Drug Administration. The industry has long fought such efforts; it waged legal war, for instance, against Kessler's claim of jurisdiction, finally winning in the Supreme Court, which ruled that only Congress could give the FDA the authority Kessler had sought. Yet since 2000, thanks in large measure to Parrish, Philip Morris USA has been calling for the regulation of cigarettes. Two years ago, Altria made a serious, sustained effort to have such a law enacted, which was strongly backed by the country's leading antitobacco lobby, the Campaign for Tobacco-Free Kids, as well as all the other big public-health groups, and fiercely opposed by the rest of the industry, including archrival Reynolds American. Although the measure twice passed the Senate, it died in a conference committee.

Among antitobacco advocates, Parrish's words are treated with varying degrees of skepticism. "Parrish is different from other tobacco executives in many ways," says Matthew Myers, president of the Campaign for Tobacco-Free Kids. "He is exceptionally bright and skillful. He has been the catalyst for Philip Morris taking a number of positions that surprise public-health advocates and that on their surface are consistent with what public-health advocates have long supported. But having said that, the jury is still out on what he really intends." Myers was quick to add, "One can look at the history here and wonder whether what Philip Morris is doing today is nothing more than a sophisticated version of what they've always done."

Paul Billings, of the American Lung Association, says: "I think Philip

Morris is aggressively trying to demonstrate it is changing, but its words don't match its deeds. In Marlboro, they still have the No. 1 brand for kids. I think they are just as despicable as the other tobacco companies."

David Kessler, now the dean of the medical school at the University of California, San Francisco, says: "I believe that Steve believes 100 percent in what he is saying. Steve is genuine. But our job is to decrease the number of people who smoke to the lowest possible level. I'm not sure that's Steve's agenda yet."

But in the months I spent talking to him and others at Altria, I came to a different view. In his own way, Steve Parrish really is trying to solve the cigarette problem. Without question, he is doing so in a way that will allow Altria and Philip Morris USA not just to survive but also to thrive—and there are many in the public-health community who view any such solution as abhorrent. But that doesn't mean that his central idea is wrong. When you dig into it, you discover there are good public-health reasons to embrace regulation—and compelling business reasons for Philip Morris USA to embrace it, too. "This isn't social work," says Michael Szymanczyk, Philip Morris USA's chief executive.

I also came to believe that Parrish has another motivation. He is 56 years old. He has been with the company for 16 years. He's not going to be doing this all that much longer. And before he moves on to the next phase of his life, he'd like a little redemption—for his company, and for himself.

This is not the first time Steve Parrish has been featured in this magazine. Twelve years ago, Philip Morris made a decision to cooperate with an article by the writer Roger Rosenblatt that examined what it was like to work for a tobacco company. The article ran in March 1994. The cover read, "How Do They Live With Themselves?" The opening photograph was of Parrish, wearing a double-breasted suit and looking warily into the camera.

Parrish no longer smokes, but he did then, as Rosenblatt pointed out. He noted that Parrish grew up in the small town of Moberly, Mo., the son of a railroad cop, and wanted to be a Democratic politician before veering off into law. As a lawyer in the late 1980s, he defended Philip Morris in the Cipollone case, famous as the first trial in which a tobacco company was ordered to pay damages to a smoking victim. (The judgment, later overturned, was against another cigarette company, Liggett, not Philip Morris.)

Parrish explained to Rosenblatt that when he was approached about working for Philip Morris, he didn't have any big moral qualms; having represented the company in the highly publicized trial, he knew the issues, and he also knew he liked the people who worked there. He conceded that it was

painful to be described as "a merchant of death," and he sometimes worried that he rationalized what he did for a living because of his "nice salary." ("I don't think I do," he concluded.) None of these thoughts were terribly different from the ones I heard recently when I plowed the same ground in my own interviews. Parrish is a thoughtful and articulate man, but there are clearly places he doesn't want to go.

He also said this to Rosenblatt: "A year or two ago, my daughter came home from school and said: 'I have a homework assignment I need you to help me with. Tomorrow we're going to talk about drugs like marijuana, cocaine, and alcohol. We're also going to talk about cigarettes and whether they're addictive. I want to know what you think about cigarettes.' And I told her that a lot of people believe that cigarette smoking is addictive, but I don't believe it. And I told her the surgeon general says some 40 million people have quit smoking on their own. But if she asked me about the health consequences, I would tell her I certainly don't think it's safe to smoke. It's a risk factor for lung cancer. For heart disease. But it's a choice. We're confronted with choices all the time. Still, I'd have to tell her that it might be a bad idea. I don't know. But it might be."

His daughter was 11 at the time of that conversation, and when I asked him not long ago about that quote, he seemed stricken that I had brought it up. In fact, he told me, that is not what he had said to his daughter. "As long as I can remember," he says now, "I thought smoking caused lung cancer, and I said that internally. And I said it was addictive and we should say that." But when Rosenblatt asked him what he said to his children about smoking, he used the opportunity to lapse, as he puts it, into "corporatespeak." "It was one thing to convey the company's position, even if I didn't agree with it. But to do it through a conversation with my daughter—that was awful." He adds: "I said a lot of things back then that make my blood curdle now. But of all the things I did and said back then, that's the one I'm most ashamed and embarrassed about."

Rosenblatt's article was one of the early markers of the tobacco wars of the mid-1990s. A few weeks earlier, the ABC newsmagazine *Day One* accused the big tobacco companies of adding nicotine to cigarettes. (Nicotine, of course, is the ingredient that addicts smokers.) Five days after the article, Kessler testified before Congress that he believed that he had the authority to regulate cigarettes as "nicotine-delivery systems." A few weeks later, the chief executives of the seven largest tobacco companies went before a Congressional committee and famously denied that smoking was addictive. And a month after that, the attorney general of Mississippi filed the first of the states' multibillion-dollar lawsuits against the big tobacco companies.

What role did Parrish play in the tobacco wars? In the beginning, he led the charge against tobacco's enemies. In the wake of the *Day One* broadcast, Parrish was put in charge of something called the Action Team to orchestrate the company's response to its mounting problems. The first decision the company made was to sue ABC for libel. Philip Morris documents from that era include a draft of a presentation Parrish made to the board describing a Tobacco Strategic Attack Plan that included lawsuits and aggressive ad campaigns. He also commissioned polls and focus groups to figure out which countermessages would work best.

And more often than not, he delivered the message himself. For instance, after Kessler asserted jurisdiction over tobacco, Philip Morris and the other companies quickly filed their lawsuit to block him. Parrish then did a video presentation for the company's employees to denounce the FDA commissioner. His language was strident and unapologetic. "Dr. Kessler has asserted that nicotine is addictive," he said, his jaw clenched angrily. "It has been called addictive because the concept of addiction has been expanded to include sex and exercise. We believe that it does not meet the common-sense notion of addiction. We believe that Dr. Kessler has described nicotine as addictive to further his own political agenda, so that he can regulate and possibly ban cigarettes." In other appearances, Parrish routinely described Kessler as a "neo-prohibitionist"—a description he says he also now regrets.

Strange as this may sound from the previous paragraph, Parrish is a likable man, with an easy laugh, a gracious manner and a desire to be liked by others. Lashing out did not come naturally, he told me. He mentioned several times how struck he is now, looking at old tapes of himself engaging in angry debates with tobacco's enemies, at his own body language. He appears distinctly uncomfortable. But of course, he was saying things he didn't believe, denying the terrible toll cigarettes take.

But why? Why didn't he just quit and find work at a company that sold something besides cigarettes? Parrish told me that he never thought seriously about quitting. But no matter how often I pressed the point, his reasons always struck me as pat and unsatisfying; this was one of those places, I wound up thinking, where he could go only so far. He still thought of himself as an advocate, just as he'd been during his career as a defense lawyer, he told me. He thought Philip Morris was a great company full of good people and felt a duty to help them. He respected the people within the company who were insisting that cigarettes weren't addictive, and he understood their reasoning even if he disagreed with it. He figured he had a better chance of changing their minds by staying than by walking away. And, of course, the longer he stayed at Philip Morris, the more his own career ambitions were

tied up with the company itself, where, it must be said, he has done very well for himself. (Last year, for instance, Parrish's compensation package, including salary, bonus, and restricted stock, was valued by the company at more than $14 million.) To the outside world, nothing could be more obvious than the fact that cigarettes were addictive; John Reed, a former CEO of Citibank and an influential Altria board member, recalls one of his own sons telling him that the industry had its head in the sand. But if you were in the tobacco bunker, it was easy to feel misunderstood, beleaguered, unfairly attacked. Parrish felt that, too.

Eventually, his role in the tobacco wars changed: he helped bring them to an end. By the spring of 1997, the tobacco industry had begun secret negotiations with the states' attorneys general. It did so not because it suddenly saw the light about the evils of cigarettes, but because it had no choice. The state suits posed an enormous threat to the companies, and the documents coming to light repulsed the country. "Today's teenager is tomorrow's potential regular customer," began one 1981 Philip Morris memo, "and the overwhelming majority of smokers first begin to smoke while still in their teens." By the mid-1990s, Reed and several other board members were telling Philip Morris management that if it continued to stay in the bunker, it risked "having society take away our license to operate."

Parrish played a key role in the negotiations with the states, and it was the turning point of his career. Once he got in the room, his essential self kicked in; he liked the people on the other side of the table, and he wanted them to like him. As he listened to what the attorneys general and their negotiators were saying, he saw how wrong Philip Morris—and he—had been in fighting the obvious: "All we knew was our own rhetoric." The people in the room weren't neo-prohibitionists; they were trying to solve a terrible public-health problem, and they were justifiably angry with the tobacco industry's historic tactics of denial, obfuscation, and trench warfare. They believed the industry needed to be punished for its behavior. To his surprise, Parrish found himself agreeing with much of what they said. He also began to feel ashamed about his earlier role in the tobacco wars.

Parrish became the tobacco executive most committed to ensuring that a deal was cut, and he took huge risks to make it happen. Matthew Myers, of Tobacco-Free Kids—the one public-health advocate involved in the secret talks—was also taking a giant risk; when word leaked out that he was one of the negotiators, he was roundly condemned by many antitobacco advocates, who insisted that their side should never sit at the same table as Big Tobacco. There was one moment, Myers would later recall to Michael Pertschuk, who wrote a book about the settlement talks, when he felt that negotiations had

nearly reached a stalemate. "Don't quit," Parrish pleaded with him, his hands shaking. "There are people on our side of the table who have staked their careers on these talks succeeding, who don't agree with the position the industry is now taking."

The deal, announced on June 20, 1997, should have been one of the great public-health triumphs in American history. The industry agreed to be regulated by the FDA, which could, among many other things, set manufacturing standards that could include the lowering of nitrosamines, an established carcinogen; mandate bigger and bolder warnings on cigarette packages; virtually eliminate tobacco marketing and advertising; and take other measures that might reduce the long-term harm tobacco causes. It agreed to pay financial penalties if youth smoking didn't decline by a certain percentage. And it agreed to pay $368.5 billion, over 25 years, to the states and the federal government, some of which would be earmarked for smoking-cessation programs, antismoking research, antismoking advertising, and other national programs to reduce cigarette consumption and, over time, perhaps eliminate the culture of smoking. In return the industry received an explicit guarantee that the FDA would not ban cigarettes outright. And it was granted relief from most liability—not just the state lawsuits but private litigation as well. At long last, the country would have a national tobacco policy.

But it wasn't to be. Both the FDA and liability-relief provisions required that Congress pass a new law, and once the settlement reached Capitol Hill, all hell broke loose. Even though the agreement embodied far more than public-health advocates had ever dreamed of, once they saw how much they had gotten, they wanted more. The money figure starting climbing, until it exceeded $500 billion. And the liability relief was gradually stripped away. Many of the deal's opponents believed that the industry needed to be punished further by the courts. But once the liability relief was out of the bill, the tobacco industry, including Philip Morris, withdrew its support, and the deal died. After which, the two sides went back to the drawing board and came away with the Master Settlement Agreement. Without the federal government's involvement, though, the new deal no longer represented a national tobacco policy; it was merely a contractual settlement with a group of aggrieved plaintiffs.

One way to think about what Parrish has been doing ever since is trying to get back to that place he and Philip Morris were on June 20, 1997, a place that could both reduce the harm caused by smoking—and rehabilitate his company.

Shortly after the tobacco wars ended, Kessler contacted Parrish through an intermediary. Kessler left the FDA in early 1997, but he remained a powerful

antitobacco voice; he was a key opponent of the 1997 deal, in large part because of the liability-relief provision, which he maintained should not be a quid pro quo for a public-health measure. Now, as he was preparing to write a memoir of his time at the FDA, he wanted to interview Parrish. Parrish quickly agreed.

"We were supposed to just meet and say hello that first time," Parrish recalls. "But we sat and talked for hours. And I had the same reaction I'd had during the negotiations: this guy I always thought was a fire-breather was really a pretty neat guy. I remember talking to him about how it felt for him when we were calling him a neo-prohibitionist. And as we talked, I started to understand a lot better why he had done the things he'd done."

Sure enough, a relationship developed. "I consider David Kessler a friend," Parrish says now; Kessler, for his part, agrees that they became close. Kessler, who had become the dean of the Yale University Medical School, invited Parrish to speak at Yale. Parrish apologized for all the invective he had once hurled at Kessler. They had a number of long talks about the past. And as Philip Morris began to change its long-held positions, Parrish made a point of getting in touch with Kessler, to apprise him personally and solicit his input. He became a one-man outreach program to anyone on the other side willing to talk to him.

After the MSA was signed, Parrish had a new stature inside Philip Morris. With the blessing of the company's CEO at that time, a tough-talking tobacco man named Geoffrey Bible, Parrish began to assert himself more forcefully. In the beginning the battles were fierce; the place was still filled with old-timers who clung to their traditional view that they shouldn't give an inch. Some of them accused Parrish of coming down with Stockholm syndrome; another once told him, "Let's not get carried away with this good-guy stuff."

In 1999, for instance, Parrish used the creation of Philip Morris' new Web site to reopen the internal debate over whether the company should acknowledge that cigarettes were addictive and caused disease. This time, he largely won that debate, but to placate the old-timers, he accepted a compromise. When the Philip Morris Web site went live, it said that cigarettes were addictive—"as that term is most commonly used today." After the change in policy, Parrish went on *Nightline* to promote the company's new position—only to be raked over the coals by Ted Koppel for the weasely sounding language.

But over time, as it became increasingly clear that Parrish had the support of the company's board and chief executive, Parrish's job got a little easier. In early 2000, Parrish was invited to a tobacco-control conference in

California, where he sat on a panel with David Kessler, who had encouraged the conference organizers to invite him. That is the venue he chose to make the announcement that the company favored federal regulation—this time without the condition of liability relief for the tobacco industry. A few months later, Parrish was being deposed in a tobacco case in New York State. When he was asked whether cigarettes were addictive and caused disease, he responded, "Yes." Was that the company's position? "Yes, it is," he replied. When he got back to the company's headquarters, he saw to it that the weaselly language was erased.

Over the intervening years, Altria has taken a number of similar steps. It stopped fighting local smoking-ban ordinances in 2004. It has chosen not to make candy-flavored cigarettes, even though Reynolds makes such a product. Unlike Reynolds, it runs no magazine advertising. The company says it has pushed the farmers from whom it buys tobacco to cure it somewhat differently so that the nitrosamine levels are lower. Recently, the tobacco companies got into a dispute with the states over whether their payments could be reduced under the terms of the MSA; Philip Morris USA was the only company to make the full payment anyway, even though an arbitrator issued an initial ruling that sided with the industry. Inside Altria, there is a palpable feeling of pride—a feeling that the company is trying hard to get it right, even as it continues to make, market, and sell cigarettes. Parrish is the person who is given most of the credit for this cultural shift. "Steve has taken a number of courageous positions," says Louis Camilleri, the company's current CEO.

Yet, of course, it does continue to make, market, and sell cigarettes, and for many people that remains the core issue, and always will. It is why virtually no one in the public-health community is willing to concede that the company has changed in any fundamental way, no matter what Steve Parrish says or does. "I feel they are belatedly admitting to what is factually accurate, and they decided that it was in their own best interests to own up," says John Seffrin of the Cancer Society, who wholeheartedly supports FDA regulation. "But I don't believe there is any responsible tobacco company today." Like many public-health advocates, Seffrin specifically mentioned another of Altria's operating companies, Philip Morris International, which accounted for 45 percent of the company's income in 2005. (Philip Morris USA accounted for 26 percent of its income.) The international business is buying foreign tobacco companies and working to build its market share—it currently has 14 percent of the world tobacco market—with no apparent qualms, in some of the world's poorest countries.

And, as Myers points out, the company is tirelessly building market share

in this country too: "Altria is the most successful marketing juggernaut in history." Indeed, what the company has done since the signing of the MSA has been to market Marlboro primarily by offering price discounts—two packs for the price of one, for example—even though it is widely known that there is a direct correlation between cigarette prices and youth smoking: the higher the price, the less likely a kid will buy it. Myers continued: "If you know that your brand Marlboro is the No. 1 brand for boys and girls, and you understand discounting, have you really discouraged tobacco use? Have you really changed?" In the years since the signing of the MSA, Marlboro's market share has increased 5 percentage points.

Partly, the refusal on the part of the public-health establishment to acknowledge any difference between Altria and, say, Reynolds, which, to judge by its actions, seems to enjoy being an in-your-face tobacco company, is rooted in a moral judgment about making cigarettes—and it doesn't matter which company makes them. "If they had a shred of ethics, they wouldn't be in business," says Stanton Glantz, a professor at the Medical School of the University of California, San Francisco, and perhaps the most uncompromising antitobacco activist in the country.

Partly, it is strategic. Since the country lacks a national tobacco policy, the efforts to bring down smoking rates is largely conducted as a kind of guerrilla warfare—local smoking-ban fights, battles to enact excise taxes, efforts to put pressure on the tobacco companies at every turn. Blasting the tobacco companies and refusing to differentiate among them is part of that ongoing warfare. During the tobacco wars, the companies became demonized, and there is a sense in the public-health community that they need to stay that way to keep the product demonized in the mind of the public. If they eased up on Altria, wouldn't that mean they were also easing up on cigarettes?

Finally, though, this position stems from Big Tobacco's sordid history. After 40 years of denying reality, deceiving the public, and working to undercut every effort to reduce smoking rates in the United States, tobacco companies simply have no credibility. Indeed, there is a school of thought within the public-health community that holds that if a tobacco company comes out in favor of something, that fact alone is enough to signal that there must be something wrong with it. It has to be some kind of trick. Which is why those among tobacco's enemies who've come to know Steve Parrish still worry about his motives. Including David Kessler.

In the memoir he published in 2001, *A Question of Intent*, Kessler recalls his astonishment when Parrish first told him he thought that he, Kessler, had been right to want to regulate tobacco. Yet, in a later conversation, when

Parrish told Kessler that the company would publicly support federal regulation, Kessler found himself questioning the effort he had once fought so hard for. On the one hand, he writes in his memoir, "all of our studies told us that regulation could cut rates of youth smoking." On the other hand, "I was nervous to learn that the tobacco companies themselves now wanted regulation."

When I spoke to him a few months ago for this article, Kessler practically renounced his old belief in the importance of regulation, fearing that it might give the tobacco companies a legitimacy they don't now have. "As much as I respect Steve," he said, "I am not sure he is really ready to see a world in which the end result is that the American cigarette market goes away." But while many in the public-health community agree with Kessler, others view regulation as the best chance to reduce the harm caused by cigarettes and create a national effort to reduce youth smoking. Just as it was on June 20, 1997.

The public-health case for the regulation of tobacco is pretty straightforward. Imagine a world in which every cigarette company—not just the big ones that have settled lawsuits—have to abide by the same set of rules. Manufacturing standards would be established by the FDA, standards that might well, over time, make cigarettes at least a little less harmful. Imagine a world in which advertising and marketing disappears completely, where cigarettes have to be placed out of sight in retail stores, where warning labels on cigarette packs are as big and scary as they are in much of Europe, where smoking in public places is outlawed everywhere, where cessation programs are national in scope and where efforts to reduce youth smoking are no longer sporadic or piecemeal. Imagine a world in which tobacco policy evolves out of a sustained national effort rather than from the vagaries of litigation, the half-measures of the MSA or the attitudes of state officials.

In California right now, the state spends about $100 million each year on antismoking efforts, and the population that smokes is around 16 percent, the second-lowest in the country. Meanwhile, in Mississippi, Gov. Haley Barbour, a former tobacco lobbyist, recently vetoed a small increase in the cigarette tax and has also taken steps that, if successful, could gut the state's antismoking program.

"We know a great deal now about how to reduce tobacco use through public education and public policy," Myers told me. "And through FDA regulation we could learn a great deal more about how it works, and change its marketing. The world we envision is one where, through public-policy change, we discourage tobacco use. If we had government regulation over

the product and the marketing of tobacco, we could reach the point where so few people would start smoking that the percentage of smokers would become a very small part of the population." The FDA is far from perfect. Drugs like Vioxx are approved and then have to be withdrawn. It sometimes bends to political winds. But even with its flaws, FDA oversight of so dangerous a product would surely be a better approach than the current mishmash.

Whenever I talked to Steve Parrish about federal regulation, he was in general agreement with many of the goals of the public-health community. But he also happily conceded that he believed regulation would be good for his company. To get a better understanding of why, I traveled to Richmond, Va., where Philip Morris USA has its headquarters.

The company's huge 1.6-million-square-foot manufacturing plant churns out 310 million Marlboros a day, in a process that begins when cured tobacco flows into one end of the plant and ends with packs of cigarette cartons being wrapped for shipping at the other end. Inside the company's headquarters a few miles away, the walls were lined with expensive art. The campus and the building all conveyed a corporation flush with cash.

To spend time there is to be reminded that cigarettes remain a big and profitable business—and that it's absurd to think the company will somehow wake up one day and shamefacedly abandon it. When I put the question directly to Parrish—Why not stop making cigarettes?—he said: "I honestly believe that if Philip Morris USA were to shut down tomorrow, it would not reduce the consumption of cigarettes at all. I think the marketplace would be turned over to the literally hundreds of companies who would be competing overnight for half of the share of the industry." Is that a rationalization? Sure it is. Is it true? Undoubtedly. One thing that the MSA has proved is that if there is a market opportunity, new companies will enter the business— even the cigarette business.

During my time in Richmond, I also saw how the company's employees carried themselves with the kind of confidence that comes of being a market leader. That is part of what makes the company so hard to grapple with: it talks about doing right by society, but competing for market share is embedded in its DNA. Smoking may be bad for you, but if people are going to smoke, by God, Philip Morris would much rather they smoke a Marlboro than a Camel.

Listening to the Philip Morris USA executives, I recalled something Matthew Myers had told me: "I remember sitting in the room negotiating with the tobacco companies in 1997 and discussing government regulation. It was clear from the behavior of the Philip Morris representatives that their

attitude was 'Just tell us what the rules are, and I can beat my competition.' It was equally true of the behavior of the R.J.R. folks that they believed, 'Just tell Philip Morris what the rules are, and they'll beat the pants off us.' " That's one reason that Altria is unruffled by prospect of regulation: it assumes Philip Morris USA can win no matter what the business environment.

But that's hardly the only reason. When I spoke to Szymanczyk, Philip Morris USA's chief executive, he made a point that's easy to miss when you're watching all those people churn out cigarettes: tobacco isn't exactly a growth business. "When I started as CEO in 1997, we had 16,000 people," he said. "Now we have 10,000. We used to have three plants. Now we have two. The industry declines 1 to 2 percent a year. It won't go away tomorrow; it makes a lot of money; it gets a decent return; but it will continue to get smaller."

In any other industry, a market leader in a declining business would begin to branch out while there was still time. It would buy other companies, redefine its basic purpose and take other steps to maneuver into faster-growing businesses. But that is very difficult for Philip Morris USA to do. Although Altria's stock price has performed well in recent years, it should be much higher based purely on its financial performance. But it's not, in part because it owns a tobacco company with a tarnished reputation, under constant attack. As a result, it is much more difficult for Altria to use its stock to buy other companies.

There is no question, then, that Parrish and Philip Morris USA are hoping that regulation could help lead the company to reclaim some legitimacy. From a business perspective, that could result in a higher stock price, which would give the company, as Parrish puts it, the ability "to increase the flexibility that the board and the senior management has in deploying the shareholders' money." He also wants to see the company accepted as having a legitimate seat at the table when tobacco policy is being debated.

As he thinks about how to get his company growing in a declining cigarette market, Szymanczyk has etched out what he calls an "adjacency strategy" pursuing new products that are "adjacent" to cigarettes. It's a common strategy for consumer-products companies—Coca-Cola once sold just Coke; now it sells all manner of carbonated and noncarbonated beverages. During the time I was in Richmond, the company was extremely hush-hush about its plans. But it was very clear that, as a first step, the company wanted to see if it could come up with "reduced harm" tobacco products—smokeless tobacco, perhaps, or less lethal cigarettes, or perhaps products that deliver nicotine, which is relatively benign, without doing so through a lighted cigarette, which is anything but benign. I saw a new $350 million research facility under construction; it will eventually house 500 scientists, engineers,

and support staff. Much of their work will involve trying to develop reduced-harm products.

In the public-health community, there are huge divisions as to whether reduced-harm tobacco products are possible, or whether it would even be a good thing if they were developed. Stanton Glantz says there is "no scientific evidence" that anyone is ever going to be able to make a reduced-harm cigarette. There are many others who think it is dangerous to begin making any health comparison among different kinds of tobacco products, because it will only encourage people to take up the habit. But another longtime anti-tobacco activist, Scott Ballin, the former chairman of the Coalition on Smoking or Health, says that such products are on the way, and that the public-health community needs to start thinking hard about how to deal with them.

One area that has received a lot of attention lately is smokeless tobacco, especially so-called "pouch tobacco," which doesn't require spitting. Jonathan Foulds, director of the Tobacco Dependence Program at the University of Medicine and Dentistry of New Jersey, School of Public Health, says that the scientific literature is overwhelming that smokeless tobacco is less harmful than lighted cigarettes. According to a review of the literature by epidemiologists published in late 2004, so-called low-nitrosamine smokeless-tobacco products carry a much lower risk of death by disease than regular cigarettes do. "In comparison with smoking, experts perceive at least a 90 percent reduction in the relative risk" of low-nitrosamine smokeless-tobacco use. This makes sense, since it is the 4,000 ingredients in the smoke that make a cigarette so lethal. Or, as the tobacco-policy expert David Sweanor, who teaches law and medicine at the University of Ottawa, puts it, "It's the smoke, stupid."

But if you're a tobacco company with no credibility, how do you introduce such a product? What do you say about it? Who would believe any studies you might conduct?

And what about all the unintended consequences of introducing such a product? Clearly, if nicotine addicts switch from cigarettes to smokeless tobacco, they've done something good for themselves. But these new products are not risk-free, and it is surely better not to ingest tobacco at all. Smokeless products might get kids hooked on nicotine and then allow them to "graduate" to cigarettes. Or smokeless products might serve "to tide smokers over when they are in places they are not permitted to smoke," says Kenneth Warner, the dean of the School of Public Health at the University of Michigan and an author of the 2004 study. "We have excellent research that shows that work sites that prohibit smoking reduce smoking rates." A product that subverted that goal would hardly be a gain for public health.

Clearly, these are not judgments a tobacco company should be allowed to make. The stench of the old "light" cigarette fiasco, in which "low tar" cigarettes were marketed 40 years ago with implicit—but false—health claims, hangs over the whole enterprise. But a regulatory body could make such judgments. In fact, that is very much what the FDA does with pharmaceutical products now. Whenever it vets new drugs, it balances the potential benefit with the potential side-effects. It can order tough language for warning labels. It can—and often does—conclude that a proposed new drug simply doesn't have enough value to be approved. With tobacco, the FDA could mandate the kinds of health claims the industry could and could not make for its products based on scientific evidence. It could make the calculation as to whether a product's potential benefits outweighed its potential drawbacks. Certainly, the FDA process for reduced-harm products wouldn't be perfect, just as it isn't perfect for pharmaceuticals. But can you really argue that it wouldn't be better than the current situation, which is nothing at all?

In May, months after I visited Richmond, Philip Morris USA announced Taboka, its first noncigarette tobacco product. The company made no health claims about the product, a tiny pouch of smokeless tobacco, which a user puts between his gum and cheek, and which it will test-market in Indianapolis next month. Indeed, it will most likely put a warning label on its Web site that says smokeless products can cause disease. But why else would it introduce such a product? And what is the consumer to make of it? All Philip Morris USA would say was that it offers "a new way to enjoy tobacco." In responding to the introduction of Taboka—and a similar product announced earlier by Reynolds—Matthew Myers had another fear: "Absent FDA authority over tobacco products," he said in a statement, "the tobacco companies are free to market their new smokeless-tobacco products in ways that encourage kids to start using tobacco and discourage smokers from quitting tobacco entirely."

And they can.

It is easy to hate Altria, and many people do. It is still, above all else, a company that makes its money from cigarettes. It still has all that history to live down. But nearly a decade after the failure to get FDA regulation, hate may no longer be an emotion we can afford.

Nobody hates the tobacco companies more than Stanton Glantz, for instance. He has been fighting them for more than two decades, leading the charge to pass smoking bans and engaging in grass-roots guerrilla warfare. He says that the way to beat the tobacco companies is through local efforts, and he has utter disdain for federal regulation, which he assumes the tobacco companies would instantly subvert. His office is the repository for the

millions of tobacco documents that have been collected over the years, and he takes pride, as he should, in the role those documents played in turning the country against the cigarette companies. He has done truly heroic work. But when I asked him what his ultimate goal was, he didn't say, "to have fewer people get sick and die from smoking." The first words out of his mouth were, "To destroy the tobacco industry."

That's a fool's errand. Philip Morris USA is not about to be destroyed. It's a big, strong, smart company, and the chief weapon its opponents still use as they try to club it into submission—litigation—is a spent force. Right now, one big legal threat facing Philip Morris USA and the other big tobacco companies is a civil-racketeering lawsuit that was tried last year by the Department of Justice. The judge has yet to issue her ruling in the case, but even if the federal government wins, the upshot will be monetary damages that the companies can easily handle, and a series of new remedies that, while helpful, would still fall far short of a true regulatory regime and wouldn't apply to the many cigarette companies that were not defendants in the suit.

Matthew Myers has done plenty of guerrilla warfare against tobacco, but he has also invested great effort trying to get regulation passed in recent years, especially in 2004, when he worked hard to shape a bill that would serve public-health goals. Conferring legitimacy on Altria through regulation is a possibility, he concedes, but by no means a sure thing; it depends on how Altria acts. He doesn't talk about trying to destroy the tobacco companies, because he knows it won't work. "The challenge to me is not to eliminate smoking, but the death and disease from smoking," Myers says. "That should be the end goal. If you had a product that addicted 45 million people and killed none of them, I would take that deal. Then you'd have coffee! I have to believe that if the marketplace incentives were such that over time someone could devise a product that would give the same satisfaction as tobacco but didn't kill them, people would flock to it."

Myers claims that the fractures that were evident in the public-health community a decade ago have largely healed. But that's not quite true. In 2004, Myers had to spend a lot of time persuading others in his camp that the bill was worth supporting. Many felt as Kessler did: that if a tobacco company was in favor of it, then there had to be something wrong with it. One antitobacco blogger went so far as to post an angry demand that Myers apologize for supporting something Altria also supported. To this day, Myers cannot admit that he and Steve Parrish have occasional contact and that they are both working toward a common goal: FDA regulation. Such an admission would lead to accusations that Myers was consorting with the enemy rather than trying to fix a terrible problem.

But what does it matter what Steve Parrish and Altria's motives are? "For us, the goal is strictly a public health one," Myers says. "If we know what we want and for whatever reason a tobacco company wants it, too, we need to be able and willing to embrace that." There is no chance that anyone is going to make another push for FDA regulation this year. But Parrish says that he hopes that next year, once the new Congress is settled in, Altria can make one more run at it. As Myers sees it, the real test of whether Steve Parrish can be believed—and whether Altria has changed—will come only after the federal government begins regulating tobacco. "Would Philip Morris fight meaningful rules?" he asks. "Would it support restrictions on content of the product? These are all unknown at this point. I wish we could find out."

He added, "That's when we'll know if Steve Parrish is truly sincere, or whether he's the most effective spokesman the industry has ever had."

CHAPTER 13

The Cufflinks That Went to China

There was a problem on the Northeast Corridor that morning, and Amtrak wasn't running from New York to Wilmington, Delaware. I found this out when I walked into the cavernous ballroom of the Hotel DuPont—the scene of Home Depot's 2006 annual meeting—and realized that the room was nearly empty. This had been billed as one of the most contentious annual meetings in years—a showdown between CEO Robert Nardelli and his many critics, who were working hard to turn him into the poster child for overpaid chief executives. Surely, it would be packed with reporters, shareholders, and activists. And yet there were only three reporters in the room, and a smattering of shareholders. The only reason I made it was because I was feeling lazy that week: not wanting to get up at the crack of dawn to catch an early morning train, I had arrived the night before. Lucky me.

As a columnist, I often wake up Monday morning having no idea whether the path I've chosen to travel that particular week will be fruitful. That was never truer than when I went to Wilmington for the Home Depot annual meeting. I had no advance knowledge that the board wasn't going to show up, or that Nardelli was going to act so petulantly. Indeed, before the meeting, I leaned toward one of the company's veteran public relations hands and whispered nervously, "I hope I can get a column out of this." Knowing what was about to transpire, he laughed. "Don't worry," he replied. "You will."

Once the board meeting was over, however, I had no doubt about how it was going to end for Nardelli. In the modern age, you simply can't thumb your nose at shareholders the way he did that day and expect to keep your job. Sure enough, eight months later, he was asked to leave by the board—which is not to say he didn't land on his feet. He is now the chairman of

Chrysler, which had been taken private by Cerebus, a big private equity firm. One of the great advantages for Nardelli is that he no longer has to disclose is salary to the SEC—or anybody else.

Most of my columns don't offer such tidy endings; as you'll see from the handful collected here, my primary goal is to illuminate some aspect of business, and perhaps allow readers a different prism through which to view, say, Wal-Mart's labor practices or globalization. But there is one other column here that has a recent denouement. A year after I wrote about Howard Schultz and Starbucks, he finally took drastic action. He and the board fired the company's CEO, and Schultz, who had been serving as chairman, retook his old job as chief executive. I wrote a column mildly skeptical of whether he is truly the right man to turn around the chain. But as a Starbucks customer, I'm rooting for him.

The Board Wore Chicken Suits

The New York Times, May 27, 2006

"A showdown could occur at the annual meeting tomorrow as firms that advise large shareholders and activist groups are urging shareholders to withhold votes from several directors." So wrote Julie Creswell on Wednesday, in her detailed front-page article in *The New York Times* about the compensation package of Robert L. Nardelli, the chief executive of Home Depot.

This was a showdown I didn't want to miss. Mr. Nardelli, you see, has become this year's version of Mr. Overpaid CEO. He's earned this status, in part, by the sheer sum of money his board has awarded him in the five years since he was recruited from General Electric to take over Home Depot: $245 million, including $37.1 million just this last year. At the same time, Home Depot's stock has fallen 12 percent, while shares of its chief competitor, Lowe's, have risen 173 percent. You've heard of pay for performance? This is the classic definition of pay for pulse.

But as Ms. Creswell's article made clear, these facts barely begin to get at the richer story that is the Home Depot scandal. There's the lead director, Kenneth G. Langone, who's never met a chief executive he doesn't want to overpay. The cozy board. The other overpaid chief executives who sit on the Home Depot compensation committee, who have every incentive to keep lining Mr. Nardelli's pockets because his good fortune will rebound to them

as well. Mr. Nardelli's compensation illustrates precisely what is so offensive about CEO pay: it's a rigged game. Heads I win, tails you lose.

So I hopped on a train Wednesday night, and headed to Wilmington, Del., where the Home Depot meeting was being held. In all honesty, I cannot characterize what I saw the next day as a showdown. But it certainly was a show.

9:15 A.M.: I see a man in a chicken suit holding a sign. He's part of a small group protesting Mr. Nardelli's pay package on behalf of the American Federation of State, County and Municipal Workers. Unions like the AFL-CIO, the United Brotherhood of Carpenters, and the government workers' union have taken aim at executive pay in recent years, and have gotten shareholder proposals on the proxies at many companies. This year, the government workers' union has put forward a proposal calling for the Home Depot board to allow shareholders to hold an advisory vote on the compensation committee's report. The union is also among those urging shareholders to withhold votes from the directors as a way of protesting Mr. Nardelli's pay.

"Home Depot is a classic case of a board being nonresponsive to shareholders," says Richard Ferlauto, who is the union's director of pension investment policy. As I walk into the hotel where the meeting is taking place, I can hear the protesters chanting, "Hey Bob, why are you chicken/while the stock price takes a lickin'?"

9:45 A.M.: The ballroom doors finally open and a few shareholders and reporters trickle in. But where are all the Home Depot people? The corporate officers? The middle managers? Maybe a few local store managers who might be asked to stand up and take a bow? Nowhere to be seen. There are a few public relations people here and there, helpfully explaining why Mr. Nardelli really, really, really deserves all that money, but otherwise what I mainly see are big, strong men, some wearing Home Depot aprons, who look as if they could be bouncers at a rowdy club. Here's something else strange. In the front of the room, facing the audience, I see two large digital timers. It also seems odd that there is only one seat on each side of the podium. Where are the board members going to sit?

10:00 A.M.: Mr. Nardelli takes the podium, and the meeting is under way. He is accompanied by two people who sit in the seats next to him—and no one else. Suddenly, we all understand what's going on: the board isn't coming to the annual meeting! In all my years as a business reporter, I have never seen that before. As Charles Elson, the corporate governance expert at the University of Delaware, will tell me the next morning: "Your one obligation as a director is to show up at the annual meeting. The fact that the directors didn't show up is disgusting."

The first item on the agenda, Mr. Nardelli says, is the election of directors. He invites comments from shareholders. "Questions are limited to one minute and one person," he adds. Sure enough, when the first person gets up to speak, the timer starts counting down. The timer is another new one for me.

"I have a question about board independence and conflicts," says the first questioner—and then proceeds to rattle off a few of the conflicts that afflict the Home Depot board. "What steps will the board take to address these conflicts?" he asks.

"This is not the forum in which to address these comments," Mr. Nardelli replies.

Mr. Ferlauto steps to the microphone. Again, the timer starts counting down. "If the candidates are up for election, can we be introduced to them?" he asks.

"They are not in attendance today," Mr. Nardelli says.

"I think it is absolutely outrageous that the board is not here," Mr. Ferlauto retorts. "The board is too chicken to face the shareholders." As he speaks, the timer hits zero—and the microphone is shut down. Mr. Ferlauto continues speaking. Two of those big burly men take a step toward him. He sits down.

10:10 A.M.: The meeting moves to its next phase—the pleadings on behalf of the shareholder proposals. There are eight in all. This time, the speakers are allowed all of three minutes to make their case.

Mr. Ferlauto jumps up to discuss his union's proposal that shareholders be allowed an advisory vote on executive pay. He goes through the litany of Mr. Nardelli's compensation abuses: the guaranteed bonuses, the $10 million loan that costs the shareholders $21 million because the company pays the tax on it, and so on. When he has finished, Mr. Nardelli replies matter-of-factly, "The board recommends you reject this proposal."

Two speakers later, a shareholder named Sam Yake stands up to talk about his proposal to have Home Depot separate the job of chief executive and chairman of the board, a practice that many companies have instituted over the last few years. But Mr. Yake is so mad he doesn't really want to talk about his proposal. "I love Home Depot," he says. "I came here wanting to buy more stock. But I am totally offended by the way you are conducting this meeting. Are we even going to have an opportunity to ask questions?"

Mr. Nardelli refuses to answer the question about asking questions. "If this is the way you are conducting this meeting, I can see why G.E. didn't pick you." He storms off.

"The board recommends you reject this proposal," Mr. Nardelli says.

Next up: A woman from the United Brotherhood of Carpenters, which has offered a nonbinding proposal calling for Home Depot to require its directors to get a majority of the shareholder votes to remain on the board. Currently, directors who run unopposed—as they invariably do—could have 99 percent of the votes withheld and still be reelected as a director. This change to majority vote is also something many companies have begun to adopt.

"Thank you, Catherine," Mr. Nardelli says when she finishes. "The board recommends that you reject this proposal."

And so it goes. "This is really disturbing," says one man, referring to the way Mr. Nardelli is conducting the meeting. "It really reflects what we have been reading in the press about the style of this board." The room bursts into applause.

"Thank you," Mr. Nardelli says. "The board recommends that you reject this proposal."

Then, the proposals finished, Mr. Nardelli asks the bouncers to hand out voting cards to anyone who wants to vote. But of course the overwhelming majority of shareholders have already voted—and Mr. Nardelli can't even be bothered to wait for those in the room to hand in their votes.

"It appears that each of the directors has been selected for a one-year term," he says. "A majority of shareholders have supported management recommendations"—except, he quickly adds, No. 6, the one concerning majority vote. "Ladies and gentlemen, that concludes our meeting." And just like that, he's gone.

10:37 A.M. I look down at my watch and I suddenly realize, Mr. Nardelli did not even tell his shareholders what the vote totals were, nor did he divulge how well the shareholder proposals did. It's mind-boggling. As for the proposal about majority vote—the one the company actually lost—it seems pretty unlikely that Mr. Nardelli and the rest of the board will abide by the wishes of the company's shareholders. If there is one thing the meeting proved, it is that they don't much care what their shareholders think.

Afterward, the words on people's mouths are "appalling," "disgraceful," and "arrogant." I would add one more: contemptuous. I'm sure there are plenty of boards and chief executives who have contempt for their shareholders, but most of them are at least smart enough to keep it to themselves. On Thursday morning, in Wilmington, Del., Mr. Nardelli and the Home Depot board let the world know exactly how it feels about the people for whom they are supposed to work.

One other thing: late yesterday, Home Depot issued a statement that said in part, "While we understand that the approach we took to the annual

meeting was a departure from past practice, it should in no way be construed as either a lack of respect for our shareholders or a lessening of our commitment to high standards of corporate governance and transparency."

Apparently, Mr. Nardelli and the Home Depot board think their shareholders are stupid, too.

Overstock's Campaign of Menace

The New York Times, February 15, 2006

"I am just sitting here with a glass of wine in my hands, reflecting on what a really bad week you and your friends have had," read the e-mail message to Herb Greenberg, a well-known columnist for MarketWatch.com.

It was Friday, Feb. 10, just after 7 P.M. Three days earlier, Mr. Greenberg had received a subpoena from the Securities and Exchange Commission, demanding that he turn over all communications between him and a handful of his sources concerning five companies he had written about. One of the companies was Overstock.com, an unprofitable retail liquidation Web site based in Utah. Patrick M. Byrne, Overstock's chief executive, was the author of the message.

For some time now, Mr. Byrne has been saying that his company is the victim of a Wall Street conspiracy intended to drive down its stock, which has fallen to the mid-20s from the mid-70s since the fall of 2004. Last August, Overstock sued Rocker Partners, a short-selling hedge fund that has been openly negative on the company, and Gradient Analytics, an independent research firm that has written consistently bearish reports on Overstock's mounting business problems. The lawsuit asserted that the two firms were acting in concert to hurt the company and manipulate its stock price. Both Donn W. Vickrey, who runs Gradient Analytics, and David A. Rocker, the managing partner of Rocker Partners, have been sources for Mr. Greenberg over the years. And Mr. Greenberg has written about Overstock and Mr. Byrne from time to time, in his typically tough-minded fashion.

Which of course makes Mr. Greenberg a charter member of the Overstock conspiracy. To hear Mr. Byrne tell it, Mr. Greenberg's role is to do the bidding of Rocker Partners and Gradient Analytics; when asked last year by Ron Insana of CNBC whether he was accusing Mr. Greenberg of "helping others front-run or trade illegally in the shares of your company's stock," Mr. Byrne replied, "That's correct, that's what I am doing." He described Mr. Greenberg to me as a "lapdog."

Although Mr. Byrne says he did not know about the subpoena, he clearly knew something was afoot. (He later told me that he had "just come from an interview with certain law enforcement people" who had been asking about Mr. Greenberg.) "As I take a sip," he taunted in his e-mail, "I find myself curious: do you guys know? Are you sitting somewhere, blithely oblivious, still chuckling about Whacky Patty, and all that? Or do you understand now that this is going to end badly for you?"

If you know anything about Patrick Byrne, it's probably his famous "Sith Lord" conference call. Held last summer, it was an hour-long monologue during which Mr. Byrne laid out a vast, overarching conspiracy, made up of dozens of Wall Street players—including the New York attorney general, Eliot Spitzer!—all under the thumb of a mysterious puppet master, whom Mr. Byrne labeled the Sith Lord. He titled the conspiracy "The Miscreants' Ball," an obvious reference to Michael Milken's old Predators' Ball.

Although Mr. Byrne told me that his Sith Lord speech ranked among "the 10 proudest moments of my life," most people, including me, thought it was loony beyond belief. Roddy Boyd of *The New York Post* recalled hearing about it from someone on Wall Street. "When he described it, I thought he was embellishing," Mr. Boyd said. But when he listened to the replay, "my jaw dropped—you cannot make up what occurred on that phone call."

In addition to his conspiracy-mongering, Mr. Byrne talked about Stinger missiles, Wayne and Garth, a mysterious Spanish phone message, stuttering, and cocaine. ("I'm not a coke head," he said, unprompted.)

But I'm not laughing anymore. I've gone from viewing Mr. Byrne as an amusing diversion to a menace, at least for anyone who cares about the First Amendment. What has become increasingly clear in the months since the Sith Lord speech is that Mr. Byrne is using the courts, the Internet, his taunting e-mails—and even his conspiracy theory—as part of a thinly disguised effort to squelch any and all criticism of Overstock, a company with $804 million in sales last year.

Mr. Boyd, for instance, decided to look into Mr. Byrne's allegations about collusion between Rocker Partners and Gradient. After concluding there was nothing to it, he called Mr. Byrne and told him, as he put it to me, "everything you've said not only doesn't stand up, it is false." From that point on, Mr. Boyd became one of Mr. Byrne's targets on the Motley Fool message board, where he often posts messages. "He would say, 'I work for *The Post* and I'm dumb as a post,'" Mr. Boyd recalled.

Fast-forward to January. Mr. Boyd sent an e-mail message to Mr. Byrne asking about Overstock's dwindling cash position. In a typically coy, sneering response, Mr. Byrne implied that Mr. Boyd was clearly doing the bidding

of the miscreants, who were ordering up articles about Overstock's cash situation. He then posted the exchange with Mr. Boyd on the Web site of an ally, a mysterious character who uses the pseudonym Bob O'Brien.

Mr. Boyd soon discovered that Mr. Byrne had dissembled in his answer about Overstock's cash, failing to subtract money owed to the company's vendors, which lowered its available cash from $112 million to $10 million. Furious, Mr. Boyd left a message on Mr. Byrne's voice mail, accusing him of lying. Again, Mr. Byrne saw to it that the voice mail message was posted on Mr. O'Brien's Web site.

"I lost my judgment," Mr. Boyd told me. "And the fact that I made that phone call constrains me. I am going to take at least three to six months before I write about him again."

This is what Mr. Byrne does: along with Mr. O'Brien, he bullies and taunts and goads the small handful of reporters who dare to write about Overstock, making it clear that there will be a price to be paid for tackling the company or its chief executive. And as a result, financial reporters have become very chary of taking him on.

A lawsuit, of course, is far more onerous than being bullied on the Internet. But the purpose is the same. As Mr. Rocker put it in an affidavit, "It is my opinion that this lawsuit represents an attempt by Plaintiff Overstock .com Inc. and its chief executive Patrick Byrne to use his family's wealth and influence to silence Overstock's critics and doubters through the burden and expense of a lawsuit." (Mr. Byrne's father, who is the chairman of Overstock, is the former chief executive of Geico.)

Rocker Partners has long had a reputation as one of the more aggressive short sellers around. But it also has a reputation for being right a lot of the time. The firm was early on Boston Chicken, on AremisSoft, on Conseco, on Lernout & Hauspie Speech Products, and any number of other companies that subsequently "blew up."

What's more, as Mr. Greenberg pointed out to me, Mr. Rocker is one of the few short sellers who will sometimes be quoted by name. "You want people to go on the record," Mr. Greenberg said. "You want your readers to know when your sources are short a stock." Now, however, the firm has instituted a policy of not talking to the news media. The lawsuit has effectively silenced Mr. Rocker.

The Gradient situation is similar. The small 10-year-old firm specializes in forensic accounting and what's called "quality of earnings"; its Wall Street clientele count on it to send early warnings about companies that might be playing games with their financials. It is thus not surprising that Gradient makes enemies among the corporations it writes about, including Over-

stock, which it has been dogging since 2003. In one recent report, Gradient dissected Overstock's "Negative Cash From Operating Activities" and "Difficulties Generating Repeat Customer Buying," among other things, and gave it an "Earnings Quality Grade" of F. No wonder Patrick Byrne is ticked off. But precisely because Gradient is small and independent, there is a limit to how many lawsuits—even frivolous ones—it can absorb and remain focused on its primary task.

And then there's Mr. Greenberg, who has been an acquaintance of mine for more than a decade, and is one of the straightest shooters I know. As you can surely tell by now, he isn't backing down an inch. "This is the McCarthyism of business journalism," he said the other day. Dow Jones, which owns MarketWatch, has objected to the subpoena, and indeed, the SEC appears to have backed away from it, at least for now. Yesterday, Mr. Greenberg broke the news of his own subpoena in a strongly worded column. If his communications with sources "aren't safe from government eyes," he wrote, "then the tools of every business reporter in this country become fair game for any company that doesn't like scrutiny and chooses to play the 'conspiracy' card." Mr. Greenberg told me that the lawsuit was simply an effort to tarnish "watchdogs of public companies who are doing their jobs." I agree with him.

The most ridiculous part of this whole story is that the SEC has taken the bait, using the allegations in Mr. Byrne's lawsuit to open an investigation into Rocker Partners and Gradient—and has also ensnared Mr. Greenberg as a witness of some sort. But the agency is looking in the wrong direction. Last fall, the SEC chairman, Christopher Cox, sent a letter to Senator Ron Wyden, Democrat of Oregon, saying that he was concerned about "issuer retaliation against research analysts." Surely, he ought to be able to see that what is going on here is a form of retaliation.

Oh, and one other thing. You may have noticed that a few days ago, a small pharmaceutical company called Biovail sued a handful of hedge funds—and Gradient Analytics—contending a stock market manipulation scheme. The next day on his Web site, Bob O'Brien wrote that he had spoken to Mr. Byrne, who told him that "he did have a hand in the Biovail lawsuit" by "sharing his wealth of information that his affiants have made available."

Which leaves only one question: Who's really running a conspiracy here?

After Five Years, His Voice Can Still Crack

The New York Times, September 9, 2006

Time passes. Time heals.

A few days before the fifth anniversary of the 9/11 attacks, I went to see James J. Dunne III, the managing partner of the small investment banking firm Sandler O'Neill & Partners. Sandler O'Neill, you may recall, was one of the hardest hit firms that day. Its primary offices were on the 104th floor of the south tower of the World Trade Center; of the 83 employees (out of a total of 171) who were in the office that awful morning, only 17 made it out alive. Among the 66 who died were two of the three men who ran the firm: Herman Sandler, the co-founder, and Christopher Quackenbush, who headed investment banking.

Jimmy Dunne was the junior member of the ruling troika. He had been spared because he was on a golf course in Westchester County that morning, trying to qualify for an amateur tournament. Truth to tell, before 9/11, he was more focused on golf than on work. At 45, he had one foot out the door.

But I learned that only later, and it came as a surprise. The Jimmy Dunne I met shortly after 9/11 was more committed to his work than anyone I'd ever known. Thrust into a role he had never expected and had never prepared for—not just to lead Sandler O'Neill, but to save it—he embraced his task with an unnerving intensity.

Back then, he was everywhere, doing everything: comforting grieving families, hiring equity traders (the equity desk lost 20 of its 24 traders), asking for help from competitors to get into deals, writing eulogies for dead partners, going on CNBC to refute a report that the firm was going out of business, figuring out how to rebuild the computer systems, and on and on.

There was something so raw about him then, so fierce, as if his life truly depended on rebuilding Sandler O'Neill. I remember especially how openly emotional he could be. He would start talking about Mr. Sandler, who had been his mentor, or Mr. Quackenbush, his best friend forever, a man who helped him quit drinking in his 20s—and his eyes would well up while his voice would start to crack. He always seemed on the verge of losing it. But he never did.

Five years later, Jimmy Dunne met me in his paneled office on Third Avenue and shook my hand. His hair was whiter than it used to be, and he'd gained a little weight. What was most apparent, though, was that the overpowering intensity that had characterized him after 9/11 had lifted.

Once we sat down, he immediately launched into a recitation about how much stronger the firm has become in recent years, with 255 employees, vastly improved research, and a better mergers and acquisitions department. Though, he quickly added, things were more difficult this year because the "flat yield curve" was making trading profits tougher to come by.

I had to smile. So did he.

No one will ever accuse Jimmy Dunne of being the perfect boss. "He's not always the most patient listener, and he can be brutally blunt," said the firm's co-chief operating officer, Michael Lacovara, who joined a few years ago. "And I think he believes he can do anybody's job as well as they can do it themselves." But, added Mr. Lacovara, "if on Sept. 12, 2001, he hadn't felt that way, we wouldn't be here today." Mr. Dunne turned out to be the exact right person to lead Sandler O'Neill out of the abyss.

"What he did was a little akin to Rudy Giuliani," said Marc Maltz, the managing partner of the Triad Consulting Group, which worked with the firm, providing both organizational and psychological assistance for two years after 9/11. "He made decisions that gave people confidence. Once Jimmy worked it through in the first 48 hours and concluded that the firm would rebuild, he gave it the kind of leadership that was necessary."

There were two instinctive decisions he made in particular that would prove enormously beneficial over the long haul. First, he and several other surviving partners—who were also thrust into new leadership roles—made the snap decision that despite its crippled state, the firm would do right by the families of its deceased employees. It extended full benefits for five years for all the families. It set up a foundation to pay for the education of the 71 children who lost a parent who had worked at Sandler O'Neill. It offered years of psychological counseling not just to surviving employees but to family members of the deceased.

And in 2001, it paid out salaries and bonuses as if the employees were still alive and working. It also paid out the deceased partners' capital to their families, even though that depleted the firm's own capital. Indeed, as it completed deals or did trades in the latter part of 2001, it shared the proceeds with the families of deceased partners who had been working on those deals before 9/11.

These acts of generosity created a tremendous amount of goodwill for the firm. It motivated employees and caused clients and competitors and just about everyone else to rally around it. But that's not why Mr. Dunne took that path. Lots of small firms like to say they're a family, but at Sandler O'Neill it was actually true. "It really was a firm founded by friends who hired friends," Mr. Maltz said. More than anything else, the culture of the place drove Mr. Dunne's decision.

Mr. Dunne's second decision, equally instinctive and heart-felt, was to cast the rebuilding of Sandler O'Neill in moral terms. Partly, Mr. Dunne used the "they can't do this to us" rhetoric, and partly he made the case that rebuilding the firm was something the deceased would want the survivors to do. But just as important, it gave the living a way to connect with one another, to do something after 9/11 that felt purposeful and important. "The organization had such a deep sense of moral purpose," marveled Mr. Maltz, who has written several papers about the underpinnings of Sandler O'Neill's revival.

Karen Fishman, one of the 17 employees who got out of the south tower before it collapsed, said: "Work was a way to deal with what happened. You needed to be with people who experienced what you experienced. You didn't want the firm to go away, because you needed it."

As with many Sandler O'Neill survivors, Ms. Fishman was suddenly handed new responsibilities. She buried herself in her work, sometimes thinking, after a 12-hour day, that she hadn't worked hard enough. But as the firm got stronger, those feelings lifted, and she began to feel instead that she should spend more time with her children. So in 2003, she left the firm. Time was passing. Time was healing.

Mr. Dunne believes that the decisions he and the other new leaders of the firm made back then gave them a confidence they hadn't had before. And that also helped Sandler O'Neill become a bigger, stronger firm. "It was like we were in a cave, and we were making decisions without having any idea what other firms were doing," he said. "And then we saw others doing the same things we did. Usually when you are a small firm, you wait to see what the big firms are going to do. But we didn't wait for anyone's lead. And I think that has given us the confidence to believe that there isn't a piece of business in our niche that we shouldn't compete for—and get."

Today, the number of employees hired since 9/11 vastly exceeds the number who were there that day. Still, I was astonished to discover that 74 of the 105 employees who worked for Sandler O'Neill on Sept. 12, 2001, are still there. But there's not much of a gap anymore between the new people and the old ones, as there inevitably was for the first year or so. And for the most part, even the old-timers now view 9/11 as an event that has slowly receded into the past.

"I don't need to go back there," said William Hickey, who now helps run the firm's M&A department. "I think about my friends all the time, but I don't think about the event itself."

Indeed, the person who probably dwells the most on 9/11 is Mr. Dunne himself. Over time, the firm took down from the walls the many letters of

support and grief it had put up after 9/11; Mr. Dunne's own collection came down last of all, and only at the urging of his sister, who told him that the time had come for him to do so.

But he hasn't taken them all down. In his office, he has several framed letters, including one from Mr. Quackenbush's brother, written shortly after the attack, urging him to rebuild the firm. Sandler O'Neill commissioned a sculpture with the names of the deceased employees, and placed it in the lobby of its office. But after a few years, some employees came to feel that it was too omnipresent a reminder of an event they were trying to move beyond. So Mr. Dunne had it moved to a small alcove just outside his own office, where he, at least, can see it every day.

Most of all, Mr. Dunne still feels a sense of moral purpose. It's just a little different now. Whereas rebuilding was once a way of honoring his deceased partners, now he feels something else. "What are our responsibilities to all the people who helped us or took an interest in seeing us do well?" he said. "We got letters from a farmer in Iowa and a teacher in South Korea. They took the time to say that they respected what we were doing. I feel a large responsibility to the world for helping us survive."

Not long ago, Mr. Dunne gathered his partners together and told them he wanted to extend the benefits to the families for another three years. Not a single one dissented.

Why did you do that? I asked him. "We did it because we feel fortunate," he replied, "more fortunate than when we first did it five years ago. It just felt like the right thing to do."

His voice suddenly cracked, just as it used to before the passage of time.

Give Me a Double Shot of Starbucks Nostalgia

The New York Times, March 3, 2007

Is it possible that there are actually two Howard Schultzes lurking around Starbucks headquarters in Seattle? I think it is.

The first Howard Schultz is the man who has coffee in his veins. He's the one who bought what was then the tiny Starbucks company in 1987 and turned it into one of the dominant brands of the age. Starbucks coffee was a step above other coffee, and it also offered a "coffee experience" that made customers willing to pay $4 for something that used to cost them 60 cents.

Starbucks was a place where people could hang out, read the paper, and make friends with the "baristas" behind the counter; Mr. Schultz used to call it the "third place," a respite from both the workplace and the home front. Starbucks had its own language and culture. Its part-time staff got stock options and health insurance. It didn't exploit its coffee growers. It had a huge social responsibility program. And Mr. Schultz, who is chairman of Starbucks, took deep pride in all the things that made Starbucks special.

Last week, this Mr. Schultz was on vivid display when an internal memo he wrote to his top executives was leaked to Starbucksgossip.com. The memo is a cri de coeur from Mr. Schultz, a lament for what has been lost as Starbucks has grown from 6 stores in 1987 to more than 13,000 stores today. He pointed, for instance, to the company's decision some years ago to install automatic espresso machines, which, he wrote, "solved a major problem in terms of speed and service," but also made buying a cup of Starbucks coffee a more antiseptic experience.

He complained about the loss of aroma because the baristas no longer scooped fresh coffee beans from bins and ground them in front of customers. He said that streamlining the company's store designs had caused them to lose "the soul of the past and reflect a chain of stores vs. the warm feeling of a neighborhood store." He said that the Starbucks experience was becoming commoditized, and he urged the executive team to "go back to the core."

The memo was widely lauded as an example of an entrepreneur who understood the importance of recapturing what made his business special before it was too late. "While I wouldn't argue that the Starbucks brand is in its death knell, I would argue that the efficiencies and economies of scale have introduced a virus in need of serious care," wrote Mike Neiss on the Web site of the Tom Peters Company. "And it looks like Howard Schultz just might be the healer they need."

Warren Bennis, the leadership guru who has served as an informal mentor to Mr. Schultz, said, "This is something every successful chief executive should do every once in a while."

But then there's the other Howard Schultz, the one who signed off on the very compromises he complained about in the memo, precisely because they would help the company grow faster. This second Howard Schultz can talk Wall Street's language: he goes on the quarterly conference calls and spits out data about same-store sales, return on investment, and, most of all, growth. Though it has lagged recently, his company's stock price has risen 5,000 percent since it went public in 1992, in large part because Mr. Schultz has been so fanatical about growth.

"Starbucks is the fastest-growing retail story of all time," said John Glass, an analyst with CIBC. "It has grown faster than McDonald's ever did."

This second Howard Schultz shows no signs of slowing down anytime soon. "I want to say this as loud as I possibly can," he told Maria Bartiromo on CNBC last November, after Starbucks released its quarterly earnings. "Three to five years, 20 percent revenue growth, 20 to 25 percent earnings per-share growth. And we're headed to 40,000 stores." Those are astounding goals for a company the size of Starbucks: no company in history has ever built 40,000 retail outlets. (McDonald's, by contrast, has 30,000 stores worldwide.) And 25 percent earnings growth is something only the most aggressive growth companies shoot for.

The quandary Mr. Schultz faces, assuming there is only one of him, is that he wants two things that are incompatible. If he wants to recapture the soul of the old Starbucks, then he has to slow down the company's growth. But if he slows the growth, the stock will collapse. He has to choose. Truth is, though, Mr. Schultz has already chosen.

Once, maybe 10 years ago, Mr. Bennis asked Mr. Schultz why it was so important to him that Starbucks grow so rapidly. "He said something to the effect that if he didn't do it, Starbucks could be cannibalized by another chain that would wipe it out," Mr. Bennis told me.

As I discovered when I asked around, Mr. Schultz is an enormously competitive businessman; I wound up thinking that the idea of relentless growth is just as powerful a driving force for him as coffee itself. In the memo, he complained that Starbucks' competitors have become emboldened to go after Starbucks customers. "This must be eradicated," were the startling words he used.

But to give him his due, Mr. Schultz has always struggled with the problem of trying to stay true to the company's roots while growing aggressively. "Last October or November, he made comments very similar to the thoughts in the memo at a dinner with investors," Mr. Glass said. And according to Anne Saunders, Starbucks' senior vice president for global brand strategy, what he wrote in the memo was nothing Starbucks executives hadn't heard from him many times in the past. "Howard is often challenging us," she said.

"We have grown as a company because we have chosen to do business in a different kind of way," she continued. "If growth comes from doing things that are out of whack, then it is not the right kind of growth." Ms. Saunders went on to say that she, and the rest of the company's managers, believed that the company had grown in ways that remained compatible with its culture.

Maybe. But from where I'm sitting, it just looks as though whenever push has come to shove, the growth imperative has usually won out.

Take, for instance, food. "I remember when Starbucks went public," said Ron Paul of Technomic, a food retail consulting firm. "I went to one of the

roadshow presentations. Howard said that they would never serve food. He thought it would dilute the experience." (A Starbucks spokeswoman said Mr. Schultz was pointing out that Starbucks was a coffee company, not a restaurant chain.)

But one of the most important metrics for Wall Street is same-store sales increases. If growth is being generated purely from the opening of new stores—and not from increased sales in stores that are already open—that's viewed as a bad sign. It means that once the company runs out of places to put stores, it will stop growing. For Starbucks, there was always going to be a limit to how much coffee it could sell in any one location, so to goose same-store sales, it began selling food. (Not very good food either, but that's a whole other story.) Most recently, it has begun selling hot breakfast sandwiches in a number of markets, yet another move it would never have made, say, five years ago. The same principle applies to music, to books, and all the other things Starbucks now sells in its stores.

The food and brand consultants I spoke to were unanimous in their feeling that Starbucks had hurt itself by expanding so far beyond its coffee and coffeehouse roots—and that it needed to return to those roots. "He is right that Starbucks is losing its soul," said Harvey Hartman, who heads the Hartman Group in Bellevue, Wash. "They were built on the coffee experience, and by moving so far beyond that, they are jeopardizing everything else."

Robert Passikoff, president of the brand consultant Brand Keys, said that Starbucks had taken its eye off the brand. "In trying to migrate from a coffee brand to a lifestyle brand, there has been a certain brand dilution." He agreed that the "whole European coffeehouse experience" was no longer how people thought about Starbucks, to the company's detriment. Mr. Passikoff's firm just completed a survey of 20,000 people by phone and in person that showed that Dunkin' Donuts now had higher customer loyalty than Starbucks. He also pointed out that *Consumer Reports* recently asserted that McDonald's coffee was superior to Starbucks'. Both Mr. Passikoff and Mr. Hartman felt that the memo made a great deal of sense.

The Wall Street folks I spoke to, though, saw the memo differently—as a kind of longing for a memory that will never return. "When you grow as big and as fast as they have, you have to make compromises," said Howard Penney, who covers the company for Prudential. "The complexity of the menu has changed dramatically since it first opened," he said. That complexity required automation and other techniques to keep waits for coffee from being too long. (As anyone who buys Starbucks coffee in New York knows, the company doesn't always succeed.)

Mr. Glass of CIBC said: "If it remained a coffee destination and nothing else, same-store sales would not increase. It's a public company. Their job is to make money for the shareholders by selling more stuff." Both Mr. Glass and Mr. Penney pointed out that Starbucks plans to open 2,400 stores this year. That's more than six new stores every day. Tell me how you're going to do that if the baristas start grinding coffee by hand again?

Of course, that's never going to happen, as Ms. Saunders of Starbucks quickly acknowledged when we spoke. "Our business has never been better," she said. "We are really doing well." But the company didn't want to ever rest on its laurels—and it didn't want to sacrifice what made it special just for the sake of growth, she said. "The question is always, How do you keep things in balance?"

For lovers of Starbucks, I suppose it's comforting to know that Mr. Schultz and his team sit around worrying about whether they are watering down the customer experience. But it would be even more comforting if they actually did something about it. Because someday, the growth will slow and the stock will slide—that's inevitable. And how will customers feel if, when that happens, their customer experience has been turned into a drive-through window, just like McDonald's?

Oops, I forgot. Starbucks has already started putting in drive-through windows.

Our Love-Hate Relationship with Wal-Mart

The New York Times, November 5, 2005

At the turn of the last century, a new phenomenon arose in America: the chain store. The most dominant chain was the Great Atlantic and Pacific Tea Company—A&P—which by 1930 had become the country's fifth-largest corporation, with $1 billion in sales, and was "opening stores at a rate unprecedented in the history of American retailing," according to Richard S. Tedlow, the author of *New and Improved: The Story of Mass Marketing in America.*

The New York Times described A&P that year as "the world's greatest retailing machine." Its president, John A. Hartford, attributed the company's success to its policy "of immediately passing on reductions in wholesale commodity prices to the consumer," as the *Times* put it. Under Hartford, writes Mr. Tedlow, "A&P had one dominant mission: to sell quality food at low prices."

Of course, the rise of A&P had other consequences as well. When A&P came to town, it usually meant that many mom-and-pop grocery stores went out of business. Food wholesalers were squeezed, and were sometimes cut out entirely, as A&P took ever greater control of the supply chain. And the company's emphasis on keeping prices low for its customers meant that it was ruthless about keeping wages low for its workers.

Can you guess what happened? Sure you can. Unions agitated, sometimes violently, to organize A&P's workers. Federal legislation was passed intended to prevent the big chains from getting price breaks from manufacturers that small stores couldn't get. More than half the states enacted "chain taxes." And anti-chain-store oratory flourished. "We can whip these chain stores," one populist radio commentator used to proclaim. "We can drive them out in 30 days if you people will stay out of their stores."

But that's precisely the point: people didn't stay out of the stores. Instead, they kept shopping at A&P even though it meant that some of their neighbors lost their businesses, and others worked for low pay. In time, the opposition to the big chains faded, and they became a part of a commercial landscape we now take for granted. The desire for low prices trumped all other considerations. In America, it always does.

These days, there is another huge chain store that finds itself under populist attack: Wal-Mart. For most of its existence, the company was lauded for its low prices, its astonishing logistical abilities, its rah-rah culture, and its rising stock price. There was a widespread feeling, very much shared by Wal-Mart's management, that it was doing God's work in making goods affordable.

Indeed, a reasonable argument can be made that over the last 10 or 15 years, Wal-Mart has done more to keep inflation in check than Alan Greenspan has. After all, Mr. Greenspan, the Fed chairman, can't force Procter & Gamble to roll back a planned increase in the wholesale price of toothpaste. Wal-Mart can—and does.

But now that Wal-Mart vies with ExxonMobil as the largest company in the country, with more employees than the United States Army, the worm has turned. Instead of embracing Wal-Mart, many communities now fight to keep the company out. Groups like Wal-Mart Watch have sprouted, bent on exposing the company's evil ways. Wal-Mart's low wages (less than $10 an hour, on average) and stingy benefits (employees often have to rely on Medicaid because they can't afford or are not eligible for Wal-Mart's health plan) have galvanized union activists.

Just last week, for instance, Wal-Mart Watch, an ally of the unions, got hold of an internal Wal-Mart memo, which it leaked to the *Times*. In it,

Wal-Mart fretted about rising health care costs and suggested that the company might start "discouraging unhealthy people from working at Wal-Mart," as the *Times* put it. And last night, an anti–Wal-Mart documentary, entitled *Wal-Mart: The High Cost of Low Price*, had its premiere in New York and Los Angeles.

The documentary, which I saw this week, is of the Michael Moore variety. A polemic intended to enrage viewers, it catalogs all of Wal-Mart's suspected sins, from forcing small businesses to close, to paying so little that its workers need food stamps, to its supposed reliance on Asian sweatshops.

Not surprisingly, Wal-Mart refused to cooperate with the film, but the movie's producer and director, Robert Greenwald, made no effort to find anyone who was remotely sympathetic to the company. The background music turns melancholy as each Wal-Mart victim tells his or her sad story.

Mr. Greenwald makes no apologies. "Here is a corporation with $10 billion in profits," he said a few days ago, and yet, in his view, it treats two huge constituencies—its workers and the communities where it does business—in ways that are deeply unfair. "It's not right," he said.

Although the movie will be shown in a few dozen theaters around the country, Mr. Greenwald's real strategy is to sell DVDs for $12.95 to activists who will screen it in an effort to gain more converts to the cause. "This is not a model for maximizing profits," Mr. Greenwald said proudly. He struck me as the modern equivalent of the radio populists during A&P's heyday.

So far, Wal-Mart's efforts to rebut its critics have been largely inept. On Tuesday, for instance, it sent its director of corporate affairs, Mia Masten, to New York to try to counter the film, which was being screened that night as a fund-raiser for a group called Wal-Mart Free NYC Coalition. But no one at Wal-Mart had actually seen the movie, so she was reduced to mouthing platitudes, which she did both nervously and unconvincingly.

And yesterday, the company held a conference for academics and journalists to examine Wal-Mart's impact on the economy. Although some of the papers presented at the conference were critical of the company, the centerpiece was a study by the economic research firm Global Insight that purportedly shows, to quote the headline of the Wal-Mart news release the company sent me, that "Wal-Mart Saves Working Families $2,329 Per Year." That may well be true, but the fact that Wal-Mart paid for the study will largely undercut its ability to persuade anyone not already in its camp.

Here's the thing, though. Whatever you might think of its tactics, its wages, its effect on communities, and its economic power, Wal-Mart, for the most part, has played by the rules we as a society have set for it. That's what the anti-Wal-Mart folks tend to leave out of their analysis.

"Wal-Mart has devised an extremely efficient way to deliver low prices to

consumers and good returns to shareholders," said Robert Reich, the former labor secretary who is now a professor at Brandeis University. "That is American capitalism," he added. "That is what the system rewards."

Mr. Reich—who, remember, was a member of the Clinton administration—doesn't even blame Wal-Mart for the fact that its workers often need to rely on Medicaid. "Medicaid," he said, "is designed for the working poor and the poor. If we are not happy about the results, then the real question we ought to be asking ourselves is whether we should be changing the rules. Wal-Mart is an invitation to have that debate."

The new documentary has a number of short clips showing the Wal-Mart chief executive, H. Lee Scott Jr., speaking to investors, employees, and others. In one clip, he says quite bluntly that the company can't raise wages without cutting into the profits that its shareholders expect it to generate. That may sound awfully harsh, but it is undeniably true. We live in an economic culture that exalts "shareholder value" above pretty much everything else. Can you really expect Mr. Scott and his company to turn its back on that?

Similarly, what was true 70 years ago remains true today: we could shut down Wal-Mart and allow small local stores to thrive by doing one simple thing: shopping at the latter instead of the former. But we don't do that. We buy our drugs at drugstore chains like CVS, our food at grocery chains like Safeway, our tools at Home Depot or Lowe's—and just about everything else at Wal-Mart—for the most basic of reasons. Americans love a bargain. Many of us who would choose not to have a Wal-Mart in our backyard still can't resist shopping there once it opens. Wal-Mart's growth is a direct result of its understanding of that fundamental fact.

Do we really want to change Wal-Mart? If the answer truly is yes, then we need to change ourselves first.

The Cufflinks That Went to China

The New York Times, January 21, 2006

Last June, my brother-in-law, Frank E. Williams, took his first trip to Asia. Along with a sales executive who worked for him at Visa Jewelry, Frank traveled to Hong Kong, which is where all the mainland Chinese costume jewelry manufacturers have their showrooms. Frank wanted to see if there was any way he could save his small costume jewelry business in Rhode Island.

Frank recently turned 70, but he's one of those people who is happiest when he's busy; as his wife, my sister Rosemary, wrote in an e-mail message to our family, "forced retirement is probably the only way Frank would consider it." He's been in the costume jewelry business since 1957, starting as an apprentice on the shop floor and rising over time to become a salesman, merchandiser, and designer. He bought his own company in 1978, and named it Visa.

Although Visa never got bigger than 50 employees and $2.5 million in revenue, it has been profitable for most of the time Frank has owned it. The last five or six years, though, have been rough. "If we broke even," my sister recalled recently, "we considered ourselves lucky." By 2005, the business was steadily losing money. Frank and Rosemary drew down the company's line of credit, and then began using their own credit to keep it going. "Customers weren't buying, and if they were buying, they were pushing us hard to lower our price," my sister said. And there wasn't much doubt about why this was happening. Globalization was taking its toll, as Chinese manufacturers have pretty much taken over the costume jewelry industry.

What Frank saw in Hong Kong only drove home the obvious. "Ten years ago," he said, "Chinese imports were terrible. But in every showroom we visited, we saw a quality product." Frank has long specialized in men's jewelry, particularly studs and cufflinks for tuxedos. "My average pair of cufflinks, taking into account overhead and a 10 percent profit, costs $6.50," he said. "I could get the same pair of cufflinks from China for $2 and change." Peter Jernquist, the Visa executive who made the trip with Frank, said, "There was nothing we could make in the U.S. that couldn't be made far less expensively in China."

After returning to Rhode Island, Frank thought he might try to become a distributor of Chinese costume jewelry. But that required additional capital, and he and Rosemary were worried they might be throwing good money after bad. Besides, becoming an importer would still mean letting go most of the company's employees, and a large part of the reason Frank wanted to stay in business was to preserve their jobs.

In August, after a long weekend of soul-searching, Frank and Rosemary succumbed to the inevitable, and decided to shut Visa. And Rhode Island lost one of its last remaining costume jewelry manufacturers.

When I was growing up in Providence, the city was known as the Costume Jewelry Capital of the nation. There were literally hundreds of jewelry factories, not just in Providence, but across the state. Many were tiny, but some had as many as 500 or 600 employees; at its peak, costume jewelry provided

jobs for 40,000 to 50,000 people, and many more in satellite industries. In high school, having a summer job in a jewelry factory was practically a rite of passage.

"We thought it would be there forever," recalled Jack Reed, Rhode Island's Democratic senator. But the industry peaked sometime around 1978, and today, according to Rich Youmans of the Manufacturing Jewelers and Suppliers of America, there probably aren't more than 500 costume jewelry jobs left in the state. What jewelry-making still exists in Rhode Island resides in the higher-margin precious metals.

High-end jewelry is different from the costume business, though, not least because it is not as cost-sensitive. Costume is fundamentally about two things: design and price. Which is to say, it is exactly the kind of American industry globalization destroys. Over the years, Frank worked hard to control costs, but there was no way he could even come close to Chinese labor costs. As everyone knows, cheap labor is one of China's competitive advantages in the global marketplace.

As for his design skills, which Frank always thought of as his competitive advantage, globalization rendered them less and less useful. Customers would buy some of his new pieces, and then send them to China to have the designs reproduced. "Three or four months later," Mr. Jernquist said, "you'd see the same design on a Chinese Web site." Senator Reed told me that he tried to help with intellectual property issues, but conceded that it was hard to rouse much interest. "The loss to the industry is huge, but to the federal government, this is pretty small stuff," he said.

Indeed, the main reason Frank's company lasted as long as it did was that he made the shrewd decision to stick with men's jewelry, which is a niche business compared with women's jewelry. China wiped out the much larger women's costume jewelry industry first, before turning its attention to the men's side of the business. "Frank did everything right," said Peter M. DiCristofaro, who runs the Providence Jewelry Museum. "The times were against him."

The American economy will not rise or fall on the fate of the costume jewelry business, of course, but it does make you think about the real-world consequences of globalization. There is no question that when Americans can buy cufflinks for $2 instead of $6.50, it's a net plus for consumers. Nor is there any question that globalization is profoundly good for the people of China and India and other emerging economies.

But does it matter that, in the process, as Senator Reed put it, "a great source of wages and employment" is being lost? Frank and Rosemary certainly think so; my sister told me that she worried about whether there would

be any manufacturing left in this country if the government didn't step in. "There have to be some industries in this country that use nonskilled labor," said Frank.

Clyde V. Prestowitz Jr., the president of the Economic Strategy Institute and a leading critic of globalization, worries that the government lacks "a sense of urgency" as not only manufacturing jobs but service jobs move overseas. "The theory has long been that we are going to make up in service jobs what we lose in manufacturing," he told me. "If you look at our own trade figures, you'll see a small and declining surplus in services."

Most mainstream economists, though, believe that globalization is not something we should fear, even if it does eliminate low-wage industries like costume jewelry. "People panicked when consumer electronics moved elsewhere," said Diana Farrell, the director of the McKinsey Global Institute. But, she said, that move not only gave consumers lower-priced goods, it also spurred innovation here and led, eventually, to better-paying, higher-value jobs. "The process of globalization," she added, "is wealth-creating for the economy."

But she conceded that there were people, and industries, that were inevitably going be left behind. The trick was not to protect the jobs, but to protect the people—by stressing education and retraining, "delinking health care from employers," and, in general, helping people make the transition from a declining industry to a growing one. No matter how you feel about globalization, you'd have to have a heart of stone to disagree with this sentiment. Which is also, I think, the most discouraging part of this story.

In the months since Visa went out of business, Frank and Rosemary have worked hard to find new jobs for their workers. They've scoured the help-wanted ads and talked to anybody they could think of who might have a job to offer. They haven't had much luck. My sister told me of one woman who found a job; the wages were lower "but at least she has health care now." Most of the other employees, however, remain out of work.

For a while, she thought she had found a great way to help them: the Department of Labor's Trade Adjustment Assistance program. In a meeting with the program's Rhode Island representative, she got more and more excited as she heard about the benefits. They included not only job search workshops, but cash to pay for faraway job interviews, tax credits to help cover health insurance premiums, money for school, up to two and a half years of unemployment benefits to someone who was in the process of learning a new skill, and more.

Then she came to the line on the application that asked which country's imports were responsible for failure of the business. The Labor Department's

agent tried to steer her answer. "If you mark down China," he told her, "it disqualifies you."

She couldn't believe it. Neither could I. But I looked it up on the Labor Department's Web site, and sure enough, it was true. The assistance was available only to workers who could show that they'd been laid off "as a result of a shift in production to a country that is party to a free trade agreement with the United States"—like Nafta. In other words, if you've lost your job because of imports from, say, Canada, you can get the benefits. But if Chinese imports are the culprit, you're out of luck.

Thanks for nothing.

CHAPTER 14

Return of the Raider

Two decades after my first business story, I came full circle. I went to Dallas and wrote another long story about Boone.

The brief synopsis of the 15 or so years during which Boone and I were estranged is included in this story. Here are a few facts, though, that I didn't put in that story: First, I was an awful ghostwriter. Agreeing to ghost Boone's memoirs in 1986 was the worst career decision I ever made; I completely lacked the ability to write in someone else's voice, and bridled when Boone began rewriting my chapters into a more folksy tone that was far better suited to him. When he fired me, halfway through the project, I was secretly relieved.

I was also, of course, furious, and I responded to the firing by filing a lawsuit to get the money I felt I was owed. By the time the lawsuit was settled, I had moved from Texas to New England. Boone hired another ghost to finish the book, installed him in his home in Amarillo, and made his deadline. When the book did poorly in the marketplace, I made no effort to hide my glee. It was not my finest moment. It took me years to realize that our falling-out was as much my fault as his.

Still, during the intervening years, I never stopped watching him out of the corner of my eye. I watched as Unocal and the courts put an end to Boone's days as a corporate raider; watched Mesa's stock slowly sink as he kept betting—and losing—that natural gas prices would rise; watched as he embarrassed himself by feuding with half of Amarillo; saw him try—and fail—to take on the Japanese corporate system; and watched him make a number of "shareholders' rights" efforts that never got much traction. I had kept in touch with Ralph Whitworth, one of Boone's former aides who had gone on to cofound a successful shareholder activist firm, Relational Investors, with another ex-Mesa executive, David Batchelder. It was Batchelder

who put Mesa in play, causing Boone to lose the company he had founded in his 20s. I watched that Oedipal battle play out too. Over the years, as my anger from the failed book project dissipated, I began to view him a sad figure. "A prophet without honor," I once described him in the early 1990s.

Which is why I was so surprised to discover in 2002 that Boone had not fallen off the face of the earth after all. Instead, he had gone back into business with a vengeance. It may not be what you or I would choose to do in our 70s, but it's what makes him happy.

Things have changed even since I wrote this story. Boone got divorced and remarried again. One of his sons, Mike, the one I met in Houston 25 years ago, was arrested a few years ago and went into rehab; the younger son, Tom, gave a lengthy interview to *Portfolio*, a new business magazine, complaining about how shabbily he was treated by his father when he was growing up. I think back to my old 1982 story in *Texas Monthly*, when I asked him about his family life. "As long as the children had something to say, we would talk," he replied. "But as soon as they started that silly stuff, well, that wasn't in the program." I remember thinking even then that it must have been tough growing up in that household. And yet it is obvious that Boone would like to repair his relations with his children, something he has done, with some success, with his daughters. As a father of grown children myself, I read that *Portfolio* story and winced.

On the business front, however, Boone has scarcely made a false step. The water project described in this story still hasn't gotten off the ground—but it has become even more ambitious, and now includes wind from the Panhandle of Texas as an alternative energy source. His natural-gas fuels company, now called Clean Energy Fuels, went public in 2007, and has had a nice little run. And Boone isn't trying to rattle corporate cages anymore, as he was in 2002. Instead, he is focused on trading equities and commodities in his hedge funds. In the intervening years since I wrote this story, his funds have done extraordinarily well—as of the fall of 2007, the equity fund had $4 billion under management, much of it Boone's money. In 2007, *Forbes* magazine ranked him 117 on its list of the richest people in the country, with a net worth of $3 billion.

I see him now a couple of times a year, whenever he is New York and has a little time to spare. We usually have breakfast in his hotel and catch up on this and that. He usually has a few funny stories and some good gossip. We avoid politics. Eventually, I get around to asking him a business question or two, usually about the oil or natural gas markets. He's 80 years old, and I've learned a lot about business from him. I still do.

Return of the Raider

Fortune, May 27, 2002

"Do you think I've changed?" Boone asked.

It was late on a gorgeous spring afternoon in Dallas, and T. Boone Pickens Jr. was in a contemplative mood. He was leaning back in his comfortable leather office chair, his hands stuffed in his pockets, his feet propped up on his desk. Though he'd been getting hammered in the natural gas futures market recently, he looked like a man without a care.

Boone has lived in Dallas since 1989, but his spacious office reminded me of the one he'd had in Amarillo, Texas, when I first met him 20 years ago, back when he was running Mesa Petroleum and preparing to take on the world. There was the sports memorabilia from Oklahoma State University, his beloved alma mater. The oil painting "Trails in the Palo Duro," by the Western artist G. Harvey. The framed Mesa stock certificates. The little mementos commemorating old deals. There were a few new things as well. Pinned against the back wall was an enormous map of a four-county area in the Texas Panhandle that includes Boone's 27,000-acre ranch. It serves as a constant reminder of his audacious—and yet unrealized—plan to drill water from the aquifer that lies under that land and sell it to some water-starved Texas city like Dallas or San Antonio. There were also at least two dozen pictures of family members in prominent places all over the office: Boone's daughter Pam with her three children; Boone hunting quail with several of his grandsons; Boone with his new wife, Nelda; Boone's new stepson with his wife and children. Maybe it's just the haze of memory, but I don't remember seeing many family pictures in his office in the old days. It certainly wasn't something he talked about much.

Of course 20 years ago Boone didn't have much truck with contemplation either. He was too busy shaking up the established order as the most feared and famous of the 1980s corporate raiders. And it wasn't his style in any case. Like most CEOs I've known, he viewed serious reflection as a big waste of time. He resisted all attempts at journalistic psychoanalysis. He seemed to harbor no doubts about anything. When he did reminisce, he tended to repeat the same well-honed stories—stories in which he always came out on top.

But Boone's approaching 74 now, and he's been through things he could scarcely have imagined back when he was taking on the likes of Gulf Oil and gracing the covers of *Fortune* and *Time*. In the mid-1990s he lost Mesa, his

life's work, a company he'd founded 40 years earlier—a deal made all the more painful by the fact that the company was put in play by a former protégé. That was followed by an ugly and protracted divorce from his second wife, Bea. He struggled with depression. Some long-standing relationships—with employees, old friends, and even some of his children—became strained to the breaking point.

I was among those whose relationship with Boone had ended badly. As a young staff writer with *Texas Monthly* magazine in the early 1980s, I wrote about him extensively, and we became friends. When, at the peak of his fame, he decided to write his autobiography, he hired me as his ghostwriter. But after we started working on the book, I could sense him souring on me, and halfway through it he fired me. I was angry and hurt, and we didn't speak for more than 15 years.

Not long ago, Boone sent me a nice note, which I took to be an olive branch, and we began to reconnect. As we got reacquainted, I started to realize that, septuagenarian or no, Boone was involved in a surprising array of businesses and deals—and not just the water deal, which has gotten a fair amount of publicity. Boone owns 25 percent of a company he founded, called ENRG, that markets natural gas as a substitute for gasoline. It's doing well enough that an IPO may be in the works next year. He runs a hugely successful commodities fund that speculates in natural gas futures. He's started an equity fund that invests in undervalued energy companies. He even has a profitable little business buying ranches, fixing them up, and then selling them to wealthy hunters.

I also couldn't help noticing the money Boone was making: an astonishing $150 million in 2000 and another $100 million or so last year, thanks largely to the success of the commodities fund. Even in his heyday Boone never earned anything close to that. After the divorce in 1998, Boone was worth $37 million. Today his net worth is upwards of $200 million; he's made more money in his 70s than in the rest of his life put together.

As we spent more time together I began to sense something else: The man I was getting to know again was in many ways different from the raider I'd met two decades before. After 30 years of knowing only success, he had spent a decade being humbled, and that experience had changed him. As to how it changed him, well, I eventually realized one last thing: answering that question—the question he'd just asked me—was what this story was really about.

He told me to meet him at the entrance of a New York office building; we could fly back to Dallas together in his private jet. "We can catch up on the ride back," he said—just like we'd always done in the old days.

The old days, indeed. Boone had come to New York on this early April morning for a meeting with the chairman of a small energy company called Penn Virginia. A few weeks earlier Boone had filed a document with the SEC disclosing that he—or more precisely, the BP Energy Equity fund, his new $125 million equity fund—had taken a 7.1 percent stake in the company. In the document Boone described Penn Virginia as "undervalued" and said that the company might be a candidate "for a leveraged buyout or sale." It was one of two stakes he has publicly disclosed, the other being an 8.4 percent ownership in a larger energy company called Vintage Petroleum. In other words, Boone was approaching his 74th birthday by getting back into the corporate-raiding game—or at least some small, genteel version of it.

By the time I got to the office building, Boone was already outside. He was wearing a tweed sports jacket and a Western-style monogrammed shirt with no tie—Boone almost never wears a tie anymore, even when he's visiting the chairmen of companies he has taken a position in. He looked older, of course, but not substantially different. A lifelong health fanatic, Boone is still in great shape, though he now has a slight paunch he can't get rid of no matter how much he exercises. He sometimes wears hearing aids, though he didn't have them in on this day. Rather, he had a cell phone pressed against his ear. I knew he had to be checking in with the office. Some things never change.

Walking next to him was his longtime consigliere, Robert Stillwell. For 33 years, as a lawyer with the Houston firm of Baker & Botts, "Bobby" Stillwell served as Mesa's outside counsel; for most of that time he was Boone's closest adviser and confidant. Boone, Stillwell says, is a man of "tremendous loyalty," but he had long demanded total loyalty in return, and his definition of loyalty could be pretty taxing. Stillwell was one of the few who always passed the test, who accepted the fact that with Boone, you had the chance to do some pretty exciting things, like lead the hostile takeover and shareholder rights movements, but you were also expected to get involved in Boone's more quixotic causes. Since joining Boone full-time at the beginning of the year upon reaching his firm's mandatory retirement age of 65, Stillwell had been deeply involved in the new equity fund, which he enjoyed. But he was also working on the water deal, which was fraught with difficulty and steeped in politics—and had as much to do with Boone's desire to stick it to his old hometown of Amarillo as it did with his desire to make money.

We drove to the airport, strapped ourselves into the plane, and headed for Dallas. Even before we were in the air, the two men began recounting the Penn Virginia meeting. They sounded like nothing so much as an old married couple.

"I think they were expecting us to make a buyout proposal right there,"

laughed Boone. Stillwell agreed. "Can't see why else they would have had all those people in the room"—including the company's lawyers and investment bankers.

"We told them we were just coming up there to introduce ourselves, now that we're shareholders," said Boone. During the meeting, he added, he had told the chairman that he had no interest in running Penn Virginia himself, no matter how the deal played out. "Those days are *over*," he said now. "No more of that Phillips Petroleum stuff." This was a reference to his 1985 takeover battle with Phillips, during which he'd said publicly that he would move to Bartlesville, Okla., where Phillips was headquartered, if he acquired the company. "Bea said she wouldn't go." He let out a small chuckle. "Boy, wouldn't that have been great?"

Boone had started the equity fund last August, seeding it with $90 million, money that was supplied not only by him but by old friends like Alan "Ace" Greenberg, the longtime chairman of Bear Stearns, and Fayez Sarofim, the wealthy Houston money manager. Boone believes strongly that the energy industry is headed for a new round of consolidation; the fund was a way to play his theory. The small team he'd assembled—all people he'd worked with in the past and with whom he was extremely comfortable—would find energy companies that seemed like potential acquisition candidates. Then they would buy stock in these companies and either wait for someone else to take them over or begin pressing for a sale or an LBO. Late last year the fund acquired stakes in several companies that wound up being bought out even before Boone had a chance to disclose his holdings. As a result the fund was up 17 percent by the end of the year, and he felt his concept had been validated.

Boone wants to make things happen pretty quickly. "At my age," he says, "you don't have time to plant small trees." But he isn't much interested in "going hostile" anymore. These days it's almost impossible to take over a company that doesn't want to be acquired. Just about every state has enacted antitakeover legislation—laws prompted, in large part, by the political reaction to Boone and other raiders like Carl Icahn and Irwin Jacobs. And antitakeover defenses such as poison pills make it awfully difficult to engage in the kind of hardball tactics Boone used in the 1980s.

On the other hand, the world has changed since Boone's raiding days. People who buy large stakes in poorly performing companies aren't called raiders anymore; they're called "shareholder activists." And company managements are now under intense pressure to get the price of the stock up and reward their shareholders. One reason Boone engaged in hostile takeovers in the old days is that whenever he became a big shareholder of a company,

management just told him to go away. ("They used to say, 'Screw the stock price, let's get *him*,'" recalls Stillwell.) That doesn't happen anymore; "creating shareholder value" is simply too important in today's business culture. Without question, Boone had a lot to do with that transformation; to my mind, helping bring about that change is his legacy. Penn Virginia may not have been happy that he was a big stockholder, but the company would certainly be looking for ways to get the share price up, even if he did nothing more. "I've got the strong sense that they're already working on a plan," said Stillwell. Boone agreed.

That subject exhausted, I asked Boone about his water deal. He controls the underground water rights to 150,000 acres in the Panhandle north of Amarillo, including his own ranch. He wants to build a pipeline that could transport that water to some parched city; depending on the pipeline's route, it could cost anywhere from $1.2 billion to $1.8 billion. Boone's plan is highly controversial in Amarillo, where many people accuse him of trying to profit by diverting water, as in the movie *Chinatown*, that "belongs" in the Panhandle. Three years since coming up with the idea, Boone has spent $4 million on studies, consultants, and lawyers, and he still doesn't have either a permit to drill for water or a customer that has agreed to buy it. But he has no intention of giving up. "We're going to win this thing," he said.

What I wanted to know was *why?* Why, at his age, was he spending so much time and effort and money on a venture with such a high degree of difficulty? Especially since, by his own calculations, he was never going to make much money on the deal.

His answer, essentially, was that he was trying to protect himself from the predations of his old hometown. One of the local water authorities had begun pumping water from the ranch adjoining his; since that water comes from the aquifer that lies under his property, eventually his water would be drained as well. "I don't need the money," Boone said. "I'll set it up so that I give anything I make to charity. But I'm in a tough spot if I don't do something. I'll get drained. I'll be damned if I'm going to let that happen." The fact that he could see a solution to a pressing problem also pushed his buttons. "If this pipeline runs through West Texas, we can solve their water problems for the next hundred years," he said. Mainly, though, it was just a lot of fun trying to pull off a deal this complicated.

What struck me most as I listened to Boone was how calm he was about everything, how at peace he seemed. Twenty years ago he had a surface calm, but he was always roiling inside. And he had a very long memory; as Wales Madden, an old Amarillo friend, puts it, "Boone was too quick to remember and too slow to forget." But he wasn't like that anymore.

I knew he was disappointed that he'd only been able to raise $125 million for his equity fund; he'd expected to have three or four times that sum by now. In part he'd assumed that his name and reputation would be enough to bring in money. But as he searched for investors, he'd discovered that a lot of 30- and 40-year-old institutional investors barely knew who he was—and were telling him his fund would have to prove itself like any other new fund. Once, Boone might have responded to questions about the fund's size with sarcasm or recriminations. Not now. "We had unrealistic expectations," he shrugged.

In the old days, too, Boone would have talked my ear off all the way to Dallas, and I would have peppered him with questions at the slightest pause in the conversation. But it's not just Boone and Stillwell who've gotten older; so have I. Which is why, after an hour or so, the talk tapered off, and by the time we were over Missouri, the three of us were fast asleep.

"I should have stopped after the Gulf deal," Boone said one night. "I would have been a folk hero."

We were having dinner at his ranch, and the subject had turned, inevitably, to the past. When I first knew Boone, his ranch had been called the 2B—the initials stood for Boone and Bea. He raised cattle on it back then, and his small, utilitarian ranch house stood on another part of the property. After he and Bea separated, he changed the name to Mesa Vista and sold off 4,000 acres that included the original house. Now his ranch house was large and even a little opulent, and though he still had a small cattle operation, he used the property primarily to hunt quail, to entertain family (especially his 14 grandchildren)—and to find solace.

"Did I ever tell you about the time Drew Lewis came up here?" he asked. Lewis, a Transportation Secretary under Ronald Reagan, was CEO of Warner Amex Cable at the time of the visit. "It was right after the *Time* cover story," Boone continued. Lewis had just come from a meeting of the Business Roundtable, and he told Boone that the organization had decided to start a public relations campaign against him. "Ol' Drew said they'd raised something like $10 million right there on the spot." The Business Roundtable, of course, comprised the big old-line companies that Pickens had made suddenly vulnerable with his takeover attempts. "He said that I'd better dig a hole and get in it, because they were coming after me," Boone said.

The *Time* magazine cover story had come out in the spring of 1985, less than a year after the Gulf deal—his most breathtaking raid by far and his most financially successful. It was the third of the six big hostile takeovers he attempted between 1982 and 1987, and though he didn't take over the

company in the end—let's be honest here; he never did land one—he did ultimately force the oil giant into the arms of Chevron, netting Mesa $404 million for its Gulf stake. The Gulf battle had been a high-stakes drama, transforming Boone, for a brief moment, into the most famous businessman in America, the folksy yet swashbuckling corporate raider. It also made him seem invincible. But he wasn't. Within a few years, Boone's world began to slowly fall apart.

Not that he could see it coming. With a hubris born of that early success, Boone launched hostile raids on Phillips and Unocal, fully expecting even greater victories. Though Mesa made a little money on Phillips, Unocal handed him a defeat so resounding that it pretty much ended his corporate-raiding career. After that, says a former lieutenant, "it was just a long, slow, grinding decline."

Mesa by the mid-1980s was the largest independent exploration company in the country. But 80 percent of its reserves were natural gas, and the price of natural gas was sinking. Boone, however, was convinced that over the long term, natural gas prices had to go up—and he bet the company on that belief. He borrowed money to purchase reserves that made economic sense only if gas prices rose, which they didn't. Worse, he had begun to pay a large distribution to Mesa's shareholders in a deliberate attempt to show that he, at least, was a CEO who put his shareholders first. As gas prices declined—and Mesa could no longer afford to pay the distribution from cash flow—Boone borrowed money to make the payments. Ultimately, Mesa paid $1.1 billion to its shareholders—and wound up saddled with $1.2 billion in debt. That debt became the noose that strangled the company.

When I asked Boone what had been his biggest mistake in business, he didn't hesitate. "Giving all that money to the shareholders," he said. "I thought there would be a huge outcry if we stopped doing it." But when, in 1990, he realized he had to stop paying the distribution, there was no outcry at all. "I was astounded," he said. "It just wasn't that big a deal." As for his bet on natural gas, the price did eventually rise, but far too late for Mesa. As he's fond of saying, "You can be dead right—and dead."

As Mesa and its stock slowly sank, so did Boone's mood. "I think he was embarrassed somewhat," says a former aide. "In 1985, Boone could say he had a 20-year record of returning shareholders a 28 percent compounded rate of return. But over the next ten years, that record got chipped away, and it wasn't so great anymore. All the people who used to slap him on the back and thank him for making them money, they weren't doing that anymore. It weighed on him."

Indeed, his relationship with the entire city of Amarillo seemed to go

bad. Boone became a polarizing figure in town, a lightning rod for criticism. When he got involved in local affairs—as with his stormy tenure as the head of the board of regents at nearby West Texas State University (now known as West Texas A&M)—his critics accused him of highhandedness. Boone, who thought he should be embraced for lending a hand to local institutions, bristled at the criticisms. Of course his view was also that he was right and his critics were wrong, and that didn't help either.

The symbol of this deteriorating relationship was Boone's feud with the *Amarillo Globe-News*. Even during the glory years, it always bothered him that the paper insisted on labeling him a raider. (He still hates the label: "I never liked being called a raider," he says. "I never destroyed anything.") Like a ballplayer who starts yelling back at the fans when he's in a slump, Boone began writing critiques of articles and sending them to the editors. He dispatched emissaries to the newsroom to complain about the coverage of him—and threatened to leave Amarillo if things didn't change. Boone even set up an organization, run by Mesa executives, urging people to cancel their subscriptions. He handed out bumper stickers that read I CANCELLED. When *Globe-News* general manager Jerry Huff was transferred to a paper in Georgia, Boone hung a banner from the top of the Mesa building that read GOOD-BYE, JERRY.

It was a sad spectacle, and for many Mesa executives, extremely distasteful. Most of them were young men who had joined Mesa in the expectation that they'd be doing bigtime Wall Street deals. In the mid-1980s, working for Mesa had been exhilarating—"the most fun I ever had in business," one of them says now. But feuding with the *Globe-News* was not what they'd signed up for, and they started to leave. In 1989, Boone decided he'd had enough. He and Mesa moved to Dallas.

By then his marriage to Bea—whom he'd wed in 1972—was in bad straits, though like his business decline, it unraveled in slow motion. His relations with his four children from his first marriage, now grown, were chilly. (His fifth child, Liz, is Bea's youngest; Boone adopted her after he married Bea.) Some nights, after he got home from a difficult day at the office, he would head for the driving range and hit buckets of golf balls, just to be out of the house.

Boone now believes his depression began in the early 1990s. "When you're depressed," he says, "you don't have any energy. I was tired all the time." At the least, he was under a lot of stress and not handling it well. Humor had long been his saving grace; now it took on a hard, unpleasant edge. He would denigrate former lieutenants after they left the company— or even before they left. He railed at those he felt had wronged him.

He also felt enormous pressure to turn Mesa around—all by himself. "He used to say, 'I got us in this ditch. I'm going to get us out of it,' " recalls Sidney Tassin, who spent 14 years at Mesa before leaving in 1994. "I isolated myself," Boone agrees. "I felt like I had to both throw the ball and catch it. That's a pretty tough thing to do."

By the mid-1990s, Mesa was in terrible shape: its cash dwindling, its billion-dollar debt coming due, its ability to raise money on Wall Street largely gone. From 1989 to 1994, Mesa lost between $60 million and $200 million annually. Anyone paying attention could see that Boone needed to restructure Mesa.

Unfortunately for him, one of the people playing closest attention was his former chief strategist, David Batchelder, who had left Mesa in 1988 under the usual strained circumstances. Smelling opportunity, Batchelder rounded up some wealthy investors, including billionaire Marvin Davis. They took a stake in Mesa and publicly demanded that Boone find a way to get the stock price up—or else. Thus it was that the student turned the tables on the teacher.

What followed was a battle that Boone never really had a chance to win. "Mesa just had a poor set of cards," says Tassin. The spat between Boone and Batchelder turned into a public humiliation. The press delighted in the irony of seeing Boone on the receiving end of a hostile takeover. When Boone pushed for poison pill and golden parachute provisions, he was mocked as a hypocrite. It infuriated him that Batchelder had set in motion events that caused him to be held up to such scrutiny and ridicule—and if the truth be known, it still bothers him. In Boone's view Batchelder had come to Mesa as a young man, learned a tremendous amount, and left with $8 million in his pocket. And *this* was the thanks Boone got?

Batchelder, for his part, claims that Boone's ire was never justified—that his motives were always benign. "Boone knows our intent was never to have the company taken over," he says. "The sole intent was to make some money off something I was convinced he would do—deleverage Mesa."

In the end, though, Mesa was taken over. In February 1996, seeing no way out of his predicament, Boone agreed to hand over control to Texas investor Richard Rainwater, whom he had known for years and with whom he cut a deal. Rainwater wound up recapitalizing Mesa with just $300 million of new equity, of which Rainwater himself put up $130 million. Though Boone stayed on the board for another year, he was effectively out. In late 1997, Boone sold his Mesa stock for $35 million. Less than a year later he left the board.

In retrospect it was good that Boone left Mesa—good for the company (which is now called Pioneer) and good for Boone, who desperately needed a

fresh start. And he's happy to admit as much. But he still can't look back without shaking his head. "Gawd almighty," he exclaims. "It only took $300 million to recapitalize the company! There's no way I couldn't have raised $300 million. But I was so beaten down. It really shows you that I wasn't thinking clearly."

He has always been a great speculator. I remember traveling with Boone in the 1980s, watching in amazement as he bet big on cattle futures, pork bellies, you name it. Eventually he abandoned those markets to concentrate on natural gas and crude oil futures. He may have been wrong about the long-term price of natural gas, but when it came to betting on short-term trends, he had few peers. Between the mid-1980s and the mid-1990s, Boone actually covered Mesa's $15 million annual administrative overhead by playing the futures market. "He used to do it out of his back pocket," marvels Stillwell. "He'd spend 15 minutes a day on it."

So it was hardly a surprise when, after exiting Mesa, Boone decided to set up a small commodities fund that would concentrate on natural gas futures. He gathered a small team of loyalists to staff it and rounded up the usual suspects to help fund it, including Ace Greenberg and Fayez Sarofim. The BP Capital Energy fund opened for business in May 1997 with $36 million in capital.

In his office one day Boone showed me a chart of the fund's five-year performance record. It goes up a little at first before making a long, steep descent; by the end of 1998, the fund is down almost 90 percent, to less than $4 million. It recovers a little in 1999, and suddenly, with the arrival of 2000, it leaps straight up. By the end of 2000, the fund is up to $252 million for an eye-popping gain of 5,400 percent. The following year—last year, that is—it's up another $148 million.

"What Boone did in 2000 constitutes one of the greatest individual trading runs of all time," says Tassin. My own view is that his performance last year was even more impressive. After all, in 2000 gas prices finally went up, just as Boone had been predicting. But in 2001, they fell—from $10 per thousand cubic feet to around $3—and Boone *still* made buckets of money. Yet as I looked at the chart, I couldn't help noticing something else. It may be just a coincidence, but its fall and eventual rise almost perfectly mirror Boone's emotional state during those years.

If the late 1980s were dominated by Boone's feud with Amarillo, and the early and middle 1990s by the troubles at Mesa, then the middle to late 1990s constituted the Years of the Divorce. It was brutal—a knock-down, drag-out battle that lasted for two years and didn't end until mid-1998. It was filled

with charges and countercharges, with bitterness and recriminations. It consumed Boone. Combined with the way he had lost Mesa, the divorce nearly destroyed him. It got to the point where people didn't want to be around him, knowing they'd be harangued about Batchelder or Rainwater or Bea. It got to the point, in fact, where Boone was spending more time talking to his divorce lawyer than to just about anyone else.

Which, it turns out, was a damn lucky thing. The man's name is John McShane; he's been doing divorce law for 35 years, and he's seen just about everything—though, he says, the Pickens case was "about the toughest I've ever been involved in." After they got to know each other, Boone and McShane became very close, and pretty soon Boone was confiding in him, expressing his deepest fears and his innermost thoughts in a way he'd never done with anyone before. McShane was thus in a position to see firsthand the emotional damage Boone was suffering—but he was also in a unique position to do something about it.

Early in 1997, McShane confronted Boone. He told Boone that he thought he was suffering from clinical depression and needed help. Once, Boone might have waved him off or made some joke to deflect his concern. Not now. "What do you recommend that I do?" he replied.

Boone went to see a psychotherapist, and he spent a short time taking antidepressants. Pretty soon he was back to his old self. Except that he wasn't his old self anymore—not really. Something happened as he emerged from the darkness, something good. As his daughter Liz puts it, "He really did become a kinder, gentler Boone." Part of it, Liz believes, had to do with the simple fact that the divorce came to an end. "I so desperately wanted them to stay together," she says. "But now it's clear that they're both so much better apart." Another part of it is that Boone started to think hard about how he'd spent his life and how he wanted to spend the rest of it. The old bitterness and resentments, most of them, went away. He abandoned old grudges. He regained his sense of humor. He just became—there is no other way to put it—*nicer*. "He knows who he is and what he's about," says one old friend, "and that hasn't always been the case." He wasn't trying to impress the world anymore, or change it, or make people see that he had it all figured out. He was instead a man in his 70s who'd lived a pretty interesting life and wanted to enjoy what was left of it. Suddenly he was a lot of fun to be around.

Of course it didn't hurt that in 1999 he met a woman named Nelda Cain and fell madly in love. They met on a blind date, and, she says, the attraction was immediate. Nelda, 52, a family therapist, has had her share of rocky times; she's twice divorced and has raised a son largely on her own. As she and Boone grew closer, she says, "we were both scared to death." They broke

up for six months, during which time she moved to Aspen. But Boone kept calling. Finally he asked her to come to Dallas for a party, and she consented. She never went back. They flew to California on a vacation and had a long talk about whether they should get married. When Boone proposed, he began with the immortal words, "Neither one of us can afford to book another loss." She laughed out loud.

I couldn't help wondering if Nelda would have fallen in love with the person Boone used to be. I have my doubts—and so does she. When she talks about him, she uses words like "openness" and "honesty." She talks about his "generous heart" and "dry wit." She says things like, "He's gotten more forgiving of himself and others." I had dinner with them one night; a year and a half into their marriage they still act like newlyweds. "It's nice to see," says McShane. "It's such a contrast to the dark days."

Boone did one other thing to repair his personal life. Two days before Christmas in 1999, he wrote a letter to his children admitting that in his quest for business success, he'd often left them behind. He asked for the chance to repair the relationship while there was still time. Even before the letter, his daughter Pam, now a broker in Tulsa, had begun the process of trying to mend her relationship with her father. "It was hard, growing up in our house," she says. "But my dad has changed. He's more giving, and more generous with his time. And he's remorseful for things that happened." She adds, "My relationship with my father is a huge part of my life, and I get a lot of fulfillment out of it." Still, Boone remains estranged from several of his children. It's the great, lingering sadness in his life.

"How's your golf game?" I asked Boone one day in the office.

"Terrible," he groaned, and then explained, with a grimace, that his swing had abandoned him. It got so bad that Boone would lift his club and then just freeze at the top. Boone has no idea why this has happened. He'd seen a golf psychologist and consulted with his friend Mike Holder, the Oklahoma State golf coach, but to no avail. He gave me a pained shrug. "I'll tell you something," he said. "If I could get my golf game back, I'd give all this up in a minute." Then he laughed.

In fact, it's hard to believe that Boone could ever give up coming to the office, even for golf. "Boone's always had the ability to make money," says Stillwell, but it's more than that. Making money is what he does for fun—for relaxation, even—and he's making more of it now than he ever has before. He's surrounded by people whom he knows and trusts and likes. He does only things that interest him. If he wants to give away millions to charity— and he does—who's going to tell him he can't?

In the old days, Boone, like most CEOs, used to be scheduled practically to the second. Now he usually comes to the office with a looser agenda—no more than a couple of planned meetings—and spends the rest of his time on the phone, which has always been his lifeline. People want to hear what he thinks about oil and gas prices, and he tells them. He trades market information and gossip with Wall Street pals. He calls friends in the Panhandle to find out what's going on up there. He constantly watches the ebb and flow of natural gas prices. Sometimes he works from the ranch, where he has a huge computer screen against a wall in his bedroom. Sometimes he even goes on vacation—though he still checks in with the office ten times a day. In the old days he used to stay late or go back to work after dinner. Now he leaves the office at a reasonable hour to get home to Nelda and his dog, Murdock.

He's even enjoying himself when he's *not* making money, which was decidedly the case in early April, when I was reporting the bulk of this story. Early in the year, sensing a temporary oversupply in the gas market, Boone had shorted gas futures. For the first two months of the year, his strategy worked beautifully. But he kept the position too long, and in March the market turned against him. As a result both of his funds were underwater. (The equity fund uses natural gas futures as a complicated hedge.) Like all great speculators, Boone was completely unruffled by the situation. His focus was on figuring out where to go from here.

So he'd gather his small team in the conference room, and they'd sit for a couple of hours, hashing over the state of the markets, the state of their funds, the state of their fundraising efforts, the state of the water deal, the state of just about anything that popped into their heads. They made lots of jokes, as often as not about their ages. They wandered in and out searching for snacks. They kept a constant eye on the big computer screen that tracks the prices of energy stocks and futures contracts. As I watched them, the image that came to mind was that movie from a few years ago, *Space Cowboys*, in which four old codgers, astronauts from an earlier era, have to go up into space one last time to save the world. Boone and his gang are the Wall Street version of *Space Cowboys*. They've all been around the block a few times, but they can still show the young whippersnappers on Wall Street a thing or two. Having the market turn against you—hell, that's just part of the deal sometimes. Indeed, by the end of April the commodities fund was back in the black, and Boone was now long natural gas. "If gas prices rise the way we think they will, we're going to have a good year," he said happily.

The only person who seemed really agitated was Boone's futures trader. Then again, he's 25. One day I was sitting in an office next to him, and I overheard him talking to a trader on the other end of the phone. "You never

heard of Boone Pickens?" he said. "He is *large*! He used to own Mesa Petroleum. He tried to take over Gulf Oil. That's my boss." I had to smile.

It was on my last afternoon in Dallas that Boone asked me the question that begins this story: did I think he had changed? I had been thinking about this for days, of course, but I was still caught off guard when he asked it, and I stumbled for an answer. I responded by ticking off the things that would seem obvious to anyone who hadn't seen him in a long time. His tongue wasn't as sharp as it used to be, I told him. He had more patience. He let things roll off him that he once would have picked at like a scab. He was easier to be around. What I didn't say—but wish I had—was that Boone finally seemed happy. And that I was happy that it had turned out this way for him.

Boone stared up at the ceiling as I recited my little litany. "I agree with all that," he said. "I'll tell you something else. I'm a better listener too. Back then, nobody could tell me anything. I knew everything." He shook his head in dismay at the memory of his former self. "I didn't, of course. But I thought I did."

Just then, his daughter Liz called. "You're smiling today," she began after he'd said hello.

"Yeah," Pickens replied with a chuckle, "we finally made some money today." She knew that he'd been taking a beating in the market recently, and they talked for a few minutes about whether natural gas prices were finally going in his direction. Then he gently changed the subject. "Listen," he said, "I got ol' Joe Nocera in here, and we're working."

"So you're cutting me off?" She laughed.

"Yeah, I guess I am."

"Well, okay. Goodbye. I love you."

"I love you too," said T. Boone Pickens Jr.

Acknowledgments

A few words about editors: I like them. In fact, I depend on them.
    I have a friend who, whenever I used to tell him I liked one of his stories, would reply sardonically: "You should have seen the one I wrote!" Maybe I've just been lucky, but I've never felt that way. From the start of my magazine career at the *Washington Monthly* in the late 1970s, I've been blessed with editors who have made my work demonstrably better. Good editors see things you don't. They find the hole in the story you missed. They force you to face squarely the flaws in your argument. To me, a good magazine story is a surprisingly collaborative process, and my editor is my partner.

And so, my thanks to the many terrific editors who worked their magic on the stories in this collection. At *Texas Monthly*, Nick Lemann first lured me to Texas, assigned me the Boone Pickens story, and then gave me a magazine-writing tutorial when he edited that story. Greg Curtis, who was *Texas Monthly*'s editor during my years there, and Paul Burka, its éminence grise, were also friends and mentors.

Lee Eisenberg was the editor of *Esquire* when I wrote the Steve Jobs story, which was my first for a national magazine. After that story was published, I went to visit Lee, who came up with the idea for the other *Esquire* story in this collection, about Fidelity Investments and the 1980s bull market. What he really wanted to understand, I remember him telling me that day, was why his mother had started following mutual funds and the stock market. My editor for both those stories was one of the real characters in the New York media world, David Hirshey, who is now an editor at HarperCollins. He—and I—got a big assist from his then assistant Laura Marmor, who, it was clear even then, was loaded with talent. Happily, she is now a colleague of mine at *The New York Times*, where she is deputy travel editor.

I'm pretty sure that Art Cooper, the late editor of *GQ*, never so much as added a comma to a sentence I wrote. That wasn't his style; Art was a force of nature who loved holding court, having lunch, and putting out a magazine that would beat the pants off *Esquire*, which, for the nearly two decades he ran *GQ*, was his goal in life. Nevertheless, I will always be indebted to him. He gave me a column—and paid me enough money for it—to allow me to finish a book I thought I would never finish. And he assigned Martin Beiser to be my editor, for which I'm also grateful. Marty is a deft editor and a good guy—a nice combination.

I thought I knew a lot about business by the time I arrived at *Fortune*, but what I quickly discovered was how little I knew. The place was filled with writers and editors—and fact-checkers and researchers and photo editors, up and down the masthead—who were passionately devoted to the subject of business, and whose depth of knowledge consistently bowled me over. I learned things just walking down the hallway—especially when I would stop into the office of Carol Loomis, *Fortune*'s most legendary writer, whose career there spans more than 50 years.

Fortune was also an exciting place to be in the mid-1990s, when I joined. That's partly because the Internet bubble had just begun, which brought in millions of dollars in ad revenue, and lots of new readers, who were devouring our coverage of not just the Internet but the broader subject of business. Mainly, though, it was because John Huey was running the place. Now the editor in chief of Time Inc., John was a savvy, charismatic editor who cared deeply about business storytelling. Early on, he handed me off to Tim Smith, one of the finest story doctors I've ever met, and we worked together for the next ten years. At *Fortune*, I also had the great good fortune to work with Norman Pearlstine, who was Time Inc.'s editor in chief before Huey; Rik Kirkland, who succeeded Huey as *Fortune*'s managing editor; and deputy managing editors Rick Tetzeli and Hank Gilman. The terrific Beth Fenner edited "Return of the Raider," the last story in this collection.

Money magazine is also a Time Inc. publication, and a few years into my tenure at *Fortune*, I was approached by Robert Safian, *Money*'s new editor, to write a regular column. Bob, who is now the editor of *Fast Company* magazine, is a first-rate magazine maker, who built a fine staff and put out a terrific magazine for a half dozen years. His right-hand woman, Denise Martin (who has since joined him at *Fast Company*), edited most of my *Money* columns.

When I first joined *The New York Times*, it felt a little like old home week: the person editing my column was Jim Impoco, who was an old *Fortune* colleague. And my editor at the magazine was Vera Titunik—who was also an

old *Fortune* colleague. It was wonderful to be working with them again. Jim, alas, left the *Times* about a year after I got there, and I've since had two other editors, Mickey Meece (who, sad for me, also left the *Times* to return to her native Kentucky) and Bruce Headlam, who currently handles the task. My thanks to both of them. I also owe a debt of gratitude to Bill Keller, the *Times'* executive editor, who hired me; Larry Ingrassia, the editor of *Times'* business section; and Gerry Marzorati, who edits *The New York Times Sunday Magazine.*

There are two editors whose handiwork is not on display in this book, but whose influence on me has been profound. The first is Charlie Peters, the founder and former editor of the *Washington Monthly*, which is one of the great training grounds for writers and editors. Charlie gave me my first magazine job, paid me next to nothing, worked me harder than I've ever worked in my life—and I've never been more grateful for anything in my life. The Charlie Peters boot camp is like nothing else in magazine journalism. He takes unformed talents and shapes them into writers who are ready to make their mark on the world.

The second influence is Dan Okrent, for whom I worked in the mid-1980s, when I moved from Texas to New England. In addition to being one of New York's great raconteurs, Dan was the founder of Rotisserie baseball (now known as fantasy baseball), the first public editor of *The New York Times*, and the author of several fine books. He is also the founding editor of *New England Monthly*, where, for a brief time, I was his executive editor. I've never met anybody who so overflowed with story ideas, and whose sense of story was so unerring. Although I didn't stay long at the magazine, Dan has remained a lifelong friend, and is the first person I turn to when I'm floundering on a story. My thanks to them both.

In Liz Darhansoff, I am fortunate to have a book agent who is also a friend; there isn't an agent in New York who so fiercely protects her authors. At Portfolio, I would like to thank my editor Adrian Zackheim, as well as Will Weisser, Allison McLean, and Courtney Young, who helped make the experience of putting this book together such an enjoyable one.

A year after I wrote my first business story in 1982, my daughter Kate was born. My two sons, Amato and Nicholas, were born a few years later, not long after I moved to New England. Throughout my career, their love has been a constant source of inspiration. I thank them from the bottom of my heart.

Finally, my thanks, and my love, to Dawn, who inspires me every day.

Index

A&P stores, 259–60
Abboud, A. Robert, 26–27
Adjacent products
  tobacco industry, 238–40
Agent Orange class-action suit, 136–37
Allardice, Barry, 25
Altair, 21
Altria. *See* Parrish, Steve; Tobacco industry lawsuits
Anderson, Fred, 70–71
Anderson, Gary, 154–55
Angelos, Peter, 128
Antitrust, Cities Service takeover, 39, 45
Apple Computer
  iPod, 65–68
  iTunes, 66
  See also Jobs, Steve
AQR Capital, 207–24
  decline during Internet boom, 219–21
  origin/growth of, 209, 218
  See also Asness, Cliff
Arbitrageurs, Cities Services takeover, view of, 25–26, 40
Asbestos lawsuits, 128
Asness, Cliff, 207–24
  "bubble logic" concept, 220–21
  computer model, use of, 216–17
  earnings of, 209
  hedge funds, view of, 210, 223
  manager secrecy, 207, 209
  market neutral approach, 213, 217
  profile/background of, 209–10, 213–17

Bailey, Fenton, 100–101
Baker & Botts, 10, 15, 17, 271
Ballin, Scott, 239

Bancroft, Bettina, 163, 176
Bancroft, Christopher, 174–76
Bancrofts versus Dow Jones
  management, 161–78
  family support of management, 169–70, 174, 176
  legal counsel, 164, 169, 173
  management mistakes, 163, 167, 170–72
  new board, requirements of, 173–74
  profile of, 175–76
  and Telerate, 171–72
  See also Cox, William III; Goth, Elisabeth
Barron, Clarence W., 109, 163
Bartiromo, Maria, 257
Bass, Sid, 35
Batchelder, David, 267–68, 277
Baxter, J. Clifford, 199
Baxter Healthcare, 128
Bear hugs, 15, 17, 23
Bennis, Warren, 256
Bent, Bruce, 80–81
Berg, Paul, 63
Berkowitz, Sean M., 203
Berkshire Hathaway. *See* Buffett, Warren
Bernick, David, 145–47, 152–53
Bible, Geoffrey, 233
Billings, Paul, 227–28
Blaise, Pierre, 146–47
Blizzard, Edward, 152
Blodget, Henry, 187–94
  Amazon stock analysis, 188–91
  fines, 192
  incriminating e-mails, 187, 192
  as writer, 192, 194
Boesky, Ivan
  and Cities Services takeover, 9
  and Milken, 101, 104–5

Bolton, Dan, 130–34
Boswell, Mike, 38
Boyd, Roddy, 249–50
BP Capital Energy Fund, 270, 278
BP Energy Equity fund, 271–72, 274
Breck, Henry, 18
Brown, Tom, 33–34, 37, 38, 41–42
Bruck, Connie, 101
"Bubble logic" concept, 220–21
Buffett, Warren, 180–86
   and Bancroft family conflict, 161, 164, 168
Buffett, Warren (*continued*)
   Berkshire Hathaway annual meeting,
      180–82
   business principles of, 183–85
   profile of, 182–83
Burenga, Ken, 170, 172
Busch, Harris, 153
Bush, George, and Enron, 198–99
Bush, John, 17, 26, 32
Bushnell, Nolan, 53
Byrne, Patrick M.
   stock price manipulation claims
      by, 248–51

Cabour, Francis, 94, 96
Cain, Nelda, 279–80
Camilleri, Louis, 234
Campaign for Tobacco-Free Kids, 225, 227,
   231
Campbell, Andrew, 147
Carr, Fred, 104
Chanos, Jim, 207, 222
Cheney, Richard, and Cities Services
   takeover, 26, 29–30
Chesley, Stanley, 135–45
China, costume jewelry manufacturing,
   263–66
Cigarette smoking
   tobacco-related disease, 226
   See also Tobacco industry lawsuits
Cities Service Company
   Occidental Petroleum takeover, 45
   Pickens takeover attempt, 10–18, 23–46
Clean Energy Fuels, 268
Cohen, Jonathan, 188–90
Cole, Robert, 7, 29–30
Coleman, Debbie, 62
Commonwealth School, 110
Cook, Ralph, 138
Cornfield, Bernie, 77
Corporate crime
   Blodget, Henry, 187–94
   Enron, 195–206
   fall and reinvention theme, 194
   Milken, Michael, 98–106

Corporate takeovers
   Cities Service Company, 10–18, 23–46
   shareholder activists label, 272–73
   See also Pickens, T. Boone; Tender offers
Cox, Christopher, 251
Cox, Jessie, 164, 168
Cox, William III
   fact-finding mission of, 168–69
   profile of, 167–68
   See also Bancrofts versus Dow Jones
      management
Cox, William, Jr., 168, 174
Creswell, Julie, 244
Cronin, Dr. Thomas, 142

Dalkon Shield, 130, 156
Davis, Marvin, 277
Denby, David, 193
Doerr, John, 158
Dow Corning silicon breast implants,
   125–57
   attorneys involved, 127–28, 130–31, 135,
      138–41, 145–46
   awards to victims, 127, 133, 145, 154
   Bristol-Myers Squibb in, 144–45
   company documentation on, 131–34
   consolidation of cases, 142–43
   Dow Chemical in, 151–54
   Dow Corning bankruptcy, 128, 154–57
   epidemiology investigations,
      138, 146–47, 153
   implants as unregulated, 131
   media coverage, impact of, 133–34,
      144–45
   product harm, nonexistent support for,
      129, 146–47, 156
   settlements, 128, 148–50, 155
   victim physical complaints, 130, 133, 144,
      148, 152
Dow Jones News Service, 163
Dunn, Bill, 167
Dunne, James J. III, 252–55

Ebbers, Bernard J., 206
Economic Strategy Institute, 265
Efficient-market hypothesis, 214–15
Eisner, Michael, 69
Elkind, Peter, 195
Elson, Charles, 245
Enderle, Rob, 67
Enron, 126, 159, 195–206
   bankruptcy of, 197
   and Fastow, 198, 201–6
   political connections, 198–99
   significance of scandal, 198–99

and Skilling, 196–203
   whistle-blower, 198
Epstein, Edward Jay, 100, 101

Fabian, Dick, 93
Fama, Eugene, 214–16
Farrell, Diana, 265–66
Fastow, Andrew S., 195, 201–6
Fastow, Lea, 205
Feinberg, Kenneth, 138, 147
Ferlauto, Richard, 245–46
Fidelity Securities
   advertising by, 82
   bull market, end of, 92–97
   Capital Fund, 79
   and crash of 1987, 75–78, 95–97
   Equity-Income Fund, 93
   Fidelity Daily Income Trust, 82
   fund manager, creation of, 78–79
   and Lynch, Peter, 77, 88–91
   Money coverage of, 87–88
   money-market funds, check-writing
      against, 81–82, 92
   phone reps operation, 82–85
   Select funds, 75, 86–88
   Trend Fund, 79
   Tsai as money manager, 78–79
Fishman, Karen, 254
Flom, Joe, 7, 9, 23–24, 27, 32, 40–45
Foulds, Jonathan, 239
French, Kenneth, 215–16

Gallagher, Mike, 140, 144–45, 147–48
Garzarelli, Elaine, 92–93
Gates, Bill, 48, 161
Gerow, Dr. Frank, 142
Giuliani, Rudy, on Milken, 98–99
Glantz, Stanton, 235, 239, 240–41
Glanville, Jim, 17, 38
Glass, John, 256–59
Gliedman, Chip, 67
Glisan, Ben F., Jr., 199
Globalization
   Chinese-made costume jewelry, 263–66
   negative impact on American
      business, 264–66
   Trade Adjustment Assistance
      program, 265–66
Goth, Elisabeth
   and Billy Cox, 167–69
   Dow Jones holdings, 163–64, 175
   fact-finding mission of, 164, 168–69, 176
   profile of, 166, 173
   See also Bancrofts versus Dow Jones
      management

Gould, George, 17–18
Greenberg, Alan, 272, 278
Greenberg, Herb, 248–51
Greenwald, Robert, 261
Grubman, Jack, 192, 194
Gulf Oil
   Boone takeover attempt, 8–9, 274–75
   and Cities Services takeover
      attempt, 12, 36–37
   and Cities Service takeover attempt, 45

Habacht, Alan, 11
Hammer, Dr. Armand, 27, 35
Hammer, Roy, 162, 169, 173–74
Hartford, John A., 259
Hartman, Harvey, 258
Hazleton, Richard, 156
Hedge funds
   Asness, Cliff/AQR Capital, 207–24
   and bull market (1982–2000), 212–13
   downturns, performance during,
      221–22
   investing methods of, 210–11, 213, 215–17,
      221–23
   manager salaries, 209
   origin of, 211–12
   rise in popularity, 208, 210–13
   transaction costs, 212
Heinen, Nancy, 69–72
Hennessey, Edward, 35
Hickey, William, 254
Hill, Leslie, 177
Hock, Dee, 74
Holder, Mike, 280
Home Depot, Nardelli, Robert, 243–48
Hopkins, Mariann, 134
Hueston, John, 204–6
Huey, John, 161–62
Hugoton Production Company, 21

Icahn, Carl, 8, 272
Investing
   Asness, Cliff, 207–24
   Buffett, Warren, 180–86
   efficient-market hypothesis, 214–15
   Fidelity Securities, 75–97
   growth stocks, 215
   intrinsic value of company, 185–86
   Johnson, Edward, III, 78–82
   Lynch, Peter, 89–91
   Merrill, Charles, 107–24
   shorting, 211
   value stocks, 215
iPod, 65–68
iTunes, 66

Jackson, David, 115
Jacobs, Irwin, 272
James, Hamilton, 7, 9, 17, 28–29, 33, 45
Jobs, Steve, 47–72
  and Apple executives, 59
  biographical information, 53
  controlling nature of, 47–48
  leadership style, 47, 52, 59–61
  leaves Apple, 47, 57–58, 63–64
  Lisa project, 59–61
  Macintosh, 60–63
  media, relationship with, 48–49
  NeXT, 47–48, 50–52, 57–58, 63–65
  personal life, stress on, 56–58
  physical demeanor, 51–52
  Pixar, 47, 57
  returns to Apple, 48
  stock option backdating scandal, 68–72
  work as self-expression, 55–57, 62–65
  and Wozniac, 53–55, 60, 62
Johnson, Carolyn, 142, 148
Johnson, Edward, II, fund manager, creation
    of, 78–79
Johnson, Edward, III, 78–82
  on bull market, 91
  money management, approach to, 78–79
  money-market funds, check-writing
    against, 81–82, 92
  takeover at Fidelity, 79–80
  See also Fidelity Securities
Johnson, Ned, 73–74
Johnstone, Bruce, 93–94
Jones, Alfred Winslow, 211–12, 215–17
Junk bonds. *See* Milken, Michael

Kabiller, David, 218
Kann, Peter, 165, 167, 170, 171–72
Kassen, Michael, 87–88
Keeley, Larry, 68
Keker, John, 158
Kessler, Andrew, 66
Kessler, David, 126, 134, 135, 156, 226, 228–
    30, 233–36, 241
Kilgore, Barney, 165
Knowles, Ralph, 139, 144, 148
Koch, Charles, 31–32
Kopper, Michael, 204–5
Kornbluth, Jesse, 101–2
Kossovsky, Nir, 153
Krail, Robert, 217, 218

Laas, Gladys, 152–55
Lacovara, Michael, 253
Ladner, Jenny, 152
Laminack, Rick, 128, 143–44, 150, 157

Lampert, Eddie, 207, 210
Lanier, Elyse, 152
Lawson, Rodger, 93
Lay, Kenneth L., 196–200
  See also Enron
Lazar, Seymour M., 157–58
Lee, James E., 41, 43–44
Lemann, Nicholas, 8
Lerach, William S., 126, 157–60
Lewin, Dan'l, 52
Lewis, Drew, 274
Lewis, Michael, 106
Liedtke, J. Hugh, 32–33
Liew, John, 217, 220
Lipton, Marty, 9, 42–45
Lisa project, 59–61
Litigation
  Bancrofts versus Dow Jones management,
    161–78
  class action suits. *See* Mass torts
  Dow Corning silicon breast implants,
    125–57
  shareholder lawsuits, Lerach as council,
    157–60
  tobacco industry. *See* Tobacco industry
    lawsuits
Loeb, Marshall, 85–87, 92
Lovejoy, Jesse R., 17, 25–26, 28, 31, 32, 34, 38–
    39, 41, 45
Lucas, George, 47, 57
Lynch, Edward, 112
Lynch, Peter
  investment books of, 179
  and Magellan Fund, 77, 89–91

McCartt, Eugene, 20
Macintosh computer, 60–63
McKenna, Regis, 63
McKennon, Keith, 135–39
McKinsey Global Institute, 265
McLean, Bethany, 195
McShane, John, 279–80
Madden, Wales, 273
Magellan Fund, and Peter Lynch, 77, 88–91
Magowan, Doris Merrill, 111, 116, 118, 123
Magowan, Dorothy, 108
Magowan, Felix, 124
Magowan, Merrill Lynch, 116, 123
Magowan, Peter, 111, 117, 123–24
Magowan, Robert A., 110–11, 116–18
Magowan, Robin, 117–20
Magowan, Stephen, 117, 118, 123
Mahood, Stephen C., 32–33
Maltz, Marc, 253
Mandel, Stephen, Jr., 209
Manhattan Fund, 79

Market neutral approach, 213, 217
Markkula, Mike, 59–60
Mass torts
  Agent Orange class action suit, 136–37
  asbestos cases, 128
  Dalkon Shield, 130, 156
  impetus for, 133–34
  lawyer profile in, 130
  multidistrict litigation panel (MDL), 139
  silicon breast implants. *See* Dow Corning
    silicon breast implants
Master Settlement Agreement (MSA),
    tobacco industry, 226–27, 232–35
Merrill, Bruce, 123
Merrill, Catherine, 121–23
Merrill, Charles, 107–24
  biographical information, 110
  children's remembrance of, 108, 110–11,
    113–16
  death of, 110
  democratization of money, 107–8, 111
  grandchildren's remembrance of,
    118–24
  and Magowan (son-in-law), 116–18
  womanizing of, 108, 112, 115
Merrill, Charles, Jr., 108, 110
Merrill, James, 108–16, 119–20
Merrill, Peter, 108
Merrill Lynch. *See* Blodget, Henry; Merrill,
    Charles
Mesa Petroleum Company, 21–22
  See also Pickens, T. Boone
Metz, Tim, 30
Milken, Lowell, 101
Milken, Michael, 98–106
  allegations against, 102, 105–6
  and Boesky, 101, 104–5
  and corporate raiding, 9
  Giuliani on, 98–99
  greed of, 104
  personality profile of, 103–4
  plea bargain, rejection of, 106
  prison routine, 99–100
  regulations, view of, 103
  revisionist view of, 101
  sentence reduced, 101
  supporters of, 99, 100
Millstein, Ira, 164, 169, 173
Mindich, Eric, 218
Mithoff, Richard, 127–28, 140, 150
Money, coverage of Fidelity Securities,
    87–88
Money-market funds
  Fidelity check-writing against, 81–82, 92
  origin and development of, 80–81
Monks, Bob, 166
Munger, Charlie, 181, 185–86

Murdoch, Rupert, 162
  Wall Street Journal purchase, 175–78
  See also Cox, William III; Goth, Elisabeth
Murphy, Tom, 164, 168, 173
Murray, Mike, 60, 64
Mutual funds
  rise in popularity. *See* Fidelity Securities
  transaction costs, 212
Myers, Matthew, 225, 227, 231, 234–35, 237–
    38, 240–42

Nardelli, Robert, 243–48
  as Chrysler chairman, 243–44
  compensation package, 244
  Home Depot annual meeting (2006),
    244–48
  leaves Home Depot, 243–44
  opponents of, 245
Neiss, Mike, 256
NeXT, 47–48, 63–65

O'Brien, Bob, 251
O'Brien, John G., 20
Occidental Petroleum, Cities Service
    takeover, 45
Och, Daniel, 209
Olin, James, 206
O'Neill, Sandler, 252–55
O'Quinn, John, 140–45, 148–55, 157
Overstock.com, stock market manipulation
    claims, 248–51

Pai, Lou L., 202
Parrish, Steve, 224–42
  cigarette smoking, view of, 227, 233–34
  industry defense/countermessages,
    229–31
  profile/background of, 228–29
  tobacco regulation, support of, 227, 233–
    38, 242
Passikoff, Robert, 258
Paul, Ron, 257–58
Penn Virginia, 271–73
Peretsman, Nancy, 164, 168–70
Perry, Nancy Ling, 120–21
Pertschuk, Michael, 231
Petrocelli, Daniel, 199, 201, 203, 204, 206
Petroleum Exploration, Inc., 20–21
Philip Morris. *See* Parrish, Steve; Tobacco
    industry lawsuits
Phillips, Kevin, 199
Phillips, Warren, 165, 167
Pickens, Beatrice, 22, 26, 29, 274, 276
Pickens, Lynn, 20, 22

Pickens, T. Boone, 10–46, 268–82
  Altair, 21
  biographical information, 20, 22, 268–70,
    276, 278–80
  BP Capital Energy Fund, 270, 278
  BP Energy Equity fund, 271–72, 274
  Cities Service Company, 10–18, 23–46
  Clean Energy Fuels, 268
  as corporate raider, 8–9, 12, 22, 46
  earnings/stock ownership, 21–22, 270
  Gulf takeover attempt, 8–9, 274–75
  as health buff, 19–20, 30, 271
  Mesa Petroleum Company, 21–22
  Mesa takeover by Rainwater, 275–78
  New York headquarters/operation,
    16–18, 26
  Penn Virginia deal, 271–73
  personal life, turnaround by, 279–82
  Petroleum Exploration, Inc., 20–21
  physical demeanor of, 11
  self-proclaimed mistakes of, 275–77
  water transport plan, 273
Pixar, 47, 57
Pointer, Sam C., Jr., 139–40, 142, 151–52,
  155
Prestowitz, Clyde V., Jr., 265
Pubco, 21

Quackenbush, Christopher, 252, 255

Rainwater, Richard, 277
Rand, Paul, 50
Rapoport, Nancy B., 199
Reagan, Ronald, 34, 36
Reed, Jack, 264
Reed, John, 231
Regulation Q, 80, 83
Reich, Robert, 262
Reserve Fund, 80
Ribstein, Larry E., 159
Rice, Ken, 202
Robertson, Julian, 212
Robes, Martha, 170
Roby, Joe L., 17, 38, 45
Rocker, David A., 248
Rosenblatt, Roger, 228–29

Salinas, Carlos, 173
Sandler, Herman, 252
Sarofim, Fayez, 272, 278
Saunders, Anne, 257, 259
Savings and loan collapse, and Milken, 102
Schultz, Howard, 244, 255–59

Schwab, Charles, 74
Scott, H. Lee, Jr., 262
Scott, Michael, 59–60
Sculley, John, 47, 51, 59, 63
Seffrin, John, 226, 234
Seraglio, The (Merrill), 110, 116
Shareholder lawsuits, Lerach as council,
  157–60
Shugart, Alan, 158
Silicone breast implants. *See* Dow Corning
  silicon breast implants
Silicon Valley
  and Apple. *See* Jobs, Steve
  workers/work ethic, 49–50, 56
Simons, James, 209
Skilling, Jeffrey, 196–203
  See also Enron
Smartest Guys in the Room, The (McLean and
  Elkind), 195, 198–99
Smyser, Craig, 205
Soros, George, 169, 212–13, 218–19
Southland Corporation, 13–14, 18
Spitzer, Eliot, 187, 192, 194, 249
Stampel, Ira, 164
Starbucks
  loss of originality, 255–59
Stein, Ben, 100–102
Steinhardt, Michael, 213, 218–19
Stempel, Robert, 169
Stern, Maria, 130, 134
Stewart, Martha, 194
Stillwell, Robert, 17, 26, 30–31, 38–39, 43, 45,
  271–73, 278, 280
Stock market
  crash of 1987, 74, 92–97
  democratization and Merrill, 107–8
  democratization of money, 111
Stock options
  Buffett's view of, 183
  Jobs backdating investigation, 68–72
Sweanor, David, 239
Swensen, David, 219, 221–22
Szymanczyk, Michael, 228, 238–39

Taboka, 240
Tassin, Sidney, 277–78
Tech boom
  Blodget, Henry, 187–94
  hedge funds during, 219–21
  Jobs, Steve, 47–72
  shareholder lawsuits, 198
Telerate, 171–72
Tender offers
  antitrust factors, 39, 45
  bear hugs, 15, 17, 23

Cities Service Company by Pickens, 10–18,
23–46
time frame, 15, 25
unfriendly, 11–12, 17
Thomas, Michael M., 91, 96
3M, 128
Tobacco industry lawsuits
failure of, 224, 226–27
first case, 228–29
industry defense/countermessages, 229–31
Master Settlement Agreement (MSA),
226–27, 232–35
Tobacco industry regulation
public-health stance, 236–37, 239–40
See also Parrish, Steve
Trade Adjustment Assistance program,
265–66
Tribble, Bud, 52, 62
Tsai, Gerry, 77–79, 91

Useem, Michael, 199

Valenti, Carl, 172
Vickrey, Donn W., 248

Waidelich, Charles J., 9, 12, 15–16, 27–29, 40
Wall Street Journal, The, Murdoch purchase,
162, 175–78
Wal-Mart, 259–62
critical documentary on, 261–62
critics of, 260–61
rebuttal of critics, 261–62
Warner, Kenneth, 239
Wasserstein, Bruce, 9, 39–40, 44, 45
Watkins, Sherron S., 198
Weill, Sanford, 69
Weinstein, Jack B., 136–37
Weisberg, Jacob, 194
Weiss, Melvin I., 158
Whitney, Richard, 197
Whitworth, Ralph, 267
Williams, Frank E., 262–65
Williams, Steven, 67
Wolfe, Sidney, 134
Wood, Kimba, 100–101
WorldCom, 206
Wozniac, Steve, and Jobs, 53–55, 60, 62
Wyden, Ron, 251

Yake, Sam, 246